CW00819520

Civil Liberties in Northern Ireland:

The C.A.J. Handbook

3rd edition

edited by **Brice Dickson**

Civil Liberties in Northern Ireland

Copyright © the Committee on the Administration of Justice, 1997
First edition published 1990
Second edition published 1993

Published by the Committee on the Administration of Justice
45-47 Donegall Street
Belfast
BT1 2FG
Tel: (01232) 232394
Fax: (01232) 246706

Website:
http://ourworld.compuserve.com/homepages/Comm_Admin_Justice/

British Library Cataloguing in Publication Data
A catalogue record for this book is available from the
British Library

ISBN 1 873285 53 1

Printed and bound in Belfast
by Shanway Distributors
461 Antrim Road
Belfast BT15 3BJ
Tel: (01232) 777979

Cover design by Walter Steele, Belfast.

Contents

The Committee on the Administration of Justice

The Committee on the Administration of Justice (CAJ) was established in 1981 and is an independent non-governmental organisation affiliated to the International Federation for Human Rights. CAJ takes no position on the constitutional status of Northern Ireland and is firmly opposed to the use of violence for political ends. Its membership is drawn from across the whole community.

The Committee seeks to secure the highest standards in the administration of justice in Northern Ireland by ensuring that the government complies with its responsibilities in international human rights law. The CAJ works closely with other domestic and international human rights groups such as Amnesty International, the Lawyers Committee for Human Rights and Human Rights Watch, and makes regular submissions to a number of United Nations and European bodies established to protect human rights.

CAJ's activities include publishing reports, conducting research, holding conferences, monitoring, campaigning locally and internationally, individual casework and providing legal advice. Its areas of work are extensive and include prisons, policing, emergency laws, the criminal justice system, the use of lethal force, children's rights, gender equality, racism, religious discrimination and advocacy for a Bill of Rights.

The organisation has been awarded several international human rights prizes, including the Reebok Human Rights Award.

Membership entitles you to receive the CAJ's monthly civil liberties newsheet **Just News**, to take part in the work of the sub-groups and to use the CAJ resource library and clippings service. If you would like to join CAJ or find out more about its activities, please contact:

CAJ
45/47 Donegall Street
Belfast BT1 2FG
Tel: 01232-232394
Fax: 01232-246706

Notes on Contributors

Christine Bell is a lecturer in law at the Queen's University of Belfast.

David Bonner is a senior lecturer in law at the University of Leicester.

Madge Davison was a barrister in Northern Ireland and a prominent civil rights activist; she died in 1991.

Brice Dickson is a professor of law at the University of Ulster at Jordanstown.

Eileen Evason is a professor of social policy at the University of Ulster at Jordanstown.

Steven Greer is a reader in law at the University of Bristol.

Anne Grimes is a solicitor employed by the Law Centre (NI).

Brigid Hadfield is a professor of public law at the Queen's University of Belfast.

Angela Hegarty is a lecturer in law at the University of Ulster at Magee.

John Jackson is a professor of law at the Queen's University of Belfast.

Beverley Jones is a solicitor in Belfast and a former Chief Legal Officer at the Equal Opportunities Commission for Northern Ireland.

Stephen Livingstone is a reader in law at the University of Nottingham.

Steve McBride is a barrister in Northern Ireland and a member of the Belfast City Council.

Gerry McCormack is a reader in law at the University of Essex.

Anne McKeown is a lecturer in social work at the Belfast Institute for Further and Higher Education.

Chris Moffat is an education materials editor with Fortnight Educational Trust.

Richard Steele is a senior lecturer in law at the Queen's University of Belfast.

Ciaran White is a lecturer in law at the University of Ulster at Jordanstown.

Acknowledgements

The contributors to the third edition of this book have once again provided their services free of charge and are to be sincerely thanked for their hard work. Besides the writers, however, many other people assisted in the book's production. First and foremost is Liz Martin, who put in a huge number of hours above and beyond the call of duty to make sure that the text was camera-ready. Her patience, helpfulness and efficiency made the editor's job a great deal easier than it would otherwise have been. Thanks too to several proof-readers: Fiona Doherty, Lesley Emerson, Rob Fairmichael, Mary Foley, Eilis Haughey, Mark Hughes, Issac May, Michael Ritchie, Dan VanDerMortel and Ellen Weaver. For help with the Index and Tables I am indebted to Maggie Beirne, Veronica Carson, Liam Lynch, Martin O'Brien and Christine Sadli. Last, but not least, my appreciation goes to Lord Lester of Herne Hill for his Foreword. It is appropriate that the person most responsible for making the European Convention on Human Rights part of Northern Ireland's law should have agreed to identify himself with this work, as Lord Scarman, the writer of the Foreword for the first and second editions, did before him.

Brice Dickson

FOREWORD

I congratulate the Committee on the Administration of Justice for publishing this third edition of its handbook on civil liberties in Northern Ireland.

I have taken a close interest in the effective protection of civil liberties in Northern Ireland ever since I had the great privilege of acting as Special Adviser to the Standing Advisory Commission on Human Rights between 1975 and 1977, when they were preparing their landmark report recommending the incorporation of the European Convention on Human Rights into domestic law.

Successive governments have been willing to enact a wide variety of specific measures to protect civil rights and liberties in Northern Ireland, but only now, two decades after the publication of the SACHR Report, has a government introduced a measure to incorporate the Convention as a fundamental law. The Human Rights Act 1998 is likely to have a dramatic impact in enhancing legal protection of the individual against the misuse of the powers of the State on both sides of the Irish Sea.

As Brice Dickson rightly observed in his introduction to the second edition, it is all very well to have laws on human rights, but if those laws are imperfectly enforced they may as well not exist. One reason for this imperfect enforcement is the complexity of the law and its lack of accessibility to ordinary men and women.

It is a particular virtue of this Handbook that it is user-friendly, explaining in plain English what everyone needs to know about their basic rights, freedoms and duties, and where to seek practical help and advice, in the context of the continuing tragic conditions of terrorist violence, emergency powers, and the suspension of democratic government in Northern Ireland. It is factual and informative rather than polemical. It is well-designed and easy to understand. And it is a bargain.

I only wish that there were a similar handbook on civil liberties in Britain.

Lord Lester of Herne Hill QC

Chapter 1

Introduction

Brice Dickson

In all democracies the law is part and parcel of a wider notion called "the rule of law". By this is meant that no-one, whether an individual, a company, a private body or an organ of the government, can be above the law: the law must apply to everyone equally, without any unfair discrimination. Hand in hand with this principle runs the understanding that all individuals have certain basic rights - or fundamental civil liberties - which the state must not take away. It is those rights and liberties which form the subject-matter of this book.

The development of human rights law

After the end of the Second World War, which brought to light horrific violations of human rights in Germany and elsewhere, nations around the world were determined to take steps to guarantee protection to human rights in international and national law. The first concrete manifestation of this was the American Declaration of the Rights and Duties of Man, drawn up by the Organisation of American States in 1948. This was followed in the same year by the Universal Declaration of Human Rights, produced under the auspices of the newly-created United Nations. The Declaration was proclaimed on 10 December, which is now known worldwide as international human rights day. In 1950 the member states of the Council of Europe, meeting in Rome, adopted the European Convention for the Protection of Human Rights and Fundamental Freedoms.

All of these documents concentrated on protecting civil and political rights, such as freedom of expression, freedom of religion and freedom of association. But the American Declaration and the Universal Declaration also embraced social, economic and cultural rights, such as the right to the preservation of health, the right to education and the right to work. In 1966, in order to supplement the general provisions of the Universal Declaration, the United Nations adopted two further International Covenants, one on civil and political rights, the other on economic, social and cultural rights. The gap in the European framework was filled by the adoption of the European Social Charter in 1961, another document prepared by the Council of Europe. It was issued in a revised form in 1996. The member states of the European Union have also agreed their own Social Charter, as part of the Maastricht Treaty of 1992. In 1997 the Labour government of the UK said it would abide by this Charter. The Treaty of Amsterdam, also in 1997, strengthened the EU's commitment to human rights even further.

In national legal systems there has been a comparable growth in human rights law. The majority of countries now have a written constitution with a Bill of Rights contained in it. The best known system is probably that of the United States of America, where the influence of the first 10 amendments to the Constitution - which were adopted in 1791 and are collectively known as the Bill of Rights - has been profound. In more recent years many other former colonies of the British Empire have marked their independence by adopting a constitution which includes guarantees for human rights. Even existing colonies, such as Gibraltar, are governed by legal provisions guaranteeing human rights.

The 1937 Constitution of the Irish Free State (now the Republic of Ireland) places Articles 40-44 under the general title of "Fundamental Rights" and includes such matters as the right to be held equal before the law, the right to one's life, person, good name and property, the right to liberty, freedom of expression, freedom of assembly and association, the right to education for children and the right to freedom from religious discrimination. The 1950 Constitution of India lays down similar legally enforceable fundamental rights. In Canada, a Bill of Rights was enacted in 1960 and this was supplanted in 1982 by a more far-reaching Charter of Rights and Freedoms. Australia - a federal state with a written constitution - does not yet have a Bill of Rights, but New Zealand - a unitary state with no written constitution - does. New Zealand's Bill of Rights, like that which operates in Hong Kong even after the handover to China, is based almost word for word on the United Nations' International Covenant on Civil and Political Rights. The most advanced

Bill of Rights in the world is now probably the one contained in the Constitution of South Africa 1996.

Nor is the tendency towards protection of human rights apparent only in countries which have an historical connection with English law. In France, the famous Declaration of the Rights of Man and of the Citizen (1789) was specifically incorporated into current law by the preamble to the 1958 Constitution of the Fifth Republic. In Germany, the 1949 Basic Law devotes the first 19 of its 146 Articles to basic rights. Moreover in both these countries the constitutional courts, or their equivalents, have gone to considerable lengths to develop the substance of these rights.

The enforcement of human rights

It is all very well to have laws on human rights, but if those laws are imperfectly enforced they may as well not exist. International agreements on human rights are especially difficult to enforce because there is, as yet, no supreme body to which governments of states can be made answerable; nor, usually, are there any sanctions which can be effectively imposed. The United Nations has tried to get round this problem by asking states to accede to what is called the Optional Protocol to the 1966 International Covenant on Civil and Political Rights. This allows citizens, in effect, to sue their own governments before the United Nations' Human Rights Committee. Likewise, the European Convention on Human Rights can be enforced by individuals in the European Commission of Human Rights and then, provided the application is referred to it, in the European Court of Human Rights (both bodies sit in Strasbourg and are to be merged into one Court of Human Rights in about a year's time). However, none of these international judgments is backed by a system of effective penalties if the state concerned chooses not to comply. Enforcement ultimately depends on political pressure, which can often take years to exert. While nearly every country in Europe has agreed to be bound by the European Convention, by the end of 1996 only 89 countries worldwide had agreed to be bound by the United Nations' Optional Protocol (including Ireland, but not the United Kingdom).

At the national level, countries differ greatly in the ways in which they permit citizens to claim their rights and liberties. In the USA, any person can challenge the constitutionality of any law in any court. If the Supreme Court confirms that a law made by Congress (the US Parliament) is invalid, then that law can be ignored by everyone in the land. In France, MPs can challenge the constitutionality of a

Parliamentary statute before it is officially published but no challenge can be mounted after publication. In Ireland, both prior *and* subsequent court challenges are permitted.

In the United Kingdom, Parliament's Acts can be challenged in court only if they run counter to a clear principle of EU law. There can be "judicial review" of lesser forms of legislation (*i.e.* Rules and Regulations), and of administrative, tribunal and some court decisions, but even then the only fundamental rights which can be relied upon by the applicant are the so-called principles of natural justice (*i.e.* "no-one should be a judge in his or her own cause" and "everyone has the right to a fair hearing"). There are at present no written constitutional guarantees in the United Kingdom, no Bill of Rights, no effective way of enforcing the government's obligations under international law in national courts. In Northern Ireland this lack of protection for human rights is particularly noticeable.

In October 1997, however, the UK's government published a Human Rights Bill, which if enacted by Parliament will make the European Convention on Human Rights part and parcel of UK law. Judges will not be able to invalidate an Act of Parliament which violates the Convention's standards, but they will be able to issue a "declaration of incompatibility" which will, in practice, force the government to introduce appropriate amending legislation.

The role of non-governmental organisations

In practice, the educational and campaigning activities of non-governmental organisations may be more effective in improving the law on human rights than court actions. A large number of non-governmental organisations now exist, the best known probably being Amnesty International, which has its headquarters in London, national sections throughout the world and a regional office in Belfast. Within the United Kingdom the two most prominent organisations are possibly Justice (which is the British branch of the International Commission of Jurists) and Liberty (formerly known as the National Council for Civil Liberties).

In Northern Ireland much valuable work in this area was carried out in the 1960s and early 1970s by the Northern Ireland Civil Rights Association. In subsequent years a number of other organisations have been formed to work on a range of specific civil liberties issues. In 1973 the government itself set up the Standing Advisory Commission on

Human Rights, to advise it on whether the law in Northern Ireland operates in a discriminatory fashion. In 1976 the Equal Opportunities Commission and Fair Employment Agency were created by Parliament in order to assist alleged victims of discrimination based on sex or marriage (in the case of the EOC), and on religion or political belief (in the case of the FEA). All of these bodies (including the Fair Employment Commission, which replaced the Agency in 1989) have performed valuable work in their own fields. In 1997 they have been joined by the Commission for Racial Equality for Northern Ireland.

In 1981 the Committee on the Administration of Justice (CAJ) was formed as an independent voluntary organisation to carry out more general monitoring of the legal system in Northern Ireland. It has acquired a reputation for accuracy and thoroughness and the present book is a further demonstration of its wish to provide information about Northern Ireland's legal system to as wide an audience as possible.

A Bill of Rights for Northern Ireland?

The CAJ has long been convinced that a Bill of Rights could play an important part in the prevention of injustice in Northern Ireland. The group believes that, unless the rights of all individuals in Northern Ireland are guaranteed equal protection, there is little prospect of a lasting solution being found to the area's problems. A Bill of Rights, in short, is a prerequisite to permanent peace and justice. At the time this book is going to press political talks about the constitutional future of Northern Ireland are taking place in Belfast: we hope that protection of human rights will be a matter about which all the participants can agree early in the process.

The Labour government's plan to satisfy the growing demand for a Bill of Rights by incorporating the European Convention on Human Rights into British law would certainly be a good first step towards improving the protection of civil liberties in Northern Ireland, but it has to be remembered that, although that Convention is the most successful of all the international human rights documents, it is still far from perfect. It proved of no avail, for instance, to the victims of Bloody Sunday in 1972 (*McDaid and Others* v *UK*, 1996), or to the mother of a boy who, while not himself directly involved in rioting, was killed by a plastic bullet in Belfast in 1976 (*Stewart* v *UK*, 1984), or to the father of a young man who was killed by the security forces when he was joyriding in 1985 (*Kelly* v *UK*, 1993). Likewise, the Convention did not assist the workers at Government Communications Headquarters in Cheltenham after the government banned certain trade unions there in 1984. Perhaps most importantly, the European Convention does not grant much, if any, protection to the rights of physically or mentally disabled people, to those lacking an education, to the unemployed, to the homeless or to the poor.

The CAJ therefore believes that a more comprehensive Bill of Rights is required for Northern Ireland, one that readily meets the expectations of ordinary people. As each of the chapters in this book will show, the law in Northern Ireland rarely confers positive rights on people but instead controls people's behaviour by placing all sorts of constraints on them: whatever is not affected by these constraints is deemed to be a liberty. The approach of the European Convention is not very different. The constraints which at present exist are so far-reaching, and the rights conferred on government agencies so all-embracing, that the resulting liberty is at times very narrow in scope. A Bill of Rights could not only increase people's confidence in the administration of justice but also improve the content of the law and make people more physically and psychologically secure. The CAJ has published its own draft Bill of Rights, and a discussion paper on how it could be implemented, and it hopes these will serve as useful models for further debate.

The content of this book

The chapters in this book offer advice and information on a wide variety of common legal problems encountered by people living in Northern Ireland. Although they are ascribed to particular authors, they have been edited and cross-referenced so as to make the book more than a disparate collection of essays. Needless to say, several of the chapters have had to take account of the "emergency" laws, but much is also said about the "ordinary" laws. The book tries to be reasonably comprehensive but inevitably there are some omissions. The third edition differs from the second in having additional chapters on children's rights and on racial discrimination. All of the other chapters have been carefully revised and updated. But still we have not been able to say as much as we would have liked about particular topics and we have excluded altogether material on the rights of consumers, hospital patients and people with environmental concerns. Greater enlightenment on all rights issues can in some instances be obtained from the publications listed in the section on Further Reading beginning on page 429.

The book begins with a description of court and tribunal structures in Northern Ireland and with an explanation of the European dimension, public law remedies and legal aid. It then moves on to describe police and army powers, where the distinction between emergency and ordinary laws is most apparent. Those powers are very extensive, especially in view of the Emergency Provisions Act 1996, so if they are abused the consequences for individuals can be dire. The next two chapters look more closely at the police's power to question suspects and at the system for handling complaints against the police: the law on the former was significantly altered by the Police and Criminal Evidence (NI) Order 1989, while the law on police complaints was subjected to a radical independent review by Dr Maurice Hayes in 1997.

In Chapter 7 the position of prisoners is examined, an area which has given rise to a large amount of litigation in Northern Ireland. The impact of the European Convention on Human Rights has often been felt in prisons, but not always to the advantage of prisoners. What amounts to a further variety of imprisonment is described in the chapter on immigration and freedom of movement, where the law relating to exclusion orders issued under the Prevention of Terrorism Act (hopefully a thing of the past) is fully explained. This leads in the next three chapters to an exposition of people's rights to expression and information, whether through demonstrations, meetings, organisations or direct speech. Some account has been taken of the Protection from Harassment (NI) Order 1997, and of the Public Processions etc. (NI) Bill, which was published just before this edition went to press.

The following three chapters which focus on discrimination, covering religious and political belief, gender, and race, illustrate the degree of sophistication which the law must attain if it is to begin to rectify human rights abuses. Northern Ireland is the only part of the United Kingdom or Ireland where discrimination based on religious or political belief is unlawful and the Fair Employment (NI) Act 1989 has considerably bolstered the original 1976 Act, even though a large-scale review of those Acts in 1997 has identified areas where improvements could still be made. Chapter 15 describes the (not so extensive) rights of disabled persons in Northern Ireland (giving full attention to the Disability Discrimination Act 1995), while Chapter 16 outlines the law affecting family and sexual life, with particular emphasis on the rights of women. Again, it should be noted that there is not yet any law which prohibits discrimination based on a person's sexual orientation, although the government did change the criminal law on male homosexuality following a decision of the European Court of Human Rights in 1981 (*Dudgeon* v *UK*). Ageism is still not unlawful.

The final chapters are devoted entirely to the category known as social and economic rights, which many would argue are even more significant than civil and political rights. The law relating to education has been affected by a number of pieces of legislation, while the more general law relating to children's rights was considerably recast by the Children (NI) Order 1995. The rights of employees were consolidated by the Employment Rights (NI) Order 1996. The rights to proper housing and to a decent level of social security are not yet fully recognised in our law, despite the terrible conditions in which thousands of people live.

Each chapter aims primarily to explain the current law and is restrained in offering a critique. At times contributors have inevitably found it difficult to conceal their objections to some of the relevant legal provisions and the CAJ endorses the points they make in this regard. As far as possible contributors have sought to ensure that their chapters accurately state the law as of 1 November 1997. If there are mistakes, please let us know.

Chapter 2

Remedies

Brigid Hadfield

An important aspect of the law concerns its procedures and remedies. Access to the courts is a central element of justice. A right conferred by law is an empty one without the means of enforcing it. Furthermore, the law should provide procedures which are appropriate for remedying the different types of grievance which may arise. As far as the criminal law is concerned, the law should both ensure a procedure suitable for the gravity of the offence and also avoid undue or oppressive punishment for those who break the law.

This chapter, therefore, sets out the court structure in Northern Ireland, including not only the criminal and civil courts but also tribunals and inquests. The European dimension, as provided by European Union law and the European Convention on Human Rights, is also explained. Particular attention is paid to the remedying of grievances against public bodies, both through judicial review and through a complaint to the Ombudsman. Finally, reference is made to the schemes of legal aid, advice and assistance which provide some people in need with financial assistance when dealing with legal problems.

The criminal courts

Criminal offences in Northern Ireland divide into four broad categories: offences which must be tried summarily, those which must be tried on indictment, those which are triable either way - formerly called "hybrid" offences - and offences which are "scheduled" under the emergency laws.

Summary offences

Offences which must be tried summarily are the least serious offences. They are tried in a magistrates' court by a resident magistrate sitting without a jury. Illustrations of summary offences are to be found in the Public Order (NI) Order 1987 (as amended) (see Chapter 9). These include organising or taking part in a public procession in respect of which the required notice has not been given, taking part in a public procession as a member of an unregistered band, trying to break up a lawful public procession or public meeting, riotous or disorderly behaviour in a public place and obstructive sitting in a public place. Common examples also include assault and many motoring offences. A person found guilty of a summary offence is liable to a sentence of imprisonment (of variable duration but usually not exceeding six months), to a fine or to both.

An appeal against a magistrate's court's decision can go either to a county court (on questions of fact and law) or to the Court of Appeal (on questions purely of law). From there an appeal can go to the House of Lords.

Offences triable on indictment

These are serious offences which have to be tried in the Crown Court by a judge and jury. They include murder, manslaughter, rape, robbery and wounding or causing grievous bodily harm with intent to cause grievous bodily harm. The committal stage for these offences - *i.e.* the preliminary hearing into whether or not the accused person should be "committed" for trial - is heard in a magistrates' court.

Appeals against decisions in the Crown Court go to the Court of Appeal and from there to the House of Lords.

Offences triable either way

An offence may be triable either summarily or on indictment in one of three situations. First, the legislation creating the offence may state that it can be tried either way. In this situation, the prosecution will decide how to proceed according to the seriousness of the offence. So, for example, under the Public Order (NI) Order 1987 a person who takes part in a prohibited procession may be tried either way depending on how grave his or her alleged misconduct was. Second, some offences normally triable on indictment, such as, theft and indecent assault, may be tried summarily if the resident magistrate who hears the case at the committal stage considers that it is not a serious case and if both prosecution and defence have no objections.   Third, a small number of statutory offences normally tried summarily (*e.g.* criminal damage) may be tried on indictment if the offence carries a potential sentence of more than six months and if the defendant asks to be tried on indictment.

Scheduled offences

The "scheduled" offences are those listed in Schedule 1 at the end of the Northern Ireland (Emergency Provisions) Act 1996, being offences most commonly committed by persons engaged in political violence. The category cuts across the distinction between summary and indictable offences. Most of the scheduled offences are indictable, in which case they are tried before a "Diplock court" , *i.e.* a single judge of the Crown Court, sitting without a jury. Some of the offences are stated by the Act to be triable either summarily or on indictment, such as membership of a proscribed organisation or display of support in public for a proscribed organisation. A prosecution in respect of an offence under the 1996 Act cannot be instituted without the consent of the Director of Public Prosecutions for Northern Ireland.

Some of the scheduled offences may be "de-scheduled" by the Attorney-General if there is no element of "terrorism" involved in a particular case, but if he or she refuses to do this there is no appeal against the decision.   Some offences cannot be de-scheduled (or "certified out" as the process is sometimes called). Some offences are treated as scheduled offences only if committed in a particular way (*e.g.* robbery where a firearm is used).

Inquests

The main legislation on inquests in Northern Ireland is the Coroners Act (NI) 1959 (as amended) and the statutory rules made under it. There are currently seven coroners and five deputy coroners in Northern Ireland, all of whom must be solicitors or barristers of at least five years' standing.

The function of a coroner is to investigate unexpected or unexplained deaths, deaths in suspicious circumstances or deaths occurring as a result of violence, misadventure or unfair means. The coroner has a discretion whether or not to order a *post mortem* examination of the body; in practice a *post mortem* will be held in any case where the explanation of a death fails to satisfy the coroner. If the investigation indicates that death was due to unnatural causes then an inquest is likely to be held; this happens in approximately one in five investigations.

The inquest is held in public and is usually held without a jury, but a jury must be summoned where the death occurred in prison, where it was caused by an accident, poison or a notifiable disease, or where it occurred in circumstances which, if they were to continue or recur, would be prejudicial to the health or safety of the public. Unlike in England, there is no requirement to summon a jury where a death has occurred in police custody or by the action of the police in pursuance of their duty, although the coroner has a discretion to summon a jury in such a case. A jury at an inquest has between seven and eleven members.

The purpose of an inquest is to ascertain who the deceased was and how, when and where the deceased came by his or her death. An inquest in Northern Ireland now returns no verdicts as such. Prior to 1981 a coroner or a jury could return a verdict of death by "natural causes", "accident", "misadventure", "his (or her) own act", "execution of sentence of death" or an "open" verdict. Since 1981 a verdict has had to take the form of factual "findings" only. Neither the coroner nor the jury is permitted to express "any opinion on questions of criminal or civil liability" (rule 16 of the Coroners (Practice and Procedure) (NI) Rules 1963). In practice an inquest is not opened until the coroner has been informed that no criminal proceedings will be brought in relation to the death. Where a person is charged with a criminal offence, the coroner must adjourn the inquest, "in the absence of reason to the contrary" (rule 13 (1)), until after the completion of the criminal proceedings, including an appeal. This can lead to delays in the holding of an inquest. The Coroner also has a discretion not to hold an inquest after criminal proceedings.

Procedures at inquests

The procedure for the conduct of an inquest is regulated by both statutory rules and the coroner's own discretion, the exercise of which may be subject to judicial review (see page 16).

The calling of witnesses at an inquest is a matter for the discretion of the coroner, although he or she is prohibited from compelling any person to give evidence "who is suspected of causing the death or has been charged or is likely to be charged with an offence relating to the death" (rule 9(2)). This rule has been upheld as lawful by the House of Lords (*McKerr v Armagh Coroner,* 1990). If such a person volunteers to offer information, it in practice tends to be done in the person's absence by way of the submission of a written statement to the inquest. It is effectively not possible to test or challenge the contents of such a statement other than by direct testimony from other witnesses at the inquest. This position has also been upheld as lawful by the House of Lords (*Devine v Attorney-General for Northern Ireland,* 1992).

Witnesses who do give evidence may be questioned (but not cross-examined) by both the coroner and by other "properly" interested parties to the proceedings, either directly or through a barrister or solicitor (rule 7(1)). Evidence is given on oath. The questions must be confined to the remit of an inquest. Hearsay evidence is admissible. The relatives of the deceased are not entitled to call witnesses, although they may suggest the names of potential witnesses to the coroner.

Documentary evidence is also placed before the inquest. Relatives of the deceased may be given a copy of the *post mortem* report before the inquest begins. There is no requirement, however, for other documentary evidence, such as forensic reports, photographs or witness statements, to be given to them before then. They may make a final statement to the jury before the inquest concludes. If the Secretary of State for Northern Ireland believes that a part of the written or oral evidence puts national security at risk, he or she can issue a Public Interest Immunity Certificate which may bar the disclosure of evidence to the inquest or control the way in which oral evidence is given (*e.g.* from behind a screen hiding the witness from the general public: see *In re McNeill,* 1994. The coroner or court on judicial review may scrutinise the ambit of the term "national security" (see *In re McNeill* and *In re Toman,* 1994).

At the conclusion of the inquest, the coroner or the jury delivers their findings, which are confined to "a statement of who the deceased was, and how, when and where" he or she died (rule 2(1)). No qualifications or additions are permitted. There can be no appeal against the decision of a coroner's inquest, although the proceedings may be subject to judicial review.

Although legal aid for inquests is contemplated by the Legal Aid, Advice and Assistance (NI) Order 1981 for those entitled to be legally represented at inquests, the relevant provision has never been implemented and legal aid is, therefore, not available at present for the inquest itself. "Green form" legal advice and assistance (see page 24) is available for those who meet the financial eligibility criteria and who want legal advice before the inquest or assistance in preparing for it.

Juries

The law dealing with the qualification for jury service and the empanelling, summoning and balloting of juries is to be found in the Juries (NI) Order 1996. Some of its provisions apply to coroners' juries. In civil cases both the plaintiff and the defendant can each challenge the presence of up to six proposed jurors without giving any reason for the challenges; other proposed jurors can be challenged provided the judge thinks satisfactory reasons have been supplied (art.14). In criminal cases the prosecution can challenge proposed jurors only if reasons are given, whereas the defence can challenge up to 12 without giving reasons and only thereafter must they "show cause" for their challenges (art.15).

The civil courts

In general terms, the criminal law is primarily concerned with the punishment of those who have broken the law. The civil courts, however, are concerned with compensation and redress, with property matters and with questions of status, such as divorce and adoption. There are three types of court for civil proceedings in Northern Ireland: they are the magistrates' courts, the county courts and the High Court. Which court a civil matter comes before depends largely on the seriousness of the issue, including the amount of money or the value of the property involved. Civil proceedings are often settled between the parties before the matter reaches the court.

Magistrates' courts

The powers of magistrates in civil matters are less extensive than their criminal law powers, on which they spend the greater amount of time. In civil matters, the procedure used is simple and speedy, and litigants are often represented by a solicitor rather than a barrister. The main civil powers of a magistrates' court relate to some domestic matters, such as financial provision orders, personal protection orders and exclusion orders (see Chapter 15). They also deal with small debts, including rent arrears (although there is some overlap with the small claims court: see below), some proceedings brought by landlords (including the Housing Executive and housing associations) to evict tenants, and licence renewal applications.

Appeals against a magistrates' court's decisions in civil matters go to a county court or (on questions purely of law) to the Court of Appeal.

County courts

The financial upper limit for most cases coming before the county courts is now £15,000. The county courts can hear claims in tort (such as personal injury claims following an accident at work or on the roads), or for breach of contract, some undefended divorce petitions, equality of opportunity and discrimination cases, other than in the field of employment (see Chapters 12 to 15) and applications to determine the proper rent for a protected tenancy under the Rent (NI) Order 1978 (see Chapter 20). The county courts have a special "small claims" procedure for many claims not exceeding £1,000. This procedure is commonly employed by business and commercial organisations for non-payment of hire-purchase installments or for money owed for goods which have been delivered or for services rendered, but consumers can also use it when claiming against shops or suppliers. It cannot be used for road accident claims, unlike in England and Wales.

The county courts also hear appeals against decisions of the Secretary of State for Northern Ireland on applications for compensation for criminal injuries and criminal damage or for compensation under the emergency powers legislation (see Chapters 3 and 4). These are applications by people who have suffered loss because of criminal or "terrorist" activities.

Appeals against county court decisions in civil matters go to the High Court or (on questions purely of law) to the Court of Appeal.

The High Court

The jurisdiction of the High Court is not limited by the value of the claim. There are three Divisions of the High Court: the Queen's Bench Division, which deals principally with claims in tort and for breach of contract; the Chancery Division, which deals mainly with property matters; and the Family Division, which deals with petitions for divorce or nullity and matters affecting those who are mentally ill. The Queen's Bench Division (Crown Side) deals with applications for judicial review. Appeals against High Court decisions can go to the Court of Appeal and from there to the House of Lords but appeals in judicial review cases involving criminal matters go directly from the Queen's Bench Division to the House of Lords.

Judicial review

Judicial review is the procedure which should be used to challenge the validity of the public decisions of public bodies. Where a solely contractual or other private relationship exists between the individual and the body, judicial review is not appropriate and other remedies must be sought. Similarly, where an alternative remedy such as an appeal to a tribunal, or to the Housing Executive's internal review/appeal system, is both available and adequate, that procedure should be followed in preference to judicial review. Public bodies subject to judicial review include the Northern Ireland government departments, government ministers, district councils, the education and library boards, the health and social services boards, the Housing Executive, the lower courts and tribunals, including coroners, and certain decisions of the Royal Ulster Constabulary. Judicial review, therefore, is available against administrative, executive and judicial decision-making. Subordinate legislation (*e.g.* Rules and Regulations) can also be judicially reviewed. Acts of the Westminster Parliament are subject to judicial review only where it can be argued that there is a conflict with European Union law.

Judicial review is concerned with the procedures employed by a public body in reaching its decision and not with the merits of the decision itself, unless the decision is particularly outrageous or absurd. Judicial review is not a way of challenging an unwelcome decision unless it can be argued that an unfair or unlawful procedure has been employed in reaching it. The grounds on which a challenge may be made include these: the body has wrongly interpreted the relevant law, taken into account irrelevant or ignored relevant factors, failed to pursue the policy and objectives of the legislation, unduly restricted its discretionary powers or followed an unfair or biased procedure. Aspects of an unfair procedure include the nature of the hearing given. A developing area of the law relates to a duty to give reasons, even where the legislation in question is silent on the matter.

A judicial review may be sought by a person or body with a sufficient interest in the matter, who seeks the permission of the court promptly and in any event within three months of the challenged decision being made. The remedies which the court may grant to a successful applicant for judicial review include *certiorari* (which quashes the public body's decision), *mandamus* (which compels a person or body under a duty to act to do so), *declaration* (which declares what the law is or the rights of the parties are) and *prohibition* (which prevents the public body from proceeding to an unlawful decision). These remedies are available at the court's discretion and the court may refuse a remedy if it believes that the applicant's conduct merits this or if it is in the interests of good administration to do so. Applications for judicial review are brought to court under Order 53 of the Rules of the Supreme Court (NI).

Appeals

In both criminal and civil matters, an appeal will lie against the decision of the original court. Although some other courts do have an appellate jurisdiction, the main appeal court is the Court of Appeal in Belfast. In criminal matters, a person convicted in the Crown Court may appeal to the Court of Appeal on a point of law, on a question of fact or against sentence. In some other situations the accused person will need the permission of the court before he or she can appeal. The prosecution cannot appeal against the acquittal of a person convicted in the Crown Court, although the Attorney-General may refer a point of law to the Court of Appeal for its opinion. This does not affect the acquittal at all, but the opinion of the Court will guide the prosecution in future trials. The Attorney-General also has the power to refer a case to the Court of Appeal where he or she believes that the sentence imposed by the Crown Court was too lenient. The Criminal Cases Review Commission, whose remit includes Northern Ireland, has the power to refer alleged miscarriages of justice to the Court of Appeal and to carry out investigations at the request of the Court of Appeal.

The Court of Appeal also has jurisdiction in civil matters, particularly on points of law. In both criminal and civil matters an appeal may lie, with leave, to the House of Lords in London. Only two or three appeals are taken to the House of Lords each year, and these are cases of major legal importance.

The enforcement of civil judgments

A person who has lost litigation may be ordered by a court to pay money to the winner of the litigation. These people are known respectively as the judgment debtor and the judgment creditor. The judgment debtor is required to pay within a reasonable time. If he or she does not do so, then the judgment creditor may ask the Enforcement of Judgments Office to send the debtor a document called a notice of intent to enforce. This orders the debtor to pay within 10 days. If the debtor still does not pay, the creditor may apply to the Office for actual enforcement of the judgment. As this can be an expensive procedure, it should be followed only if the creditor is sure that the debtor has assets with which to pay. If the debtor does not have the means with which to satisfy the order, the creditor must accept that the original judgment in his or her favour may be worth nothing. The Enforcement of Judgments Office is at: Bedford House, Bedford Street, Belfast BT2 7NR, tel: 01232-245081.

Tribunals

Tribunals are now very much a part of the legal system, dealing with thousands of cases every year. A tribunal is established (by legislation) where the intention is to provide a system of dispute resolution which is both specialised and also relatively speedy, cheap, informal and accessible. A tribunal is often composed of three people, of whom only one, the chairperson, is legally qualified. The best known tribunals are industrial tribunals (which deal with employment rights, including those relating to equality of opportunity: see Chapter 19), social security appeal tribunals (see Chapter 21) and the Mental Health Review Tribunal.

An appeal often lies on a point of law from a tribunal decision to the Court of Appeal, although there may also be an intermediate appeal before this stage is reached. Where the legislation provides an individual with recourse to an appeal tribunal, he or she should, as a general rule, follow that procedure rather than judicial review. Tribunal decisions are themselves also subject to judicial review, but an applicant will be successful only if one or more of the factors mentioned above is present.

European Union law

The law of the European Union is also part of the domestic law of the United Kingdom. EU law deals with many matters concerning economic and social activity, most notably the free movement of goods, the free movement of workers and the Common Agricultural Policy. It also deals with matters designed to protect the enjoyment of these freedoms, such as the freedom to provide and to receive services, freedom of establishment, social security and sex discrimination (see more particularly Chapter 13). EU law is to be found in the Treaties of the European Community, including the Treaty of Rome, the Single European Act, the Maastricht Treaty and the Treaty of Amsterdam, in the Community's Regulations and Directives and in the decisions of the European Court of Justice (the ECJ) and Court of First Instance (CFI). The ECJ is the Community's main court and sits at Luxembourg.

If a matter comes before a Northern Ireland court or tribunal involving EU law, one of two procedures may be followed. If the EU law is clear, the domestic court must follow and apply it (and if necessary not apply any conflicting domestic laws). If the meaning of the EU law is not clear, the domestic court may make a reference under Article 177 of the Treaty of Rome to the ECJ (see *e.g. Johnston v Chief Constable of the RUC*, 1987). While the reference is pending, the domestic proceedings are suspended. The ECJ gives its ruling on the meaning of EU law only (not on the domestic law), leaving the domestic court to apply the ruling on EU law to the facts before it. Lower courts and tribunals have a discretion whether or not to make an Article 177 reference, but domestic courts and tribunals against whose decisions there is no judicial remedy under domestic law *must* make a reference on questions concerning the interpretation or application of EU law. The Article 177 procedure cannot be invoked in those areas of domestic law not actually or potentially affected by European Union law.

The European Convention on Human Rights

The European Convention on Human Rights (the ECHR) is an international treaty which has been ratified by the United Kingdom government and which is, therefore, binding upon it in international law. It is not yet a part of domestic law, which means that its provisions cannot, unlike European Union law, be directly invoked by an individual before the domestic courts. It may, however, be used by the courts to resolve any ambiguities which may exist in domestic statutory law, or where the common law is uncertain or incomplete. The Human Rights Bill, at present before parliament in Westminster, *will* make the ECHR part of domestic UK law.

The ECHR deals with the protection of rights, such as the right to life, to liberty, to a fair trial and to respect for one's private and family life. It also seeks to protect fundamental freedoms, including freedom from torture or inhuman or degrading treatment or punishment, freedom of thought, conscience and religion, freedom of expression and freedom of peaceful assembly.

Those states which have ratified the ECHR are required to secure to "everyone within their jurisdiction" the rights and freedoms set forth in the Convention (Article 1). These states - known as High Contracting

Parties - may be proceeded against for an alleged breach of the Convention either by another High Contracting Party or by an aggrieved individual. This latter right exists only if the state has accepted the right of individual petition, which the United Kingdom government has done since 1966.

The individual lodges his or her complaint with the European Commission of Human Rights at Strasbourg, and the Commission must first decide whether the petition is admissible. The Commission's address is: Palais de L'Europe, 67006 Strasbourg, France. It will be inadmissible if all domestic remedies have not been exhausted or if it is out of time, anonymous, substantially the same as a matter already examined by the Commission, manifestly ill-founded or an abuse of the right of petition. The petition must also relate to a matter covered by the Convention, in terms of substance, location and time of the alleged violation. Usually it needs to be lodged within six months of the final decision on the matter in the national courts.

If the petition or complaint is admissible, the Commission will undertake an inquiry and try to secure a "friendly settlement", which must be compatible with the terms of the Convention. If it is not possible to secure a friendly settlement, the Commission will draw up a report indicating whether or not there has been a breach of the Convention. The matter may then, within three months, be referred to the Court of Human Rights, which also sits at Strasbourg. If the matter is not referred to the Court, it is resolved by the Committee of Ministers of the Council of Europe.

The Court's decision is binding on all the states involved in the case, although in practice most states delay before changing their law or administrative practice to bring it into line with the requirements of the Convention. The Court may also order the High Contracting Party to pay compensation or "just satisfaction" to the successful petitioner, as well as his or her legal costs.

Protocol 11 to the ECHR, when it becomes operative, probably in a year or two's time, will make changes to Convention procedures. Protocol 11 will create a permanent full-time Court, replacing the current two-tier system of Commission and Court. The Court will sit in Committees of three judges, in Chambers of seven judges and in a Grand Chamber of 17 judges. A consequence of this reform is that an individual will have the right to bring an alleged human rights violation directly before the European Court of Human Rights. Under the new system, once a case is registered, it will be assigned to a Chamber. The application will then be considered by a Committee which will deal with the majority of admissibility decisions, determined under the existing criteria. If a case is declared admissible the Chamber will deal with the case, securing, where feasible, a friendly settlement. If it is impossible to do this, the Chamber will proceed to judgment in the case. The case may, before judgment, in certain circumstances and if certain conditions are fulfilled, be referred to the Grand Chamber, especially in those cases involving serious questions involving the interpretation of the Convention. The Committee of Ministers retains its role of overseeing the execution of the judgments of the new Court.

So far several cases from Northern Ireland have led to judgments from the European Court of Human Rights, including *Dudgeon* (1981, on homosexuality), *Murray (Margaret)* (1994, involving Article 5 rights with regard to arrest and detention) and *Murray (John)* (1996, involving Article 6 rights and access to a lawyer).

The Ombudsman

The term "Ombudsman" in Northern Ireland covers two distinct offices, although they are in practice held by the same person. There is, first, the office of Parliamentary Ombudsman and, second, that of the Commissioner for Complaints. The relevant legislation is the Ombudsman (NI) Order 1996 and the Commissioner for Complaints (NI) Order 1996.

The function of the Parliamentary Ombudsman is to investigate complaints of maladministration made against Northern Ireland government departments and the Office of the Director-General of Electricity Supply. The administrative staff of tribunals listed in the legislation are also subject to investigation by the Ombudsman. The complaint must be made by a person who feels that he or she has suffered injustice as a result of the maladministration and the complaint should be made within 12 months of the action or inaction in question. "Maladministration" is not defined in the relevant legislation but covers matters such as neglect, inattention, delay, incompetence, ineptitude, perversity and arbitrariness.

The complaint should be made to the Ombudsman via a Westminster Member of Parliament, who has a discretion whether or not to refer the complaint to the Ombudsman. He or she may decide to deal with the matter instead. If a person writes directly to the Ombudsman, he or she will, where the complaint merits further investigation, ask the complainant to refer the matter back through an MP.

The Ombudsman is completely independent of government departments and the service provided is free of charge. He or she has full access to all files and records. The purpose of an investigation is to ascertain whether or not there has been maladministration; the Ombudsman has no jurisdiction to investigate the merits of decisions reached without maladministration. The Ombudsman does not usually investigate complaints where there is an alternative remedy, particularly an appeal to a tribunal or judicial review, although if an individual appeals to a tribunal and believes that the injustice remains unremedied, the Ombudsman may then investigate the complaint.

Once an investigation has been completed, the Ombudsman sends a report of the investigation to the complainant, the referring MP and the relevant government department. If the Ombudsman upholds the complaint, hc or she will try to effect a fair settlement, perhaps by securing appropriate redress for the complainant, such as an apology or the payment of compensation. In some cases, as a result of an Ombudsman investigation the department concerned will change its procedures. The Ombudsman (whose reports are in turn considered by Westminster's Select Committee on the Parliamentary Commissioner) cannot, however, compel the government department to provide any redress to a complainant.

The Ombudsman can also investigate complaints about personnel matters in the Northern Ireland Civil Service. Complaints against Westminster government departments are within the jurisdiction of the United Kingdom Parliamentary Commissioner, whose jurisdiction therefore includes the Northern Ireland Office, the Northern Ireland Court Service, the Inland Revenue and the Ministry of Defence. The Northern Ireland Parliamentary Ombudsman would be called the Assembly Ombudsman, if there were devolution to Northern Ireland again.

The second office held by the Northern Ireland Ombudsman is that of Commissioner for Complaints. In that capacity he or she investigates complaints of maladministration made by an aggrieved individual against local and public bodies in Northern Ireland. These bodies include the district councils, the education and library boards, the health and social services boards, the Housing Executive (although its own internal complaints procedure should be resorted to first), the Labour Relations Agency, the Local Enterprise Development Unit, the Council for Catholic Maintained Schools, the Equal Opportunities Commission and the Fair Employment Commission.

There is direct access to the Commissioner for Complaints, whose services are again both free and independent, but the complaint usually needs to be made, at the latest, within 12 months. The Commissioner cannot question the merits of a decision taken without maladministration, nor will he or she usually investigate a complaint which could be the subject of legal proceedings or an alternative investigatory procedure. Certain matters also fall outside his or her jurisdiction, including the commencement or conduct of civil or criminal proceedings.

If the Commissioner's investigations disclose that there has been maladministration, he or she will try to secure a settlement, such as an apology or the payment of compensation. If this is unsuccessful, the complainant may apply to a county court for compensation. The Attorney-General may also, at the request of the Commissioner, seek an injunction or a declaration from the High Court to restrain a public body from persistent maladministration. The law has recently been altered by the Commissioner for Complaints (Amendment) (NI) Order 1997 which extends the Commissioner's powers with regard to (amongst others) actions taken by health professionals in the exercise of their clinical judgment and action taken by general health service and independent providers in connection with the provision of those services.

With regard to the various Citizen's Charters, individuals, when dealing with a public body operating under the provisions of a Charter, should note that the body itself may have introduced a complaints mechanism.

- The Northern Ireland Ombudsman is:

   Mr Gerry Burns,
   Progressive House,
   33 Wellington Place,
   Belfast BT1 6HN
   tel: 01232-233821.

- The UK Parliamentary Commissioner is:

   Mr Michael Buckley,
   Office of the PCA,
   Church House,
   Great Smith Street,
   London SW1P 3BW
   tel: 0171-276 3000.

Legal aid, advice and assistance

There are various types of legal aid schemes designed to provide financial assistance in legal matters. The controlling legislation is the Legal Aid, Advice and Assistance (NI) Order 1981 and the regulations made under it. The schemes are "means tested" in terms of both disposable income and disposable capital and in 1993 the financial limits were altered so as to make help available primarily to people who are on income support.

- The "Green Form" scheme (its popular name) allows a solicitor to offer advice on any area of the law of Northern Ireland. The advice may be written or oral; it includes preparation of all types of documents but does not extend to representation at hearings. The assisted person may be required to make a financial contribution to the assistance, which in any event cannot exceed a value of £86.50.

- "ABWOR" - assistance by way of representation - is based on the green form scheme and is available for the Mental Health Review Tribunal and disciplinary hearings before Boards of Visitors in prisons (see Chapter 7).

- Civil legal aid covers most civil proceedings in the higher courts (excluding libel actions) but it is not available for either inquests or tribunals. The Department of Health and Social Services assesses financial eligibility for civil legal aid. The Law Society's Legal Aid Department also applies a "merits" test to determine whether or not it is reasonable for the party concerned to take or defend the proceedings in question. An assisted person may be required to make some financial contribution.

- Criminal legal aid relates to the defence of criminal proceedings by a solicitor or barrister. If granted by the court concerned it is entirely free in Northern Ireland, unlike in England and Wales.

Chapter 3

Powers of the Police

Brice Dickson

This chapter sets out the powers of the Royal Ulster
Constabulary which people in Northern Ireland are most likely
to encounter in everyday life. Readers should note that the
powers of soldiers in the army (see Chapter 4) are often different. The
specific topic of police questioning is dealt with in Chapter 5.

Much of the law on police powers was altered by the Police and
Criminal Evidence (NI) Order 1989 - the PACE Order - which came
into force in January 1990. This Order is similar in many respects to the
Police and Criminal Evidence Act 1984, which governs the position in
England and Wales. Books on that Act are therefore relevant to the law
in Northern Ireland as well. The position regarding police powers in
relation to "terrorist" offences in Northern Ireland is governed by the
Prevention of Terrorism (Temporary Provisions) Act 1989 (the PTA)
and by the Northern Ireland (Emergency Provisions) Act 1996 (the
EPA). Only the first of these applies in other parts of the United
Kingdom as well as in Northern Ireland. Throughout this chapter the
police's powers are first described as they exist under the ordinary law
and then as they exist under the emergency laws.

The power to stop and question under the ordinary law

Contrary to popular belief, the general rule is that the police do not
have a general power to stop and question people. This is true not only of
pedestrians but also of people in cars or any other form of transport. The

police can, of course, *attempt* to stop and question people, and many of us may well comply with the police's request and will readily answer questions, but there is no legal obligation to stop when asked to do so or to answer questions put by a police officer. The PACE Order confers powers on the police to stop people for the purpose of searching them (these are dealt with below), but it does not remove a person's right not to be stopped for questioning.

To stop a person lawfully the police have to carry out an arrest. During the period of detention after an arrest the police can ask questions but the person arrested is still under no legal duty to reply. In fact, when questioned at any time it is very often sensible to remain silent until a solicitor is present. As England's Lord Chief Justice Parker put it in *Rice v Connolly* (1966): "the whole basis of the common law is the right of the individual to refuse to answer questions put to him (*sic*) by a person in authority". However, as explained more fully in Chapter 5, one of the consequences of the Criminal Evidence (NI) Order 1988 is that the silence of a detained person may later constitute corroborative evidence that that person is guilty of an offence. The law on this point in England and Wales is now the same as in Northern Ireland, as a result of the enactment of sections 34-38 of the Criminal Justice and Public Order Act 1994.

After the police have collected information from persons whom they have stopped and questioned, they can immediately destroy it or store it, indefinitely if they wish and on computer if necessary. The Data Protection Act 1984 prevents citizens from gaining access to data which is "required for the purpose of safeguarding national security" or "held for the prevention or detection of crime". The latter phrase would cover most of the information held by the police. The 1984 Act also does not apply to non-computerised records: a card-index system, for instance, is immune from the access provisions (see Chapter 11).

There are a number of important exceptions to the general rule that the police cannot arbitrarily stop people. These mainly concern road traffic and "terrorist" incidents. The law on the former is identical to that in England and Wales: it permits a police officer to control traffic and, provided the officer is in uniform, to require drivers to stop their vehicles (art.180 of the Road Traffic (NI) Order 1981).

The power to stop and question under the emergency laws

The chief exception to the general rule in the context of "terrorist" incidents is section 25 of the Northern Ireland (Emergency Provisions) Act 1996. According to this, any constable may stop and question any person for as long as is necessary in order to put questions about his or her identity and movements or what he or she knows concerning any recent explosion or any other recent incident endangering life or concerning any person killed or injured in any such explosion or incident. If a person fails to stop when required to do so under section 25, or fails to answer to the best of his or her ability any question addressed under this section, he or she may be fined in a magistrates' court up to £2,000.

There is some doubt over the exact scope of section 25. No-one knows for sure, for instance, whether in law the "identity" of a person includes his or her date of birth and address; the answer may depend on whether or not the person has a common name. The section also gives no indication as to how much detail a person must provide about his or her movements, although the duty to answer to the best of one's ability probably means that one must be as detailed as the police wish. The locality a person is coming from and going to must be disclosed, but it would be unreasonable to have to give the names of the people just visited or about to be visited. Nor is the meaning of "recent" in section 25 clear. But the questions asked do not have to be related to acts of "terrorism", so "any other incident endangering life" could refer to a fire or a car accident. There is no obligation to answer questions relating to one's occupation, family or friends.

The power in section 25 can be used to stop pedestrians but is most frequently used at vehicle check points (VCPs). There is no legal obligation to show a driving licence at a VCP, but it is an easy way of proving your identity. As yet there has been no authoritative ruling as to what exactly constitutes "stopping" within section 25. Knocking on a person's door and putting questions to the person who opens it may not qualify, but temporarily preventing someone from moving from his or her position in a queue or at a counter would probably be enough. Being approached while standing at a street corner would certainly constitute being "stopped" in this context.

The power to arrest under the ordinary law

The Police and Criminal Evidence (NI) Order 1989 contains provisions governing "arrestable" offences, a category which includes offences carrying a sentence (for those over 21) of five years or more, as well as some less serious offences for which Acts of Parliament provide a separate arrest power. The full list is in article 26 and Schedule 2 of the Order. It includes the following:

- smuggling offences under the Customs and Excise Acts;
- offences under the Official Secrets Acts 1911 and 1989;
- indecent assault upon a female;
- taking away a motor vehicle;
- "going equipped for stealing";
- loitering and importuning by a prostitute;
- impersonating a voter at a polling station;
- failing to provide a breath test, or being in charge of a motor vehicle while under the influence of drink or drugs; and
- public order offences under the Public Order (NI) Order 1987.

The PACE Order also provides that the police can arrest without a warrant any person who is reasonably suspected of attempting or conspiring to commit any of the listed offences, or of inciting, aiding, abetting, counselling or procuring their commission. Article 27, moreover, makes it clear that the police may arrest someone for a non-arrestable offence if the service of a summons (requiring later attendance at court) is not practicable or appropriate. Service will not be practicable or appropriate if a person's name or address cannot be readily ascertained or is doubtful, if a child or other vulnerable person needs to be protected, or if the person to be arrested would otherwise suffer or cause injury or damage to property, commit an offence against public decency or cause an unlawful obstruction on a road. Altogether the RUC arrested 26,062 people under the PACE legislation in 1996.

There also exists a judge-made power to arrest someone for a breach of the peace. To be more exact, according to the leading case on the point (*R v Howell*, 1981), there is a power of arrest (1) where a breach of the peace is committed in the presence of the arresting officer, (2) where the arresting officer reasonably believes that such breach will be committed in the immediate future by the person arrested, or (3) where a breach of the peace has been committed and it is reasonably believed that a renewal is threatened. The courts have even said on occasions that the police can arrest people who are not themselves threatening to commit a breach of the peace but whose conduct is likely to provoke others to do so. A breach of the peace was defined in *R v Howell* as "an act done or threatened to be done which either actually harms a person, or in his presence his property, or is likely to cause such harm, or which puts someone in fear of such harm being done". A person arrested for breach of the peace may be "bound over" by a magistrate. This means that he or she will not be further punished provided he or she commits no further breach of the peace, or some other crime, within a stipulated period.

The 1989 Order maintains the rule that the police may arrest any person so long as a warrant for that purpose has been issued to the police by a Justice of the Peace. The JP must be satisfied that the police reasonably suspect the person of a crime and that his or her voluntary co-operation is unlikely. Once a person has been dealt with by a court for the offence alleged in a warrant, the warrant ceases to be valid and cannot be used to justify a later arrest (*Toye v Chief Constable of the RUC*, 1991).

In all situations a police officer is entitled to use reasonable force when carrying out an arrest. The 1989 Order says that in exercising any power under the Order, the police "may use reasonable force, if necessary" (art.88). However, the use of unreasonable force, or of reasonable force in circumstances where it is not necessary, will not make the arrest unlawful. It will only make possible a claim for compensation, under the civil law, for assault. Using force to effect what is in any event an unlawful arrest may lead to the police having to pay so-called exemplary damages to the victim, as in *Carroll v Chief Constable of the RUC* (1988).

An arresting officer must also indicate that the arrest is taking place and give a reason for it (unless the reason is very obvious). This was made clear in *Christie v Leachinsky* (1947) and confirmed by article 30 of the PACE Order. If it later turns out that the reason for the arrest was not a good one, the person arrested can claim compensation for "false imprisonment" and "malicious prosecution". But if the police show that they had "reasonable and probable cause" for acting as they did, perhaps because the person arrested had confessed to the alleged crime, no compensation will be awarded (*Cooke v Chief Constable of the RUC*, 1989).

It remains the case that an ordinary citizen has the power to make what is popularly known as "a citizen's arrest", though the extent of this power is not as great as in the case of the police. It does not permit a citizen to arrest someone who is *about to commit* an arrestable offence, and it does not allow an arrest for an arrestable offence which the citizen reasonably believes has been committed but which *in fact has not been* (*R v Self*, 1992). Given the difficulty of knowing which offences are arrestable and which are not, it is unwise for ordinary people to try to take the law into their own hands in this way.

The power to arrest under the emergency laws

Ever since the creation of Northern Ireland in 1920 there have been special powers conferred on the police. After the Northern Ireland Parliament was abolished in 1972, the Northern Ireland (Emergency Provisions) Act 1973 was passed (the EPA). In 1974 this Act was supplemented by the Prevention of Terrorism (Temporary Provisions) Act (the PTA), which was enacted for the whole of the United Kingdom but designed to deal only with violence connected with the political affairs of Northern Ireland. The EPA in force today is that enacted in 1996; the current PTA was enacted in 1989 and it now applies to "international terrorism" as well. The present government has said that it wishes to replace the PTA with permanent anti-terrorist legislation.

The main arrest powers conferred on the police are in section 18 of the EPA 1996 and section 14 of the PTA 1989. Section 18 permits a police officer to "arrest without warrant any person whom he or she has reasonable grounds to suspect is committing, has committed or is about to commit a scheduled offence or an offence under this Act which is not a scheduled offence". When the list of scheduled offences and other offences created by the EPA is compared with the list of offences for which a person can be arrested without warrant under the PACE (NI) Order 1989 (see above), there is almost a complete overlap. There is therefore a good case for allowing section 18 to lapse. The annual statistics on the EPA show that in any event it has not been used since 1990 because the arrest power in the PTA is much more wide-ranging.

The arrest power in section 14(1) of the PTA 1989 is so important that the exact wording deserves to be set out in full:

Subject to subsection (2) below, a constable may arrest without warrant a person whom he has reasonable grounds for suspecting to be (a) a person guilty of an offence under section 2, 8, 9, 10 or 11 above; (b) a person who is or has been concerned in the commission, preparation or instigation of acts of terrorism to which this section applies; or (c) a person subject to an exclusion order.

The section applies to all acts of terrorism except those connected solely with a part of the United Kingdom other than Northern Ireland. This means that people such as animal rights protestors in England, or arsonists of English holiday homes in Wales, cannot qualify as terrorists however terrible their behaviour. The offences referred to in section 14(1)(a) are membership of or support for a banned organisation, failing to comply with an exclusion order (see Chapter 8), contributing to acts of terrorism or to the resources of banned organisations, and assisting in the control of terrorist funds. But it is section 14(1)(b) which is by far the most all-embracing provision, for it allows arrests for unspecified crimes provided only that the police reasonably suspect involvement in acts of terrorism. "Terrorism" itself, therefore, is not an offence, but suspected terrorists can be arrested. The government claims that this power is necessary because it helps to *prevent* terrorism; the arrest powers in the PACE Order, including the one which authorises arrest of any person reasonably suspected of being about to commit an arrestable offence, are deemed inadequate. It is clear, moreover, that, just as in the case of the PACE Order's powers, a police officer can be said to have "reasonable suspicion" for the purposes of section 14 if he or she is acting on information supplied and instructions issued by a superior police officer (see *O'Hara v Chief Constable of the RUC*, 1997).

If the police arrest a person under the emergency laws, they still have to indicate why the arrest is occurring and under what power. If subsequent questioning - or the lack of it - shows that there were no real grounds for reasonably suspecting a connection with terrorism, an action in the civil courts for compensation for false imprisonment may succeed. It is a fact that, during the last 10 years, three-quarters of the persons arrested in Northern Ireland under section 14 of the PTA have later been released without being charged. This might suggest that the arrest powers are being used not just for the legitimate purpose of rounding up genuine suspects but for the illegitimate purpose of harassing people or fishing for snippets of incriminating evidence about other people. Alternatively, it might mean that people who are arrested supply no evidence which the police can rely upon to found a charge.

The use of arrest powers just for the gathering of information is possibly a contravention of Article 5(1)(c) of the European Convention on Human Rights, which says that arrest or detention must be for the purpose of bringing the person "before the competent legal authority on reasonable suspicion of having committed an offence or when it is reasonably considered necessary to prevent his (*sic*) committing an offence". In *Brogan v UK* (1988), however, the European Court of

Human Rights held that the PTA's definition of "terrorism" ("The use of violence for political ends, including any use of violence for the purpose of putting the public or any section of the public in fear") was well in keeping with the Convention's notion of an "offence".

What is clear is that, if the police arrest someone under paragraphs (a) or (c) of section 14(1), the precise grounds for the arrest must be notified at the time. This is a rule laid down by judges and it has not been expressly abolished by the PTA. Unfortunately, there is nothing to stop the police from arresting someone under paragraph (b) even though they may have enough suspicion of more particular offences to make an arrest under one of the other two paragraphs. But if a person disputes the lawfulness of an arrest under paragraph (b) the police must still supply details ("in general terms") of the matters which constituted reasonable grounds for the arresting constable's suspicion that the person was involved in terrorism (*Clinton v Chief Constable of the RUC*, 1991).

In the first six months of 1997, 319 people were arrested under the PTA in Northern Ireland; 89 of these were charged with a criminal offence, but 230 (72%) were released without charge.

The power to stop and search people under the ordinary law

The police do not possess a general power to stop and search anyone at will. A person may, of course, consent to being stopped and searched, but if consent is withdrawn the search must cease immediately. The consent may also be limited, for instance, to a search of a person's pockets or handbag. In this case any more extensive search will be an assault, for which compensation can be sought.

The police do possess limited stop and search powers conferred by legislation, in particular the Police and Criminal Evidence (NI) Order 1989. For a useful list of other relevant legislation see Annex A to the Code of Practice on this topic, referred to at page 50 below. As a rule, because it can be difficult to know whether the police are acting within their powers when conducting a search, it is better if the person being searched, rather than resisting the search and risking a prosecution for obstructing the police in the execution of their duty or for assault, submits to the search while informing the police that he or she is not consenting voluntarily. The police should be asked to name the exact power under which they are acting so that its terms can be checked later. If the police act in a high-handed fashion, or in breach of the powers conferred upon them, the person searched should lodge a complaint (see Chapter 6) or think about bringing a civil action (see Chapter 2).

A person can also be lawfully searched once he or she has been arrested. Any weapon or evidence of a crime discovered can be seized. The person's home can be searched too, or the place where the arrest has occurred, provided that there is some connection between that place and the suspected offence. If the police uncover evidence relating to a crime during the course of an unlawful search, that evidence is still admissible in a court of law but a civil action against the police for compensation can be begun.

The PACE (NI) Order 1989 empowers police officers to stop, detain and search any person if they have reasonable grounds for suspecting that they will find stolen or prohibited articles. An article is prohibited if it is an offensive weapon or something intended for use in a burglary or theft. Any such item may be seized and need not be returned. The power can be exercised only in a public place. People who are in a garden or yard connected with a dwelling cannot be searched unless the police have reasonable grounds for believing that those people do not reside in the dwelling and are not there with permission.

Before a search is begun, the constable must prove that he or she is indeed a police officer (by displaying a card or giving his or her police number and station). The constable must also indicate the purpose of the proposed search, the reasons for making it and the fact that a written record will be made available to the person if requested within the next year. During the search a person cannot be required to remove any item of clothing in public, except an outer coat, jacket, headgear and gloves. Strip-searching is permitted at police stations in exceptional circumstances (see page 47). A person cannot be detained for longer than is reasonably required for the search to be carried out.

The duty to make a written record and the prohibition on requiring clothes to be removed do not apply to searches following an arrest, although an arrested person can be searched only if the custody officer considers it necessary to permit a record of the person's possessions to be taken. The search must be conducted by an officer of the same sex as the person searched and special conditions apply to "intimate" searches (see below). In any event, after a person has been arrested and taken to a police station, the station's custody officer must record everything which the person is carrying. Any of these things may be retained by the custody officer provided reasons are given, though clothes and personal effects may be seized only if the officer believes that the arrested person may use them to inflict injury, damage property, interfere with evidence, assist an escape, or if there are reasonable grounds for believing that the items may be evidence relating to an offence.

Intimate searches

An intimate search is defined as "a search which consists of the physical examination of a person's body orifices". It requires the written authorisation of a police officer of at least the rank of superintendent, who must first have reasonable grounds for believing that an arrested person may have concealed on his or her body a "Class A" drug or anything which could be used to cause injury while in custody. "Class A" drugs include heroin but not amphetamines or cannabis and they can be searched for only by a registered doctor or nurse and not at a police station. Other intimate searches should also be conducted by a doctor or nurse unless a police officer of at least the rank of superintendent considers that this is not practicable, in which case they must be carried out by a constable of the same sex as the person searched; they can be conducted at police stations.

A written record must be kept by the custody officer of the parts of the body that have been searched, and why. Anything found during an intimate search may be retained only in the circumstances outlined above in relation to clothes and personal effects. In 1996 the RUC conducted just two intimate searches under these powers.

The power to stop and search people under the emergency laws

By virtue of section 20(6) of the EPA 1996 any police officer may stop any person in any public place and search him or her for explosives, firearms, ammunition or wireless transmitters. This power can also be exercised elsewhere than in a public place if the police officer has reasonable grounds to suspect the presence of these items. If a person fails to stop when required to do so he or she may be fined up to £2,000. A search cannot take place under this power for other items (see *Carlisle v Chief Constable of the RUC*, 1989). Explosives inspectors also have the power to stop a person in a public place and search for explosive substances (s. 22(2) of the EPA 1996). If any of the items mentioned are found during a search, they may be seized.

Section 15(3) of the PTA allows a constable to stop and search anyone whom he or she has the power to arrest under section 14 of that Act. The search must be for evidence justifying an arrest, but there must still be independent grounds for the arrest besides whatever is found during the course of a search. People who have already been arrested under section 14 of the PTA may also be searched (s.15(4)). In both instances the search must be carried out by a person of the same sex. Strip-searching, other than in a public place, is nowhere specifically prohibited by the law.

The power to stop and search vehicles under the ordinary law

Curiously, the exact legal position regarding the stopping of vehicles (a term which for present purposes includes vessels and aircraft) is unclear, even though the relevant powers are largely conferred by legislation - see article 180 of the Road Traffic (NI) Order 1981. In an English court case in 1982 (*Steel v Goacher*) it was held that the police had a power under the common law (*i.e.* not based on any statute) to stop traffic in order to prevent criminal activity. Failing to stop a car when requested to do so by the police is therefore a more risk-laden thing to do than failing to stop walking when approached by the police, although it is uncertain what offence is being committed if one disobeys a police command to stop (other perhaps than obstructing the police in the execution of their duties).

The ordinary law already set out above in relation to searches of persons also applies to searches of vehicles. Thus, a car can be stopped, detained and searched if the police have reasonable grounds for suspecting that they will find stolen or prohibited articles. If a vehicle is parked on land connected to a dwelling, it may not be searched unless the police have reasonable grounds for believing that it is there without the permission of a person who resides there. The rules about the police having to identify themselves before making the search also apply, but no police officer can stop a vehicle unless he or she is in uniform. Persons inside a vehicle can be searched only if the conditions mentioned at pages 34-36 are satisfied. Altogether 1,135 persons and vehicles were searched by the RUC under the PACE (NI) Order in 1996; 149 people were arrested as a result of these searches.

Whenever the police search an unattended vehicle they have to leave a notice stating that it has been searched, the date of the search and the identity of the searching officer. The notice also has to indicate that a written record of the search can be requested within a year and that an application can be made for compensation for any damage caused. This duty does not apply to searches of vehicles at an airport, railway, dock or harbour, to searches of air cargo, or to searches conducted under the emergency laws.

The PACE (NI) Order 1989 contains a second power relating to vehicle checks (art.6), but it deals with searches for wanted people rather than for stolen goods or weapons. It authorises a police officer to stop and check vehicles to see if they are carrying people who are unlawfully at large or who are intending to commit, have committed, or are witnesses to an offence (except a road traffic offence). The vehicles to be searched can be chosen in accordance with any criterion, *e.g.* the colour or age of the car, or the appearance of its occupants. The authorisation for a road check of this nature must come from a senior police officer and can last for no longer than seven days at a time. In 1995 the power was used on just four occasions.

The power to stop and search vehicles under the emergency laws

Because the space inside a vehicle constitutes a "place", the emergency laws conferring powers to enter and search premises or other "places" (see page 39) mean that the police have extensive powers to enter and search cars, buses, vans and lorries. Bags or boxes carried by bicycles and motorbikes can also be searched. Persons in or on a vehicle can be searched only if the conditions mentioned at pages 34-35 are satisfied.

By virtue of section 17 of the EPA 1996, a police constable may enter and search any vehicle if he or she has reasonable grounds for suspecting that it contains a person who could be arrested under the PTA because he or she is reasonably suspected of involvement in terrorism. A similar power is conferred by section 18(2), and section 18(3) allows the police to seize anything which they have reasonable grounds to suspect is being, has been or is intended to be used in the commission of an offence created by the EPA or listed in Schedule 1 of the Act. To enable the police to look for people who may have been kidnapped, and whose lives are in danger, section 23 permits the police to enter any place and search for the missing persons.

The main vehicle search power under the emergency laws, however, is section 20 of the EPA 1996, which allows the police to enter and search any vehicle to look for explosives, firearms, ammunition or wireless transmitters. Caravans may be searched only if an officer not below the rank of inspector authorises it. As always, items found may be seized.

A police officer may interfere with the use of a highway, any right of way or the use of a waterway. Anyone who meddles with materials used in the exercise of this power is guilty of an offence carrying a maximum penalty of six months' imprisonment and a fine up to £2,000 (s. 26(4) of the EPA 1996).

The power to enter and search premises under the ordinary law

The police have no general power to enter and search private premises in order to investigate criminal acts. Only in relation to some road traffic offences may they do so. Otherwise they may enter and search only if they have the permission of the occupier, if a breach of the peace is involved or if the requirements of the PACE Order are satisfied.

The relevant provisions of the PACE (NI) Order 1989 are articles 10-25. They deal only with searches of "premises", but this term is defined so as to include any place. It therefore covers outdoor as well as indoor premises, movable and stationary premises, occupied and unoccupied premises, and public and private places. The power to search carries with it the power to enter in order to conduct the search.

Entry with a warrant

The police will normally have to obtain a search warrant from a Justice of the Peace in order to enter and search premises and a JP can grant a warrant only if he or she is satisfied that a serious arrestable offence has been committed and that there is material on the premises which is likely to be relevant to its investigation. The JP must also be satisfied that it is not practicable for the police to obtain permission to enter the place, or that a search may be frustrated unless a police officer is allowed to enter immediately.

Applications for warrants must specify the reasons for the proposed search, the premises to be searched and the articles to be looked for. The warrants themselves must be just as specific. They can authorise entry on one occasion only, which must occur within a month of the issue of the warrant and be at a reasonable hour unless this would frustrate the search.

If the police wish to search for personal medical records, documents dealing with counselling or with assistance given by a voluntary organisation, journalistic material or confidential business information, they must obtain either a production order or a warrant, not from a JP but from a county court judge. Before issuing an order or a warrant the judge must normally be satisfied that access to the material is in the public interest. Otherwise similar preconditions apply to the issue of a warrant as in the case of applications to a JP. The only material which is totally exempt from search is that which is subject to legal privilege; in the main these are communications between solicitors and their clients (art.12).

Entry without a warrant

Under articles 19 and 20 of the PACE (NI) Order, the only situations where a police officer is able to enter and search premises without a warrant are the following:

- where the officer wishes lawfully to arrest a person whom he or she reasonably suspects is present on the premises;
- where the police wish to search premises occupied or controlled by a person who has been arrested for an arrestable offence because they have reasonable grounds for suspecting that the premises contain evidence relating to that or some other connected arrestable offence;
- where entry is necessary in order to prevent serious personal injury or serious property damage;
- where entry is necessary in order to deal with or prevent a breach of the peace;
- where any statutory provision so permits, *e.g.* the Food Safety (NI) Order 1991, article 33.

The power to seize objects

The police can seize and retain anything they are looking for during a lawful search. In addition, by virtue of article 21 of the PACE Order, an officer who is lawfully on any premises may seize anything found there (even if it is not being looked for) provided he or she has reasonable grounds for believing that it has been obtained as a result of an offence, or that it is evidence in relation to any offence, and that seizure is necessary in order to prevent it being concealed, lost, damaged, altered or destroyed. Even information accessible through a computer can be seized under this power.

Whenever anything has been seized, a written record must be provided, if requested, to a person who was the occupier of the premises or who had custody or control of the thing immediately prior to the seizure. Access to items seized, even if only in order to photograph or copy them, must be permitted by the officer in charge of the investigation unless he or she has reasonable grounds for believing that this would prejudice criminal proceedings. Otherwise items seized may be retained by the police for as long as is necessary. Under section 1 of the Police (Property) Act 1897 a person can apply to a magistrates' court for an order for the return of property or for a statement from the police as to why they think retention is still justified.

Anything seized during an unlawful search may nevertheless be used in court as evidence of an offence. Judges have a discretion to exclude the evidence because of the adverse effect on the fairness of the proceedings (art. 76 of the PACE Order), but the person searched can seek compensation for infringement of his or her rights only by taking action in the civil courts (see Chapter 2). He or she can also lodge a complaint against the police (see Chapter 6).

The power to enter and search premises under the emergency laws

Under the EPA 1996, searches of any place can be made by the police as follows:

- to arrest a suspected terrorist (s.17);
- to arrest a person suspected of offences listed in the 1996 Act (s.18 (1));
- to look for explosives, firearms, ammunition or transmitters (s. 20);
- to look for persons who have been kidnapped (s. 23).

If the place to be searched is a dwelling-house then, as far as the section 20 and 23 powers are concerned, authority to conduct the search must be granted by a police officer not below the rank of inspector, and, in the case of section 20 searches, only if the police have reasonable grounds for suspecting the presence of what is being sought. In the three years 1994-96 there were 3,791 recorded searches by the RUC but there are no published figures on the quantities of weapons, ammunition or transmitters revealed by searches of homes. It has been held by the European Court of Human Rights that searches under the section 20 power are *not* a breach of the European Convention on Human Rights (*Murray (Margaret) v UK*, 1993).

Under section 20(4) and (5) of the EPA 1996, the police may require any person who is in the place being searched to remain in a part of it for up to four hours, though a police officer of the rank of superintendent or above may extend that period by a further four hours if he or she reasonably believes that it is necessary to do so. The police can use reasonable force to ensure that the requirement is complied with and anyone wilfully failing to comply runs the risk of two years' imprisonment and an unlimited fine. The police can arrest anyone reasonably suspected of committing this offence, which is triable without a jury; it seems, however, that no-one has ever been charged under this provision or its predecessor in the EPA 1991. A challenge to the legality of detention during a house search was unsuccessful before the European Commission of Human Rights (*O'Neill and Kelly v UK*, 1992).

Although section 20 of the EPA 1996 authorises the police to search only for explosives, firearms, ammunition and transmitters, if they find other incriminating items during the course of any search the person in possession of these items can be arrested and charged. Under section 32 of the EPA it is an offence to have in one's possession *any article:*

> *in circumstances giving rise to a reasonable suspicion that the item is in [one's] possession for a purpose connected with the commission, preparation or instigation of acts of terrorism connected with the affairs of Northern Ireland.*

The items most likely to be involved in this offence are everyday things which can be used in the making of a bomb, *e.g.* rubber gloves, adhesive tape, bell-pushes, coffee-grinders and kitchen scales. It should also be noted that under section 33 of the EPA it is an offence to have in one's possession, unless one has a lawful excuse, any information which is likely to be useful to terrorists in planning any act of violence. The maximum penalty for the offences in sections 32 and 33 is 10 years' imprisonment.

When the police are searching premises they can be assisted by specially appointed civilians such as forensic scientists and police photographers. Unless it is not practicable to do so, a written record has to be made of the search specifying the name or description of the apparent occupier of the place searched and of the place itself, the date and time of the search, any damage caused and items seized during the search and the service number of the searching officer. The apparent occupier must be supplied at once or as soon as is practicable with a copy of any such record (s. 21 of the EPA 1996).

If, in the exercise of their powers under the EPA 1996, the police take or damage any property (*e.g.* during a house search), the Secretary of

State must pay compensation provided a claim is submitted no later than four (or exceptionally 12) months after the incident (s.55 of the EPA 1996). Special rules have been issued governing the procedures to be followed when making a claim (see the Emergency Provisions (Compensation) (NI) Rules 1988), and the right to compensation under section 63 replaces any other legal right to claim compensation (see *Deehan v Chief Constable of the RUC*, 1990).

The power to detain under the ordinary law

The PACE (NI) Order 1989 made radical changes to the law on detention. By article 32 an arrested person has to be taken to a *designated* police station if it may be necessary to keep him or her in detention for longer than six hours. In Northern Ireland the 22 designated stations are in Antrim, Armagh, Ballymena, Banbridge, Belfast (Antrim Road, Grosvenor Road, Musgrave Street, Strandtown), Coleraine, Cookstown, Derry (Strand Road and Waterside), Downpatrick, Dungannon, Enniskillen, Larne, Limavady, Lisburn, Lurgan, Newtownards, Omagh and Strabane. Any other station may be used if detention is to be for less than six hours, or if otherwise there might be an injury caused to any person. Article 32(13), however, makes it plain that the duty to take an arrested person to a police station as soon as practicable after the arrest does not apply if the presence of the person is necessary elsewhere in order to carry out immediate and reasonable investigations.

Having been arrested and taken to a police station, a person can be arrested there for a further offence (art.33) but, if a person voluntarily attends a police station - to help the police with their inquiries - he or she must be allowed to leave whenever wanting to - unless first placed under arrest (art.31). An arrested person can be detained for questioning or released on bail. If the arrest took place under a warrant, the warrant itself may have been endorsed with a note authorising bail. Otherwise the police officer in charge of the station concerned may release the person on bail if satisfied that this would not lead to an injustice.

The maximum period of ordinary detention without charge is 24 hours (art.42(1)). Detention beyond 24 hours is possible only for "serious arrestable offences", a category defined in article 87. It comprises:

- offences which are always serious arrestable offences, such as manslaughter, kidnapping, most sexual offences, firearms offences and causing death by reckless driving (Sched. 5 of the Order);
- offences for which a person can be arrested under the PTA 1989;

- arrestable offences which lead to, or are intended or likely to lead to, any of the following consequences: serious harm to the security of the state or to public order; serious interference with the administration of justice or with the investigation of an offence; the death of any person; serious injury to any person; substantial financial gain to any person; serious financial loss to any person;
- arrestable offences consisting of making a threat which, if carried out, would be likely to lead to any of the above consequences (*e.g.* blackmail or intimidation).

In the case of these offences, a police officer of at least the rank of superintendent and who is responsible for the police station concerned may authorise detention for a further 12 hours, provided there are reasonable grounds for believing that this detention is necessary to secure evidence and that the investigation is being conducted diligently and expeditiously (art. 43(1)). In relation to serious arrestable offences the police are therefore able to detain a person without charge for up to 36 hours. In 1996 only two persons were kept in police detention in Northern Ireland for more than 24 hours under this power and then released without being charged. The average detention period for all persons arrested was about seven hours.

Detention beyond 36 hours is allowed only if authorised by a magistrates' court. In 1996 there were just five applications for extensions of detention, all of which were granted; of the detainees involved only one was later released without charge. The court can initially require further detention for up to 36 hours. A second court order can be applied for, but the total period of detention since the time of the arrest must not exceed 96 hours (arts. 44 and 45). Before the 1989 Order came into force the maximum detention period was 48 hours.

Throughout the period of detention the position of the arrested person must be reviewed. The first review must be carried out six hours after the detention begins and later reviews must be conducted at least once every nine hours. The review officer must be a police officer of at least the rank of inspector who has not been directly involved in the investigation up to that point. As soon as the grounds for detention cease to exist, the arrested person must be released or charged. Once charged, he or she must be released on police bail or brought before a magistrates' court on that day or on the following day. Until his or her release the arrested person is the responsibility of the station's "custody officer", who must have at least the rank of sergeant. It is this officer who must authorise the initial detention and any release.

The power to detain under the emergency laws

The PACE (NI) Order did not alter the law concerning detentions under section 14 of the PTA 1989. This section allows detention without charge for up to 48 hours, but the period can be extended for up to five days by order of the Secretary of State.

Detentions under the PTA have to be supervised in accordance with Schedule 3, which requires a review officer to review the detention as soon as practicable after it has begun and thereafter at intervals of not more than 12 hours. The detention cannot continue unless authorised and unless the person detained or his or her solicitor has been given the opportunity to make representations about the detention. But two vital factors make this review process a very different thing from that which is required by Article 5(1)(c) of the European Convention on Human Rights. In the first place, it is conducted by a police officer; although this must be an officer who has not been directly involved in the matter to date, he or she would not constitute a "competent legal authority" for the purposes of Article 5(1)(c). Secondly, no review needs to be conducted if an application has been made to the Secretary of State for an extension to the 48 hour period (although in practice such reviews do occur). Schedule 3 is therefore not a satisfactory response to the decision of the European Court of Human Rights in *Brogan v UK (*1988)*,* where unreviewed detentions for longer than four days and six hours were held to contravene the European Convention. It is still necessary for the government to rely on the notice of derogation which it issued under Article 15 of the Convention and which excuses the United Kingdom's continuing breach of the Convention. The validity of this derogation notice was upheld by the European Court of Human Rights in *Brannigan and McBride v UK* (1993).

Detention for a period longer than that permitted by the law will leave the police open to be sued in a civil action for false imprisonment (see Chapter 2). In one case, where a woman was detained from 9.30pm to 10.05pm simply so that she could then be medically examined (having already been at the police station all day), compensation of £300 was awarded (*Petticrew v Chief Constable of the RUC*, 1988). In *Moore v Chief Constable of the RUC* (1989), where Mr Moore was arrested early one morning and held for most of the rest of the day while being interviewed several times, the judge held that it was reasonable for the police to hold him from 6.30am to 8.00pm in order to dispel or confirm the arresting officer's reasonable suspicion that he was guilty of the attempted hijacking of a vehicle, but there were one or two hours' detention which the police had failed to justify and damages of £150 were awarded. The Court of Appeal has said that the sum to be awarded for unlawful detention should be £600 per hour for up to the first 12 hours; thereafter a lesser hourly sum should be awarded if it appears that the distress caused has lessened (*Oscar v Chief Constable of the RUC*, 1992).

The power to take photographs and fingerprints

As a person has no right to his or her own image, the police can photograph people as much as they want. This does not breach the European Convention on Human Rights (*Murray (Margaret) v UK*, 1993). Article 61 of the PACE (NI) Order 1989 provides that fingerprints (and palm prints) may be taken without a person's consent if a police officer of at least the rank of superintendent authorises them to be taken or if the person has been charged with, or is to be reported for, an offence. In both of these situations the person must already have been detained at a police station. There is no power to fingerprint someone who has not been arrested and if an arrested person has not yet been charged or told that he or she is to be reported there must be reasonable grounds for suspecting that the person is involved in an offence and that the fingerprints will tend to confirm or disprove this involvement. In the absence of consent, the police may use reasonable force to take fingerprints, but a written record must be kept of the reason for taking the prints.

If, after fingerprints have been taken, the person is no longer suspected of having committed an offence, the prints taken, and any copies, must be destroyed as soon as practicable, in the presence of the person involved if so requested. The person can even apply for a certificate to show that access to computer data relating to the fingerprints has been made impossible.

Under the PTA - in Great Britain as well as in Northern Ireland - a police or prison officer, or immigration officer, "may take all such steps as may be reasonably necessary for photographing, measuring or otherwise identifying" a person arrested under the PTA (s.15(9)). However section 48 of the EPA 1996 confirms that in Northern Ireland fingerprints can be taken without consent only if a police officer of the rank of superintendent or above is satisfied that this is necessary to help determine whether the suspect is involved in terrorism or is subject to an exclusion order (see Chapter 8). But any prints taken in these cases do not have to be destroyed later.

A person has no right to know what photographs and other information the police possess. In *Re Gillen* (1990) the applicant was told that his photograph had gone missing from a police station. He sought further details about the loss but the court held that he had to be satisfied with the police's offer of advice on personal safety.

The power to take samples

Under the ordinary common law the police have no power to take samples from a person's body. To do so without the person's consent would be an assault. An important statutory exception is the Road Traffic (NI) Order 1981, under which it is an offence to refuse to supply a sample of breath, blood or urine in cases of alleged driving while under the influence of alcohol or drugs. The PACE (NI) Order creates further important exceptions in articles 62 and 63. The Order distinguishes between intimate samples, which can be taken only with the person's consent, and non-intimate samples, which can be forcibly taken.

"Intimate samples" are samples of blood, semen or any other tissue fluid, urine or pubic hair, or a swab taken from any of a person's body orifices except his or her mouth. "Non-intimate samples" are hair other than pubic hair, material taken from a nail or from under a nail, saliva, a mouth swab or any other body swab, a footprint or any other impression of a part of a person's body other than the hand. Peculiarly, mouth swabs are classified as non-intimate samples in Northern Ireland, but as intimate samples in England and Wales.

All samples require the written authorisation of a police officer of at least the rank of superintendent, who must have reasonable grounds for suspecting the involvement of the person in a serious arrestable offence and for believing that the sample will tend to confirm or disprove this involvement. A written record must be kept of the sampling. Intimate samples must be consented to in writing and (except for urine samples) be taken by a doctor. If a person refuses to consent to the taking of an intimate sample, then in any proceedings against that person the magistrate, judge or jury may "draw such inferences as appear proper" (art.62(10)).

The power to use force

Whenever they are carrying out their "ordinary" function of preserving the peace, the RUC are not entitled to use force. They must act with restraint, resisting pressure rather than applying it. Even when controlling crowds or patrolling a procession or parade they must not apply force in an active manner. If they do so, they can be sued for assault.

However, if the police are preventing crime or effecting a lawful arrest, they can use "such force as is reasonable in the circumstances" (s.3(1) of Criminal Law Act (NI) 1967). The burden of proving that the force used was reasonable lies on the police. For example, in *Wasson v Chief Constable of the RUC* (1987), since the RUC could not prove that their version of how Mr Wasson came to be injured by a plastic bullet was more likely to be true than Mr Wasson's version, they were held liable to pay compensation. But it seems that, even in the absence of any proof that the police knew that the person they fired at was committing an offence (such as driving a stolen car), a judge may still regard the use of real bullets as reasonable force whenever someone drives through a vehicle checkpoint. In *Magill v Ministry of Defence* (1988) it was held that a soldier's act in firing at a 15-year-old driver was reasonable use of force in the prevention of crime. A police officer would probably enjoy a similar immunity in such circumstances, though much would depend on the particular features of each case.

In relation to police powers expressly conferred by the PACE (NI) Order 1989, article 88 says that the police "may use reasonable force, if necessary, in the exercise of the power". The term "reasonable" suggests that the force used must be in proportion to the gain the police hope to achieve through exercising the power. The term "necessary" implies that other means of exercising the power must be attempted first. This would seem to impose a stricter test than that contained in the 1967 Act, but as yet no court has ruled on how the two provisions inter-relate.

The power to interfere with property

Section 26(2) of the EPA 1996 is the provision which legalises the actions taken by the security forces whenever private property rights are interfered with in order to counter unlawful paramilitary activities. It permits any police officer, if authorised by the Secretary of State, to take possession of any property, to place any structure in a state of defence, to detain, destroy, or move any property, and to do any other act interfering with any public right or with any private rights of property. It is therefore perfectly lawful for the police to take over, say, a house for the purpose of keeping an eye on a nearby building. Land, too, can be requisitioned so that look-out posts or fences can be constructed.

Furthermore, under section 26(3) of the EPA 1996, any police officer may wholly or partly close a highway if he or she considers this immediately necessary for the preservation of the peace or the maintenance of order. To permit more permanent measures to be taken, section 27 empowers the Secretary of State to order the closure of any highway.

Interference with any of this work is a crime, punishable by up to six months in prison and a fine of up to £2,000.

Codes of Practice

Article 65 of the PACE (NI) Order 1989 obliges the Secretary of State to issue codes of practice to cover (a) searches of persons or vehicles without first making an arrest, (b) the detention, treatment, questioning and identification of persons, (c) searches of premises and (d) the seizure of property found on persons or premises. The codes which have been issued in Northern Ireland are almost identical to those in England and Wales. They first came into effect in January 1990, but a new edition has been operative since 29 July 1996. Under article 60 a code must also be issued on the tape-recording of interviews at police stations. This came into effect for the first time on 29 July 1996. The codes are not themselves pieces of legislation - and are not therefore to be found in official collections of legislation - but they can be purchased in booklet form from the Stationery Office and they must be made available in all police stations for consultation by members of the public. Their status is comparable to that of the Highway Code (see Road Traffic (NI) Order 1995, art.51(6)).

For the most part the codes simply repeat in clearer language the provisions of the main legislation, but occasionally they are fuller. For instance, the code on searches of premises says that:

Searches must be conducted with due consideration for the property and privacy of the occupier of the premises searched, and with no more disturbance than necessary (para. 5.9).

Likewise, the code on the treatment of detainees provides that:

A strip search may take place only if the custody officer considers it necessary to remove any article which a person would not be allowed to keep, and the officer reasonably considers that the person might have concealed such an article (para.10).

There are also special provisions dealing with the treatment in custody of vulnerable and mentally disordered people (see Annexes D and F to the code on treatment). In the case of certain countries (including France, Germany, Italy, Spain and the USA) the police must give notice to the foreign consulate that one of their nationals has been arrested and detained.

A breach of the codes will not automatically render the police liable to criminal or civil proceedings (art.66). The only available penalty will be disciplinary proceedings. A court, however, can "take account" of a code's provisions when hearing any criminal or civil case, so it might refuse to admit a piece of evidence if it considers that it was obtained in breach of a code.

A very important difference between the codes in England and those in Northern Ireland is that the former (apart from the code on tape-recording) apply also to persons and incidents being dealt with under the PTA 1989. In Northern Ireland such persons and incidents are excluded from the scope of the codes (see art.66(12) of the Order). Instead they are governed by a code issued under section 52 of the EPA 1996. This code covers only the detention, treatment, questioning and identification of persons detained under the PTA and it contains fewer safeguards for detainees than the equivalent PACE code. PTA detainees do not have the right, for instance, to know the identity of their interrogators, nor can they obtain a copy of their custody record. As yet the Secretary of State has not issued codes dealing with the exercise of other police powers conferred by the EPA, despite being given the right to do so under section 52.

A draft code governing the use of video-cameras in the holding centres (where persons arrested under the EPA are interrogated) was issued early in 1997, but it has not yet been published in its final form.

Chapter 4

Powers of the Army

Steven Greer

The current legal powers of the army in Northern Ireland are to be found almost exclusively in the Northern Ireland (Emergency Provisions) Act 1996 (the EPA). Powers had been conferred upon the army by the Stormont Parliament in the Civil Authorities (Special Powers) Act 1922, but in 1971 the legality of these powers was successfully challenged in the High Court by two Stormont MPs, on the grounds that the Government of Ireland Act 1920 reserved the making of laws concerning the armed forces in Northern Ireland to the Westminster Parliament (*R (Hume and Others) v Londonderry Justices*, 1972). Almost immediately the Westminster Parliament passed the Northern Ireland Act 1972, which bestowed new powers on Stormont to make laws concerning the armed forces, provided they were necessary for the maintenance of peace and order in Northern Ireland. The legislation also conferred retrospective validity on any actions taken before its enactment which would otherwise have been invalid because of the High Court's decision. The statutory framework was changed again by the passing of the Northern Ireland (Emergency Provisions) Act 1973. This has since been modified and supplemented on several occasions, notably in 1975, 1978, 1987, 1991 and 1996. All subsequent references are to the 1996 Act.

Although the policy of successive British governments since the mid-1970s has been to promote "police primacy", limiting the army to a supportive role, the Royal Irish Regiment (formerly the UDR) has had a pervasive presence throughout Northern Ireland, with other army units being the principal law enforcement agency in parts of West Belfast, parts of Derry City and in certain border areas. All members of Her Majesty's forces on plainclothes duty are required to produce documentary evidence that they are soldiers if requested to do so when exercising any power conferred by the EPA (s. 28(11)). The powers of the military police (the "red caps") used to be the same as those of constables. But since the 1991 Act came into effect they have been the same as those of other members of the army.

The legal powers of the army in Northern Ireland will be considered here under the following heads:

* stop and question;
* personal searches;
* searches of private and other premises;
* examination and seizure of documents;
* arrest;
* detention;
* miscellaneous powers; and
* the use of force.

It should be noted that the search powers are combined with powers to seize munitions, and transmitters (this includes scanning receivers). Some suggestions are offered by way of conclusion as to how complaints against the army may be made and legal rights enforced.

Stop and question

In Northern Ireland, soldiers on duty have the power under section 25 of the EPA to stop people at any time, including when they are travelling in a vehicle, and to question them for the purpose of ascertaining:

* their identity;
* their movements;
* what they know concerning any recent explosion or other recent incident endangering life or concerning any person killed or injured in such an explosion or incident.

It is a criminal offence to fail to stop when required to do so or to refuse to answer such questions to the best of one's knowledge and ability (s. 25(2)). A person can be arrested on the spot by a soldier for this offence and tried later by a magistrates' court. The maximum penalty is a fine of £2,000. Elsewhere in the United Kingdom the army has no power whatsoever to stop and question civilians.

It is important to realise that under section 25 the power to stop and question can be legally exercised only for one or more of the purposes listed. There is, however, some uncertainty about precisely what sort of questions a person is obliged to answer. For example, the term " identity" is not legally defined and may include not only name but also address and perhaps even age, since two members of the same family may have the same name and address. It is not clear how detailed the answers to questions concerning movements must be. Strictly speaking a general answer should be sufficient, since the purpose of this particular aspect of the provision is to oblige people to explain why they happen to be at the specific place at which they were stopped and questioned, and not precisely where they have been or are going. There is therefore probably no legal requirement to give the exact address one is coming from or going to.

Having legally been stopped and asked about identity, movements etc, people may be asked questions by the army about any other matter, but there is no legal obligation to reply. Refusing to answer, however, though entirely legal, may result in suspicions being aroused, will probably prolong the encounter and, in certain circumstances, may also result in an increase in stopping and questioning on other occasions. Harassment of this kind is not legally prohibited: the army can stop and question anyone under section 25 as often as they like.

People are not legally required by section 25 to fill in forms of any kind nor to be photographed. If asked to do so, a person may lawfully refuse. However, if a photograph is taken against a person's will, there is nothing in law that can be done about it.

Personal searches

A soldier's legal power to conduct a personal search varies according to whether the person searched is in a public place or in a private home or other premises. A public place is defined by the EPA as "a place to which for the time being members of the public have or are permitted to have access, whether on payment or otherwise" (s.58). This includes such obvious public places as the street, a shop, a pub or a cinema but it also includes centres to which suspects arrested by the army are brought, as well as hotels, guest houses and hostels.

In public places

Any soldier on duty may stop and search anyone in any public place at any time in order to ascertain whether or not he or she unlawfully possesses any munitions or transmitters (s.20(6)(a)). This power permits entirely random, and legally unchallengeable, searches: the soldier involved need not entertain any particular suspicions about the person searched. There is no legal reason why women cannot be frisked by male soldiers, or men by women soldiers, although there is no evidence that this often happens.

In non-public places

In order to conduct a legal personal search somewhere other than in a public place the army must first lawfully gain entry to the premises. The legal requirements are discussed in the next section. If admittance to any premises including private dwellings has been lawfully obtained, soldiers on duty may legally search anyone found there if they have reasonable grounds to suspect that they may possess a transmitter or be in unlawful possession of munitions (s.20(6)(b)). Anyone entering or found in a dwelling-house may also be searched in the absence of such suspicions, although entry to dwelling-houses is more tightly controlled than entry to other premises.

Seizure of munitions and transmitters

During the course of personal searches either in public or non-public places munitions, transmitters and documents may be found. "Munitions" are items which can be used in the manufacture of explosives, firearms or ammunition, and could include apparently innocuous items such as sugar or wire (s.20(9)). Munitions unlawfully held may be seized and destroyed (s.20(7)(a)), while transmitters may be seized but not destroyed (s.20(7)(b)). Documents or records discovered may be examined or retained for further examination but not destroyed (see page 54).

Searches of private and other premises

Details of searches carried out in both private dwelling-houses and other places must be recorded in writing unless it is impracticable to do so (s. 21). The occupier (or presumed occupier) is entitled to a copy of this document "at once" or "as soon as is practicable". It is an offence punishable by a sentence of two years' imprisonment and/or a fine wilfully to seek to frustrate the object of a search.

In order to conduct a legal search of premises lawful entry must first be obtained. Different rules govern the legality of entry depending upon the purpose of the search and whether or not a dwelling-house is involved.

The general power of entry

Under section 26 (1) any soldier on duty has the power to enter any premises if he or she considers it necessary to do so in the course of operations for the preservation of the peace or the maintenance of order, or if authorised to do so by the Secretary of State. Anything found as a result may be seized and detained for up to four hours if there are reasonable grounds for suspecting that it is being, has been, or is intended to be used in the commission of an offence (s. 19(4)).

Entry and search to effect an arrest

The power to enter and search in order to make a legal arrest, using reasonable force if necessary, is confined to two circumstances:

- The army may enter and search any premises, including private homes, provided that a person suspected of any offence (not necessarily a "terrorist" offence) is actually to be found there (s. 19(3)(a)).

- The army may enter any premises to search for persons reasonably suspected of being "terrorists" or of having committed offences involving the use or possession of explosives or firearms. There must, however, be reasonable grounds to suspect that such persons are to be found there even though they are in fact elsewhere (s. 19(3)(b)).

In both cases the army also possesses ancillary powers to deal with resistance from on-lookers and to search the premises, following an arrest, to confirm or dispel suspicions which prompted the arrest (*Murray v Ministry of Defence*, 1987).

Entry to search for munitions etc other than in dwelling houses

Any soldier on duty may enter and search any premises, other than a dwelling-house, in order to discover whether they unlawfully contain munitions (s.20(1)). These items, if found, may be seized (s.20(7)). This search power amounts to a power to search at will, although the restraints described at page 52 apply here too.

Entry of dwelling-houses to search for munitions etc

In order to enter a dwelling-house to carry out a search, a soldier on duty must obtain authorisation from a commissioned officer. This must be refused unless there are reasonable grounds to suspect that munitions are unlawfully on the premises in question or that a transmitter is being kept there (s. 20(2)). Any of these items found in such a search may be seized (s. 20(7)). Systematic house searches in given areas are unlawful unless the requisite suspicion exists in relation to each house.

Details of the army's formal procedures for house searches under an earlier version of section 20(2) of the 1996 Act were revealed in the case of *Kirkpatrick v Chief Constable of the RUC and Ministry of Defence* (1988). Army search teams consist of a leader, a number of search units (in the *Kirkpatrick* case one unit of two soldiers for upstairs and another of two soldiers for downstairs), plus a "scribe" whose function is to keep a log. On gaining entry a cursory search of the entire house is made, the doors are locked, the curtains are drawn and the occupants are assembled in one room usually under "house arrest" (see page 56). Then, in the presence of the occupants, the team leader searches the search units and he himself is searched by the scribe. The occupants are then formally asked if they possess munitions or transmitters. Next the team leader invites the head of the household to make a tour of inspection so that any pre-existing damage can be recorded. Only then does the search proper commence, with the occupants confined in one room.

Entry to search for persons unlawfully detained

Any soldier on duty may at any time enter and search any place, other than a dwelling-house, in order to discover whether anyone whose life may be in danger is unlawfully detained there (s.23). Searches of dwelling-houses for this purpose require the authorisation of a commissioned officer. This power has been most visibly used to rescue alleged informers from paramilitary interrogation.

Examination and seizure of documents

When conducting any lawful search of persons or premises any documents or records, except those protected by legal privilege, may legally be examined if reasonably necessary to ascertain whether they contain information, including details about certain public officials, likely to be useful to "terrorists" when planning or carrying out acts of violence (s. 24(1)). They may also be removed for examination for periods of up to 48 hours, extendable on the authority of an officer of the RUC not below the rank of chief inspector to a total of 96 hours, but may not be photographed or copied (s. 24(2), (4), (9) and (10)). A written record of the examination must be kept, a copy of which must be supplied to the person in whose possession, or on whose premises, the document was found (s. 24(8)). Wilful obstruction of the exercise of these powers is an offence punishable by imprisonment for up to two years and/or a fine (s. 24(11)).

Arrest

Any soldier on duty in Northern Ireland can arrest anyone at any time, using reasonable force if necessary, provided that he or she has reasonable cause to suspect that that person "is committing, has committed or is about to commit any offence" (s. 19). To the extent that an arrest may be made for any offence (not necessarily a "terrorist" offence), soldiers have more extensive powers than the police possess under both ordinary and emergency laws.

No warrant is required for an arrest by the army, but two basic conditions must be fulfilled:

• If called upon after the event to justify the arrest (for instance in a claim for compensation for unlawful arrest) it is not sufficient for the soldier in question to have genuinely believed that the person arrested was committing, had committed, or was about to commit, an offence. The court must be persuaded that there were *reasonable* grounds for believing that the person arrested was, for example, acting in a suspicious manner. The mere order of a superior officer would not constitute reasonable grounds for the purpose of an arrest. But an order supported by some reasons, though scanty, would suffice (see Chapter 3).

• The soldier carrying out the arrest must usually state that he or she is making the arrest "as a member of Her Majesty's forces" (s.19(2)). Unlike in the case of arrests by the police, the offence in question need not be disclosed at the time of the arrest nor during the subsequent period of detention in army custody. In *Murray (Margaret) v UK*, (1994), the European Court of Human Rights found the predecessor of the current section 19 power of arrest (s. 14 of the 1978 Act), and the army's arrest process, including the photographing of those under arrest with or without their consent, to be compatible with the European Convention on Human Rights.

Detention

The army in Northern Ireland possesses two separate detention powers:

- detention during the course of a search and
- detention following an arrest.

Detention during the course of a search

The army has the power to hold under "house arrest" people found in, or entering, both private dwellings and other places while searches are being conducted for munitions and radio transmitters (s.20(4)). Such detentions are lawful provided those carrying out the search reasonably believe that they are necessary for the purposes of the search. The initial period of detention can last for up to four hours, but it can be extended for a further four hours if a police officer of at least the rank of superintendent reasonably believes this is necessary. Any person who is not resident in the place being searched can be stopped from entering it. Reasonable force can be used to enforce these requirements and wilful failure to comply with them is an offence punishable by up to two years' imprisonment and/or a fine (s. 21(5)).

Detention following an arrest

Under section 19 of the EPA the army has the power to detain people whom it arrests for up to four hours. During this period the person arrested has no legal right of access to a solicitor or to have a friend or relative notified about the arrest. At the end of the four hours detainees must either be released or handed over to the police for re-arrest.

There is still some doubt about precisely what powers the army possesses over persons it has lawfully arrested and detained (see generally *Murray v Ministry of Defence*, 1987). It is of course illegal for detainees to be assaulted, tortured or subjected to inhuman or degrading treatment. But minor indignities, such as being made to sit facing the wall of a small cubicle while the detention is processed, have been tolerated by the courts. Detainees may legally be frisked upon arrival at detention centres, but not as a matter of routine. Such searches have been held to be unlawful when the detainee was asleep in bed before arrest and was watched getting dressed by a member of the arrest squad.

It is lawful for detainees to be questioned about the offence(s) which motivated the arrest, but the person arrested has an obligation to answer only those questions concerning identity and movements, recent explosions and any other recent incident which endangered life. It is not an offence to refuse to reply to other questions nor, strictly speaking, should a refusal to reply be to the disadvantage of an accused at a subsequent trial. The provisions of the Criminal Evidence (NI) Order 1988, which effectively abolish the right to silence (see Chapter 5), apply only to silence in the face of police, not army, questioning.

It is not clear if the power to inspect documents discussed on page 54 applies to civilians under military arrest, although it is available prior to arrest. Photographing those arrested and detained by the army is not legally prohibited.

Miscellaneous powers

Under section 26 of the 1996 Act the army has a number of miscellaneous powers most of which require the authorisation of the Secretary of State, or someone to whom he or she has delegated the decision. Those which do not require such approval are the powers wholly or partly to close a road or divert traffic and to prohibit or restrict the use of any waterway if it is considered immediately necessary for the preservation of the peace or the maintenance of order. Those which require the Secretary of State's consent are the powers under section 26 (2) to:

* take possession of any land or other property;
* take steps to place buildings or other structures in a state of defence;
* detain any property or cause it to be destroyed or moved;
* interfere with any public or private rights, including carrying out work on any land which has been seized under the Act.

Anything found as a result of the exercise of these powers may be seized and detained for up to four hours if there are reasonable grounds for suspecting that it is being, has been, or is intended to be used in the commission of an offence (s. 19(4)). Impeding the exercise of these powers is an offence triable by a magistrates' court and punishable by a maximum sentence of six months' imprisonment and/or a £400 fine (s.26(4)).

The use of force

Under section 3(1) of the Criminal Law Act (NI) 1967, any person in Northern Ireland is legally entitled to use:

such force as is reasonable in the circumstances in the prevention of crime, or in effecting or assisting in the lawful arrest of offenders or of persons unlawfully at large.

By and large this includes the right to defend oneself, since lawful self-defence is also crime prevention. The army possesses an extra power under the EPA to use force if it is needed to gain lawful entry (s.28(4)). If the necessity for the use of force is in dispute, a court's view of whether it was necessary must prevail, not that of the army. But in practice these are unlikely to diverge.

"Reasonable in the circumstances"

Controversy has raged over how the courts and the prosecuting authorities in Northern Ireland have interpreted this key phrase, particularly when the lethal use of firearms by the security forces has been at issue. In theory, the unreasonable use of force for the purpose of law enforcement exposes the soldiers concerned to a criminal prosecution, and their "employers", the Ministry of Defence, to a civil suit for compensation. However, in practice, there is often an official reluctance to drag army personnel through the criminal courts. Even where prosecutions are brought for the lethal use of firearms, the trial is conducted by a "Diplock" court, where the reasonableness of the force is decided by a judge sitting alone, without a jury.

Diplock judges have considered a wide range of factors relevant to such decisions. The result has been, in almost all cases, that particular uses of force have been characterised as "reasonable" and, therefore, legal. These factors have included: the "general wartime situation" in Northern Ireland, the character of the area in question and the problems it poses for the security forces, whether the accused honestly and reasonably believed it was his duty to open fire because he believed his target was a member of a "terrorist" organisation, and whether the accused honestly and reasonably believed he, or other colleagues, were about to come under fire even though the suspects in question may not have been armed (see *R v MacNaughton*, 1975; *Attorney-General for Northern Ireland's Reference*, 1976; *Farrell v Secretary of State for Defence*, 1980; *R v Clegg*, 1995).

In civil cases, where damages are sought, settlements are often reached out of court without admission of liability, so it is not possible to say that the army has accepted the legal blame. But where such cases do reach court the crucial issue, as in a criminal trial, is whether the force used was "reasonable in the circumstances". Civil courts, however, accept a lower standard of proof than criminal courts because the consequences for the defendant are less serious. Until 1987, the reasonableness issue could have been decided by a civil jury if either party chose this mode of trial. But in that year the civil jury was largely abolished in Northern Ireland for the trial of personal injury and fatal accident cases.

Pursuing complaints and enforcing rights

It can be seen that in relation to all the powers available to the army the law imposes certain limits. Breaches of these limits, if proven, can have significant legal consequences. The action which may be taken by a party aggrieved by an alleged violation of the army's legal powers will depend upon whether the complaint concerns damage to property or some other alleged wrong, such as injury to the person or illegal arrest and detention.

Damage to property

Persons whose property is taken through the operation of the EPA have a statutory right to compensation, provided that they were not committing an offence on the relevant occasion. Section 55 sets out the procedure for making a claim. Applications should be made to the Secretary of State, usually within four months of the incident in question, but up to a year can be allowed in special circumstances. Appeals against the Secretary of State's decision can be lodged at a county court.

Other wrongs

Other wrongs may amount to criminal offences and create other non-statutory rights to compensation. It is virtually impossible to pursue a private prosecution against the army (*i.e.* without the assistance of the police or the Director of Public Prosecutions), since there will be enormous problems in obtaining adequate evidence. In any event, the DPP and the Attorney-General, who is a member of the government, can intervene in any private prosecution and terminate it. Public prosecutions of military personnel will involve the DPP for Northern Ireland and, therefore, may be subject to political considerations. Taking a civil claim for compensation against the army is easier and in many cases, including those involving the use of firearms, the Ministry of Defence has settled out of court, generally without an admission of liability. There is some chance of success even in those cases which do go to court.

Certain basic guidelines are worth following when seeking redress for alleged wrongs committed by the army:

- The more that is known of the real extent of the army's legal powers the better, because this heightens awareness of possible violations as they occur. This, in itself, may be sufficient to vindicate rights. For instance, if a soldier attempts to destroy documents during a street search, a question concerning his or her legal authority to do so may be enough to prevent it from happening.

- If a breach of the law is suspected, notwithstanding attempts to prevent it, the victim should try to take note of what is happening and write down the details as soon as this becomes possible (times, exact locations, who was involved, etc). He or she should also ask for the names, numbers and units of the soldiers in question. Every army patrol is now required to carry cards identifying their regiment number with a phone number where complaints may be lodged. Soldiers are under orders to distribute the cards to anyone seeking to make a complaint against them.

- Legal and political representatives should be contacted and a complaint lodged with the local army commander. The address of the army's headquarters is Thiepval, Lisburn, Co. Antrim. The Northern Ireland (Emergency Provisions) Act 1991 established an Independent Assessor for Military Complaints Procedures to review the manner in which the army deals with complaints but not to investigate complaints independently. The Independent Assessor should be contacted if a complaint against the army is not dealt with satisfactorily by the army itself. The police should be involved if the complainant suspects that what has occurred amounts to a criminal offence, such as an assault. The Independent Assessor, unfortunately, has no official role to play in those cases. The Assessor's address is: Hampton House, 47/53 High Street, Belfast BT1 2QS (tel: 01232-237161).

Pursuing legal actions against the army is not easy, even when the complainant is obviously in the right. But it is not impossible. A few people have done so with success. The army's own recent figures show that nearly 10% of all complaints of non-criminal behaviour are substantiated. In 1996 the army's Central Complaints Office investigated just 24 non-criminal complaints, and 264 informal complaints were also dealt with.

Chapter 5

Questioning Suspects

John Jackson

The investigation of crimes was originally the responsibility of jurors, then of magistrates. During the nineteenth century the task was given to the police. As explained in Chapter 3, the police do not have a general power to stop a person for questioning unless he or she is placed under arrest. Nor do they have a general power to detain someone for the purpose of getting "help with police inquiries". There is no half-way house between voluntary co-operation with the police and arrest for a specific offence.

The absence of any duty to reply to police questions is usually referred to as "the right of silence". It also protects defendants (*i.e.* the persons accused of crimes) from having to give evidence at their trial. We shall see, however, that this right has been limited by the Criminal Evidence (NI) Order 1988. A person other than a defendant is protected by the right of silence at a trial only to the extent that he or she can claim the privilege to decline to answer a question which may incriminate him or her in a criminal offence (see page 78).

The "voluntariness" principle

The police must conduct their questioning of suspects within the law and it is always open to a person who has been assaulted in the course of police questioning, perhaps for the purpose of extracting a confession, to bring a civil action against the police officers involved. In one case involving a man whose ear-drum was perforated, the High Court of Northern Ireland held that if a person is lawfully arrested for the purpose of questioning, but is subsequently assaulted during questioning, the detention becomes unlawful and the person is entitled to a writ of *habeas corpus* to secure release (*Ex parte Gillen*, 1988).

For many years, the most significant restriction on the power of the police to question suspects was the rule that a statement could be used as evidence only if it had been made voluntarily. This meant that, when an accused person challenged the validity of a confession which he or she had allegedly made, the prosecution had to prove beyond a reasonable doubt that the statement had not been obtained "by fear of prejudice or hope of advantage held out by a person in authority". This test was later extended to require the prosecution to show that the statement was not obtained by "oppression". "Oppressive questioning" was defined by one judge as:

> *questioning which by its nature and duration or other attendant circumstances (including the fact of custody) excites hopes such as the hope of release or fears, or so affects the mind of the subject that his (sic) will crumbles and he speaks when otherwise he would have stayed silent.*

Whether there was oppression in an individual case depended on many elements, including the length of time intervening between periods of questioning, the length of any specific period of questioning, whether the accused had been given proper refreshment and the characteristics of the person who made the statement.

Article 74 of the PACE Order

In a major modification of the voluntariness principle under article 74 of the Police and Criminal Evidence (NI) Order 1989, the prosecutor now has to prove that the statement was not obtained by oppression of the person who made it or in consequence of anything said or done which was likely to render it unreliable The voluntariness principle, therefore, no longer applies. Yet another test is used where the accused is charged with a serious scheduled offence under the Northern Ireland (Emergency Provisions) Act 1996 (the EPA) (see page 66).

The "admissibility" of a confession (*i.e.* whether it can be accepted as proper evidence in a court of law) is frequently tested at what is known as a "*voir dire*" or a "trial within a trial". This is when the judge asks the jury to withdraw so that it cannot be influenced by hearing evidence which the judge might rule to be inadmissible. If an alleged confession is ruled inadmissible by the judge, the prosecution may not adduce evidence of what was said by the accused at the *voir dire* at a later stage of the trial, provided the evidence was relevant to the issue at the *voir dire*. If what the accused says at the *voir dire* were to be admissible at the trial, it might significantly impair his or her right of silence at the trial.

For the purposes of article 74 of the PACE Order, "oppression" is defined to include torture, inhuman or degrading treatment and the use or threat of violence, whether or not amounting to torture (arts. 74(8)). This seems a narrower definition than at common law, but the word "includes" in article 74(8) entitles the courts to extend the categories of oppression to the kinds of conduct and circumstances considered oppressive at common law. In their interpretation of the equivalent English provision, however, the English courts have restricted oppression to the exercise of authority or power in a burdensome, harsh or wrongful manner, to unjust or cruel treatment, and to the imposition of unreasonable or unjust burdens in circumstances which would almost always entail some impropriety on the part of the interrogator (*R v Fulling*, 1987).

The other kind of evidence which is wholly excluded under article 74 is a confession made in consequence of conduct likely to render it unreliable. This extends the categories of behaviour which may exclude a confession beyond threats and inducements, but makes it clear that a confession will be excluded only where the conduct was *likely* to render unreliable any confession which the accused might have made as a result. Much will depend on what is considered by judges to make a confession unreliable.

Rules on police questioning

The conduct of police questioning used to be governed by what were known as the Judges' Rules, so called because they had their origin in a set of rules formulated and approved by the judges of the English King's Bench Division in 1912 and 1918. A second version of them was approved in 1964 and these were adopted in Northern Ireland in 1976. Appended to them was a set of Administrative Directions, which were concerned with affording persons questioned with reasonably comfortable conditions and adequate breaks and refreshment, and with creating special procedures for persons unfamiliar with the English language or of immature age or feeble understanding. It is important to realise, however, that neither the Judges' Rules nor the Administrative Directions had the force of law; they were merely statements of good practice which judges were entitled to take into account when deciding whether a police officer had acted lawfully or not.

Guidance and Codes

In December 1988, as a consequence of the Criminal Evidence (NI) Order 1988, the Northern Ireland Lord Chief Justice, on behalf of all the judges in Northern Ireland, issued a Practice Note cancelling the Judges' Rules and announced that to replace them the Secretary of State had issued written guidance to the Chief Constable of the RUC. This guidance has been incorporated in a Code of Practice for the Detention, Treatment and Questioning of Persons by Police Officers, issued under article 65 of the PACE Order. The Code of Practice issued under PACE applies to all suspects except those arrested under the Prevention of Terrorism (Temporary Provisions) Act 1989 (the PTA). A separate Code of Practice issued under section 52 of the Northern Ireland (Emergency Provisions) Act 1996 deals with persons arrested under the PTA. There are differences in the degree of protection offered to suspects under each of these Codes (see page 69).

The Code of Practice under PACE, which was revised in July 1996, requires all arrested persons and all persons who are being questioned regarding their involvement or suspected involvement in an offence to be cautioned in the following terms:

You do not have to say anything, but I must caution you that if you do not mention when questioned something which you later rely on in court, it may harm your defence. If you say anything it may be given in evidence.

Suspects who are in custody must in addition be given a written notice setting out the terms of the 1988 Order so as to ensure that they are fully aware of the consequences of their action.

The Code contains detailed rules on how interviews are to be conducted. It requires that an accurate record be made of each interview with a person suspected of an offence and that the record be signed by the suspect as correct. Interviews in police stations cannot be conducted without the consent of the custody officer, who is an officer not involved in the investigation of the offence but who has the responsibility for the treatment of detained persons.

In any detention period of 24 hours, a suspect must be allowed a continuous period of at least eight hours for rest. When an interviewing officer considers that there is sufficient evidence to prosecute a suspect and that the suspect has said all that he or she wishes to say about the offence, the officer must bring him or her before the custody officer, who is then responsible for considering whether he or she should be charged. On being charged the suspect should again be cautioned and given a written notice showing particulars of the offence and stating the terms of the caution. Questions relating to the offence should not be put to him or her after charge unless they are necessary to prevent harm to some other person or to clear up an ambiguity in a previous answer.

A further Code of Practice has been issued under article 60 of the PACE Order requiring that interviews be taped in certain circumstances at police stations where approved tape-recording facilities exist. The Code does not apply to persons arrested or detained under the PTA or the EPA. Under the Code interviews should be taped where a person has been cautioned in respect of any indictable offence (including an offence "triable either way" – see Chapter 2) other than a driving offence. The only exceptions are where the person is being questioned in respect of an offence under section 1 of the Official Secrets Act 1911 or where there are reasonable grounds for suspecting that the offence is connected to terrorism. A uniformed officer not below the rank of inspector may also authorise an interview not to be taped where the equipment is faulty and the interview should not be delayed.

Young and mentally handicapped persons

The Code of Practice for Detention etc. requires that a person under the age of 17, or a person who is mentally handicapped, must not be interviewed or asked to provide a written statement in the absence of an "appropriate adult", unless an officer of the rank of superintendent or above considers that delay would involve an immediate risk of harm to persons or a serious loss of property. An "appropriate adult" means, in the case of a juvenile, the juvenile's parent or guardian, a social worker or a responsible adult over 17 who is not a police officer.

Article 58 of the PACE Order creates a new section 52 of the Children and Young Persons Act (NI) 1968, so that there is now a duty, where a juvenile is in police detention, to take such steps as are practicable to ascertain the identity of a person responsible for his or her welfare and to inform that person, unless it is not practicable to do so, why and where the juvenile is being detained.

Enforcement of the rules on questioning

Judges have discretion under the common law (*i.e.* non-statutory law) to exclude from court proceedings any statement which has been obtained unfairly. It is their duty to see that the accused has a fair trial according to law (*R v Sang*, 1979). In one Northern Irish case other matters which were considered relevant to the judge's discretion included the reason that led the accused to say what he or she did, whether the police had acted improperly in order to get him or her to crack under the strain, and the unlawfulness of the police conduct, but it was stressed that the "paramount criterion" was the fairness of the accused's trial (*R v McBrien and Harman*, 1984).

Article 76 of the PACE Order states that in any criminal proceedings the court may refuse to admit evidence on which the prosecution proposes to rely if it appears that, having regard to all the circumstances, including the circumstances in which the evidence was obtained, the admission of evidence would have such an adverse effect on the fairness of the proceedings that the court ought not to admit it. The effect of this is that, just as the courts have a broad common law discretion to exclude statements obtained unfairly, the courts have a broad statutory discretion to exclude statements obtained in breach of a Code issued under the Order. It is worth noting that the courts in England have been much more prepared to use their power to exclude statements under the statutory discretion (which has been in force there since 1986) than they have ever been prepared to do under their common law discretion.

The Codes of Practice issued under the PACE Order, like the earlier Judges' Rules, do not have the full force of law. Article 66(7) states merely that a police officer shall be liable to disciplinary proceedings for a failure to comply with any provision in a code. As regards whether a statement obtained in breach of a code can be used as evidence, article 66(10) states in effect that in all criminal and civil proceedings the courts may take such account of any breach as they think fit. In some cases this will mean excluding the statement.

Questioning under emergency legislation

A number of emergency powers were enacted for Northern Ireland in 1973 on the recommendation of the Diplock Commission. These powers are now enshrined in the EPA 1996. The Diplock Commission believed that, as regards police questioning, the voluntariness principle was, with its technical rules, hampering the course of justice. In particular, the decision in *R v Flynn and Leonard* (1972) had excluded statements obtained as a result of questioning which was designed to build up an atmosphere in which the initial desire to remain silent was replaced by an urge to confide in the questioner. The Commission considered that, if human lives were to be saved and destruction of property prevented in Northern Ireland, the security authorities must have the power to build up an atmosphere of this kind. To this end it proposed that admissibility of confessions should depend on the much lower standard of the absence of torture or inhuman or degrading treatment, a standard derived from the European Convention on Human Rights.

The current rules

The position today is that if a person being tried on indictment (*i.e.* in the Crown Court) for a scheduled offence (*i.e.* one listed in Schedule 1 of the EPA) wishes to challenge the admissibility of a statement allegedly made by him or her, he or she must adduce evidence which on the face of it shows that he or she was subjected to torture or to inhuman or degrading treatment or to any violence or threat of violence in order to induce the making of the statement. The prosecution must then satisfy the court that the statement was not obtained in this manner (1996 Act, s.12).

The insertion of the words "violence or threat of violence" clarifies one of the difficulties with the European Convention's standard, which was whether it precluded the use of violence altogether. Another difficulty is what degree of psychological pressure is permitted within the standard. It seems that statements made by a suspected member of a "terrorist" organisation after periods of searching questioning *are* to be admitted, notwithstanding that at the outset the suspect did not wish to confess and that the interrogation caused him or her to speak when otherwise he or she would have stayed silent (*R v Dillon and Gorman,* 1984). Whilst such questioning would have constituted oppression at common law, it is not in itself considered "degrading" within the European Convention standard.

Judges' discretion and other rules

Shortly after the enactment of the emergency legislation in 1973, the then Chief Justice explained that:

> there is always a discretion, unless it is expressly removed, to exclude any admissible evidence on the ground that (by reason of any given circumstance) its prejudicial effect outweighs its probative value and that to admit the evidence would not be in the interests of justice (*R v Corey,* 1973).

This discretion has since been written into section 12 of the 1996 Act, which states that the court has discretion to exclude a statement if it appears that it is appropriate to do so in order to avoid unfairness to the accused or otherwise in the interests of justice.

An early case under the emergency legislation suggested that the involuntariness of the confession at common law was a ground for the exercise of the discretion to exclude the confession, although it was emphasised that the mere fact that a confession had been obtained involuntarily did not necessarily mean that it would have to be excluded (*R v Tohill*, 1974). More recently, the courts have been cautious to ensure that the discretion is not exercised so as to defeat the will of Parliament, which was to admit statements made after periods of searching questioning by persons suspected of "terrorist" involvement (*e.g. R v Cowan*, 1987).

Reforming interrogation procedures

Concern about the treatment of suspects held under emergency legislation by the security forces led to an inquiry in 1978 by Amnesty International and in 1979 a Committee of Inquiry into Police Interrogation Procedures in Northern Ireland, chaired by Judge Bennett, made a number of recommendations on interrogation procedures. One of these was that there should be a Code of Conduct applying specifically to interviewing officers. The Code should prohibit certain kinds of conduct and regulate the length and time of interviews. In June 1979 the Secretary of State announced that the Chief Constable had with his approval issued "Instructions" to implement the recommendations of the Bennett Committee. As mentioned above, the Code of Practice issued under the PACE Order for the Detention, Treatment and Questioning of Persons does not apply to persons arrested under section 14 of the PTA, but codes of practice on the detention, treatment, questioning and identification of such persons have been issued under section 52 of the EPA 1996 and revised versions came into force in July 1996.

Like the Codes of Practice issued under the PACE Order, the EPA Codes lack the full force of law, but failure by police officers to comply with them (the Codes do not apply to arrests made by the army) may make them liable to disciplinary proceedings (unless criminal proceedings are pending against them) and the provisions of the Codes may be taken into account by the courts when deciding whether to admit confessions. In view of the courts' discretion under section 12 of the 1996 Act, to exclude statements which are otherwise admissible, it would also seem that the courts may exercise their discretion to exclude statements obtained as a result of a breach of the Codes.

The EPA Code on Detention, Treatment and Questioning offers levels of protection which are similar to but not as extensive as those in the Code of Practice issued under the PACE Order. The most significant differences relate to the extent of access to legal advice (see below). Other differences worth noting are that persons arrested under the PTA are not permitted to talk on the telephone with anyone, to have writing materials or to receive visits, although there are restricted rights of access to a lawyer. The EPA Code makes provision for the possibility of examination by a medical practitioner of the detained person's choice, but unlike the PACE Code this can take place only in the presence of the Medical Officer called by the police.

Apart from differences in the detention and questioning codes, there are other differences between the ordinary and emergency questioning regimes. As mentioned above (page 65), the government has traditionally refused to extend tape-recording to suspects arrested under the PTA, although interviews take place in rooms fitted with closed-circuit television cameras. In the latest Northern Ireland (Emergency Provisions) Bill, currently going through Parliament, there is at last a proposal to introduce audio-recording of these interviews, but this will not come into effect for at least another year. Section 53 of the EPA 1996 requires the Secretary of State to make a code of practice in connection with the *silent* video-recording of interviews and to order the silent video-recording of interviews in accordance with such a code. A draft code was circulated for comment early in 1997 and video cameras are due to be in operation early in 1998. The government has refused to extend the lay visiting scheme introduced in 1991 to monitor the treatment of PACE suspects to suspects detained under the PTA. Instead it appointed an "Independent Commissioner" in 1992 to pay random visits to the interrogation centres and oversee the conditions under which detainees are held. This Commissioner (and his Deputy) can also sit in on interviews. The Commissioner's address is: Hampton House, 47/53 High Street, Belfast BT1 2QS (tel: 01232-237161).

Despite these changes, there continues to be international criticism of the treatment of PTA suspects in the three interrogation centres to which they may be taken (Castlereagh, Gough, or Strand Road in Derry). Recently, criticism has focused on the restrictions which are placed on such suspects' access to legal advice.

The right of access to a lawyer

Under article 59 of the PACE Order, a person arrested and held in custody is entitled to consult a solicitor privately at any time if he or she so requests. The police may delay in complying with the request only if the person is in detention for a serious arrestable offence and if an officer of at least the rank of superintendent authorises the delay. In 1996, of the 26,062 persons arrested under the PACE (NI) Order, 9,401 requested access to a solicitor. In only 18 of these cases was access delayed. In any event, delay is permitted only for up to 36 hours from the beginning of the person's detention. The allowable reasons for delay are:

- that there are reasonable grounds for believing that the exercise of the right will lead to interference with evidence or witnesses, or to the alerting of other suspects; or
- that it will hinder the recovery of property or the proceeds of a crime.

Article 57 also entitles a detained person to have someone informed that he or she has been arrested, subject to the same grounds of delay as in article 59. In 1996 there were 4,371 requests for such information to be communicated and in only five cases was communication delayed. Arrested persons have no absolute right to be told of their entitlements under articles 57 and 59, but the Code of Practice says that they should be told. Articles 57 and 59 specifically exclude from their scope persons arrested or detained under section 14 of the PTA.

A person detained under section 14 has a right under section 47 of the 1996 EPA to consult a solicitor privately if he or she so requests and section 46 of the same Act enables a detained person to have someone informed of the fact that he or she has been arrested. The detainee must be informed of these rights as soon as practicable after being arrested. The police may delay in complying with any request under sections 46 and 47 only if such delay is authorised by an officer of at least the rank of superintendent and the delay must not extend beyond 48 hours from the beginning of the detention. The grounds of delay are broader than those allowed under article 59 of the PACE Order, extending to interference with the gathering of information about the commission of acts of terrorism and to alerting any person so that it will be more difficult to prevent an act of terrorism or to apprehend a person in connection with an act of terrorism. The Northern Ireland Court of Appeal has held that it is sufficient that the police reasonably believe that there is a real risk of a legal adviser being used as an unwilling agent to convey information of use to "terrorists" (*R v Harper*, 1990). The police do not need to cease questioning until the lawyer arrives. Moreover, the access permitted need not be unrestricted, provided consultations are allowed at intervals of 48 hours.

The right of access to a lawyer has been described in one English decision as "one of the most important and fundamental rights of a citizen" (*R v Samuel*, 1988). But the English courts appear to require some causal connection between any breach of the right and any resulting confession before they are inclined to exclude confessions on the grounds of denial of the right of access to a lawyer and the Northern Ireland Court of Appeal has approved of this approach (*R v Harper, 1990*). The Northern Ireland courts have, however, recognised that the decision of a police superintendent to delay access to legal advice or to delay a suspect's right to have someone informed of detention is clearly one of an official affecting public rights and is therefore liable to judicial review (*In Re Duffy's Application*, 1992; *In Re McKenna's Application*, 1992).

In *Murray (John) v UK* (1996) the European Court of Human Rights held that the denial of legal advice for 48 hours in combination with the right of silence provisions in the Criminal Evidence (NI) Order 1988 (see page 78) amounted to a violation of Article 6 of the European Convention on Human Rights. After being cautioned under the Order, the applicant had been interviewed 12 times without access to a solicitor. The Court held that, even though the restrictions on legal advice had been lawfully exercised, they were capable of violating the fair trial provisions in Article 6. The scheme contained in the 1988 Order was such that it was of "paramount importance" for the rights of the defence that an accused had access to a lawyer at the initial stages of police interrogation.

Statistics illustrate that despite section 47 of the 1996 Act solicitors have increasingly been given access to suspects arrested under the PTA. More recent legal challenges have centred on the refusal to allow solicitors to be present during police interviews. Under the PACE Code, suspects are allowed to have their solicitor present while being interviewed, but the EPA Code grants no such right. In the *Murray* case the European Commission on Human Rights considered that applicants were entitled to have their solicitor present during police interviews, but the European Court did not consider it necessary to decide this.

A number of Northern Ireland cases have refused to recognise any right of legal access to police interviews in emergency cases. One of these is *In re Russell's Application* (1996), where Lord Chief Justice Hutton said it was the general intent of parliament that the police should be able to "create a situation in which a guilty man is more likely than he would otherwise have been to overcome his initial reluctance to speak and to unburden himself to his questioners". This approach has very recently been endorsed by the House of Lords in *Ex parte Begley* (1997). The House did not, however, expressly disagree with Hutton LCJ's view that the police do have a discretion to allow solicitors to be present in exceptional circumstances and that the application of a fixed policy of refusing solicitors access to interviews would be unlawful.

The right of silence before trial

Research indicates that only a minority of subjects in fact exercise their right to say nothing when questioned by the police, which suggests that the right may not be the valuable safeguard it is often claimed to be. The provisions of the Criminal Evidence (NI) Order 1988, however, which allow adverse inferences to be drawn from a person's silence in a number of circumstances, make it even less likely in the future that silence will be maintained in the face of police questioning.

A number of laws impose a duty to answer questions or provide information:

* Section 26 of the Official Secrets Act 1939 provides that a policeman of at least the rank of inspector may be authorised to require a person to furnish information regarding an offence under section 1 of the Act.

* Under road traffic legislation, the police have a right to require the driver of a car to present his or her driving licence, and, if the driver is alleged to be guilty of an offence under the legislation, to give his or her correct name and address and those of the owner of the car (Road Traffic (NI) Order 1981, 177 and 180).

* As regards emergency legislation, section 25 of the EPA 1996 has already been dealt with in Chapters 3 and 4. Another emergency law exception to the right of silence is section 18 of the Prevention of Terrorism (Temporary Provisions) Act 1989, which makes it an offence for a person who has information about an act of terrorism or about people involved in terrorism to fail to disclose it without reasonable excuse.

Even when there is no statutory duty to answer questions, there is nothing to stop the police asking them and, if at any stage a person indicates that he or she wishes to remain silent, there is no obligation on the police to stop asking questions, although the Code of Practice for Detention etc. requires police officers not to ask questions after a suspect has been charged, unless the circumstances are exceptional.

Enforcement of the right of silence

The citizen's right of silence in the face of police questioning has traditionally been enforced by two general rules. One was laid down in *Rice v Connolly* (1966), where the court held that silence cannot lead to a charge of obstructing the police in the execution of their duty. The second general rule states that, at a trial, the prosecution and the trial judge should not suggest to the jury that an adverse inference may be drawn from an accused person's silence when questioned by the police. The only common law exception to this rule was where two persons are speaking on even terms and one charges the other with something which the other says nothing to repel. In this instance the judge may make some comment, but even here he or she must be careful, for it has been held that to ask the jury to consider whether the person's silence in these circumstances indicates guilt or innocence is to short-circuit the intellectual process that has to be followed. Where the accuser is a police officer, the parties cannot normally be said to be on even terms, although everything depends on the circumstances.

Restrictions on the right of silence

The most serious dent in the general rule that adverse inferences should not be drawn from silence is created by the Criminal Evidence (NI) Order 1988, which defines three situations when adverse inferences may be drawn in court from an accuser's silence *before* trial. Article 3 provides that, when an accused relies in his or her defence on some fact which he or she failed to mention when questioned or charged by the police, then if the fact is one which the accused could reasonably have been expected to mention, the court or jury may draw such inferences from the failure as appear proper.

The other two situations when adverse inferences may be drawn are more limited. Article 5 provides that a court or jury may draw such inferences as appear proper where, after being arrested, a person fails to account to the police for the presence of an object, substance or mark on his or her person or in a place where he or she was arrested if the object, substance or mark is reasonably believed by the police to be attributable to the person's participation in an offence. Article 6 permits inferences to be drawn from a refusal by a person when arrested to account for his or her presence at a particular place at the time the offence was committed.

The Codes of Practice issued under both the PACE Order and the EPA require that persons who are questioned by the police be warned about the effect of article 3 (see page 64). In addition, the Codes require that before a constable questions a person about the matters in articles 5 and 6, he or she must inform the person that there is reason to believe that what has been found is attributable to the person's participation in an offence or that the person's presence at the time of the alleged offence is attributable to his or her participation in it. The person must then be asked to account for what has been found or for his or her presence and warned that a failure to do so may result in a court deriving such inferences from the failure as appear proper.

The courts have in a number of decisions drawn adverse inferences against accused persons from their failure to respond to police questioning. In one of the first cases article 3 was invoked against the National Director of Publicity for Sinn Féin when he refused to reply to police questions after being arrested with seven others for unlawfully detaining a man suspected of being a police informant. The accused denied the charge and explained his silence on the ground that as a Sinn Féin spokesperson he had advised other people to remain silent and had to maintain this stance himself. But the Lord Chief Justice held that the failure to speak gave rise to very strong inferences against him that the innocent explanation which he offered in court was false (*R v Martin and Others*, 1991).

One of the accused in this case subsequently claimed that the drawing of inferences from silence violated Article 6 of the European Convention on Human Rights, as it infringed his privilege against self-incrimination. In *Murray (John) v UK* (1996) the European Court of Human Rights held that the right to remain silent under police questioning and the privilege against self-incrimination were recognised international standards which lay at the heart of a fair procedure under Article 6. But the right of silence was not absolute and it could not prevent a court taking into account an accused's silence in situations which clearly called for an explanation. On the facts of the case before it, the Court held that, having regard to the weight of the evidence against the applicant, the drawing of inferences from his refusal to explain his presence in the house where the alleged informer was being held captive was a matter of common sense and could not be regarded as unfair and unreasonable. As mentioned above, however, the failure to grant the applicant access to legal advice before he was questioned by the police did constitute a violation of Article 6 as the effect of the Order makes it vital that an accused has access to a lawyer at the initial stages of police interrogation.

Questioning at the trial

The general rule, subject to an important exception in the case of an accused person, is that if a person is a "competent" witness, *i.e.* if his or her evidence may lawfully be admitted by the court, then that person may be lawfully *compelled* by the court to give evidence or to suffer the penalty for contempt of court. This means that he or she will be required to answer any questions put in court, unless some objection is taken by a party that the question cannot be answered on the ground that it would infringe the rules of evidence such as the hearsay rule, or the rule prohibiting opinion evidence, or the rules on character evidence.

Privileged communications

The witness can also object to answering a question if able to claim a "privilege". There are privileges connected with self-incrimination (see page 78), professional legal communications, and "without prejudice" negotiations.

Professional legal privilege extends to all communications passing between a client and his or her legal adviser in the course of seeking or giving legal advice. Also covered are communications between a party or his or her legal adviser and a third party which are made for the purpose of pending litigation. In addition, all good faith offers of compromise between parties are privileged where litigation is pending or contemplated. A husband or wife could formerly also refuse to disclose any communication made to his or her spouse during the marriage, but this privilege ceased to have effect when article 79(8) of the PACE Order 1989 came into force.

One issue which the Northern Irish courts have not yet had to face is whether communications between priests and penitents are privileged. The courts in England do not seem to recognise such a privilege but the Supreme Court in the Irish Republic has held that communications made in confidence to a parish priest by his parishioners are privileged.

Communications between doctors and their patients and between journalists and their informants are not privileged. Section 10 of the Contempt of Court Act 1981, however, states that no court may require a person to disclose the source of information contained in a publication for which he or she is responsible unless that disclosure is necessary in the interests of justice, or national security, or for the prevention of disorder or crime (see also Chapter 11).

Evidence through TV links

Article 81 of the PACE Order allows three categories of person, with the court's permission, to give live evidence through television links in the Crown Court. The three categories are witnesses outside Northern Ireland, witnesses aged less than 14, and witnesses who will not give evidence in open court through fear. The second category is restricted to cases involving certain offences of a sexual nature, cruelty and offences of assault or causing or threatening injury. The comparable English provision (s. 32 of the Criminal Justice Act 1988) does not cover persons in the third category.

Children as witnesses

Since the general rule is that no testimony can be admitted as evidence unless it is given under oath, the common law position was that no child could give evidence unless he or she appreciated the solemnity of taking an oath and understood that taking an oath involved an obligation to tell the truth over and above the ordinary duty of doing so. However, Parliament has intervened over the years to make it possible for children to give unsworn testimony. Children under 14 may now give evidence unsworn and under article 3 of the Children's Evidence (NI) Order 1995 a child's evidence shall be received unless it appears to the court that that the child is incapable of giving intelligible testimony. There is no minimum age below which a child cannot give evidence. Whether a child should give evidence or not is a matter for the judge's discretion depending upon the circumstances of the particular child.

Video-recordings of interviews with child witnesses are admissible as prosecution evidence in violent or sexual offences (art. 5 of the Children's Evidence (NI) Order 1995). Children must be under 14 in the case of violent offences and under 17 in the case of sexual offences.

Accused persons and their spouses as witnesses

Accused persons have been competent to give evidence on their own behalf in Northern Ireland only since 1923, but an accused person is not a competent witness for the prosecution in any criminal case. If the Crown wishes to rely on the evidence of an accused person who is prepared to give evidence against a co-accused, it has four options available to it. First, it can file a *nolle prosequi* with reference to his or her case, *i.e.* discontinue the prosecution. Second, it can state that no evidence will appear against the accused, in which case an acquittal will follow. Third, it can obtain an order for separate trials and, fourth, it can get the accused to plead guilty, in which case it is desirable that he or she be sentenced before being called on behalf of the prosecution.

Article 79 of the PACE Order changed the law by making each spouse competent to give evidence against the other in all cases. The spouse can testify on behalf of a co-accused spouse where the offence charged involves an assault on the spouse or on a person under 17.

Informers as witnesses

Informers are perfectly competent to give evidence against accused persons, but there is a rule that an accomplice (*i e.* an actual participant in the crime which the accused is alleged to have committed) must not be called on behalf of the prosecution unless the accomplice has already been prosecuted or it is made clear that a current prosecution will be discontinued. Without this rule a person against whom proceedings were pending would have every inducement to make his or her story sound as convincing as possible when giving evidence against co-participants. In fact, of course, even when an accomplice has been prosecuted, there may still be a considerable inducement to make his or her story sound convincing, such as when he or she has made a deal with the authorities ensuring an early release from prison, police protection on release or a financial reward. The trial judge has a discretion, which is rarely exercised, to exclude the evidence of an accomplice who is operating under "powerful inducements".

A number of "terrorist" trials in Northern Ireland have proceeded on the basis of accomplice evidence. The accomplices involved have been called "supergrasses" in view of the large number of defendants implicated on their evidence. These trials caused a number of concerns, notably that many of the supergrasses were granted complete or partial immunity from prosecution or were given promises of having to serve only short sentences, and that their testimony was in a number of cases uncorroborated (*i.e.* not backed up by other evidence). There is no law which says that the testimony of suspects needs to be corroborated in this manner, and a number of defendants were convicted on the uncorroborated evidence of supergrasses. But these convictions were almost all overturned on appeal and there have been no major supergrass trials since 1983.

The accused's right of silence at the trial

Article 4 of the Criminal Evidence (NI) Order 1988 provides that, at the trial of any person over 14, the court or jury may, in determining whether the accused is guilty of the offence charged, draw such inferences as appear proper from the accused's failure to give evidence or from his or her refusal, without good cause, to answer any question. Before doing this, however, the court must at the conclusion of the evidence for the prosecution satisfy itself that the accused is aware that a failure to give evidence or to answer questions may result in this consequence. The effect of the article is to make it less attractive for accused persons to exercise their right of silence at the trial and to limit the right of an accused person to force the prosecution to prove the offence charged unaided by the accused.

In a number of cases the courts have drawn adverse inferences against accused persons who have not testified in a number of cases. In *Murray v DPP* (1994) the House of Lords upheld the view of the Court of Appeal in Northern Ireland that the 1988 Order changed the common law regarding the comments and inferences which could be drawn from an accused's silence at trial. The House of Lords held that once the prosecution has made out a *prima facie* case and the defendant refuses to testify, a judge or jury may draw such inferences from his or her silence as are dictated by common sense and may in a proper case draw the inference that he or she is guilty of the offence charged.

Article 78 of the PACE Order 1989 abolished the right of an accused person to make a statement from the dock without swearing an oath. The advantage to an accused of making an unsworn statement was that it permitted him or her to put a defence to the jury without having to submit to questions in cross-examination. The disadvantage was that the judge and jury were unlikely to be impressed by a defendant who did not submit to questioning.

The privilege against self-incrimination

One important occasion when a witness who is compelled to give evidence may refuse to answer a question is when there is, in the opinion of the court, a danger that the answer would expose the witness to prosecution for a crime. This privilege, known as the privilege against self-incrimination, extends to answers which would incriminate the witness's spouse. No adverse inference should be drawn by the judge or jury from the fact that the privilege is claimed.

A significant restriction on the privilege is contained in section 1(e) of the Criminal Evidence Act (NI) 1923, which provides that any accused person who elects to give evidence may be asked any question in cross-examination notwithstanding that it could tend to make him or her appear guilty of the offence charged. Section 1(f)(ii) and (iii), however, prevent the defendant being asked about his or her previous misdeeds if the intention is to damage his or her credibility, unless the defendant gives evidence of his or her good character, or casts imputations on the character of the prosecutor, the witnesses for the prosecution or the deceased victim of the crime, or gives evidence against any other person charged in the same proceedings.

Chapter 6

Complaints Against the Police

Brice Dickson

The law on the handling of complaints against members of the Royal Ulster Constabulary was changed quite significantly by the Police (NI) Order 1987, the RUC (Complaints) Regulations 1988 and the RUC (Discipline and Disciplinary Appeals) Regulations 1988. The 1987 Order created a new monitoring body called the Independent Commission for Police Complaints (referred to here as the ICPC or as the Commission). This replaced the Police Complaints Board, which operated between 1977 and 1988. Other relevant legal provisions are contained in the Police Act (NI) 1970 and in the Police and Criminal Evidence (NI) Order 1989. One or two further changes to the complaints system were introduced by the Police (Amendment) (NI) Order 1995.

The complaints system deals only with the alleged misconduct of individual members of the RUC and applies if, for instance, a person has been assaulted, treated uncivilly or placed under arrest without good reason. The system differs if the complaint is against an officer above the rank of chief superintendent or if the grievance is of a more general nature (see pages 92-95). It should be noted that in Northern Ireland, as elsewhere in these islands, the system for handling complaints against the police is often the object of public criticism. In recognition of this the British government asked Dr Maurice Hayes, a former Ombudsman for Northern Ireland, to conduct a wholescale review of the system. His report, entitled *A Police Ombudsman for Northern Ireland?*, was published early in 1997 and makes radical proposals for reform, including the use of non-police officers to investigate complaints and the appointment of a person of the quality of a senior judicial figure to be a full-time Police Ombudsman (with two full-time deputies). Although the report's recommendations were widely welcomed, even in official circles, they are unlikely to be enshrined in legislation immediately. The flawed existing system will probably continue to operate for at least another 18 months. This chapter therefore focuses on that system but makes reference where appropriate to likely changes.

How to make a complaint

As a guide to the operation of the complaints system, the ICPC has issued a leaflet entitled "Complaints Against the Police", copies of which are available from the Commission itself, police stations, public libraries and Citizens' Advice Bureaux. A complaint may be lodged in any of the following ways:

- writing to the Chief Constable at RUC Headquarters, Brooklyn, Knock Road, Belfast BT5 6LE;
- calling at any police station;
- writing to or calling at the ICPC at 22 Great Victoria Street, Belfast BT2 7LP (tel: 01232-244821);
- going to a local advice centre or to a solicitor, from where the complaint can be forwarded to the Chief Constable or to the ICPC; depending on the complainant's means, legal aid may be available to help pay for advice from a solicitor;
- asking a friend to do any of the above on the complainant's behalf.

Complaints cannot be officially lodged with bodies such as the General Consumer Council, a local district council, or the Ombudsman. The Hayes Report recommends that such an anomaly should be removed and that a freephone number for lodging complaints should be set up. It is important when making a complaint not to exaggerate, to be sure of all the facts and, if possible, to have at least one reliable witness. A complaint is unlikely to succeed if the only evidence is the complainant's word against that of a police officer. The complainant should always keep a copy of any letter he or she has written setting out the details of the complaint.

In practice, complaints about incidents which occurred more than 12 months prior to the lodging of the complaint will not be investigated unless there is a good reason for doing so. The Hayes Report suggests that the time limit for lodging complaints should be reduced to six months but that the Police Ombudsman should have a discretion to extend this.

What happens to a complaint

Wherever a complaint is initially lodged, it will be passed on to the Chief Constable. The Chief Constable must decide whether the matter in question does indeed constitute a complaint (rather than, say, a mere opinion); Hayes has recommended that this power should be transferred to the Police Ombudsman. If the decision is that it does not constitute a complaint then the "complainant" has no way of challenging this, except perhaps by seeking judicial review (see Chapter 2). If the matter *is* classified as a complaint the Chief Constable (or in practice his Deputy) must take steps to preserve evidence relating to the conduct complained of. If the complaint relates to a senior officer the Chief Constable must refer it to the Police Authority for Northern Ireland and explain this to the complainant (see page 92). If the complaint relates to any other officer the Chief Constable must record it and decide whether it is suitable for informal resolution. He may appoint another member of the RUC to help him make this decision.

Informal resolution

The sorts of cases which are appropriate for informal resolution are those where a preliminary investigation shows that the conduct complained of was lawful and reasonable and simply requires explanation. But the legislation makes it clear that a complaint is not suitable for informal resolution unless, first, the complainant gives his or her consent and, second, the Chief Constable is satisfied that the conduct complained of, even if proved, would not justify a criminal or disciplinary charge. Hayes proposes that the cases most suitable for informal resolution are those which raise an issue concerning merely the quality of service provided by the police

If the complaint is suitable for informal resolution the Chief Constable must try to resolve it informally and again may appoint another police officer to do this on his behalf. In practice this means that a meeting will take place between this supervisory police officer (of at least the rank of inspector) and the complainant, at which an attempt will be made to resolve the matter to each side's satisfaction. No statement made by any person for the purpose of the informal resolution of a complaint can be used as evidence in any subsequent court or disciplinary proceedings, unless it amounts to an admission of some conduct other than that being dealt with by the informal resolution procedure. This gives some reassurance to participants in informal resolutions that evidence they provide will not later be used against them.

If the complaint is not suitable for informal resolution or if informal resolution of the complaint is unsuccessful the Chief Constable must appoint a police officer to investigate it formally and must refer the complaint within 48 hours to the ICPC. As soon as it appears that a police officer may have committed a disciplinary or criminal offence, the Chief Constable may suspend him or her from duty until the matter has been fully dealt with.

Who investigates complaints?

Regrettably, the power to investigate complaints is given only to the police themselves. The investigating officer (the IO) will usually be from the RUC's Complaints and Discipline Branch, which currently employs about 60 officers (its organisational structure is outlined at page 102 of the Hayes Report). He or she will be of at least the rank of inspector and will normally be two ranks above that of the police officer who is being investigated. The Chief Constable, the Deputy Chief Constable, and any member serving in the same sub-division or branch as the officer being investigated cannot be appointed as the IO. If he wants to, the Chief Constable may appoint an IO from another police force in the United Kingdom, but this discretion is rarely exercised. The Hayes Report, crucially, has recommended that the Police Ombudsman's office should employ about 30 independent investigators, people who do not have a concurrent involvement in police operations. He thinks that all serious complaints, including those where a criminal offence may have been committed, however minor, should be investigated by these independent officers, with less serious complaints usually being remitted to the police themselves to investigate (though sometimes under the supervision of the Police Ombudsman's office).

Under the present system the IO will contact the complainant (usually within one week of the complaint being made) and ask to interview him or her. If the complainant feels unhappy about going to a police station, he or she should ask that the interview take place, preferably in the presence of a witness, at his or her own home or somewhere else, such as a local advice centre or a solicitor's office. The police will usually agree to any reasonable arrangement which is suggested. When a complainant makes a statement to the IO, he or she should ensure that the final version sets out accurately what was said and should request a copy. If the complainant is not satisfied with the statement, he or she should ask for it to be changed before signing it .

If there are witnesses who saw the incident being complained about, their names and addresses should be given to the IO so that they too can be interviewed. These witnesses should again make sure that they get a copy of any statement they make to the police.

Co-operation by the complainant

If a complainant refuses to co-operate with the investigation of his or her complaint, the Chief Constable may ask the ICPC to dispense with the need to take any further action. Should this happen the complainant will receive a letter from the Commission informing him or her of the fact. If the complainant feels that he or she *has* co-operated or that there has been a misunderstanding, contact should be made with the Commission immediately.

Some complainants are reluctant to co-operate with investigations because they fear that the statements they make may later be used against them by the police in related civil or criminal proceedings. The courts have held that complainants do not have an absolute right to have their statements kept secret (*Ex parte Wiley*, 1994). At the same time complainants do not as a general rule have any right of access to other statements or documents collected during the course of the investigation into their complaint: they have this right only if they can show that access to the written information is "necessary for disposing fairly" of their civil claim for damages (*Lanigan, McCotter and Tumelty* v *Chief Constable of the RUC*, 1991). Unfortunately, the Hayes Report does not make any recommendation to get round these particular difficulties, but he does state that there is a strong argument for all reports into complaints to be published. At present there is no legislative provision which protects statements made during formal investigations in the way that statements made during the informal resolution of a complaint are protected (see above).

The Commission for Police Complaints

The main function of the Commission is to supervise the investigation of complaints. It does not itself do the investigating. The Commission presently consists of a chairperson, two deputy chairpersons and five other members, all appointed by the Secretary of State. They serve for up to three years at a time, all but one on a part-time basis. As they must not be current or former members of any police force in Britain or Ireland, they are meant to serve as independent monitors of the way in which complaints against the police are handled.

There are some investigations which the Commission *must* supervise; all others it *may* supervise if it wishes to do so. Those which it must supervise are complaints alleging that the conduct of a police officer resulted in death or serious injury (*i.e.* a fracture, damage to an internal organ, impairment of bodily function, a deep cut or a deep laceration). In 1995 a complainant sought judicial review of the ICPC's decision not to supervise the investigation of his complaint; although the judge held that the reasons advanced for not supervising it were adequate, he found for the complainant on the basis that only one member of the Commission had been involved in taking the decision when in law at least two should have been involved.

Where an investigation is to be supervised by the Commission, the person appointed to conduct the investigation must be approved by the Commission. The Commission can then impose requirements as to how the investigation is to be conducted. For instance, it can insist that the investigation be provided with additional staff and resources, that particular persons be interviewed or that certain forensic evidence be sought. The supervising Commission member does not, however, become directly involved in the process of investigation itself. He or she does not usually attend interviews with the accused police officer or with witnesses. These interviews, by the way, usually take place inside police stations. Understandably, many complainants and witnesses are reluctant to attend police stations in Northern Ireland and the Hayes Report therefore recommends that interviews should more frequently be held in more neutral venues.

Once the supervised investigation is complete, the investigating officer must submit a report to the ICPC and send a copy to the Chief Constable. It will usually contain a recommendation as to whether the complaint can be substantiated or not. The ICPC, or rather the supervising officer at the ICPC, considers the report and submits to the Chief Constable a statement as to whether the investigation has or has not been conducted to the Commission's satisfaction. At no point does the Commission as a whole consider the report. The Commission sends copies of this statement to both the complainant and the police officer whose conduct has been investigated. This may be the first documentation the complainant receives about the complaint; Hayes has proposed that complainants should receive monthly updates on how the investigation into their complaint is progressing. He also states that the usual target time for clearing up a complaint (provided it has not led to the laying of criminal charges against a police officer) should be six months.

As a general rule no disciplinary or criminal charges can be brought against a police officer who is the subject of a supervised investigation until the ICPC has issued a statement on the investigator's report. The only exception to this is where the Director of Public Prosecutions (the DPP) thinks that there are exceptional circumstances which make it undesirable to wait before bringing criminal charges against the officer concerned. If an investigation of a complaint is not supervised by the ICPC, the IO will send his or her report directly to the Chief Constable.

Criminal charges

When the Chief Constable receives a report (whether or not the investigation has been supervised) he must decide whether it indicates that a criminal offence may have been committed by a police officer. If it does, the Chief Constable must send a copy of the investigator's report to the DPP, who will then decide whether to prosecute the officer in the criminal courts.

If the officer is charged

If the DPP decides to prosecute, the disciplinary aspects of the case will be delayed until the criminal proceedings are completed. The criminal trial will be conducted in the same way as cases against non-police officers (see Chapter 2). If it is a summary (*i.e.* fairly minor) offence it will be dealt with entirely at a magistrates' court, with a right of appeal to a county court (and if necessary to the Court of Appeal). If the offence is an indictable one (*i.e.* a major offence), it will be dealt with initially at a magistrates' court, but the magistrate will simply decide, in so-called "committal proceedings", whether there is a *prima facie* case against the police officer. If there is, the officer will be committed for trial at the Crown Court. In cases related to "terrorist" incidents, this trial may be before a judge sitting without a jury (a "Diplock" court). There is no right of appeal, in either side, against a magistrate's decision in committal proceedings, but after the Crown Court trial the accused (but not the prosecution) has a right of appeal to the Court of Appeal.

In criminal proceedings the person who lodged the complaint against the accused police officer may well be called as a prosecution witness, but otherwise he or she will probably not be involved in the trial.

If the officer is not charged

If the report of the investigator is not sent to the DPP, or if the DPP directs that no prosecution should take place, there is little that the complainant can do to initiate criminal proceedings. He or she can send letters and evidence to the DPP with a request that further consideration be given to the laying of criminal charges, but because the DPP is under no legal obligation to give reasons for his or her decisions - and in practice rarely if ever does so - it is virtually impossible to mount a legal challenge against them, even by way of judicial review (see Chapter 2). The complainant would need to be able to show that there was very convincing evidence of a criminal offence having been committed before a judge would be prepared to overrule the DPP's exercise of discretion. The complainant can also contemplate bringing a private prosecution, but this will be expensive (no legal aid is available in such cases) and in any event the DPP still has the power to take over private prosecutions and then to terminate them (*Ex parte South Coast Shipping Co. Ltd,* 1992).

If criminal charges are not laid against the police officer, or are laid and then withdrawn, the Chief Constable must consider whether to bring disciplinary charges against the officer under the RUC's Discipline Code. This Code is set out as Schedule 1 of the RUC (Discipline and Disciplinary Appeals) Regulations 1988 and is described in more detail below.

Until quite recently, the practice, in accordance with the Home Secretary's Guidance to Chief Constables, had been to apply the so-called "rule against double jeopardy" to cases which the DPP had decided not to prosecute. According to this rule, if a person has been tried in a court of law and acquitted, he or she must not be tried at a later date for the same offence. The Home Secretary was of the opinion that this meant that even though a police officer had not been placed on trial, he or she could not be charged with a disciplinary offence which was in substance the same as the criminal offence which the DPP had decided not to prosecute.

The legality of this practice was successfully challenged in England in *Ex parte Madden and Rhone* (1982) and it is now clear that in deciding whether to press disciplinary charges the Chief Constable must consider afresh the merits of each case. In doing so he will still take the views of the DPP into account, especially if the Director has decided that there is insufficient evidence to warrant a criminal prosecution, as this may suggest that the evidence would also be insufficient for disciplinary proceedings. On the other hand, there may be cases where the alleged misconduct is fairly trivial when viewed as a criminal offence but is much more serious when viewed as an offence against police discipline; in such circumstances the Chief Constable would be at liberty to press disciplinary charges. The Police (Amendment) (NI) Order 1995 allows the Secretary of State to issue further guidance to the Chief Constable as to when to press disciplinary charges; if the Secretary of State follows the recommendation of the ICPC itself (made in its Triennial Review Report 1994-97) she will suggest that the rule against double jeopardy should be ignored.

Disciplinary charges

The RUC's Discipline Code (as amended in 1989 and 1996) lists and describes 18 disciplinary offences with which a police officer may be charged. The names of the offences are:

- discreditable conduct (*e.g.* acting in disorderly manner)
- misconduct towards another police officer
- disobedience to orders (including breach of the Police Regulations, which contain restrictions on the private lives of officers, and breach of the codes of practice issued under the Police and Criminal Evidence (NI) Order 1989)
- neglect of duty
- wilful or careless falsehood
- improper disclosure of information
- corrupt practice (*e.g.* accepting a bribe)
- improper practice (*e.g.* writing a job reference for someone without the Chief Constable's consent)
- abuse of authority (*e.g.* using unnecessary violence)
- discriminatory behaviour
- neglect of one's own health
- improper dress or untidiness
- damage to police property
- drunkenness or drug taking (if it renders the officer unfit for duty)
- drinking on duty or soliciting drink
- entering licensed premises while on duty
- criminal conduct (if an officer has been found guilty by a court of law)
- being an accessory to a disciplinary offence.

In many cases there will be room for argument as to whether a police officer should be charged with one of these offences, for it is not always clear, for instance, what amounts to "neglect of duty" or to "improper practice".

If the officer is charged

In complaint cases (unless the accused officer has already admitted guilt) the Chief Constable must send to the ICPC a memorandum indicating whether he is preferring disciplinary charges, and if so which ones. After receiving the memorandum, the Commission must itself decide whether the investigator's report indicates that a criminal offence may have been committed and whether an officer ought to be charged with that offence. If it decides that an officer should be so charged it must tell the Chief Constable to send the investigator's report to the DPP, together with a copy of the original complaint. But the ICPC cannot itself direct that criminal charges should be laid against a police officer. If the ICPC disagrees with the Chief Constable's decision not to prefer disciplinary charges, it may recommend that charges should be brought, and which ones. If the Chief Constable is still unwilling to act against an officer, the Commission can then direct that disciplinary charges be brought. In *In re Marshall* (1996) a detective constable sought judicial review of the ICPC's decision to direct that a disciplinary charge be brought against him, but he failed.

The disciplinary hearing

The procedures for dealing with disciplinary offences are laid down in the 1988 Discipline Regulations, as amended. They apply in all disciplinary cases, not just those where breaches of discipline allegedly arise out of complaints from members of the public. The disciplinary charges will be formulated by the Chief Constable and all relevant documents must be supplied to the police officer. The House of Lords recently decided that officers under investigation cannot sue the Chief Constable for negligence if the investigation has not been properly conducted (*Calveley v Chief Constable of Merseyside,* 1989).

At the disciplinary hearing the officer can be represented by another police officer or, in specified cases, by a solicitor or barrister. The specified cases are those where the officer who has formulated the charges against the accused is of the opinion that the charges, if proved, could lead to the accused being dismissed from the force, required to resign or demoted. The hearing will usually be conducted either by an internal disciplinary board (consisting of two members of a rank not lower than assistant chief constable) or by a single officer of the RUC appointed by the Chief Constable. Some cases, such as those connected with the Stalker-Sampson inquiry of 1986-87, where allegations of collusion between police officers and Loyalist paramilitaries were investigated, may instead be considered by the Chief Constable of a police force in Great Britain. If the case is one where the ICPC has directed the bringing of disciplinary charges, or which the Commission sees as exceptional, it will be heard by a disciplinary *tribunal* consisting (usually) of the RUC Chief Constable as chairperson and two members of the ICPC.

Disciplinary hearings are held in private and a word-for-word record of what is said is kept. A complainant can attend and can be accompanied, if the officer-in-charge considers it appropriate, by a friend or relative who is not to be called as a witness. But, unlike in criminal trials, if the complainant is to be called as a witness, he or she cannot attend at any time before being called, and the officer-in-charge may always tell the complainant and his or her companion to withdraw if sensitive information might be about to be disclosed. The complainant is also allowed to put relevant questions to the accused officer and powers exist to compel the attendance of witnesses. The accused officer, like all defendants in a criminal trial, retains in theory the right to silence (and must be appropriately cautioned when interviewed in advance of the hearing), but if he or she says nothing then the disciplinary board is entitled to draw inferences about his or her guilt.

All disciplinary charges must be proved beyond reasonable doubt (the same standard of proof as in a criminal trial). This is a difficult standard to attain and is probably the main reason why so few complaints against police officers are upheld. Official moves are supposedly afoot to reduce the standard to "on the balance of probabilities", which applies in nearly every other profession where complaints about misconduct have been lodged, but the necessary regulations to effect the change have not yet been issued. The ICPC would like to see a "sliding scale" of proof, so that a higher standard would be required as the severity of the possible punishment for the breach of discipline increases. Hayes was of the same view.

It is the officer in charge of the hearing who decides what punishment to impose if the officer is found guilty of a breach of discipline, though in a disciplinary tribunal the views of the two members of the ICPC must be taken into account. If the hearing has been chaired by a Chief Constable from a force in Great Britain, the power to punish still lies with the RUC Chief Constable. The punishments available are dismissal, a requirement to resign, reduction in rank, reduction in salary (for up to 12 months), a fine, a reprimand and a caution. So that complaints are not rejected on the basis that no officer could be pinpointed as the one(s) responsible for the conduct complained about, both the ICPC and Hayes have recommended that disciplinary hearings should be able to issue verdicts which state "substantiated, but officer(s) unidentified".

Disciplinary appeals

An officer can appeal to the Chief Constable within 14 days of being notified of the punishment imposed by a disciplinary board. There is a further right of appeal to the Secretary of State, who, unless he is satisfied that there are sufficient grounds for allowing the appeal without an inquiry, may appoint three persons to hold an inquiry and report to him. An inquiry must be held if an officer who has been punished by dismissal, a requirement to resign or demotion, so requests. The persons appointed to conduct an inquiry will be (a) a barrister or solicitor (to act as chairperson), (b) a serving or retired inspector of constabulary or a retired chief officer, and (c) a retired RUC officer of a rank similar to that of the accused officer.

In most cases the appeal tribunal will hold a hearing to take evidence. The complainant (if the case involves a complaint, for as noted below some disciplinary charges, indeed the majority, are laid as a result of internal police procedures not involving members of the public) will be given at least 28 days' notice of the hearing and the rules governing participation in the proceedings are essentially the same as those outlined above in connection with disciplinary hearings, though any evidence given will be taken on oath. The appeal tribunal reports to the Secretary of State, who may allow the appeal, dismiss it, or substitute a less severe punishment. This decision is final, unless, for instance, the accused officer can prove a breach of natural justice, in which case he or she could bring an application for judicial review in the High Court (see Chapter 2).

If the officer is not charged

Even if the Chief Constable accepts that a complaint has been substantiated by the IO's report, and that there is sufficient evidence to support disciplinary proceedings, he may decide it is inappropriate to press disciplinary charges, and the ICPC may confirm this. In cases such as these the complainant will receive a letter from the ICPC offering an explanation.

If the letter states that the complaint has not been substantiated, this may be because the complainant's account of the incident has not been accepted or because the evidence available to support the complaint is felt to be insufficient to meet the required standard of proof. If the ICPC's letter indicates that the complainant's account of the incident has been substantiated but that no officer has been charged with a disciplinary offence, this may be because it proved impossible to identify the officer involved or because the offence was very minor. The letter may convey the Deputy Chief Constable's apologies or indicate that, although no formal disciplinary action has been taken, the officer concerned will be spoken to by his or her divisional commander; this is known as "action short of the Code" or "informal disciplinary action". If the case is covered by the rule against double jeopardy (see page 87), this will be mentioned.

If the complainant is not satisfied with the explanation offered as to why no disciplinary charges have been laid against the officer concerned, he or she should contact the ICPC, who may then offer to send a member of staff to the complainant's home to help clarify why the complaint has not resulted in disciplinary action.

Complaints against senior officers

If a complaint is made against one of the few officers in the RUC above the rank of chief superintendent, it should still be lodged in one of the ways mentioned on page 81. But the procedures to be followed thereafter differ from those already outlined for junior officers. It remains the duty of the Chief Constable to obtain and preserve evidence relating to the conduct complained of, but he sends particulars of the complaint to the Police Authority for Northern Ireland, the body given the general duty by the Police Act (NI) 1970 to maintain an adequate and efficient police force in Northern Ireland. It consists of a chairperson, a vice-chairperson and between 14 and 20 other persons, all appointed by the Secretary of State. As well as its particular role in relation to complaints against senior officers, the Authority has a statutory duty to keep itself informed (which it does through its Complaints and Public Relations Committee) as to the manner in which complaints from members of the public are dealt with by the Chief Constable.

Once the Police Authority has received a complaint against a senior officer it must record it. If it is satisfied that the conduct complained of, even if proved, would not justify a criminal or disciplinary charge, the Authority may deal with the complaint according to its discretion. In any other case it must appoint another member of the RUC or of another United Kingdom police force to investigate the complaint. The Investigating Officer cannot be the Chief Constable or any police officer serving in the same sub-division or branch as the senior officer under investigation. The Authority must also refer the complaint to the Independent Commission, which has the same duties and powers concerning supervision of investigations as it has in relation to complaints against junior officers.

The IO submits his or her report to the Police Authority and (if it has been a supervised investigation) to the Commission. The Commission (if involved) must in turn submit a statement to the Authority indicating whether it is satisfied with the conduct of the investigation. The Authority must then send a copy of the investigator's report to the DPP unless it is satisfied that no criminal offence has been committed. When the question of criminal proceedings is out of the way the Authority will consider whether disciplinary proceedings need to be taken. The senior officer may be suspended from duty as soon as it appears to the Chief Constable that a criminal or disciplinary offence may have been committed.

If the senior officer admits a disciplinary offence, the Police Authority may impose a punishment immediately. Otherwise the Authority will instruct a solicitor to draw up the particulars of the alleged offence. The charge will be heard by a tribunal consisting of a single person appointed by the Police Authority with the approval of the Secretary of State. To assist the tribunal the Authority must also appoint one or more assessors, approved by the tribunal, who must not be the Chief Constable, a civil servant, an inspector of constabulary or someone working for the Police Authority. After the hearing, the tribunal submits both to the Police Authority and to the accused a report with its findings and any recommendations for punishment. It is the Authority which finally decides what action to take. The punishments available are dismissal, requirement to resign or reprimand. As in the case of junior officers, a senior officer can appeal to the Secretary of State, who may appoint one or more persons to hold an inquiry and to report to him or her.

We are not aware of any complaint ever having been substantiated against a senior officer in the RUC. The Hayes Report recommends that in future no distinction should be made between the ways in which junior and senior police officers are dealt with in this context; he proposes that the Police Authority's role in the complaints system should come to an end, except in relation to general complaints about police policy.

General complaints against the RUC

It must be noted that the criminal and disciplinary procedures outlined in this chapter, whether for junior or senior officers, are applicable not just in cases arising out of complaints lodged by members of the public. They also apply (with the exception of the involvement of the ICPC) where suspicion of the commission of offences derives from other sources, *e.g.* from reports submitted by fellow police officers, media allegations or information submitted by politicians. In such cases investigations and hearings may be conducted even though there is no specific complainant involved. Nevertheless, the ICPC may still have a role to play.

For a start, the Commission *must* supervise the investigation of any matter which, in the opinion of the Secretary of State or Police Authority, indicates that a police officer may have committed a criminal or disciplinary offence and which ought in the public interest to be investigated under the Commission's supervision. The Commission *may* also supervise the investigation of a matter indicating the commission of an offence which has been referred to it by the Chief Constable or the Police Authority and which, in the opinion of all three bodies, should in the public interest be subjected to a supervised investigation. All of these supervised investigations will proceed in the manner already indicated in relation to complaints. Only in the past few years have matters been referred to the ICPC under the latter headings mentioned in this paragraph. These have usually been cases involving death or injury caused by the use of police firearms and have been referred to the ICPC by the Chief Constable. As far as we are aware, no matter has yet been referred by the Secretary of State or Police Authority.

The ICPC must make a report every year, and a more general one every three years, to the Secretary of State. It must also, at his request, report on such matters relating generally to its functions as he may specify. In addition, the Commission may issue a report to the Secretary of State on any matters coming to its notice to which it considers that his attention should be drawn because of their gravity or other exceptional circumstances. Copies of such a report must be sent to the Police Authority and to the Chief Constable. As yet, however, no reports other than annual and triennial reports have been deemed necessary. As part of its 1988-91 Triennial Review Report the ICPC did make nine recommendations for improving the complaints system, but the government accepted only six of these. In particular the government has refused to give the ICPC a power to supervise in the public interest any matter considered by the ICPC to be of a grave or exceptional nature. In its subsequent Triennial Review Reports for 1991-94 and 1994-97 the ICPC reiterated its call for reform. All that the Police (Amendment) (NI) Order 1995 says in this regard is that the ICPC may draw to the attention of the Secretary of State any matter which it thinks the Secretary of State should refer to the Commission (art.20(4)).

The Hayes Report recommends that the new Police Ombudsman should be able to comment on those aspects of complaints which concern operational or general policies but that the overall responsibility for dealing with such issues should reside with the Police Authority for Northern Ireland.

Compensation

Even if a complainant succeeds in having his or her complaint upheld as a result of an investigation, this does not mean that he or she is entitled to any compensation for losses or injuries sustained. If the police officer concerned is found guilty of a disciplinary charge or a criminal offence, as a general rule the complainant will obtain compensation only if he or she brings separate proceedings in a county court or the High Court. In such court actions the complainant need only prove his or her case on a balance of probabilities, not beyond all reasonable doubt. However in practice it can be difficult to persuade a judge that one has been mistreated by the police. Although several people have succeeded in obtaining compensation for police misconduct (it is the Police Authority which pays the money), usually the claims are settled out of court. Compensation for false imprisonment or assault will often be relatively high (see Chapter 3). Hayes has suggested that the proposed Police Ombudsman should be given the power to recommend the payment of *ex gratia* amounts to complainants; he also thinks complainants should be reimbursed their travelling expenses if they have to attend interviews and hearings.

Statistics

Compared with its much larger counterpart in England and Wales (the Police Complaints Authority), the ICPC is kept busy. The number of cases referred to the ICPC in 1996 for possible supervision was 2,544; the number referred to the PCA in 1996-97 was 2,199 (this excludes some 8,000 cases where supervision was not even considered). The ICPC undertook supervision in 390 cases while the PCA did the same in 998. As regards the outcome of cases, in Northern Ireland just 39 formal disciplinary charges were laid against police officers in 1996, a ratio of one charge for every 65 cases referred; in England and Wales 216 formal disciplinary charges were laid, a ratio of one charge for every 10 cases referred. In a further 112 cases, 153 "informal disciplinary actions" were taken in Northern Ireland; the figure for England and Wales was 993 such actions. In Northern Ireland the DPP directed just 11 criminal charges, one for every 74 cases referred to his office; in England and Wales, 16 officers were prosecuted in 1996. On these figures the substantiation rate for complaints in Northern Ireland was therefore 8%; in England and Wales it was 12%.

Of all the cases considered by the ICPC during 1993-96, 9% (929 out of 10,132) resulted from complaints made by people arrested under the Emergency Provisions Act or Prevention of Terrorism Act. Of the allegations made in these complaints (a total of 1,118), 384 (34.3%) were of assault during an interview with the police. A further 65 (5.8%) alleged assault prior to arrival at the police station. It is a fact difficult to believe, but nonetheless true, that the ICPC has not been able to substantiate even one of these allegations before a disciplinary tribunal; in 1995 a detective sergeant in one case was "admonished" for his interviewing technique and in two other cases "constructive discussions" took place with four officers. The reason repeatedly given for the lack of substantiation, apart from the complainant's refusal to co-operate with the investigation, is "insufficient evidence". This again highlights the very high standard of proof currently required to be satisfied, as well as the inadequacy of the systems in place for obtaining evidence.

Chapter 7

Prisoners' Rights

Stephen Livingstone

Northern Ireland currently has four prison establishments. These are at Maze, Maghaberry (male and female prisons), Magilligan and Hydebank Young Offenders' Centre. The last official statistics (in the 1995-6 Prison Service Report) give an average daily prison population of 1703 (of which 1670 were men and 33 women). Of these:

- 296 were on remand;
- 166 were young offenders;
- most of the remand prisoners were held at the Maze prison; and
- all women prisoners were held at Maghaberry.

Prisons in Northern Ireland are under the authority of the Secretary of State, who appoints the governors, medical officers and all other officers. Since 1995 the Prison Service has been an executive agency headed by a Chief Executive who has responsibility for "operational" matters. The Chief Executive in return reports to the Secretary of State, who in turn makes an annual report to Parliament on the working of the prison service. For each prison the Secretary of State must also appoint a Board of Visitors from members of the public. These Boards have three functions:

- to inspect the prison regularly and make an annual report to the Secretary of State;
- to hear prisoners' complaints; and
- to adjudicate upon the most serious disciplinary charges.

Legal rights of prisoners

In 1982, in the House of Lords case of *Raymond v Honey*, Lord Wilberforce said:

> *Under English law a convicted prisoner, in spite of his (sic) imprisonment, retains all civil rights which are not taken away expressly or by necessary implication.*

This was certainly a great advance on earlier pronouncements, some of which had stated that the courts would not hear the claims of "disgruntled" prisoners. But it still left prison law in a state of uncertainty because in the absence of a Bill of Rights or written constitution it is not clear what "civil rights" *any* of us have. It is also unclear what rights are removed by "necessary implication".

Perhaps the first place to look for an indication of what rights and duties prisoners have is the Prison and Young Offenders' Centre Rules (NI) 1995. These relate to a wide range of matters such as letters, visits, medical treatment, food, religion and discipline. On entry to a prison a prisoner should be given information about these rules and may consult the rules at any reasonable time (rule 23). Families can obtain a copy of them from the Stationery Office. The rules, however, are very vague on many points and are normally amplified by Standing Orders issued by the Northern Ireland Office. Several of these have now been published.

The vagueness of the rules, and the secrecy which surrounds Standing Orders, obviously limit their usefulness as a source of prisoners' rights. Another limitation is the fact that courts have held on a number of occasions that a breach of the rules by the authorities does not of itself give a prisoner a right to sue. Advocates of prisoners' rights have consistently criticised this position and called for a legally enforceable code of rights.

Courts have nevertheless held that they will look at the Prison Rules when deciding whether a right asserted by a prisoner, such as to a fair hearing in a disciplinary procedure, or to privacy as regards correspondence, has been breached. Therefore a prisoner who feels that the authorities have done something that they have no right to do, or have prevented the prisoner from doing something that he or she has a right to do, might look at the Prison Rules when framing a legal claim. The 1995 rules also contain (in rule 2) a set of general principles to guide their interpretation. Although the legal status of these principles is unclear, several of them (such as the requirements that all prisoners are treated equally and that reasons are given when a decision affects a prisoner) may be relevant to determining a prisoner's rights under the rules where a dispute arises. A claim might take one of a number of forms, *e.g.*:

- that the rules have nothing to say on the issue, *e.g.* where a prisoner is injured by another prisoner and claims compensation from the prison authorities;
- that the rules do cover the issue but are being interpreted wrongly, *e.g.* where the authorities claim that the rule entitling a prisoner to a fair disciplinary hearing does not entitle him or her to call a witness;
- that the rules are themselves invalid because they contravene the Prison Act (NI) 1953 or the European Convention on Human Rights, *e.g.* where the authorities claim that they can intercept all correspondence with lawyers.

Asserting prisoners' legal rights is not therefore a simple business, as it may require reference to private law, public law or European law. In addition, nearly all cases will involve claims by the authorities that the right asserted must be denied on security grounds. Prisoners who feel that their rights have been infringed are thus well advised to seek legal advice, a topic discussed later in this chapter.

Rights automatically lost on conviction

Things have changed from the days when conviction for a felony automatically led to a prisoner forfeiting all his or her property. By section 9(1) of Criminal Justice Act (NI) 1953, legal restrictions on the property of convicted prisoners were abolished. Currently the most important rights lost by convicted prisoners are public rights:

- they are disqualified from voting in Westminster elections during the period of their imprisonment;
- they are disqualified from becoming members of the House of Commons if they are serving a sentence of a year or more in prison; this does not of course apply to prisoners on remand, who remain entitled to vote or stand for election at all times;
- there appear to be no express disqualifications from either voting or standing at local elections, but electoral law relating to proxy and postal voting disables prisoners from casting votes they may be entitled to;
- any person sentenced to five years or more or to detention at the Secretary of State's pleasure is permanently disqualified from jury service;

- any person who serves a sentence of three months or more is thereafter disqualified from jury service for 10 years.

Internal grievance procedures

For a variety of reasons a prisoner may wish to complain about prison conditions or prison authorities' actions without resorting to legal proceedings. If so, he or she may wish to use the internal complaints procedure. This is an alternative procedure: there is no obligation to pursue a grievance internally before taking legal action.

Any prisoner with a grievance can request to see the governor, a member of the Board of Visitors or an officer of the Secretary of State. This request must be noted and reported to the governor as soon as possible (rule 74). The governor must see prisoners who have made such requests at a convenient hour every day, except at the weekends and on public holidays. When a member of the Board of Visitors or an officer of the Secretary of State visits the prison, they must be told of any requests to see them and Board members must see any prisoner who has made such a request. However, there is no clear indication in rules or standing orders as to whether and how quickly a reply must be given to a prisoner's complaint.

A prisoner may also wish to write to an MP, an MEP or the United Kingdom Ombudsman (the Northern Ireland Ombudsman's jurisdiction does not include prisons). However, if the complaint relates to a particular case and especially if it alleges misconduct by a member of prison staff, the correspondence is likely to be stopped or censored by the governor unless the matter has first been raised through the appropriate channels. These are:

- for adjudications or misconduct by staff, a petition to the Secretary of State;
- for all other matters, an application to the Board or a visiting officer of the Secretary of State.

Since 1995 prisoners in England and Wales have been able to complain to a specific Prisons Ombudsman but the remit of this Ombudsman does not extend to Northern Ireland and no similar institution exists in Northern Ireland. In England and Wales the Secretary of State must also appoint an Inspector of Prisons to investigate conditions and report to the Secretary of State. The Inspector's remit does extend to Northern Ireland, and in 1997 a report was prepared on Maghaberry.

Security classifications

Unlike the rest of the United Kingdom, all Northern Ireland's prisons (with the exception of Hydebank Young Offenders' Centre) are classified as high security prisons, but power exists for the Secretary of State to classify individual prisoners within a prison into higher and lower security classifications. As a result of recommendations by the Hennessey Committee report on the escape of 38 paramilitary prisoners from Maze prison in 1983, a further informal classification was established. This is usually known as being on the "Red Book". Such prisoners are moved within Maze prison every two to three weeks. Since the decision of the English Court of Appeal in *Ex parte Duggan* (1994) it would appear that the higher the security classification of a prisoner the greater his or her right to make representations and be given the gist of the reasons on which that classification was based.

Access to legal advice

The European Court of Human Rights has recognised that a prisoner's access to justice under Article 6 of the European Convention on Human Rights includes access to lawyers. A prisoner may therefore write to a legal adviser with a view to taking legal proceedings over any matter. Where this concerns an allegation of ill-treatment against a prison officer or the prison authorities, such a letter cannot be stopped on the grounds that the complaint has not been raised through normal channels. A prisoner may also write directly to the courts about a complaint and such a letter cannot be stopped.

When a prisoner writes to a lawyer in connection with any legal business this correspondence may not be read or stopped unless the governor has reason to believe it contains material which is not relevant to the legal business (rule 72(4)). Prison authorities are also required to provide reasonable facilities for lawyers to discuss pending proceedings with prisoners. A prisoner need give only 24 hours' notice that he or she wishes to discuss proceedings with a legal adviser and need only disclose that such a meeting relates to such proceedings. Standing Orders indicate that all legal visits should be in the sight but not the hearing of a prison officer and rule 71(1) requires this where the prisoner is a party to legal proceedings (*i.e* when a writ has been issued). Prisoners who are party to proceedings may also be examined by a doctor of their own choice in the sight but out of the hearing of a prison officer (rule 72(5)).

The right to correspond and to read

Prisoners have a right to correspond with:

- their close relatives;
- their MP and MEP;
- the Ombudsman; and
- the European Commission of Human Rights.

A prisoner can write to any other person or organisation but the governor may stop any letter where he or she thinks that such correspondence would constitute a genuine and serious threat to the security or good order of the prison.

A prisoner on remand has the right to send and receive as many letters as he or she wishes. Convicted prisoners may send and receive one letter after entering prison and thereafter one "statutory" letter a week. Postage on this letter will be paid for out of public funds and statutory letters cannot be withdrawn or withheld as a punishment. A prisoner can also send one extra letter a week on which the postage is paid at public expense. Subject to the discretion of the governor, a prisoner can write additional extra letters. Postage on these will normally be at the prisoner's expense but in a case of need a prisoner can apply to the governor to have these paid for out of public funds. The number of letters allowed varies from prison to prison.

All letters to and from a prisoner (except those relating to legal proceedings) can be read by the prison authorities and may be stopped if their content is found to be prejudicial to "discipline, good order, the prevention of crime, the interests of any persons or the security of the prison" (rule 67(4)). Further guidance on when letters may be read or stopped can be found in Standing Order 5.3.3. The main grounds are that the letter contains:

- material relating to an escape;
- threats of violence to someone inside or outside the jail;
- coded messages;
- specific allegations of ill-treatment not previously raised with the governor, Board of Visitors or the Secretary of State (though complaints or comments about prison conditions should not be stopped); or
- material intended for publication for payment.

Where a letter is stopped, a prisoner should be told and given an opportunity to re-write it. In some prisons in England and Scotland prisoners may purchase phonecards and make telephone calls subject to the same type of restrictions that apply to letters. These facilities are now also available in Northern Ireland. Mobile phones are not, officially, permitted.

Books, newspapers and periodicals are all regarded as privileges. However, it is clearly arguable that denying a prisoner access to a particular document violates his or her right to receive information, as guaranteed by Article 10 of the European Convention on Human Rights, unless justified under the qualifications in Article 10(2). According to Standing Order 4, prisoners can receive newspapers or periodicals from visitors or can order them by subscription directly from a newsagent or publisher. Subscriptions must cover a period of not less than two weeks for newspapers and not less than three months for periodicals. As the entitlement to newspapers and periodicals is regarded as a privilege, Standing Order 4 indicates that they may be removed as a punishment or if the governor feels that the content of the newspaper or periodical could prejudice the security, good order or discipline of the prison, could put at risk the lives of prison staff, is wholly or mostly in a language other than English or Irish (except where the prisoner is wholly unfamiliar with English) or in the medical officer's opinion could have an adverse affect on the prisoner from a medical or psychological point of view. A prisoner will normally be allowed to keep a "reasonable" number of books and periodicals in the cell.

A prisoner may obtain soft-backed books either from a friend or relative or directly from a newsagent or publisher, but he or she will not normally be allowed to retain more than six books in a cell in addition to a Bible, library books, a dictionary and approved texts issued by the prison education officer. Books are regarded as privileges and Standing Order 4 indicates that they may be removed on the same conditions as newspapers and periodicals.

Visits

Convicted prisoners are entitled to one statutory and three "privilege" visits per month. Remand prisoners are entitled to as many visits as they wish; in practice they are normally allowed three per week. Visits usually last for 30 minutes. Where a prisoner is sentenced to solitary confinement as a punishment, the statutory visit should still

104 Civil Liberties in Northern Ireland

be allowed unless the governor feels that the prisoner's behaviour and attitude are such that removal from solitary confinement would be undesirable or impracticable. If this does happen the statutory visit should be postponed and a prisoner should receive all the missed statutory visits at the end of the period of solitary confinement.

Prisoners may receive visits from close relatives and any other person, subject to the Secretary of State's and governor's discretion. In *McCartney v Secretary of State for Northern Ireland* (1987), the courts upheld the Secretary of State's decision to prevent a Sinn Féin councillor from visiting a friend in prison on the basis of evidence of Sinn Féin's support for violence. A prisoner must give the name and address of each adult person whom he or she wishes to have as a visitor and must be informed if any application for a visiting permit is refused. Visits between close relatives where both are in prison will be permitted provided this does not pose a threat to the security or good order of the prison.

Up to three people will normally be allowed to visit a prisoner at each visit. Visits should take place with visitors seated at a table and will be in the sight of a prison officer, but for domestic visits they should be outside the hearing of a prison officer. Visits can be stopped if a visitor attempts to pass any unauthorised article to a prisoner and visitors cannot carry recording equipment, cameras or videos; they can make notes during a visit but these can be taken out of the prison only with the permission of the governor or of the prison officer instructed by the governor to decide upon such matters.

Clothes and food

Both remand and convicted prisoners are entitled to wear their own clothes. The governor may, however, prohibit the wearing of certain clothing if this is judged to be prejudicial to the good order or security of the prison. Limits on the amount of clothing a prisoner can possess are set by each prison, but generally prisoners are allowed up to three of each item of clothing. Clothes can be left for a prisoner as part of a parcel. Convicted prisoners are generally allowed one parcel per week while remand prisoners can receive a parcel each day (except Sunday). These parcels may also contain food, confectionery, tobacco and toiletries. Special parcels are allowed at Christmas, Easter and Hallowe'en.

Prisoners on remand can be supplied with food at their own, or friends' or relatives', expense. All prisoners should be provided with prison food which is wholesome, nutritious and well prepared (rule 82(1)). Prisoners with special dietary requirements should inform the prison medical officer, who is required to inspect prison food regularly. Standing Order 14 instructs governors properly to observe the relevant provisions of food and drugs laws.

Education

Educational classes have to be established at every prison and the prison authorities are required to encourage every prisoner able to profit from educational activities to do so. The prison authorities are also required to provide facilities for private study of correspondence courses, though the Secretary of State has power to determine what books and papers may be received from outside.

Religion

Where a prisoner belongs to a denomination for which no chaplain has been appointed to that prison, the governor is required to do what is reasonable, if requested by the prisoner, to arrange for visits by a minister or priest of that denomination.

A prisoner may also be allowed an occasional visit by a family priest or minister, or by the priest or minister of the area where he or she last resided. Such visits do not require a permit and should take place either in the sight but out of the hearing of a prison officer or in the presence of a prison chaplain.

Medical treatment and hygiene

A prisoner who feels unwell should be allowed to see the prison medical officer. Where the medical officer feels a prisoner's health is endangered by imprisonment, he or she should inform the governor and Chief Medical Officer. A prisoner can refuse any medical treatment unless it is an emergency and must give written consent before any major form of treatment is begun. Time spent in hospital counts as part of a prisoner's sentence.

The Prison Rules also contain a number of provisions relating to general hygiene, *e.g.* requiring every prisoner to have a hot bath or shower once a week and placing a duty on the prison authorities to provide prisoners with toilet articles necessary for health and cleanliness. Standing Orders instruct governors to observe the provisions of the Health and Safety at Work (NI) Order 1978 with regard to washing and bathing facilities.

Prisoners are entitled to one hour's outdoor exercise a day (weather permitting; if the weather is bad the exercise can be taken indoors). Prisoners segregated for punishment retain normal exercise privileges.

In law the Northern Ireland Office owes a "duty of care" to protect prisoners from injury. Therefore, if a prisoner is injured, *e.g.* while working, or as the result of an assault by another prisoner or a prison officer, he or she may be able to claim against the prison authorities.

Searches

Prisoners and their visitors can be searched by the prison authorities. Searches may be carried out at such times as the governor orders but must take place according to the directions of the Secretary of State (rule 16). The courts have ruled that there is no requirement to give reasons for a search. Where a prisoner is required to undress for a search it can be conducted only by and in the presence of officers of the same sex as the prisoner and must be conducted in as seemly a manner as is consistent with anything being discovered. Full or strip searches should be conducted only on reception, after contact with someone outside a prison or where the governor has grounds to believe that a prisoner is in possession of an unauthorised article which cannot be discovered by other means. The rules do not permit body cavity searches but a prisoner may be required to open their mouth for visual inspection (rule 16(8)). Searches should be conducted only on arrival, final departure or after the prisoner has left the prison and returned for whatever reason (such as to make a court appearance, go to hospital or visit a prisoner in another jail), though the governor has power to order a search on other occasions. Searches carried out in a way which violates these guidelines could constitute an assault.

Removal from association

The governor may segregate a prisoner from other prisoners where he or she feels it is in the prisoner's own interests or where it is desirable to maintain good order and discipline in the prison. Cases have suggested that failure to segregate some prisoners, such as known sex offenders, may breach the authorities' duty of care if they have no other policy for reducing risk to the prisoner and that prisoner is subsequently assaulted. However, a governor may not segregate a prisoner for more than 48 hours without the authority of a member of the Board of Visitors or the Secretary of State (rule 32(2)). If such authority is given, the position must be reviewed every month. Prisoners in segregation must be visited every day by the medical officer and if he or she so advises the governor must return a prisoner to association.

This type of individual segregation for security reasons is different from a policy of segregating prisoners from different religions or factions. Such a policy seems neither to be prohibited nor required by law.

Women prisoners

Because the number of women prisoners in Northern Ireland's jails is declining (down from 75 in 1977 to 33 in 1996) and makes up a small proportion (only about 2%) of the total prison population, their legal position is often ignored. Such small numbers may have a detrimental effect on women prisoners' access to work and education programmes. Failure to accord work and education facilities equal to those given to men may amount to unlawful sex discrimination.

In general, prison rules and circular instructions apply equally to women as to men. But there are some differences. Rule 91(1) indicates that in matters of work, education, recreation or privileges governors may provide a different regime for female prisoners. However rule 91(2) indicates that this does not permit discrimination which would be unlawful if it occurred outside prisons.

The most significant difference relates to pregnancy and young children. Under rule 92(1), prisoners expected to give birth before the end of their sentence should be removed from the prison to a suitable hospital for whatever period the medical officer considers necessary. A mother and baby unit exists at Maghaberry prison and prisoners may keep their babies with them in the unit until the baby is nine months old. But the courts have upheld a governor's discretion to remove a baby from the mother's custody, without giving her a hearing, where he or she considers it necessary for the welfare of the child or the good order of the prison.

Discipline

Prisoners may be subject to disciplinary punishment only for a limited and specific number of offences. These offences have a definable content and convictions on disciplinary charges may be challenged if a governor or Board of Visitors has misinterpreted the rule setting out an offence.

A prisoner should be given notice of the charges as soon as possible. The governor must normally inquire into the charge on the next day and at that inquiry give the prisoner a fuller account of what is alleged (rule 36). A prisoner must be given sufficient time to prepare a defence; if he or she feels that the time allowed was insufficient, an adjournment should be asked for at any subsequent hearing.

If the charge is regarded as a minor one it will be heard by a prison governor or assistant governor, who, if he or she finds the prisoner guilty, may impose a range of punishments including loss of up to 28 days' remission, loss of privileges for up to 28 days or solitary confinement for up to three days (rule 39(1)). Where the charge is regarded as more serious (in practice this normally means any assaults on prison officers or repeated offences), the governor may refer the case to the Secretary of State, who always delegates the power to deal with it to the Board of Visitors. The Board may impose more severe punishments, including loss of up to 90 days' remission and solitary confinement for up to 56 days (rule 40(2)).

Whether a case comes before a governor or a Board, a prisoner is entitled to a fair hearing and to put his or her own case fully (rule 36(4)). He or she should be allowed to see all the statements made in the case, to call witnesses (except where these are called only to disrupt the proceedings), and to cross-examine witnesses who have given evidence (especially where hearsay evidence has been given, or there are inconsistencies in the evidence).

A prisoner can also ask for legal representation. This is very unlikely to be granted before a governor and there is no right to legal representation before a Board. However, the governor or Board must consider carefully a number of factors (in particular the seriousness of the offence, whether any difficult points of law are involved, and the prisoner's capacity to conduct his or her own defence) before deciding whether or not the prisoner should be legally represented. Court decisions have indicated that, if a governor or Board unreasonably refuses representation, this may be a reason for overturning a disciplinary conviction. If representation is granted, a prisoner will be entitled to free legal advice and assistance.

In deciding whether a prisoner is guilty, a governor or Board must seek proof "beyond all reasonable doubt". A number of cases have come before the Northern Irish courts on the application of this standard to cases where an offence has been committed but is denied by two prisoners who share a cell. The courts appear to have ruled that the governor or Board can convict both prisoners if there is evidence of collusion, such as an organised protest campaign, but may not do so where no such evidence exists. If a governor or Board finds the standard of proof is not satisfied on a serious charge it may not substitute a conviction on a less serious one. Also, any punishment given must be clearly set out in the decision of the governor or Board; it cannot be added to by a subsequent action of the governor. In a recent case, for instance, it was held that a governor could not remove a prisoner's bedding while the prisoner was serving a disciplinary punishment in solitary confinement: removal of bedding was in effect an extra punishment which had not been awarded by the Board.

If a prisoner feels that any of the above requirements have not been met and that he or she has been denied a fair hearing, he or she may seek to have the conviction quashed, though failure to comply with a procedural requirement does not automatically ensure that a conviction *will* be quashed on judicial review (see Chapter 2). Courts have generally been fairly strict about quashing decisions where there have been procedural errors by Boards of Visitors but have refused to quash decisions by governors despite procedural errors where they feel the same result would have been arrived at even if the right procedure had been followed.

A prisoner may also petition the Secretary of State to quash or mitigate a disciplinary conviction where he or she feels that the conviction was unfair or the punishment too severe. The Secretary of State also has the power to review disciplinary convictions or punishments of his or her own volition (rules 44-45).

Life sentence prisoners

Given the high proportion of Northern Ireland's prisoners serving life sentences, the release procedures for such prisoners are of particular importance. Although there is provision for judges to recommend that prisoners should remain in jail for the rest of their lives, this power is very rarely used and nearly all prisoners sentenced to life are released after a number of years.

Life is the mandatory sentence for an offence of murder, and is the maximum sentence available for a range of other crimes including attempted murder, manslaughter, causing an explosion and the most serious firearms and sexual offences. Those convicted of murder who were under 18 at the date of the commission of the crime can be sentenced to detention at the Secretary of State's pleasure (and are commonly known as "SOSP" or "pleasure" prisoners).

The decision as to when to release such prisoners is that of the Secretary of State. However, to advise the Secretary on such matters the Life Sentence Review Board (LSRB) has been created. This body is composed of Northern Ireland Office officials, a senior DHSS medical officer, a psychiatrist and the Chief Probation Officer. The LSRB normally first reviews a case after 10 years, though it may consider it earlier, and decides whether to recommend that the prisoner should be released or that the case should be reviewed later (usually after a period of between one and five years). Though the grounds on which this decision is based have not been expressly stated in law, officials have frequently referred to two criteria:

- the seriousness of the offence; and
- the likelihood that, if released, the prisoner will commit another violent offence.

In reaching its decision the LSRB considers material such as:

- information about the prisoner's offence;
- any comments by the trial judge in passing sentence;
- the prisoner's age and background (including any previous offences);
- reports made by the prison staff;
- relevant medical or psychiatric reports; and
- written submissions by the prisoner or comments made during a pre-hearing interview with a governor.

Neither the prisoner nor any representative is allowed to attend the LSRB hearing. If the Board refuses to recommend release, the prisoner will not be given any reasons but will simply be told that his or her case will be reviewed again in a specified number of months or years. Even if the Board does recommend release, the case must still be considered by the trial judge, if available, or by the Lord Chief Justice, who will also make recommendations to the Secretary of State. Ultimately, the decision to release is for the Secretary of State.

Prisoners released from a life sentence are released on licence and are subject to recall at any time, even if they have not committed another offence. In England the position has been changed by the Criminal Justice Act 1991, passed in response to a number of European Court cases, and prisoners may now challenge the lawfulness of their recall. Discretionary life sentence prisoners in England also have the right to know the "tariff" set by the sentencing judge and to a hearing where they are detained beyond the expiry of that tariff. These provisions do not apply in Northern Ireland but judicial review may be available in some situations.

Transfer of prisoners

Where prisoners who originally come from Northern Ireland are imprisoned in Great Britain they may apply to be transferred to Northern Ireland. They have no legal right to transfer and the European Commission of Human Rights has stated that only in "exceptional circumstances" will failure to transfer breach the right to privacy and family life contained in the European Convention on Human Rights.

Nevertheless there does exist a power to transfer prisoners between Northern Ireland and the rest of the United Kingdom. The authorities must consider all transfer requests and they have indicated that they will grant them where the prisoner is sentenced and (1) has more than 6 months of his or her sentence still to serve, (2) was ordinarily resident in Northern Ireland before imprisonment or has close relatives in Northern Ireland and it is reasonably believed that he or she has a firm intention of taking up residence on release, (3) both sentencing and receiving jurisdictions are satisfied that the prisoner will not be disruptive if transferred. However, even if all of these criteria are satisfied the guidelines allow transfer to be refused if it is believed that the prisoner is seeking transfer only to get a reduction in sentence or where so serious are his or her crimes that he or she is "undeserving of public sympathy and should not benefit in any reduction in time to serve". (For offences committed between 1973 and 1989 those convicted in Northern Ireland generally have more favourable remission arrangements than people convicted of similar offences in Great Britain.) The "undeserving of sympathy" requirement does not apply to temporary transfers as, unlike permanent transfers, release arrangements for prisoners on temporary transfer are governed by the law of the sentencing jurisdiction. However, from 1 October 1997, temporary transfer prisoners are entitled to the same home leave and compassionate leave arrangements as other prisoners in Northern Ireland (Crime (Sentences) Act 1997, s.41).

The position of ex-prisoners

A prison sentence can continue to have a legal effect on someone even after he or she has left prison. Under the Rehabilitation of

Offenders (NI) Order 1978 a person can be dismissed or a job offer withdrawn if he or she fails to provide information, when asked, about previous criminal convictions. There is no obligation to declare a conviction if the employer does not ask about previous convictions but many employers do so at the application or interview stage.

There is also no obligation to declare a conviction and sentence if it has become "spent" under the terms of the 1978 Order. The Order contains a complex set of rules for determining when convictions are spent, especially in relation to those with several criminal convictions, and anyone applying for a job with a criminal record would be wise to seek advice on their application. Some basic guidelines, however, are:

- a prison sentence, including a suspended sentence of more than two-and-a-half years is never spent;
- a prison sentence of between six months and two-and-a-half years is spent only after 10 years where someone was over 17 at the time of the conviction (five years if under 17);
- a prison sentence of less than six months is spent after seven years (three-and-a-half if under 17 when convicted);
- shorter time periods apply to those who were sentenced to a fine, community service, probation or received an absolute discharge.

Some forms of employment are deemed to be "excepted" and when applying for these a person with a criminal record is required to declare their convictions even if they are spent. These include:

- jobs (including voluntary posts) which give substantial access to people under 18;
- certain professions which have legal protection (*e.g.* lawyers, doctors, nurses, accountants);
- certain occupations which are regulated by law (*e.g.* managers of insurance companies or nursing home owners); and
- appointments where national security may be at risk (*e.g.* some civil service posts, police, armed forces, some sensitive posts in the BBC or Post Office).

If the job is in the "excepted" category it should say this on the application form. Specific advice on whether or not to declare a criminal conviction can be obtained from:

- The Coping with Convictions Unit
  NIACRO (Northern Ireland Association for the Care and Resettlement of Offenders)
  169 Ormeau Road
  Belfast BT7 1SQ
  tel: 01232-320157

Former prisoners can also obtain advice and assistance from:

- Extern
  Graham House
  1-5 Albert Square
  Belfast BT1 3EQ
  tel: 01232-240900

- EPIC
  33a Woodvale Road
  Belfast BT13 3BN
  tel: 01232-748922

- Tar Anall
  539 Falls Road
  Belfast BT11 9AB
  tel: 01232-603368

Chapter 8

Immigration and Freedom of Movement

Anne Grimes and David Bonner

United Kingdom immigration laws

Immigration law is the system of rules and laws which govern who can enter and live in the United Kingdom, under what conditions and for how long. It applies uniformly throughout the UK. The Immigration Acts 1971 and 1988 set out the system of immigration control and provide for officials to enforce it. Section 3(2) of the 1971 Act empowers the Secretary of State to make Immigration Rules. The current rules came into effect on 1 October 1994. There have been several amendments since then. The Immigration Rules set out in detail the circumstances in which "leave" (*i.e.* lawful permission) to enter or remain in the UK is to be granted or refused to persons subject to immigration control. The Asylum and Immigration Appeals Act 1993 and the Asylum and Immigration Act 1996 largely govern the system for dealing with applications for political asylum and appeals.

Immigration control

Only certain people are subject to the control of the immigration system, and to differing degrees.

No control

Certain categories of people are not subject to immigration control and can freely enter and remain in the UK. These are:

- *British citizens:*
  Before 1 January 1983 all people born in the UK were British citizens. Since that date, children born in the UK are British citizens only if one of their parents is "settled" in the UK (*i.e.* has permission to reside in the UK indefinitely) or if one parent was a British citizen at the time of the child's birth. People who are not British citizens by birth may be registered or naturalised as British citizens in certain circumstances.

- *People with the "right of abode" in the UK:*
  Certain Commonwealth citizens have the "right of abode", *i.e.* those who (a) were born before 1 January 1983 and have a parent born in the UK, or (b) are women who were Commonwealth citizens on 31 December 1982 and were married before 1 January 1983 to men who are British citizens or are Commonwealth citizens with a parent born in the UK.

- *Irish citizens travelling from Ireland:*
  The Republic of Ireland, the UK, the Isle of Man and the Channel Islands form a Common Travel Area (CTA). No system of immigration control exists for nationals of these areas travelling within the CTA. However Irish nationals can be refused entry to the UK if the Home Secretary directs that their exclusion is conducive to the public good in the interests of national security. Non-Irish citizens are governed by the Immigration (Control of Entry through Republic of Ireland) Order 1972. This provides that certain people travelling to the UK from Ireland are automatically given leave to enter for three months with a prohibition on employment. As there are no immigration officials at the border this will not be stamped on their passports but if they wish to stay longer they must apply to the Home Office for an extension of their leave to remain. This does not apply to visa nationals (see page 116) or people who have previously entered or remained in the UK. People who leave the UK for Ireland whilst having limited leave to remain in the UK and whose leave expires whilst in Ireland are automatically given leave to enter the UK for seven days upon their return.

Limited control

European Economic Area (EEA) nationals who are citizens of the European Union (EU) or of three countries of the European Free Trade Association (EFTA) *i.e.* Norway, Liechtenstein or Iceland are subject to limited control. They are free to enter the UK to exercise their EU rights to freedom of movement, *i.e.* to work or seek work, to enter into business or self-employment, to provide or receive services as a student, of it they are retired or self-sufficient. They can be refused entry or deported on the grounds of public policy, public security or public health. An EEA national may be accompanied by his or her family no matter what their nationality. If such family members are coming to the UK from abroad they must obtain an "EEA Family Permit" from a British Consular post before travelling.

Full control

The following categories of people are subject to full immigration control and must, therefore, obtain leave to enter or remain in the UK:
- Commonwealth citizens without the "right of abode" (see page 115);
- British nationals who are not British citizens, *i.e.* British Overseas Citizens, British Dependent Territories Citizens, British Protected Persons, British Subjects and British Nationals (Overseas); and
- "aliens", *i.e.* all other nationalities.

Immigration control before entry

Prior to travelling, nationals of certain countries listed in the Appendix to the Immigration Rules ("visa nationals"), as well as people wishing to come to the UK for certain purposes (such as to settle as a spouse), are required to obtain entry clearance (often known as an entry certificate or visa) from a British Consular post overseas. The list of visa national countries consists mostly of so-called third world countries and is regularly amended. Visa nationals who have already been granted leave to enter or remain in the UK for more than six months, or people who have been granted indefinite leave to remain and who are returning for settlement after an absence of two years or less, need not obtain visas when returning to the UK.

Another form of immigration control imposed by the law is contained in the Immigration (Carriers' Liability) Act 1987. This provides for airlines to be fined for each passenger they bring to the UK who does not have the correct documentation, *i.e.* a valid passport and visa. The maximum fine is £2,000 per passenger. This means that airline staff act as unofficial immigration officials This provision has particularly affected refugees who wish to come to the UK to seek asylum. Often they are unable to obtain passports from their own governments and checks by airline staff effectively stop many refugees from getting to the UK where they could claim asylum. When many refugees have come to the UK from a particular country, the UK has made it into a visa country. People cannot get visas as refugees as they must be outside their own country in order to claim asylum.

Immigration control at time of entry

Immigration officers at the port of entry have the power to grant or refuse leave to enter the UK. Leave to enter is endorsed on the person's passport and may be limited in time and have all or any of the following conditions attached to it: a prohibition or restriction on employment, a condition requiring the person to maintain and accommodate himself or herself and any dependants without recourse to "public funds" (see below) or a condition requiring the person to register with the police.

Immigration control after entry

After entry to the UK limited leave to enter may be extended or varied by the Secretary of State at his or her discretion. In practice, the power is exercised by staff at the Immigration and Nationality Department of the Home Office at Lunar House, 40 Wellesley Road, Croydon CR9 2BY. Applicants may apply for an extension of their "leave to remain" in the UK in the same category as their leave to enter was granted. They may also apply for a change of status. It is sometimes possible to switch from one category to another and to have time limits or other conditions changed. Applications may also be made for "settlement", *i.e.* a removal of all time limits and conditions attached to the applicant's leave.

Applications for variation of leave should be made to the Home Office before the expiry of existing leave, otherwise the applicant becomes an "overstayer" and can be liable to prosecution. Additionally, if his or her application is refused, there is no right of appeal. Applications for leave to remain must be made on the mandatory application form and must include all documentation requested on the form. Application forms are available from the Application Forms Unit of the Home Office (tel: 0181 760 2233). A failure to complete the form properly or to include all documentation without good excuse will lead to the form being returned; the application must then be resubmitted and may be late.

The Home Office will grant an application for variation of leave if the applicant satisfies all of the conditions for the particular category as set out in the Immigration Rules. The Secretary of State always has an overriding discretion to grant leave to remain despite the Rules, for instance when the applicant does not satisfy all of the requirements of the Rules or where there is no provision in the Rules for the granting of leave in the applicant's circumstances. In practice, any request for the exercise of that discretion is dealt with by the Home Office.

The Immigration Rules

Full details of the conditions for entry and stay are set out in the Immigration Rules. They differ depending on whether the person comes to the UK for temporary purposes, to work, to join members of his or her family, to seek asylum or for other purposes.

Temporary purposes

Persons who are "visa nationals" (see page 116) require entry clearance from abroad to enter the UK in a temporary capacity. Persons in some other categories must also obtain entry clearance before travelling. All others must obtain leave to enter from an immigration officer upon arrival. Those entering in a temporary capacity may sometimes, but not always, switch to another category.

- *Visitors:* The maximum period of a visit is six months; applicants must be able to support and accommodate themselves without working or claiming "public funds" (defined as income support, housing benefit, family credit, income-based jobseeker's allowance, attendance allowance, severe disablement allowance, invalid care allowance, disability living allowance, disability working allowance, child benefit or housing executive housing). They must intend to leave the UK at the end of their visit. Visitors may be permitted to stay to receive private medical treatment.
- *Students:* who are enrolled on a full-time course of day-time study at a publicly funded institute of further or higher education or a *bona fide* private education institution or an independent fee paying school must produce evidence of financial support without working or

claiming public funds. They must also intend to leave the UK upon completion of their studies.

- *Trainees:* Persons wishing to come to the UK for training or work experience may apply to enter on a temporary basis. Again there must be an intention to leave the UK at the end of the period. Training permits are obtained from the Department of Economic Development's Training and Employment Agency, ES2 Branch, Clarendon House, 9-21 Adelaide Street, Belfast BT2 8DJ.
- *Au pairs:* Young people aged between 17 and 27 from certain countries (currently Andorra, Bosnia-Herzegovina, Croatia, Cyprus, Czech Republic, the Faeroes, Greenland, Hungary, Macedonia, Malta, Monaco, San Marino, Slovak Republic, Slovenia, Switzerland or Turkey) may come to live in the UK for a maximum period of two years as *au pairs* in order to learn English.
- Working holiday-makers: Commonwealth citizens aged between 17 and 27 may come to the UK for a maximum period of two years on an extended holiday. They may work if it is incidental to their holiday. They must be in a position to support and accommodate themselves without claiming public funds. The person must be unmarried or married to a person who also meets the working holiday-maker requirements and they intend to take a working holiday together. The applicant must not have any dependant children over five years old. He or she must obtain entry clearance before travelling and cannot switch to this category after entry.

Work

Work permits are obtained by the employer from the Department of Economic Development (see above for the address). They are granted only for certain categories of skilled employment where no other suitable candidates can be found in the UK or EEA. The potential employee should be outside the UK when the application is made. It is not usually possible for someone in the UK in another capacity to switch to a work permit. Work permits are initially granted for a period of up to four years. A work permit entitles the holder to be employed in a particular job for a particular employer. The holder cannot switch job or employer without the permission of the DED. After four years, a work permit holder may apply for "settlement", *i.e.* permission to reside in the UK indefinitely without any time limits or restrictions.

Certain jobs do not require a work permit, *e.g.* ministers of religion, missionaries or representatives of overseas newspapers. But applicants must obtain entry clearance from abroad before travelling.

Business people and the self-employed need to have at least £200,000 available for investment in business in the UK and must show that employment will be created for people already settled here. They must also obtain entry clearance before travelling.

Writers and artists who can show that they will be able to support and accommodate themselves from their art, writing or savings and will not do any other work or claim benefits may be given entry clearance before travelling.

Joining family

Family members may apply to come to the UK to "settle" here. "Settlement" or "indefinite leave to remain" in the UK means that the person is legally in the UK without any time limits or restrictions on working. People coming to settle must obtain entry clearance before travelling. Sometimes people who are here in a temporary capacity may be allowed to change to a category leading to settlement.

- *Spouses and fiancé(e)s:* A spouse of a British citizen or of someone settled here can obtain leave to enter or remain for an initial period of 12 months and thereafter indefinite leave to remain. Both parties to the marriage must have met, they must be lawfully married and intend to live together permanently. The couple must be able to support and accommodate themselves without "public funds". The "primary purpose" rule, which meant that a couple had to show that they did not marry for immigration purposes, no longer applies. Similar principles apply in respect of fiancé(e)s, who must apply for entry clearance abroad.

  Many people born in Northern Ireland are dual Irish/British citizens. For the purpose of an application for leave to enter or remain by a spouse, an Irish/British national may elect to be dealt with as an Irish national, and therefore as an EEA national. If he or she does so his or her spouse is dealt with under European law. This means that if the Irish national is exercising an EU right in the UK, *e.g.* by working or studying here, then his or her spouse is entitled to apply for an "EEA Family Permit" to join him or her in the UK. The Northern Ireland spouse may elect to have an application dealt with in this way even though he or she has not actually moved from one EEA country to another; simply having citizenship of another EEA country brings European law into play.

- *Children:* Children under 18 who are unmarried (in certain circumstances daughters under 21) will be allowed to settle in the UK if both parents have been accepted with a view to settlement in the UK or are already settled here. The rule prohibiting public funds applies. In limited circumstances children may join one parent who is settled here.

- *Parents and grandparents:* Those over 65 who are wholly or mainly financially dependent on a son, daughter, grandson or granddaughter who is a British citizen or settled in the UK may be granted indefinite leave to remain here. Applicants must show that they have no close relatives in their own countries to turn to. Widowed mothers and grandmothers under 65 may also be admitted in this category.

- *Other relatives* must apply for entry clearance abroad and show that they are wholly or mainly financially dependent on their relative in the UK, that they have no other relatives in their own country to turn to, that they are living alone in the most exceptional compassionate circumstances and that they can be supported in the UK without claiming public funds.

- *Cohabitees and same sex relations:* since 13 October 1997 unmarried partners may apply to stay if they can be supported without public funds and have been living together in a relationship akin to marriage which has existed for four years or more.

Seeking asylum

Political asylum is granted to those who can show that they have a well-founded fear of being persecuted for reasons of race, religion, nationality or membership of a particular social group or political opinion and that they are therefore unwilling or unable to return home.

Applications for asylum are made to the immigration officer at the port of entry or, after entry, to the Home Office if the refugee has come into the country in another capacity (such as a visitor or student). Anyone who applies for asylum is entitled to have his or her claim considered by the Home Office and to remain in the UK pending a decision. However, people who come to the UK through a "safe" third country may be refused asylum without their claim being considered and returned to that country.

Those who apply for asylum on entry may be detained or given temporary admission. The Home Office takes many months, often years, to make a decision. The Asylum and Immigration Act 1996 restricted access to benefits to asylum-seekers who claim asylum upon entry to the UK. Those who claim after arrival in the UK and all people refused asylum and awaiting an appeal are no longer entitled to benefits. Many are not entitled to work pending a decision on their applications or an appeal. If the Home Office grants asylum the refugee's spouse and children under 18 can join the refugee. After four years a refugee may apply for settlement. Sometimes refugees are not granted asylum but are allowed to remain in the UK anyway. This usually takes the form of a grant of "Exceptional Leave to Remain", this can be renewed up to a maximum of seven years, after which indefinite leave to remain is normally granted.

The introduction of the Asylum and Immigration Appeals Act 1993 and the Asylum and Immigration Act 1996 has meant that stricter criteria are used in assessing asylum claims and that shorter time limits are applied for appeals against refusals of applications. These changes mean that it is even more difficult than before for an asylum-seeker to make a successful application.

Other purposes

* *UK born grandparents:* Commonwealth citizens who have a grandparent born in the UK can be granted leave to remain for four years, following which they can be granted settlement.
* *Returning residents:* A person with indefinite leave to remain in the UK will generally be allowed back for settlement if he or she returns within two years of leaving. People with limited leave to remain in the UK of at least six months will generally be allowed back into the UK subject to the same time limits and conditions after an absence abroad.
* *Retired persons of independent means:* A person with close connections with the UK, aged over 60, may come here if he or she has a guaranteed income of at least £25,000 a year. He or she must obtain entry clearance before travelling and is prohibited from claiming public funds and from doing any work or business. Settlement can be obtained after four years in this category.
* *Investors:* Investors who have £1 million and intend to invest £750,000 by way of government bonds, share capital or loan capital may come to the UK..
* *Access to a child:* A person with rights of access to a child resident in the UK may apply for entry clearance in order to enter the UK to

exercise those rights. He or she must be able to support and accommodate himself or herself without working or having recourse to public funds and may stay for a maximum period of 12 months.

There are a number of well-established practices within the Home Office which are not written in the Immigration Rules but whereby, in appropriate circumstances, leave to remain is normally granted. For example, people who have been in the UK legally for a period of 10 years may apply for settlement, and settlement is also normally granted to those who have been here for more than 14 years, even if some of their stay has been unlawful.

Enforcement of immigration law

There are a number of ways in which immigration laws are enforced.

Removal

Someone who has been refused leave to enter at a port of entry may be removed to his or her country of origin or to the country from which he or she travelled. Apart from asylum-seekers, people who are removed normally have no right of appeal within the UK and can only appeal from abroad after removal.

Deportation

This is removal after entry due to one of the following:
- a person has overstayed leave or breached a condition of leave;
- a person's removal is deemed by the Secretary of State to be conducive to the public good; or
- a criminal court recommends deportation following conviction of a crime punishable by imprisonment.

If the Home Office intends to deport someone a two-stage process is followed. First, a decision to deport is issued. For those who have been in the UK for less than seven years there is a limited right of appeal following a decision to deport, but they can win an appeal only if the facts on which the Home Office based its decision to deport were not correct. People who have been in the UK continuously for more than seven years can put forward family, compassionate and other reasons at their appeal hearing. It is possible to apply to the Chief Immigration Officer or to an immigration adjudicator for bail pending the appeal hearing. The second stage is the issuing of a deportation order. There is no further right of appeal against a deportation order except by way of an objection to removal to the destination named on the order. If an order is made, it is not normally revoked for at least three years. Until it is revoked the person subject to the order may not return to the UK. In certain circumstances the Home Office may also deport the person's spouse and children under 18.

Illegal entry

This is entry in one of the following ways:
- without obtaining leave to enter from an immigration officer upon entry;
- entering in breach of a deportation order; or
- entering the UK by deception or misrepresentation.

Alleged illegal entrants can be apprehended and removed without any formal right of appeal until after removal, unless they claim asylum (in which case) an appeal will arise upon refusal. Otherwise the only way to challenge a decision to remove is by way of judicial review (see Chapter 2).

Criminal offences

The Immigration Acts create criminal offences for breach of the laws, *e.g.* overstaying or breaking conditions of leave. Suspected offenders can be arrested by immigration officers and the police. If convicted they can be fined, imprisoned and recommended for deportation. Offences introduced by the Asylum and Immigration Act 1996 include obtaining leave to enter or remain by deception, knowingly facilitating the entry of illegal entrants and employing immigrants who are not entitled to work.

Challenging decisions

There are a number of ways in which immigration decisions can be challenged.

Reviews

The Secretary of State has discretion to reverse a previous decision to refuse leave to enter or remain or to deport someone and may direct the grant of entry clearance or leave to enter. The discretion is generally exercised only in exceptional or compassionate circumstances, however where there is no right of appeal, for instance where an application for leave to remain is made after the previous leave expires, it is still worth asking the Home Office to reconsider the decision.

Appeals before entry to the UK

It is possible to appeal to an adjudicator against the refusal of entry clearance. The appeal is heard in the UK, generally at a venue close to the UK-based sponsor (*i.e.* the fiancé or spouse in a marriage case, or the family member in a dependants case). The appeal must be served on the relevant embassy within three months of the date of the refusal. People refused entry clearance after 2 July 1993 in the following categories no longer have a right of appeal:

- visitors,
- prospective students,
- students for courses lasting less than six months,
- mandatory refusals, *i.e.* where a person has applied to enter or stay in the UK in a situation which is not permitted by the Immigration Rules his or her application must be refused; these situations are:
  (a) where the applicant does not have a relevant document which is required by the Immigration Rules,
  (b) where the applicant does not satisfy a requirement of the Immigration Rules as to age, nationality or citizenship, or
  (c) where the applicant is seeking entry, or an extension of stay, for a period longer than that permitted by the Immigration Rules.

Appeal upon entry to the UK

A person refused entry to the UK at a port of entry has a right of appeal against the refusal except where he or she falls into one of the following categories:

- visitors,
- prospective students,
- students for courses lasting less than six months,
- mandatory refusals (see above).

People not in the above categories who have a valid entry clearance or visa upon entry have a right of appeal within the UK against a refusal of leave to enter and can stay in the UK while waiting for the hearing. Those without a valid entry clearance or visa have a right of appeal which can be exercised only after they have left the UK. In both cases the time limit for serving the appeal on the relevant immigration service is 28 days.

Appeal after entry to the UK

A person has the right to appeal against a refusal of an application to extend or vary leave to enter or remain in the UK only in the following circumstances:

- the application for variation or extension was made whilst the applicant still had leave to remain in the UK, *i.e.* before the expiry of the date on the last stamp in his or her passport, and was received by the Home Office on the correct form (with all required documents) within 14 days; and
- the refusal is not a mandatory refusal (see above).

People refused *asylum* before 26 July 1993 had rights to appeal against the refusal under the ordinary immigration appeals system. Since 26 July 1993, those refused asylum have appeal rights under the asylum appeals system set up by the Asylum and Immigration Appeals Act 1993. This provides for "special adjudicators", who deal only with asylum appeals. There are very strict time limits for appeal and the Home Office may deal with asylum cases on a "fast track" system where the claim for asylum is decided to be "without foundation", *e.g.* where the asylum-seeker has been in another country on his or her way to the UK and could have claimed asylum there.

All appeals

For all appeals there is a two-tier system laid down in the legislation. An initial appeal lies to an adjudicator with a second appeal to an Immigration Appeal Tribunal on a point of law. Leave is required before the appeal to the Tribunal. The grounds for appeal to the adjudicator are narrow; the appellant must show one of the following:

- the decision was wrong in law;
- the decision was not in accordance with the Immigration Rules;

- the decision involved an exercise of discretion which should have been exercised differently.

The appeal process is quite slow and it can take up to one year for an appeal to be listed for hearing. An adjudicator comes to Northern Ireland every one to three months to hear appeals. Legal aid is not available for representation at appeal hearings but it may be available for advice and assistance from a solicitor in preparing the appeal.

Judicial review

Judicial review (see Chapter 2) is available against decisions of immigration officers, the Secretary of State or appellate bodies if such decisions are illegal or unreasonable.

Representations to the Secretary of State

Due to the limitations of the appeal procedures and judicial review, further representations to the Secretary of State are often the only remedy available to the applicant. The Secretary of State can consider such representations under his or her general discretion to reverse previous decisions or grant leave. It is possible to enlist the help of a Member of Parliament to take up the case with the Home Office Minister when all other appeals and reviews have been exhausted.

International laws on freedom of movement

Freedom of movement is recognised by a number of international instruments dealing with human rights. Article 13 of the Universal Declaration of Human Rights (1948) states that everyone has the right to freedom of movement and residence within the borders of each state and to leave and return to any country, including his or her own. Article 12 of the United Nations' International Covenant on Civil and Political Rights (1966) provides that persons lawfully within the territory of a state shall have the right to liberty of movement within it and the freedom to choose their residence. The Covenant goes on to say (in Article 13) that no one is to be arbitrarily deprived of the right to enter his or her own country and that an alien legally within the territory of a state can be expelled from it:

only in pursuance of a decision reached in accordance with law and shall, except where compelling reasons of national security otherwise require, be allowed to submit reasons against his or her expulsion and to have his or her case reviewed by, and be represented for the purpose before, the competent authority or a person or persons especially designated by the competent authority.

All these rights are to be secured regardless of race, colour, national, ethnic or social origin, gender, language, religion or opinion (Article 26), but, apart from that of nationals to enter their own country, they can legally be restricted where necessary to protect national security, public order, public health or morals or the rights and freedoms of others.

The most explicit recognition of freedom of movement in the European Convention on Human Rights (the ECHR) is in Protocol 4. The United Kingdom has not agreed to be bound by this, largely because it would require changes to the country's immigration laws and, arguably, to the Prevention of Terrorism (Temporary Provisions) Act 1989 (the PTA). However, several other provisions in the ECHR are also relevant to free movement:

- Article 3 prohibits inhuman and degrading treatment, which may come into play when someone is expelled from the country, or where returning someone to a particular state may seriously affect his or her safety;

- where the matter concerns the separation of families, the rights to respect for family life (Article 8) and to marry and found a family (Article 12) may be at issue;

- detention for the purposes of exclusion or expulsion could contravene Article 5, which guarantees liberty and security of the person subject to limitations to secure certain purposes (*e.g.* to prevent crime).

In time of war or other public emergency threatening the life of the nation, a government can derogate from these Convention obligations (other than those in Article 3) "to the extent strictly required by the exigencies of the situation" (Article 15). If the Human Rights Act 1998 becomes law, persons in the United Kingdom will be able to enforce the Convention's Articles in UK courts, no derogation having been issued in this context.

European Union law

Article 48 of the Treaty of Rome 1957 (which created what is now known as the European Union) guarantees the freedom of movement of workers within the (now 15) member states of the EU. There must be no discrimination between workers on the basis of their nationality. The protection extends to a worker's husband or wife and to his or her dependent relatives, who all have the right to reside with the worker in the state where he or she is working. There cannot be a system of work permits for EU workers. Even if someone does not yet have a job but wishes to look for one in another member state of the EU, he or she must be allowed to enter that state (and to draw unemployment benefit) for at least three months. People living in the Republic of Ireland but working in Northern Ireland, or vice-versa, should be issued with special permits by the state they are working in.

It is to be noted that Articles 48(3) and 48(4) of the Treaty of Rome allow states to discriminate against workers from other member states for reasons of public policy, public security, public health or whenever employment "in the public service" is in issue. These exceptions are narrowly interpreted by the courts, but there can be no doubt that service in the police or army would fall within them, as would discrimination on the basis of a person's previous (if recent) conviction of a "terrorist" offence.

The Treaty of Rome contains separate provisions to regulate the freedom of movement of self-employed persons within the EU. By Articles 52-57 individuals and companies must be allowed to set themselves up in business in any member state on the same conditions as nationals of that state. Similarly, by Articles 59-66, an EU national must be allowed to provide his or her services in any member state under the same conditions as those imposed by that state on its own nationals. Articles 55, 56(1) and 66 create exceptions to the rights of establishment and provision of services similar to those in Articles 48(3) and (4) for employed persons. These are also narrowly interpreted by the courts. The "public policy" exception, for instance, cannot be used by authorities in Northern Ireland to deny rights to an EC national if the conduct of that person would not be stiffly penalised within Northern Ireland if perpetrated by a British citizen.

Travel controls under the PTA

The PTA 1989 is exceptional legislation, especially because of its marked impact on freedom of movement, even on that enjoyed by full citizens of the United Kingdom. Its inroads are effected by travel controls and the power to make exclusion orders. The Act superimposes an immigration-type security control on the immigration control already exercised against most entrants, not having the right of abode, at United Kingdom ports of entry. This security control, however, also extends to journeys within the Common Travel Area (see page 115), including travel between Great Britain and Northern Ireland.

Powers of examination under the PTA

The PTA 1989 provides for the regime of travel controls in section 16 and Schedule 5. It creates a set of designated ports of embarkation and disembarkation, and equips examining officers with powers of search, examination of passengers and arrest and detention of "terrorist" suspects. Examining officers may be police officers, immigration officers or customs officials. In practice, most are police officers from the Special Branch of the local police force for the area. A person who knowingly contravenes or fails to comply with the travel controls commits an offence punishable with three months' imprisonment and a fine up to £2,500.

The powers have been little used within Northern Ireland but have been frequently applied to persons who are travelling on passenger transport from Northern Ireland or Ireland to Great Britain, and vice-versa. The Act establishes a set of designated ports and airports listed in Schedule 6, including Heathrow, Gatwick, Manchester, Birmingham, Luton and East Midlands airports, and seaports such as Liverpool, Holyhead and Stranraer. The captains of ships, aircraft and hovercraft must ensure that passengers and crew embark and disembark in accordance with arrangements approved by examining officers.

Examining officers' powers

Passengers may be required to complete landing or embarkation cards. The extent to which this is enforced is variable (e.g. passengers to and from Heathrow tend not to have to do so). Cards will be supplied on the plane or boat but, if not, may have to be completed at the port or airport if an examining officer so requests.

Examining officers are given extensive powers to search baggage and cargo including a power of random search and examination of unaccompanied cargo on ships and aircraft to see whether any person is or has been involved in the commission, preparation or instigation of acts of terrorism. They may authorise the search to be carried out by persons who are not examining officers, such as airport security staff. Anything found may be detained for examination and kept for seven days. If the examining officer considers that it may be needed for use as evidence in criminal proceedings or in connection with exclusion order or deportation order processes, he or she may detain it until satisfied that it is in fact not needed.

Examining officers have wide powers to examine passengers who have arrived in or are seeking to leave Great Britain by ship, aircraft or hovercraft. The power to examine also extends to transit passengers and crew. Because of its land frontier with the Republic, in Northern Ireland the powers extend to those entering or leaving Northern Ireland by land. Furthermore, an examining officer can examine any person found in Northern Ireland within one mile of the border to ascertain whether he or she is in the course of entering or leaving. Rail passengers entering Northern Ireland may be examined at the first stop. These powers supplement already extensive powers of stop and search exercisable by the security forces under the Emergency Provisions Acts (see Chapters 3 and 4).

Grounds for examination

In Great Britain, the power of examination may be exercised to determine:

- whether a person is subject to an exclusion order barring him or her from Great Britain or the United Kingdom;
- whether there are any grounds for suspecting that a person is in breach of an exclusion order;
- whether the person is or has been concerned in the commission, preparation or instigation of acts of terrorism connected with Northern Ireland affairs or acts of international terrorism (we shall refer to this as "involvement in terrorism").

Exercise of the power requires no prior suspicion that a person fits any of these categories; it is there to ascertain whether he or she might do so. So long as the power is exercised in good faith, it is effectively a power of random examination of travellers and is not likely to be reviewed by the courts, although it has been said that in an extreme case a court might be prepared to interfere if the decision to examine a person was one that no reasonable person could have taken (*Re Boyle, O'Hare and McAllister*, 1980).

A person examined must give any information in his or her possession which the examining officer requires for the purpose of carrying out the examination. He or she must, if the officer requests, produce either a valid passport with a photograph or some other document which satisfactorily establishes his or her identity, nationality or citizenship. Technically, this imposes no obligation to carry a passport or any such document, but prudence and a desire to avoid delay might dictate that one should. If asked to do so, a person examined must also declare whether he or she is carrying documents of a type specified by the officer. The documents must be ones relevant to the officer's functions, but could include documents of a political nature. Refusal to comply with these requests would appear to amount to a criminal offence.

Powers of detention under the PTA

Examination of a person cannot last for more than 12 hours unless the examining officer has reasonable suspicion of the person's "involvement in terrorism". Where the officer has that suspicion, he or she may serve on the examinee a written notice requiring him or her to submit to further examination. No formal arrest is involved. Although reasonable suspicion is required, since it need not be of a specific criminal offence but only of something vaguer, the prospects for effective judicial review of the officer's decision are remote.

Once a notice has been served, anyone examined may be detained on the authority of an examining officer for up to 48 hours, pending consideration of whether to make an exclusion order (see page 134). However, if a Secretary of State (in practice the Home Secretary or the Scottish Secretary) so authorises, that 48 hour period can be extended by a period up to five days. Within the initial 48 hour period, detention must be reviewed every 12 hours, by a senior police officer not directly concerned with the ground for the detention. He or she must check that matters are proceeding diligently and expeditiously and that there are still reasons for detention (Sched. 3). The person detained or a solicitor must have an opportunity to make representations to the review officer about the detention.

An examining officer can require the captain of a craft to prevent the disembarkation of a person who is subject to an exclusion order or whom the Secretary of State is considering for one. To do so the captain may hold such a person in custody on the craft. An examining officer can also order the removal from a craft of anyone liable to examination or to be considered for an exclusion order. Persons may be detained in such places as the Secretary of State from time to time directs, and examining officers, or persons acting under their authority, can convey in custody persons under examination from one place to another for purposes of examination and control. In practice, except at ports with proper detention facilities, most detentions for examination will be in nearby police stations.

Persons liable to be detained can be arrested without a warrant by an examining officer, and a warrant can be issued by a Justice of the Peace to permit a search of premises in order to carry out the arrest. Apparently, although in law not so restricted, these powers are aimed at persons who have entered Great Britain secretly, without going through the controls, rather than at persons being examined at a port, who may well not be formally arrested at all.

Do the powers contravene European laws?

In *McVeigh, Evans and O'Neill v UK* (1981), applied in *Lyttle v UK* (1987), the European Commission of Human Rights, whose opinion was affirmed by the Committee of Ministers of the Council of Europe, considered that these powers of examination and detention at ports were permissible under Article 5(1)(b) of the European Convention on Human Rights, which allows "the lawful arrest and detention of a person ... in order to secure the fulfilment of any obligation prescribed by law". In this situation the legal obligation in question is to submit to examination at the ports. The Commission took into account that the obligation arose only in the limited circumstances of travel across a clear geographical or political boundary and:

> that the purpose of examination is limited and directed towards an end of evident public importance in the context of a serious and continuing threat from organised terrorism.

The searching, questioning, fingerprinting and photographing of the applicants were said to be legitimate interferences with their right to private life, justified under Article 8(2) of the ECHR as measures which were necessary in a democratic society for the prevention of crime. The retention of fingerprints, photographs and information obtained from the suspects, kept separate from criminal records where the suspect did not have a criminal record and reserved exclusively for use in the fight against terrorism, was similarly held necessary in the interest of public safety and for the prevention of crime.

The refusal to allow two of the applicants to contact their wives was, however, a breach of the right to family life not justified under Article 8 (2). This defect was remedied by the enactment of a statutory right of contact (subject to delay in appropriate circumstances) in the Criminal Law Act 1977, which, however, did not extend to Northern Ireland. The matter is now regulated in Great Britain by sections 56 and 58 of the

Police and Criminal Evidence Act 1984 (the PACE Act) and in Northern Ireland by sections 46 and 47 of the Northern Ireland (Emergency Provisions) Act 1996 (see Chapter 3).

The PTA powers may also conflict with the rights to free movement conferred by the Treaty of Rome 1957 (which created what is now the EU). However, those rights to free movement can be limited or denied on grounds of public security or public policy, provided that this is based exclusively on the personal conduct of the person concerned (which may include his or her present associations with a particular group regarded as socially harmful - *Van Duyn v Home Office*, 1974) and that the conduct constitutes a genuine and sufficiently serious threat to the interests of the society.

Exclusion orders

Powers to make exclusion orders are conferred by sections 4-8 and Schedule 2 of the PTA 1989. An exclusion order expels a person from a particular territory (the United Kingdom, Great Britain or Northern Ireland) or prohibits a person from entering it. Such an order can be made by any Secretary of State, but in practice the powers have been exercised by the Home Secretary in relation to persons in, or seeking to enter, Great Britain, and by the Northern Ireland Secretary in respect of those in, or seeking to enter, Northern Ireland. Orders have a three year life, but fresh orders can be issued at or before the end of each three year period. The powers can be used whether or not the persons are subject to deportation under the Immigration Act 1971, and can create a form of internal exile for British citizens within the United Kingdom. In October 1997, however, the government revoked all existing orders and stated its intention to repeal the powers to make new orders in 1998.

Subjecting someone to an exclusion order has an impact on the individual and his or her family markedly similar to that of imprisonment. While it is true to say that the person excluded is not necessarily confined to a particular territory as a result of exclusion, in practice that will often be the end result. Exclusion to Northern Ireland of a person resident in Great Britain, in particular, may involve loss of employment, problems of accommodation and separation from friends and loved ones. At the very least it will create heightened pressures on family life, transfer to a potentially hostile if not lethal environment, and the stigma of perceived "involvement in terrorism" which may make the person a target for paramilitary groups on the other side of the sectarian divide (see *e.g. Ex parte McQuillan*, 1995).

When the powers can be exercised

Persons subjected to exclusion orders will usually be held under the PTA, the majority being detained under the port powers. But they may also be held under other powers, such as persons arrested under ordinary police powers or serving a term of imprisonment. Indeed, there is no requirement that the person be in custody at all. Orders can be, and are, made against persons not in the relevant territory in order to keep them out of it.

The power to exclude may be used in "such way as appears to the Secretary of State expedient to prevent acts of terrorism connected with the affairs of Northern Ireland" (PTA, s.3). This suggests that the test for whether an order should be made against a person is whether it would be advantageous for this public policy goal rather than whether the order is necessary for that goal. The Secretary of State must be satisfied that the person:

- is or has been concerned in the commission, preparation or instigation of acts of terrorism connected with Northern Ireland affairs, or
- is attempting or may attempt to enter the territory with a view to being concerned in such activities.

How an order is made

In Great Britain, applications to the Home Secretary for an exclusion order, which are made by police forces, are filtered through the National Joint Unit (NJU) at Scotland Yard. This is made up of Special Branch officers from the Metropolitan Police and provincial police forces. The NJU has a general co-ordinating role with regard to investigating and preventing acts of Irish terrorism. If the applications survive the "filter" of the NJU, they will be considered in the Home Office by civil servants up to Deputy Secretary level, providing a further "filter" to weed out unsuitable applications. The submissions will then be presented to the Secretary of State by a junior minister. A similar process, without the NJU, operates in Northern Ireland.

Consequences of an exclusion order

An order may expel the person from the territory or prohibit him or her from entering it. Where an individual is ordinarily resident in the territory, the Secretary of State must have regard to his or her connection with another territory and consider whether it is such as to make it appropriate that an order be made. What constitutes a sufficient connection for this purpose remains obscure. Persons subject to an exclusion order may be held in custody pending its enforcement. An order is given effect by the Secretary of State giving directions to passenger carriers to secure the person's removal to the appropriate destination, in custody if necessary and at public expense.

Breach of the order is an offence punishable in the Crown Court with a maximum of five years' imprisonment and an unlimited fine or, in a magistrates' court, imprisonment not exceeding six months and a fine not exceeding £5,000 (s. 8).

Exemptions

Certain individuals are exempt from exclusion from a particular territory. No British citizen may be excluded from the United Kingdom (s.7). Nor may a British citizen be excluded from Great Britain or Northern Ireland if he or she is at the time ordinarily resident in that part of the United Kingdom and has been throughout the preceding three years. A British citizen cannot be excluded from Great Britain or Northern Ireland if he or she is already subject to an order excluding him or her from the other of those places. Citizens of the Republic of Ireland not also holding British citizenship do not qualify for these exemptions, even though they may be exempt from deportation under the Immigration Act 1971.

Interviews with an adviser

As a result of a ruling by the European Court of Justice in the *Gallagher case* (1995), currently the Secretary of State now serves on the person he or she is intending to exclude (who can be detained pending the outcome of the process) written notice that he is considering making an exclusion order, then refers the matter to one or more advisers appointed by the Secretary of State (to whom the individual can make representations and with whom he or she can have a personal interview), and takes into account the advisers' advice when making a final decision. Unfortunately, in an area of fundamental importance to human rights, the decision in *Gallagher* has not proved a catalyst for subjecting exclusion orders to a binding process of review by an independent judicial body.

The individual can have a personal interview with the adviser to discuss the case, and that interview can even take place after the person has consented to being removed in the meantime. The individual who consents to interim removal has 14 days in which to make representations and request an interview. The period is seven days where the person is awaiting removal. In practice, legal representation is permitted at the interview, but the review is not intended to be a judicial process in the sense of a court of law, with adversarial procedures and full disclosure of the case against the suspect.

The adviser apparently does not interview relevant police or intelligence officers or their sources of information. He or she may have some independent discretion as to how much information to disclose to the individual, but the latter's main problem lies in having to make representations without knowing the real substance of the case against him or her. In any event, the adviser's report is not binding on the Secretary of State, merely an element to be taken into account when reconsidering the original decision. However, the Secretary of State usually follows the advice. Discontent with such procedures for review may be one reason for the low take-up rate, although a one-in-three success rate is apparent from the statistics.

Taking court proceedings

A person affected by the exclusion order can test its legality in the courts. If the contention is that he or she falls within a category exempt from exclusion, then, provided he or she can prove this point, a court will have no difficulty in striking down the order. But if, as is more likely, the ground of challenge is that the person is not "involved in terrorism", the position is problematical. It is open to the court to review the decision, ask the Secretary of State to give the reasons for making the order, and consider whether he or she had sufficient basis in law for making the order. However, given the "security" context of the power, its subjective wording ("is satisfied that"), the status of its wielder (a principal Secretary of State responsible to Parliament), and the existence of a review mechanism in the legislation itself, the court is likely to be satisfied by a sworn statement that the decision was made personally by the Secretary of State on the basis of reports from trusted subordinates founded on information from intelligence operatives, the details of which cannot for security reasons be disclosed to the court. The court itself would be unlikely to probe behind that, the individual would not be able to identify from it any defect, and it would be impossible to establish that the Secretary of State had made the order and the statement in bad faith (*Ex parte Cheblak,* 1991; *Ex parte McQuillan,* 1995; *Ex parte Adams,* 1995).

Any challenge on grounds of procedural fairness directed towards getting further reasons for the making of the order would similarly fail. In view of the "security" context, it is left to the Secretary of State to decide how much information can safely be disclosed to the individual (*Ex parte Stitt*, 1987; *Ex parte McQuillan,* 1995). In many cases all the individual receives is a printed form stating the Secretary of State's satisfaction that he or she falls within the particular statutory criteria indicated on the form.

Do the powers contravene European laws?

While exclusion orders may contravene Protocol 4 of the European Convention on Human Rights this does not help a person in the UK because the UK government has not signed that Protocol. Enactment of the Human Rights Act in 1998 will make no differences. Nor would claims made under Articles 5 or 8 of the Convention be likely to succeed, except perhaps on the ground that there are no effective means of challenging in a court the lawfulness of detention prior to the issue of an exclusion order.

Exclusion orders can have an impact on European Union nationals (especially Irish citizens) and their families, who are within the protection of Treaty of Rome provisions on the free movement of workers, the right of establishment and the right to provide and receive services (see page 128). The case of *R v Saunders* (1979), however, suggests that the protection of those provisions does not extend to cover restrictions on the movement within the state of a state's own nationals, at least where the restriction is imposed as a form of punishment. Even if it did, exclusion orders against them or other Treaty-protected persons could probably be justified on public policy or public security grounds, in much the same way as was refusal of entry to a Dutch scientologist in *Van Duyn v Home Office* (1974).

Directive 64/221/EEC provides that measures taken on these grounds must be based exclusively on the personal conduct of the individual (though this may include his or her present associations with a particular group regarded as socially harmful) and that previous criminal convictions do not in themselves constitute grounds for taking such measures. The conduct must constitute a sufficiently serious threat to the fundamental interests of the society. All of these matters would be subject to final decision by the European Court of Justice at Luxembourg in an individual case. However, it is difficult to envisage its scrutiny of the reasons for individual orders going deeper than that likely to be employed in the UK's High Court in judicial review proceedings. Unfortunately, the ECJ has been denied the chance to consider these matters more fully in that the references to it made by the national court in *Ex parte Adams* (1995) were withdrawn when the order against Gerry Adams was revoked.

Chapter 9

Meetings and Marches

Brice Dickson

As with many of the other "freedoms" dealt with in this book (and pending the incorporation of the European Convention on Human Rights into UK law by the proposed Human Rights Act 1998), there is at present no law in any part of the United Kingdom which expressly guarantees a person's right to associate with others or to be part of an assembly. The "right" is what is left after the law has laid down preconditions on a person's ability to go wherever he or she pleases. In Northern Ireland there are more of these preconditions than in other parts of the United Kingdom and as a result the extent of the remaining freedom is not as wide as in Great Britain. This is partly because the freedom has sometimes been abused in Northern Ireland.

The law on this whole area is intricate. There is not one set of rules for, say, holding a public meeting and another for organising a parade or protest march. Instead there is a core of law which is relevant to all situations and in addition a few rules which are special to particular sets of circumstances. In Northern Ireland a lot of the relevant rules are laid down in the Public Order (NI) Order 1987, which updated and replaced the Public Order (NI) Order 1981. Some rules derive instead from decisions of judges in reported cases (the common law). The European Convention on Human Rights must be borne in mind too.

Of course the law can only do so much in this field: if people flout the law in sufficient numbers there is little that the police or anyone else can do to preserve public order. In 1997 an Independent Review of Parades and Marches in Northern Ireland was published (the North Report); this led to the creation of a Parades Commission and to a promise of legislation on the issue in the 1997-98 Parliamentary session. The recommendations of the North Report are referred to where appropriate in this chapter, as are the provisions of the Public Processions etc. (NI) Bill, published in October 1997.

European Convention law

Article 11 of the European Convention on Human Rights provides as follows:

(1) Everyone has the right to freedom of peaceful assembly and to freedom of association with others, including the right to form and to join trade unions for the protection of his (sic) interests.

(2) No restrictions shall be placed on the exercise of these rights other than such as are prescribed by law and are necessary in a democratic society in the interests of national security or public safety, for the prevention of disorder or crime, for the protection of health or morals or for the protection of the rights and freedoms of others. This Article shall not prevent the imposition of lawful restrictions on the exercise of these rights by members of the armed forces, of the police or the administration of the State.

Article 17 of the Convention says that the Convention must not be interpreted so as to give any state, group or person the right to engage in activities aimed at limiting other people's rights.

To date, the European Commission and the European Court of Human Rights at Strasbourg have not had to interpret Article 11 very often, but when they have done so they have usually been reluctant to allow a government to rely on Article 11(2) in order to restrict either of the freedoms. Thus, in *Christians Against Racism and Fascism v UK* (1980), the Commission held that the right to assemble (in that case, to organise a demonstration) could not be taken away just because there was a possibility of a violent counter-demonstration. The thinking behind such a decision is that, in the long term, it is healthier for a society to allow all views to be expressed, even if their content is disgusting to the vast majority of the general public.

The European Commission also held in the *Christians Against Racism* case, however, that it was permissible for the United Kingdom to have a law which in effect prevented the authorities from imposing bans on single processions but allowed them to ban all public processions, or a class of public procession, for a period not exceeding three months. That is the power which now exists both in England and in Northern Ireland

(Public Order (NI) Order 1987, art.5). It is also contained in the proposed Public Processions etc. (NI) Bill (clause 11). It is difficult to understand how blanket bans of this nature can, within the terms of Article 11(2) of the European Convention, be "necessary".

Most of the cases taken to Strasbourg on Article 11 have involved the activities of trade unions. As with other matters, however, it is difficult to discern a definite pattern in the judgments handed down. On the one hand, the European Court has said that Article 11 "safeguards freedom to protect the occupational interests of trade union members by trade union action, the conduct and development of which the Contracting States must both permit and make possible". On the other hand, it has pointed out that the Article "does not secure any particular treatment of trade unions, or their members, by the State, such as the right that the State should conclude any collective agreement with them". Nor does the Article guarantee the right to strike.

The European Commission of Human Rights was involved in the GCHQ case - *Council of Civil Service Unions v Minister for the Civil Service* (1987) - where workers at Government Communications Headquarters at Cheltenham were banned from belonging to certain trade unions. The unions involved were unsuccessful in persuading the English courts of the justice of their case. They also lost at the European level, where the European Commission held that their complaint could not be considered because the ban was a "lawful restriction" necessary in the interests of national security.

In an earlier case (*Young, James and Webster v UK*, 1983) the European Court placed a general query over closed shop agreements between employers and one or more trade unions. In *Sibson v UK* (1993) the Court held that an employer could require an employee belonging to a particular union to work at a separate site from that used by employees belonging to a different union.

Associating with others

The effect of the various rules concerning freedom of association in Northern Irish law is to confer upon individuals the right to associate with whomsoever they please. Of course, people who feel that they are being harassed or unduly annoyed by another person's company may well have a remedy in the law of trespass (which is an intentional interference with someone else's land, person or property), or they may qualify as the victims of other specific civil wrongs or crimes, but these are all wrongs which can be committed just as much by individuals as by people acting in consort. Under the Protection from Harassment (NI) Order 1997 the victim or potential victim of harassment can claim damages for (among other things) anxiety and financial loss, as well as seeking an injunction to prevent the harassment from continuing. This Order also makes harassment a crime, punishable by up to six months prison and a fine of up to £5,000.

The chief exceptions to the right to freedom of association are as follows:

(1) An association to plan the commission of a crime

It must not be an association to plan the commission of a crime. This would amount to the offence of conspiracy, which is committed (under art.9 (1) of the Criminal Attempts and Conspiracy (NI) Order 1983):

if a person agrees with any other person or persons that a course of conduct shall be pursued which, if the agreement is carried out in accordance with their intentions, either (a) will necessarily amount to or involve the commission of any offence or offences by one or more of the parties to the agreement, or (b) would do so but for the existence of facts which render the commission of the offence or any of the offences impossible.

Under article 9(3) of the 1983 Order there is an exception for acts that are to be done in contemplation or furtherance of a trade dispute, provided the offence is a minor one triable only before magistrates. A husband and wife cannot alone be charged with conspiracy, nor can a person be charged with conspiring with a person who is under 10, but a person can be, and often is, charged with conspiracy with a person unknown. Incitement or attempt to conspire are not punishable as crimes. Conspiracies to commit a minor offence are punishable by an unlimited fine; conspiracies to commit a serious (*i.e.* "indictable") offence (see Chapter 2) can be punished with the same maximum term of imprisonment as the indictable offence itself (art.11 of the 1983 Order).

Actually associating in a crime, as opposed to a plan for a crime, makes a person guilty of aiding, abetting, counselling or procuring the crime. In Northern Ireland the idea of counselling and procuring has sometimes been interpreted by the judges in a way which attributes guilt even to people involved at an early stage in an incident. In 1990 three men were convicted of counselling and procuring the murder of two British soldiers because the men were said to be part of a "common purpose" or "joint enterprise" which culminated some time later in the soldiers being killed at a different location (*R v Kane, Kelly and Timmons*). The House of Lords has recently expressed the law differently (*R v Powell and English,* 1997), which should mean that there will be fewer convictions of this type in the future.

(2) An association specifically banned by legislation

It must not be an association which has been specifically banned by legislation. An example is the ban imposed at GCHQ by the Civil Service Order in 1982 (see page 142). In Northern Ireland several associations are banned (or "proscribed") by section 30 and Schedule 2 of the Northern Ireland (Emergency Provisions) Act 1996. These are the Irish Republican Army, the Irish National Liberation Army, the Irish People's Liberation Organisation, Saor Eire, Cumann na mBan, Fianna na hEireann, the Continuity Army Council, the Ulster Defence Association, the Ulster Volunteer Force, the Ulster Freedom Fighters, the Red Hand Commando, the Protestant Action Force and the Loyalist Volunteer Force. In England and Wales only the first two of these are proscribed. In Northern Ireland the maximum penalty for belonging to a proscribed organisation, or for inviting support for it, is 10 years' imprisonment and an unlimited fine. If the support invited relates to money or other property, the maximum penalty is 14 years' imprisonment and an unlimited fine.

It is unlawful to be a member of a quasi-military organisation (s. 7(1) of the Public Order (Amendment) Act (NI) 1970) and any person who takes part in the control of such an association is also guilty of an offence. There is an exemption for employment by the organisers of any lawful public procession or meeting of a reasonable number of people as stewards to assist in the preservation of order. The maximum penalty for membership of a quasi-military association is three months' imprisonment and a fine of £5,000; that for managing or training such an association is five years' imprisonment and a fine of £1,000. See too the Unlawful Drilling Act 1819 (page 160).

(3) Unlawful assembly

The association must not be an "unlawful assembly" under judge-made law. In Northern Ireland the old common law offence of unlawful assembly remains. A person is guilty of it if he or she is a member of an assembly of three or more people which is either causing a disturbance or giving rise to a reasonable apprehension of a breach of the peace. "Breach of the peace" means conduct causing a reasonable apprehension (to someone present) of violence against persons or property (see too Chapter 3). The offence can be committed both on private property and in public places, and the assembly need not be densely packed in order to be unlawful: persons illegally occupying 70 houses over a five week period have been held to constitute an unlawful assembly (*McKibben v Belfast Corporation*, 1936).

(4) Association forbidden by order

Associating with others is illegal if it has been forbidden by administrative or judicial order. These orders are sometimes called exclusion orders. One notorious variety is that issued by a Secretary of State under the Prevention of Terrorism (Temporary Provisions) Act 1989 (see Chapter 8) but the type most relevant here is that issued by magistrates in cases of domestic violence, for the purpose of excluding someone, usually a man, from premises occupied by that person's spouse or cohabitee (see Chapter 16).

Controls on private meetings

When considering the law on meetings it is necessary to distinguish between private and public meetings. As regards the latter, it is also important to distinguish between public meetings in general and those held in the open air. Election meetings and council meetings are in a special position too.

Meetings on private premises and restricted to a "private" group are virtually uncontrolled by the law. They are never unlawful, unless one of the exceptions mentioned at pages 143-145 above is relevant or unless certain offences are committed during the meeting. If, for instance, a breach of the peace is being committed, the police can enter private premises in order to break up a meeting. The police can also enter private premises in order to arrest a suspected criminal, which is why groups of after-hour drinkers in public houses are at risk.

Members of the public have no right to attend private meetings unless they are invited or given express permission to enter. "Gate-crashers" will be guilty of trespass, which is not a crime if it takes place on private premises but it allows the occupier of the premises to sue in the civil courts for compensation even if the trespassing has caused no damage. Even when permission to enter has been granted, it may later be withdrawn. If a club or society holds a meeting and tries to exclude certain members, those members, if they have the opportunity, are entitled to apply for a court order (called an "injunction") to compel the organisers to grant them admission.

Public meetings in general

In 1936, the Lord Chief Justice of England said that "English law does not recognise any special right of public meeting for political or other purposes" (see *Duncan v Jones*). This principle continues to apply in both England and Northern Ireland. All public meetings are subject to the rules set out below, and open-air public meetings are subject to even further restrictions. Meetings on public highways are particularly susceptible to controls. A speaker at any meeting must also "take the audience as he or she finds it": if the audience is hostile, the speaker must be careful not to "occasion" disorder. Note that the organisers of public meetings are under no legal obligation to notify the police that such a meeting is scheduled to take place, unlike in the case of public processions (see page 153), but the North Report recommended that a notice regime for open-air public meetings should be introduced if the potential for clashes between parades and such meetings develops so as to cause concern (para.12.81).

A "public meeting" is defined by article 2 of the Public Order (NI) Order 1987 as including any meeting in a public place and any meeting (even in a private place) which the public or any section of the public is permitted to attend, whether on payment or otherwise. In turn, "public place" is defined as meaning any street, road or highway and any place to which the public or any section of the public has access, on payment or otherwise, as of right or by virtue of express or implied permission. "Meeting" is also defined in the same article: it means a meeting held for the purpose of discussing matters of public interest. A few points need to be made about these definitions.

- First, they apply only to the defined words when they are used in the 1987 Order. It would be possible for a judge or a law-enforcement officer to place a different interpretation on the same words when they appear in another piece of legislation or in a law laid down by judges.
- Second, whereas "public place" and "meeting" are given exclusive definitions, "public meeting" is defined only so as to *include* certain categories of meeting. It is conceivable that a judge or law-enforcement officer could apply the term to other categories of

meeting as well, such as meetings run by an organisation for its own members and their friends.

- Third, in the definitions of "public place" and "public meeting", the phrase "public or any section of the public" is used. In English cases on race discrimination legislation this phrase has been interpreted so as not to cover clubs and societies with some form of membership system. To get round this interpretation Parliament had to amend that legislation in 1976 so that it could extend to many of these clubs and societies. It remains to be seen whether a court in Northern Ireland will take as restrictive a view of the meaning of this phrase as the English courts have done, though even if they do, because of the point made in the preceding paragraph, it may not make the 1987 Order inapplicable.

- Fourth, the definition of "meeting" certainly excludes most of those meetings held merely for the purpose of discussing the internal matters of a particular group or association. The internal workings of a large political party may be a matter of public interest, but not perhaps the discussions of a parent-teacher association or a student society. Whether a matter is or is not of public interest is a question which can ultimately be tested in court. Comparisons with other areas of the law, such as contempt of court and defamation, would suggest that virtually any matter could, in the proper circumstances, be of public interest.

- It should be noted that a meeting can consist of two or more people; there is no higher minimum number required, as there is for "assemblies" in England (where there have to be at least 20 people).

Offences connected with public meetings

Needless to say, any behaviour which constitutes an offence in a private setting will not be any less criminal simply because it occurs at a public meeting. There are also some offences which can be committed only at public meetings (just as there are other offences, especially those concerning indecency and sexual relations, which can only be committed in public places).

Under article 7(2) of the Public Order (NI) Order 1987, a person is guilty of an offence, punishable in a magistrates' court by up to six months in prison and a fine up to £2,000, if he or she at a lawful public meeting "acts in a disorderly manner for the purpose of preventing the transaction of the business for which the meeting was called together".

Two other offences currently regulated by the Public Order (NI) Order 1987 need to be mentioned. Under article 19 it is an offence "at or in relation to any public meeting" (or indeed in any public place) if a person:

(a) uses threatening, abusive or insulting words or behaviour, or (b) displays anything or does any act, or (c) being the owner or occupier of any land or premises, causes or permits anything to be displayed or any act to be done thereon, with intent to provoke a breach of the peace or by which a breach of the peace or public disorder is likely to be occasioned (whether immediately or at any time afterwards).

The House of Lords has said that behaviour does not qualify as threatening, abusive or insulting just because it gives rise to a risk that immediate violence will be provoked, nor is it enough that the behaviour gives rise to anger, disgust or distress: *Brutus v Cozens* (1972), where the defendant had merely run on to the No. 2 court at Wimbledon Lawn Tennis Club and distributed leaflets.

In England it is an offence to display "any writing, sign or other visible representation", while in Northern Ireland it is an offence to display "anything". Some would argue, therefore, that in England it could not be a criminal act, *e.g.*, for a Protestant to wear or carry an orange lily in a strongly Catholic area at a time of sectarian tension (since the lily is real and not just a sign or representation), but this could clearly be a crime in Northern Ireland. Conversely, Northern Ireland has no direct equivalent to section 5(1) of England's Public Order Act 1986, which outlaws threatening, abusive or insulting behaviour "within the hearing or sight of a person likely to be caused harassment, alarm or distress thereby." The Protection from Harassment (NI) Order 1997 outlaws a "course of conduct" amounting to harassment of another; this is now both a crime and a civil wrong (see page 143).

Dressing up

Article 21 of the 1987 Order prohibits a person in any public place or at any public meeting from wearing a uniform signifying an association with any political organisation or with the promotion of any political object. The Chief Constable of the RUC may, with the Secretary of State's consent, permit exceptions to this prohibition, but only for ceremonial, anniversary or other special occasions. There is no definition of "uniform" in the 1987 Order, so the courts will have to decide whether, for instance, wearing a beret or some kind of sash is enough to constitute a uniform. In the English case of *O'Moran v DPP* (1975) it was held that the wearing of dark berets, dark glasses, dark pullovers and other dark clothing, when escorting the coffin of an IRA supporter through London streets, could be regarded as a uniform.

It is also necessary to note that, under section 31 of the Northern Ireland (Emergency Provisions) Act 1996, it is an offence for any person in a public place to dress or behave in such a way as to arouse reasonable apprehension that he or she is a member or supporter of a proscribed organisation (see the list at page 144). The maximum penalty is one year's imprisonment and an unlimited fine. This same maximum penalty applies to offences under section 35 of the 1996 Act, which prohibits the wearing without lawful authority or reasonable excuse in a public place or dwelling-house (other than the person's own residence) of any hood, mask or other article which has been made, adapted or used for concealing the identity or features. It remains uncertain what constitutes a reasonable excuse for wearing a mask; presumably it is permissible to put on a funny face at Hallowe'en or when performing a play!

Public meetings on private premises

The definition in article 7 of the 1987 Order makes it clear that a meeting may constitute a public meeting even though it is held on private premises, whether outdoors or indoors. Police officers can attend such meetings in a purely private capacity, but their right to be there in a professional capacity is not certain. One well-known English case, *Thomas v Sawkins* (1935), suggests that the right exists in situations where the police reasonably apprehend a breach of the peace. But whether the police's apprehension is reasonable could be tested in the courts.

Election and council meetings

Some special rules apply to election meetings by virtue of the Electoral Law Act (NI) 1962 and the Representation of the People Act 1983. Under Schedule 9, paragraph 13, of the 1962 Act, a person who acts in a disorderly manner for the purpose of preventing the transaction of business at a local election meeting is guilty of an "illegal practice", which is an offence punishable with a fine of £5,000. The same kind of disturbance at a meeting connected with a forthcoming election for a Westminster seat is punishable with a fine not exceeding £500. At election times in Great Britain all candidates have the right to use certain schools and halls for public meetings free of charge, and to inspect the list of halls available in the area. In Northern Ireland these rights do not appear to exist.

By law, all meetings of district councils in Northern Ireland, and all meetings of committees of those councils, are open to members of the public whether or not they reside in that council area (s. 23 of the Local Government Act (NI) 1972). But by the same section, a council may decide by resolution to exclude the public when publicity would be prejudicial to the public interest because of the confidential nature of the business or for other special reasons. The power to exclude persons from a meeting in order to suppress or prevent disorderly behaviour also exists (s. 27(a)). Newspapers can require copies of the agenda to be sent to them in advance of meetings (s. 24), but no person can insist on being allowed to take photographs at, or to record or relay, the proceedings (s. 27(b)) (see too Chapter 11).

Open-air public meetings

Controls on open-air public meetings are stricter in Northern Ireland than in England. The Public Order Act 1986 allows the police in England to impose conditions on the holding of such meetings, but does not permit them to be banned. In Northern Ireland the police's power to impose conditions has existed since 1951 and the grounds for imposing them were extended by the 1987 Order. The power to ban open-air public meetings was first introduced by the Stormont Parliament as a reaction to the troubles of 1969-71 (see the Public Order (Amendment) Act (NI) 1971). At that time the banning power was vested in the Minister of Home Affairs, but now it is vested in the Secretary of State (see below). Although the North Report was primarily concerned with parades and marches, it recommended that the guidelines and Code of Conduct which it wanted to see adopted by the Parades Commission (see page 155) should also be adopted and applied by the police in relation to open-air public meetings (para. 13.55).

Public open spaces are usually regulated by bylaws issued by the relevant district council or public body; these bylaws may completely disallow public meetings in those spaces or require prior special permission (see also page 158).

Conditions

The power to impose conditions on open-air public meetings is at present conferred by article 4(2) of the Public Order (NI) Order 1987. This requires a senior police officer reasonably to believe that the meeting may result in:

- serious public disorder,
- serious damage to property,
- serious disruption to the life of the community,
- or that its purpose is the intimidation of others with a view to compelling them not to do an act they have a right to do or to do an act they have a right not to do.

The police officer may then impose such conditions as to the place where the meeting may be held, its maximum duration, or the maximum number of persons who may constitute it, as appear necessary to prevent such disorder, damage, disruption or intimidation. The directions given by the senior officer must be in writing, except in cases where people are already assembling for the meeting. A person who knowingly fails to comply with a condition imposed under article 4 is punishable with up to two years in prison and an unlimited fine. It is a defence for the accused to prove that the failure arose from circumstances beyond his or her control.

Bans

The power to prohibit open-air public meetings is now conferred by article 5(1) of the Public Order (NI) Order 1987, which requires the Secretary of State to be of the opinion that the meeting is likely to:

- cause serious public disorder,
- cause serious disruption to the life of the community, or
- make undue demands upon the police or military forces.

The Secretary of State may then make an order prohibiting for up to three months the holding in that area of all or specified open-air public meetings. It is strange that "serious damage to property" is expressly mentioned as one of the grounds for the police imposing conditions on meetings, yet not as one of the grounds for the Secretary of State imposing a ban, but the phrase "serious public disorder" could perhaps be interpreted as embracing serious damage to property.

The 1987 Order provides that a statement made by the Secretary of State as to the need to prohibit a meeting "shall be conclusive evidence of the matters stated therein" (art.5(3)). This probably means, alarmingly, that the reasonableness of the Secretary of State's opinion cannot be challenged in court by judicial review. This distinguishes Northern Irish law from English law, where there is no equivalent to article 5(3) as far as the imposing of conditions on public meetings is concerned. Nor is there any requirement in Northern Ireland that the Secretary of State must obtain the consent of the Chief Constable or of the Police Authority before a banning order is issued, but the Police Authority is, wherever practicable, to be "consulted" (art.5(2)) and in practice the view of the Chief Constable will be given great weight too.

A person who knowingly organises or takes part in a banned open-air public meeting is guilty of an offence for which the maximum penalty is two years in prison and an unlimited fine.

Picketing

Some of the rules on picketing are described in Chapter 19. For the present it is necessary to note that if two or more pickets are acting together they may well constitute a public meeting and so be subject to the rules set out above. In England and Wales this will be the case only if the numbers picketing are 20 or more, because only then will they constitute an assembly under English law.

One of the tests which the police must consider before deciding to impose conditions on an open-air public meeting in Northern Ireland is whether its purpose is the intimidation of others (art.4(2)(b) of the 1987 Order). This is partly aimed at the control of picketing and in such a context "intimidation" will probably be interpreted as it has been under the Conspiracy and Protection of Property Act 1875, section 7 of which first imposed specific controls on picketing (expanded for Northern Ireland by the Trade Disputes and Trade Unions Act (NI) 1927, s.3). That gives it a wider meaning than the one attributable to the same term in section 1 of the Protection of the Person and Property Act (NI) 1969 (see page 159). However, in a case arising out of the News International dispute at Wapping, an English court held that abuse, swearing and shouting did not of itself amount to intimidation (*News Group Newspapers Ltd v SOGAT '82*, 1986).

Controls on public processions

The laws on association and on public meetings will normally also be relevant to public processions. But in some respects the rules vary a little and there are, in addition, other rules which are relevant only to processions. New legislation on the control of parades in Northern Ireland, the Public Processions etc. (NI) Bill which is currently going through Parliament, adds to the special provisions.

Article 3 of the Public Order (NI) Order 1987 requires the organiser(s) of a public procession to give not less than seven days' notice to the police, but there is no obligation to advertise the procession in the press. The North Report recommended that the notice period should be extended to not less than 21 days (para.12.69) and that the Parades Commission it was proposing should consider how to require some processions to be advertised (para.12.86). The new Bill requires organisers of public processions to give 28 days' notice to the police, but does not require advertisements.

The present notice requirement applies regardless of whether the procession consists of people walking, running, cycling or motoring. The notice must specify the following information:

- the date and time when the procession is to be held;
- its route;
- the number of persons likely to take part in it;
- the number and, where reasonably practicable, the names of any bands likely to take part in it;
- the arrangements for its control being made by the person proposing to organise it; and
- the name and address of the organiser.

The obligation to give notice does not apply if the procession is a funeral procession (see page 156) or is of a description specified by the Secretary of State. There is no exemption just because the procession is one commonly held in the area in which it is proposed to be held. "Traditional" marches organised by the Orange Order or the Ancient Order of Hibernians therefore have to be notified. But less than seven days' notice can be given if it is not reasonably practicable to give the full notice (and there is a similar exception to the 28 days' notice requirement in the new Bill). This means that spontaneous demonstrations are still lawful. It is ultimately up to the law-enforcement agencies to decide whether the failure to give notice in a particular case was "not reasonably practicable".

A person who organises or takes part in an unnotified public procession is punishable with up to six months in prison and a fine up to £5,000 (arts. 3(5) and (8) of the Public Order (NI) Order 1987). It is, however, a defence to prove that the accused did not know of, and neither suspected nor had reason to suspect, the failure to satisfy the notice requirements (art. 3(6)). If the alleged offence relates to a failure to keep to the notified date, time or route for the procession, it is also a defence to prove that the failure arose from circumstances beyond the accused's control. In England, Wales and Scotland, only the organisers of, not the participants in, unnotified processions can be guilty of offences, and the maximum punishments are less severe.

People taking part in a public procession in Northern Ireland are given a certain amount of protection by article 7(1) of the Public Order (NI) Order 1987:

> *A person who for the purpose of preventing or hindering any lawful public procession or of annoying persons taking part in or endeavouring to take part in any such procession hinders, molests, obstructs or acts in a disorderly manner towards, or behaves offensively and abusively towards, those persons or any of them shall be guilty of an offence.*

There is no exact equivalent to this offence in English law. It is punishable, in a magistrates' court only, with a maximum of six months' imprisonment and a fine up to £5,000, but the North Report noted that there had only ever been one prosecution for the offence, perhaps because it requires proof of a "purpose of preventing or hindering" a procession. The North Report could not come up with an improved wording but it recommended that the government should consider amending article 7. Clause 14 of the proposed Public Processions etc. (NI) Bill 1997 re-enacts article 7(1) almost word-for-word.

On the other hand, Northern Irish law has no equivalent to sections 4 and 5 of England's Public Order Act 1986. Section 4 makes it an offence to use threatening words or signs with intent to cause a person to believe that immediate unlawful violence will be used against him or her. By section 5 it is an offence to use threatening words or signs within the hearing or sight of a person likely to be caused harassment or distress. These offences can be committed in private places but not private homes. The Protection from Harassment Act 1996 (in England) and the Protection from Harassment (NI) Order 1997 (in Northern Ireland) now provide additional legal mechanisms for dealing with disruptive influences in or near parades (see pages 143 and 148 above). But these laws are directed at persons who have pursued a "course of conduct", meaning conduct on at least two occasions.

Conditions and bans

The powers to impose conditions or bans on public processions arise in the same circumstances as the powers concerning public meetings, except that the conditions which can be imposed include those which re-route the procession or prohibit it from entering any place specified in the police directions. The power to impose conditions rests with the police, but the North Report recommended that it be shifted to the Parades Commission (leaving the power to ban with the Secretary of State) and this is what the new Bill does.

At present a court will interfere with a senior police officer's discretion on whether to allow a procession only if there is evidence that he or she failed to consider proper matters, considered irrelevant matters or reached a decision which no reasonable person could make. If the Scottish law is followed by judges in Northern Ireland, a court may uphold a ban on a public procession if it is based on the likelihood of disorder emanating from opponents of the procession: *Loyal Orange Lodge No. 493 v Roxburgh District Council* (1979). However, opposition to the procession will not be enough to re-route it unless there is also a belief on the part of the police that the result may be (at the very least) serious disruption to the life of the community: *In re Murphy's Application* (1991).

In line with suggestions in the North Report, the Public Processions etc. (NI) Bill expands the statutory criteria for determining whether conditions should be imposed on a planned parade, or whether a parade should be banned, to include consideration of the impact of the parade on relationships within the community (clauses 8 and 11). The Bill also requires the Parades Commission to publish guidelines setting out the factors which it will take into account when determining whether a procession should be made subject to conditions. A draft set of guidelines has been published, together with a Code of Conduct providing guidance to persons organising a public procession and regulating the behaviour of persons taking part in it. This Code deals with matters such as the stewarding of parades and protests, the consumption of alcohol, and respect for places of worship, memorials and cemeteries. The Parades Commission does not have the power to impose fines for breaches of the Code.

To help reduce the chances of trouble at marches, the North Report thought it would be sensible to extend to Northern Ireland the laws at present in force in Great Britain to control the taking of alcohol to sporting events (see Sporting Events (Control of Alcohol etc.) Act 1985).

This has been done, to some extent, by clause 13 of the new Bill, which permits the police to confiscate alcohol being carried by those marching, about to march or about to view a march.

Funerals

Funeral processions have been exempted from the notice requirements of the Public Order (NI) Order 1987. Nevertheless, under regulations made in 1991, the police can require mourners to travel in vehicles. However, at the point where, or when, a funeral procession loses its connection with the interment or cremation of a body, it will be liable to the controls laid down in the 1987 Order for other types of public processions.

Bands

Northern Ireland also has a unique provision for the control of bands, which are defined as "a group of two or more persons who carry for the purpose of playing or sounding, or engage in the playing or sounding of, musical or other instruments". Article 6 of the Public Order (NI) Order 1987 allows the Secretary of State to require bands to be registered and anyone knowingly parading with an unregistered band would be guilty of an offence punishable with up to six months' imprisonment and a fine up to £5,000. In fact, no registration requirement has yet been made and there would be great difficulties in creating one which could not be easily evaded. It is, in any event, open to question whether restrictions on band-playing are necessary in Northern Ireland. Even if article 6 did come into effect, it would not apply to bands playing at a public meeting rather than in a public procession. However the North Report recommended that the government should give active consideration to the introduction of a registration scheme for bands and clause 12 of the new Bill empowers the Secretary of State to do so by order.

Additional public order offences

Many of the offences which might be committed during the course of meetings or processions have already been referred to. It is now necessary to describe some further offences:

Riot (or riotous assembly)

In Northern Ireland this is still a common law offence committed whenever three or more people, in execution of a common purpose, use force or violence which alarms or terrifies at least one person "of reasonable firmness", and with an intent to assist one another, by force if necessary, against any person who may oppose them. The maximum penalty is life imprisonment.

Affray

This is still a common law offence in Northern Ireland but not in England and Wales. It consists of unlawful fighting, or a display of force, in such a manner as to terrify a person "of reasonable firmness" (who does not have to be present at the scene). It can be committed by one person acting alone, but is commonly charged whenever the police break up street fights or pub brawls. The maximum theoretical penalty is life imprisonment, though the Northern Ireland courts may follow the sentencing guidelines issued by the English Court of Appeal in *R v Keys and Others* (1986), where it was said that the leaders and organisers of serious affrays can anticipate sentences of seven years' imprisonment or more.

Riotous, disorderly or indecent behaviour

In what is a partial re-enactment of the Criminal Justice (Miscellaneous Provisions) Act (NI) 1968, section 9, it is an offence under article 18 of the Public Order (NI) Order 1987 for a person in any public place to use behaviour which is riotous, disorderly or likely to occasion a breach of the peace. The maximum penalty is six months' imprisonment and a fine of £5,000. In *Clinton v Watts* (1992) the Northern Ireland Court of Appeal held that words alone can constitute disorderly behaviour (*e.g.* swearing and shouting) and that it is enough if the behaviour is seen by a police officer; the behaviour does not have to be directed towards any particular person provided it at least seriously infringes the values of orderly conduct held by right-thinking people. The amended version of section 9 of the 1968 Act (see Sched. 1, para. 3 of the 1987 Order) criminalises, in addition, indecent behaviour in any public place and behaviour, on premises where intoxicating liquor is sold, which is riotous, disorderly, indecent or likely to occasion a breach of the peace.

Obstructive sitting etc. in public places

Under article 20 of the 1987 Order a person is guilty of an offence - maximum penalty one month's imprisonment and a fine of £1,000 - if he or she sits, stands, kneels, lies down or otherwise conducts himself or herself in a public place so as wilfully to obstruct traffic or to hinder any lawful activity. There is also the offence known as obstruction of the highway (see art. 88 of the Roads (NI) Order 1993):

> *Any person who, without lawful authority or reasonable excuse, in any way intentionally or negligently obstructs the free passage along a road shall be guilty of an offence and liable on summary conviction to a fine not exceeding £500.*

These offences can obviously be committed not just by people opposing a march but also by those taking part in it. Just because a march has not been rerouted or banned does not mean that the people taking part in it have complete freedom to cause any obstruction they like.

Breach of council bylaws

District councils and some other authorities have power to issue bylaws (which require confirmation by the Secretary of State) to regulate activities in public places. Council bylaws can be inspected free of charge at council premises and generally speaking the maximum penalty for contravening them is a fine of £20, plus £2 for each day that the offence continues after conviction (Local Government Act (NI) 1972, s. 92).

Persons employed by the district council and members of the RUC may be authorised by the council to secure the enforcement of bylaws. Under section 21 of the Town Police Clauses Act 1847, still in force in Northern Ireland, it is an offence (punishable now with a fine up to £1,000) wilfully to breach an order made by a local authority "for the route to be observed by all...persons, and for preventing obstruction of the streets,...in all times of public processions, rejoicings or illuminations ...".

Carrying offensive weapons in public places

Under article 22 of the 1987 Order a person is guilty of an offence if, without lawful authority or reasonable excuse (proof of which lies on the accused), he or she has in any public place an offensive weapon, meaning "any article made or adapted for use for causing injury to the person, or intended by the person having it...for such use..." The maximum penalty is two years' imprisonment and an unlimited fine.

Offences in relation to public buildings

Under article 23 of the 1987 Order, it is a criminal offence to be a trespasser in a public building (a term which is widely defined and includes the Stormont Estate) or knowingly to interfere with the carrying on of any lawful activity in any public building. The maximum penalty is two years' imprisonment and an unlimited fine.

Obstructing a police officer

Obstructing or impeding a police officer in the due execution of his or her duty is an offence under section 7 of the Criminal Justice (Miscellaneous Provisions) Act (NI) 1968. The obstruction must be intentional, but virtually any act qualifies if it makes the job of the police more difficult to carry out. A police officer can himself or herself be guilty of the offence, especially if he or she colludes with a suspect to mislead an investigation (*Clinton* v *Kell*, 1991). However, a refusal to give information is not obstruction (though it may amount to a separate offence: see Chapter 3). If a police officer is exceeding his or her duty at the time, no obstruction can occur in law. It is also an offence, under the same section, to assault a police officer in the due execution of his or her duty. For the purposes of these offences a traffic warden is classified as a police officer. The maximum penalty is two years' imprisonment and an unlimited fine.

Intimidation

By section 1 of the Protection of the Person and Property Act (NI) 1969 it is an offence if a person unlawfully causes another in any way whatsoever to do or refrain from doing any act. This widely worded provision carries a maximum penalty of five years' imprisonment and an unlimited fine. Participants in a provocative and disorderly demonstration can be prosecuted under it if, for instance, their actions cause someone to stay indoors for a prolonged period. As so often, the impact of the section depends greatly on the prosecution policies of the police and the Director of Public Prosecutions (see also Chapter 10.)

Breach of the peace

According to Lord Justice Watkins in *R v Howell* (1982), a breach of the peace arises:

whenever harm is actually done or is likely to be done to a person or in his (sic) presence to his property or a person is in fear of being so harmed through an assault, an affray, a riot, unlawful assembly, or other disturbance .

It can occur on private premises even though no member of the public outside the premises is involved: *McConnell v Chief Constable of the Greater Manchester Police* (1990).

A breach of the peace is not itself a criminal offence, but it can very easily constitute some other offence and therefore the police and courts have significant powers to prevent breaches of the peace. A magistrate has power under article 127 of the Magistrates' Courts (NI) Order 1981 (and under the Justices of the Peace Act 1361) to "bind over" any person to keep the peace and/or be of good behaviour for a period up to two years, on pain of paying a sum of money if he or she fails in this duty. If this sum is not paid, the court may send the person to prison for up to six months. The time and money specified in a binding-over order must be reasonable (usually the time period is 12 months); appeals can be made to the Crown Court and judicial review proceedings may be taken in the High Court (see Chapter 2).

There have been many attempts to have the law on breach of the peace abolished or reformed, because it represents a grave risk to basic freedoms. As yet all such attempts have been unsuccessful.

Unlawful drilling

Parts of the Unlawful Drilling Act 1819 are still in force in Northern Ireland. Section 1 prohibits:

all meetings and assemblies of persons for the purpose of training or drilling themselves, or of being trained or drilled to the use of arms, or for the purpose of practising military exercise, movements, or evolutions, without any lawful authority from His Majesty, or the lieutenant, or two justices of the peace of any county.

The maximum penalty for persons conducting the training is seven years in prison; for those being trained it is two years. Prosecutions have to be brought within six months of the commission of the offence (s. 7). Training in the making or use of firearms or explosive substances is also an offence under section 34 of the Northern Ireland (Emergency Provisions) Act 1996, the maximum penalty being 10 years' imprisonment and an unlimited fine.

Chapter 10

Freedom of Expression

Steve McBride

Freedom of expression is one of the most widely invoked human rights. Because communication is such a fundamental aspect of our humanity, protecting the right to speak freely is vitally important. However, defining what is meant by freedom of expression is difficult, and setting the proper limits to what should be protected by the law can be especially so. This is even more the case in Northern Ireland, where the language of politics is often extreme.

As with other rights, the exercise of one person's right of speech may conflict with the same or other legitimate rights of other individuals or of society as a whole. Drawing the right line between art and pornography, between free debate and mere insult, between investigative journalism and invasion of privacy, between protecting democracy and protecting those who want to overthrow it, is not easy. A realistic assessment of the position may be that it is essential for democratic society that there should be as little restraint as possible on the free discussion of ideas and of current events, but that certain restraints may be imposed in order to protect the rights of others.

The legal background

Article 19 of the Universal Declaration of Human Rights states that:

Everyone has the right to freedom of opinion and expression; this right includes freedom to hold opinions without interference and to seek, receive and impart information and ideas through any media and regardless of frontiers.

The United Kingdom and Ireland are both signatories to the Universal Declaration, although it has no standing in domestic law

Article 10 of the European Convention on Human Rights states that:

1. Everyone has the right to freedom of expression. This right shall include freedom to hold opinions and to receive and impart information and ideas without interference by public authorities and regardless of frontiers. This Article shall not prevent States from requiring the licensing of broadcasting, television and radio.

2. The exercise of this freedom, since it carries with it duties and responsibilities, may be subject to such formalities, conditions, restrictions or penalties as are prescribed by law and are necessary in a democratic society, in the interests of national security, territorial integrity or public safety, for the prevention of disorder or crime, for the protection of the reputation or rights of others, for preventing the disclosure of information received in confidence, or for maintaining the authority and impartiality of the judiciary.

The European Convention cannot yet be directly relied upon in British or Irish courts, but the decisions of those courts can be reviewed by the European Commission and Court of Human Rights. In spite of the extensive qualifications in the second paragraph of Article 10, a number of aspects of British and Irish law have been successfully challenged, including the rules on telephone tapping and contempt of court. The status of Article 10 and of freedom of expression in general were extensively discussed in the English courts in *Derbyshire County Council v Times Newspapers Ltd* (1992), where the House of Lords held that there was a vital public interest in protecting the right to criticise official bodies.

The law within Northern Ireland relating to freedom of expression must be sought in a wide variety of sources.

- The criminal law punishes various offences which involve threatening or inciting comments, comments deemed to be offensive to public morals, breaches of official secrecy or the prejudicing of court proceedings.

- The civil law, through the rules on defamation (*i.e.* libel and slander), allows an individual to protect his or her reputation and also provides remedies for, amongst other things, breach of confidence and breach of copyright.

Not only individuals but also the mass media are subject to most of these restraints, and the mass media are in some cases subject to others also.

Criminal offences

Incitement

It is an offence under judge-made law to incite another person, whether by threats or encouragement, to commit any criminal offence. The incitement can be by words or conduct. There must be an intention that the other person commit the offence, but it is irrelevant whether or not the offence is actually committed.

Conspiracy

It is an offence under article 9 of the Criminal Attempts and Conspiracy (NI) Order 1983 to agree with any person to commit any criminal offence. Conspiracy is committed as soon as there is such an agreement; it need not be formal, explicit or detailed.

Threats

A threat to kill someone, communicated to that person or another, is a criminal offence, carrying a sentence of up to 10 years' imprisonment. It is also a crime, carrying the same maximum sentence, to threaten without lawful excuse to damage or destroy the property of another. There are specific criminal offences of procuring sexual intercourse by threats or false pretences, and of obtaining entry into any premises by violence or the threat of violence.

Intimidation

Section 1 of the Protection of the Person and Property Act (NI) 1969 provides that a person shall be guilty of an offence if he or she:

unlawfully causes, by force, threats, or menaces or in any way whatsoever, any other person (a) to leave any place where that person is for the time being resident or in occupation; or (b) to leave his employment; or (c) to terminate the services or employment of any person; or (d) to do or refrain from doing any act.

There is a penalty of up to five years' imprisonment for such intimidation (see also page 159).

Incitement to hatred

Article 9 of the Public Order (NI) Order 1987 makes it an offence to use or display threatening, abusive or insulting words or behaviour, with intent to stir up hatred or fear of a section of the Northern Ireland community, or where such fear or hatred is likely to be stirred up. The fear or hatred must be directed against a group of persons defined by religious belief, colour, race, nationality or ethnic or national origins. It is not an offence to use such words or behaviour in a private dwelling, provided that the person concerned has no reason to suppose that the words or behaviour will be seen or heard outside.

It is similarly an offence under articles 10 and 11 of the Public Order (NI) Order to publish, distribute, play or show written or taped material which is threatening, abusive or insulting, with the intention of stirring up fear or hatred or where such fear or hatred is likely to be aroused. It is an offence under article 13 to possess such material with a view to publishing, displaying or distributing it.

Rumours

Article 14 of the Public Order (NI) Order 1981 makes it an offence to publish or circulate any statement or report likely to stir up hatred or fear of any section of the public in Northern Ireland on the basis of race, religion or national origin, knowing that report or statement to be false and intending to provoke a breach of the peace at any time.

Poison pen letters

The Malicious Communications (NI) Order 1988 makes it an offence to send or deliver articles with the intention of causing distress or anxiety. The maximum penalty is a fine of £2,500.

Bomb hoaxes

It is an offence under article 3 of the Criminal Law (Amendment) (NI) Order 1977 intentionally to cause or communicate a false bomb warning. The maximum penalty is five years' imprisonment.

Support for proscribed organisations

It is an offence under section 30 of the Northern Ireland (Emergency Provisions) Act 1996 (the EPA) to solicit or invite support for an organisation proscribed (*i.e.* prohibited) under the EPA. It is also an offence to organise or address a meeting knowing that it is to support or further the activities of such an organisation or that it is to be addressed by a person professing to belong to a proscribed organisation.

Public order offences

These are dealt with in Chapter 9.

Sedition

The old offence of sedition (also called seditious libel) makes it a crime to speak or publish words which are likely and intended to provoke public disorder and violence against the monarch, government or constitution of the United Kingdom. In practice, conduct which might once have been charged as sedition is now likely to be dealt with under one of the other headings mentioned here.

Incitement to disaffection

The Incitement to Disaffection Act 1934 makes it an offence punishable by two years' imprisonment to endeavour to seduce any member of the armed forces from his or her duty or allegiance to the Crown, while the Mutiny Act 1797 makes it an offence punishable by life imprisonment to incite any member of the armed forces to mutiny or commit traitorous acts. The 1934 Act also criminalises possession of a document inciting disaffection with the intention of using it for that purpose.

Defamation

The law of defamation causes a great deal of difficulty for journalists and others making public comment. Defamation is essentially the publication of a statement about someone which is both untrue and likely to be damaging to his or her reputation. Publication simply means the communication of the statement to another person (other than the person defamed) and the statement need not be in words; a drawing or cartoon may suffice.

Defamation may be either libel or slander; libel is defamation in a permanent form, notably in printed form, but also including film, tape, television and theatre. Slander is defamation in non-permanent form, usually unrecorded speech. There is only one important difference between the two forms of defamation: for slander, but not for libel, there is a need to prove financial loss. The exceptions are slanderous words concerning a person's competence in his or her trade or business, or suggesting that a woman is "unchaste" or that a person has a contagious disease or has committed a criminal offence. In these cases financial loss need not be proved.

Two particular aspects of suing for defamation discourage the making of such claims and encourage the settlement of those that are made. First, legal aid is not available either to take or to defend a defamation action. Second, defamation is one of the very few civil issues which must be tried by a jury (unless both parties agree to trial by judge only). The jury (consisting of seven people in Northern Ireland) has to decide whether the plaintiff (*i.e.* the person bringing the action) has been defamed and, if so, the amount of damages to be awarded. The issues involved may be very complex, making for an uncertain outcome and a long and expensive trial. The amounts awarded by juries for defamation may vary from the colossal (£1.5 million in one recent case) to the contemptuous (1p in Albert Reynold's recent clash with the Sunday Times). Defamation actions are usually a risky business for all concerned.

Proving defamation

A person who alleges defamation must show that the comments in question diminish his or her reputation in the eyes of "right thinking members of society". The judge must decide whether the statement is capable of bearing a defamatory meaning, but the jury must decide whether it actually does carry such a meaning and whether it could reasonably be taken to apply to the plaintiff.

The intentions of the person making the statement are normally irrelevant; in most circumstances it will be no defence to say that no defamatory meaning was intended, or that the statement was not intended to be taken as referring to the plaintiff. Nor need the plaintiff show that anyone did in fact read such a meaning into the statement, or thought any less of the plaintiff because of it. It is enough if they might have done.

The court is entitled to consider innuendoes and hidden meanings, and it is not necessary for the defamation to be obvious to the general public: it is sufficient if some other person with particular knowledge is able to identify the plaintiff as the subject of a defamatory statement. A statement about a broad group, such as a racial grouping, will not normally be actionable, but a statement about a specific grouping, or an unidentified member of such a grouping (such as a committee) will be actionable by any member of that group.

Defences to defamation

It is a defence to prove that on the balance of probabilities the statement was true (this is known as the defence of "justification"). But it is not enough that the defendant believed that the statement was true, or had reasonable grounds for believing that it was true, or was merely repeating what he or she had been told by someone else. It is also a defence to prove that the statement was fair comment, *i.e.* that it was the expression of an opinion held honestly and without malice by the defendant on a matter of public interest. The statement must be an expression of opinion, not of fact, and the facts on which it is based must be substantially correct. Matters of public interest include politics, books and plays.

The defence of "privilege" exists so that people may be free, in appropriate circumstances, both public and private, to communicate without fear of being sued for defamation. "Absolute" privilege covers statements made in Parliament, in parliamentary papers or in court, and extends to fair, accurate, and contemporaneous newspaper reports of judicial proceedings; the makers of such statements and reports cannot be sued for defamation. "Qualified" privilege, which means that the maker of a statement cannot be sued provided that the material is published without malice, attaches to a wide variety of other situations, including reports of parliamentary proceedings and non-contemporaneous reports of judicial proceedings. Fair and accurate reports of public meetings or meetings of a range of public or semi-public bodies, including local authorities, and reports of the decisions of trade, professional, religious, educational and sporting bodies are protected by qualified privilege, provided that anyone aggrieved by such a report is given a reasonable right of reply. It has been held in Northern Ireland that a press conference is not a public meeting for these purposes (*Turkington and Others v The Telegraph plc*, 1996). Qualified privilege also covers situations where one person is under a moral or legal duty to give information and another to receive it. This might cover complaints to the police, to social workers or to an employer about an employee.

In 1991 the Neill Committee Report recommended a number of amendments to the law aimed at simplifying and speeding up defamation actions. The Defamation Act of 1996 enacted some of these recommendations, and in particular established a procedure whereby the publisher of a defamatory statement can offer to publish a correction and apology and, if necessary, have damages set by a judge rather than by a jury. The Act provides that anyone who may be associated with a defamatory statement, but is not the author or publisher of that statement - such as a printer, distributor or live broadcaster - has a complete defence provided that he or she took reasonable care and had no reasonable notice of any defamatory content. The Act also reduces the time limit for bringing an action to one year in most cases, and provides a summary procedure for dealing with some cases where there is no prospect of success or where no realistic defence can be offered.

Injunctions

Anyone who anticipates that a defamatory statement will be published about him or her may apply for an injunction to prevent publication. The courts, however, acknowledge the importance of protecting free speech and will not normally grant such an injunction where the defences of justification or fair comment are likely to be pleaded.

Malicious falsehood

There may be occasions when people suffer damage through incorrect statements being made about them, even though those statements do not strike at their reputation and hence are not defamatory. For example, a professional person may lose business through an incorrect report that he or she has retired or gone on a long holiday. Anyone in such a position may be able to sue for malicious falsehood where it can be shown that the person making the statement acted from malicious or improper motives. In *Kaye v Robertson* (1990) an injured actor successfully sued a tabloid newspaper under this heading.

Criminal libel

Libel may also be a crime if it is so serious as to require criminal prosecution in the public interest. Proceedings against a newspaper or periodical can be initiated only with the consent of a High Court judge, and such consent is likely to be granted only in exceptional circumstances.

Broadcasting and television

Broadcasting in the UK, and hence in Northern Ireland, requires a government licence under the Wireless Telegraphy Acts. All television broadcasting in Northern Ireland is under the authority of either the BBC or the Independent Television Commission (the ITC), a regulatory and supervisory body which grants the franchises under which all independent television companies operate, and which was set up in 1990 to replace the former Independent Broadcasting Authority. The Independent Radio Authority has a similiar role in respect of independent radio stations, and the Cable Television Authority deals with cable television. Satellite television based in the UK is subject to the authority of the ITC, with the Home Secretary having a power to proscribe any unacceptable foreign satellite service.

The BBC was established by Charter and the ITC by the Broadcasting Act 1990. Both have ultimate responsibility for programmes broadcast under their authority. The ITC is under a statutory duty to ensure that news reporting is fair and impartial and that nothing is broadcast which offends against good taste or decency or which is likely to incite crime or disorder or be offensive to public feelings. The BBC has bound itself to a similar standard. Unlike its predecessor, the ITC does not have the right to call in programmes for pre-transmission vetting, but it does have significant sanctions in respect of independent television companies, including the power to impose financial penalties.

The 1990 Act makes the Obscene Publications Act 1959 and, in Northern Ireland, the incitement to hatred laws (see page 165), applicable to broadcasting. In Northern Ireland a senior police officer, suspecting that an offence has been or is likely to be committed under the incitement to hatred laws, has the right to demand access to any relevant scripts, films or tapes.

The Broadcasting Standards Commission

The Broadcasting Standards Commission was established by the Broadcasting Act 1996, replacing the Broadcasting Standards Council and the Broadcasting Complaints Commission. It has a statutory duty to monitor broadcasting and to draw up codes of practice in respect of sex, violence, good taste and decency in broadcasting, and also in respect of the avoidance of unjust and unfair treatment and the unwarranted infringement of privacy. Broadcasting bodies are under an obligation to take account of the Commission's codes when establishing their own practices. The Commission has the power to receive complaints about standards in broadcasting and can require broadcasting bodies to publicise its findings in respect of such complaints.

The address of the Commission is 7 The Sanctuary, London SW1P 3JS (tel: 0171 233 0544).

The broadcasting ban

Both the BBC and the ITC are subject to reserved government powers. These include the power, vested in the Home Secretary, to order both bodies to include or exclude specific matters in their broadcasts. This power was invoked in October 1988 when Douglas Hurd, the then Home Secretary, instructed the BBC and the IBA to:

refrain at all times from sending any broadcast matter which consists of or includes any words spoken, whether in the course of an interview or discussion or otherwise, by a person who appears or is heard on the programme in which the matter is broadcast (a) where the person speaking the words represents or purports to represent an organisation specified below, or (b) the words support or solicit or invite support for such an organisation.

The notice then specified eight organisations proscribed under emergency legislation including:

* the Irish Republican Army
* the Irish National Liberation Army
* the Ulster Volunteer Force
* the Ulster Freedom Fighters and
* the Red Hand Commandos
  as well as three otherwise legal organisations:
* Sinn Féin, Republican Sinn Féin, and the Ulster Defence Association (made illegal in 1992).

The notice stated that the ban did not apply during election campaigns or to words spoken in Parliament. The Home Office also indicated that it did not prevent the showing of pictures of an affected speaker while a reporter read a paraphrase or even a word-for-word report of what the speaker was saying. Nevertheless the ban was still broad-ranging, and because it was imposed by the Home Secretary exercising powers under existing legislation, it was not readily subject to legal challenge or clarification. One legal challenge was rejected by the House of Lords (*R v Home Secretary, ex parte Brind*), and again by the European Commission of Human Rights. Decisions on implementation of the ban were in the final analysis a matter for the broadcasting authorities. Members of the public, persons affected by the ban, and even journalists and programme makers had very little means of redress over any particular decision. The ban was rescinded shortly after the declaration of the first recent IRA ceasefire, in September 1994. Legally, it could be re-imposed at any time.

Newspapers and periodicals

There are no licensing requirements for the publishing of newspapers or periodicals; the phrase "registered with the Post Office as a newspaper" relates only to postal rates.

Complaints against newspapers can be made to the Press Complaints Commission (the PCC), which was set up in 1991 following the Calcutt Report of 1990. The PCC has published a code of practice covering issues such as accuracy, the right to reply, invasion of privacy, harassment and misrepresentation, but its real powers are very limited. Even after the death of Diana, Princess of Wales, no formal laws were introduced to replace the industry's self-regulatory code.

The address of the PCC is 1 Salisbury Square, London EC4Y 8AE (tel: 0171 353 1248).

Advertising

Complaints about advertisements may be made to the Advertising Standards Authority (Brook House, 216 Torrington Place, London WC1E 7HN; tel: 071 580 5555). This is an independent body sponsored by the advertising industry itself. It has published a Code of Advertising Practice, among the requirements of which are that advertisements should be legal, decent, honest and truthful. The ASA rules on complaints and in extreme cases may instruct subscribing media organisations not to accept the advertisement. The ITC (see page 170) applies similar rules in respect of advertising on commercial television and radio.

Films and videos

The British Board of Film Classification censors and classifies films and video tapes. In respect of video tapes it has statutory powers under the Video Recordings Act 1985, which allows massive fines for selling or distributing videos which have not obtained a Board classification. Most local authorities, which have a licensing role in respect of cinemas in their areas, make it a licensing requirement that no film can be shown which does not have a BBFC certificate but they have the right to ban even films which do have a classification. Local authority licensing requirements do not apply to private cinema clubs.

Copyright

Copyright law prevents the use of protected material without the copyright owner's consent. Material protected may include original literary works (very broadly defined and including almost anything written down), artistic and musical works, photographs, films, sound and video recordings, and television and radio broadcasts. It is not a breach of copyright to make fair use of a copyrighted work for the purposes of criticism or reporting of current events, provided that the author of the work is properly acknowledged. Use of copyright material may also be justified where the public interest is best served by publication. Breach of copyright is not a crime, but it allows the copyright owner to sue for compensation.

Obscenity

In England and Wales the judge-made law on obscenity was largely superseded by the Obscene Publications Act 1959, but that legislation has never been extended to Northern Ireland. The common law still applies here, making it a criminal offence to publish what is technically called "an obscene libel."

The common law test of obscenity is whether the material in question has a tendency to "deprave or corrupt" those who are likely to see it. Whether a particular publication is obscene is for the jury (if there is one) or the judge to decide, applying the current standards of ordinary decent people. "Deprave or corrupt" means something which is more than merely shocking or offensive. Although obscenity is normally taken to apply to pornographic matter it can cover other material as well, such as publications advocating drug-taking or glorifying violence.

To break the law it is sufficient, as in defamation, to "publish" the material to one other person, but it is not necessary to prove that any person has actually been depraved or corrupted. Having an intention to publish, knowing that the material would have a tendency to deprave or corrupt, is enough. The Obscene Publications Act provides a specific defence for publications if they are for the public good in that they are in the interests of science, literature, art or learning, or are other objects of general interest. The common law position is less clear, but there is probably a basis for an essentially similar defence.

Indecency

A variety of statutes and local by-laws deal with indecent behaviour, publication or display. "Indecent" lacks any clear legal definition but would seem to include anything offensive to the standards of ordinary reasonable people, though lacking the element of depravity necessary for obscenity (see too Chapter 16).

The customs and excise authorities have wide powers to seize indecent or obscene material brought into the United Kingdom, though the effect of a ruling by the European Court of Justice has been to restrict these powers to material which would be deemed obscene rather than merely indecent. The Post Office Act 1953 makes it an offence to send any indecent or obscene article through the post, while the Unsolicited Goods and Services (NI) Order 1976 prohibits the posting of unsolicited sexual publications. The British Telecom Act 1981 criminalises telephone calls which are grossly offensive, indecent, obscene or menacing. The Protection of Children (NI) Order 1978 makes it an offence to take, distribute or possess indecent photographs of children.

Blasphemy

The judge-made law on blasphemy once made it a crime to deny the truth of the Christian religion. In its modern form, however, blasphemy simply covers comment which amounts to an insulting or abusive attack on the Christian religion. The intention of the person making or publishing the comment is irrelevant; it is only necessary to show that he or she is responsible for comments which the court deems to be sufficiently offensive.

The offence remains extremely vague and unsatisfactory. As has been confirmed by a case arising out of the Salman Rushdie affair (*Ex parte Choudhury*, 1990), it does not protect non-Christian religions, and there is even doubt as to whether it extends beyond protecting the doctrines of the Church of England. With modern legislation now providing racial and religious groups with some measure of protection against abuse and discrimination, it would be best if the crime of blasphemy were either abolished altogether or limited, as the Law Commission has recommended, to disruptive or abusive behaviour at a religious service or on church premises. Recently, however, the European Court of Human Rights upheld a ban on a British film on the basis that it was blasphemous (*Wingrove v UK*, 1997).

The Elected Authorities Act

The Elected Authorities (Northern Ireland) Act 1989 provides that any candidate for election to a district council or to the Northern Ireland Assembly (currently suspended) must sign a declaration when submitting his or her nomination papers, and again, if elected, before taking his or her seat. The declaration states that:

> *if elected, I will not by word or deed express support for or approval of (a) any proscribed organisation or (b) acts of terrorism (that is to say, violence for political ends) connected with the affairs of Northern Ireland.*

This requirement does not apply to elections to Westminster.

The declaration covers comments at public meetings or in circumstances where the person concerned can reasonably be expected to know that his or her comments will become public knowledge. The relevant test is whether the comments can reasonably be understood to express support or approval for an illegal organisation or for acts of terrorism.

The Act states that a district council, or any member of that council or any elector for that council, may take legal proceedings in the High Court for a judicial determination that a member of that council is in breach of the declaration. If such a ruling is granted, that member will be disqualified from holding office and will not be permitted to stand again for election for a period of five years. No such proceedings have yet been taken.

Contempt of court

The law on contempt of court protects the fair and impartial administration of justice. It is particularly concerned with preventing juries from being exposed to prejudicial comment. The modern law is largely to be found in the Contempt of Court Act 1981, which was passed after criticism of existing United Kingdom law by the European Court of Human Rights in the *Sunday Times* case (1979).

The 1981 Act makes it an offence to publish anything which creates a substantial risk that the course of justice in any particular case will be substantially impeded or prejudiced. This covers any speech, writing or broadcast addressed to the public or any section of it, and the rule applies when any proceedings are "active" (*i.e. sub-judice*, to use the old phrase). Criminal proceedings are active from the time when someone is arrested or an arrest warrant or a summons has been issued. Civil proceedings are active from the time when a date is set for trial. Appeals are active from the time when leave to appeal is applied for or notice of appeal lodged.

Liability is "strict", *i.e.* the intention of the publisher is not normally relevant. It has been held, however, that the 1981 Act has not affected the common law position concerning material published with the intention of prejudicing or interfering with court proceedings: it can still be contempt to publish such material, even when no proceedings are active (*Attorney-General v News Group Newspapers*, 1988).

Publication of an accused's criminal record or comment on his or her character or that of a witness, or linking an accused to other offences, would probably constitute a substantial risk of prejudice, as would publication of a photograph of an accused where identification may be an issue. But fair, accurate and contemporaneous reports of proceedings in court cannot be contempt and discussion in good faith of public affairs or matters of public interest is not contempt if any risk of prejudice to particular proceedings is only incidental to the discussion.

Any attempt to bribe, intimidate or otherwise improperly influence witnesses, jurors or judges would be contempt of court. Abusive criticism of judges, or accusations of prejudice or partiality against them, may amount to the old form of contempt known as "scandalising the court", though the Court of Appeal has said that criticism in good faith of a judgment, however vigorous, should not constitute contempt.

Section 8 of the 1981 Act completely outlaws any approaches to jurors, however innocuous. It declares it to be contempt of court to obtain, disclose or solicit any particulars of statements made, opinions expressed, arguments advanced or votes cast by members of a jury during their deliberations.

Contempt of court also covers disorderly behaviour in court, failure to comply with court orders or to observe an undertaking given to the court, and obstructing court officers in the course of their duties. It was held in the course of the "Spycatcher" litigation that a newspaper could be in contempt of court for publishing material which was the subject of injunctions preventing publication by other newspapers. In *Home Office v Harman* (1983) a solicitor allowed a journalist to see some documents concerning prisons which the court had ordered the Home Office to disclose to the court. The House of Lords decided that this behaviour was contempt, but when the solicitor took the case to the European Commission of Human Rights the government agreed to settle it. Under the terms of this settlement the government promised to change the law so that it would no longer be a contempt to disclose documents already produced in court pursuant to a court order.

Other restrictions on court reporting

Most legal proceedings in Northern Ireland take place in open court, and can be reported by the press. The press and public can be excluded from prosecutions taken under official secrets legislation and in a number of circumstances where publicity would defeat the interests of justice, such as blackmail cases. Similarly, the Contempt of Court Act 1981 allows courts, in exceptional circumstances, to order that the names of parties or witnesses, or other relevant information, must not be mentioned in open court or the press.

There are a number of other circumstances where press reporting of court proceedings is subject to limitations. The names of rape victims are protected from publication by the Sexual Offences (NI) Order 1978 (see Chapter 16). Only very limited factual information can be published about committal proceedings in magistrates' courts (which precede criminal trials), unless the defendant asks for reporting restrictions to be lifted. In a jury trial the press cannot report legal arguments heard in the absence of the jury. Juvenile court proceedings can be reported on condition that the identity of the defendant or witnesses is not revealed (see Chapter 17). Most matrimonial proceedings are held in private and are subject to substantial reporting restrictions.

Journalists' sources

The Contempt of Court Act 1981 provides a measure of protection for journalists' sources. Section 10 says that a court can order a journalist or editor to disclose a source only where such disclosure is necessary in the interests of justice or of national security, or for the prevention of disorder or crime.

The police may in some circumstances seize documents and other journalistic material. Under the Police and Criminal Evidence (NI) Order 1989 they may obtain a court order granting access to such material where they can satisfy a judge that the necessary conditions have been met (see Chapter 3). They may also be able to obtain such material, including films and photographs, under section 18 of the Prevention of Terrorism (Temporary Provisions) Act 1989, which requires the disclosure of any information which may be of assistance in preventing terrorism. This law was first used against Channel Four after it broadcast a programme in 1992 concerning alleged collusion between RUC officers and Loyalist paramilitaries (*DPP v Channel Four Television Co. Ltd*).

Official secrets

Official secrecy has often been the subject of very considerable controversy. Section 1 of the Official Secrets Act 1911, which is still in force, makes what would commonly be called spying an offence; it deals with collecting or revealing information likely to be useful to an enemy, for any purpose prejudicial to the safety or interests of the state. The Official Secrets Act 1989 essentially creates two kinds of offence:

* It makes it an offence for any member or former member of the security services, or anyone associated with security or intelligence activities, to disclose any information about such activities. The Home Secretary may by notification make anyone who comes into contact with intelligence activities subject to this restriction. Journalists who assist or encourage such disclosure, or who publish such information with grounds for believing that it has been disclosed without permission, may be prosecuted as accomplices.

- It is an offence to disclose other kinds of government information where damage is caused or likely to be caused by unauthorised disclosure. The categories of information covered include anything which would endanger British interests abroad, prejudice the capabilities of the armed forces, or impede the work of the police. Confidential information obtained from another state or international organisation is also protected. Where information about intelligence, security, defence or international issues has been communicated to other governments or international organisations and has been leaked abroad it is an offence to repeat it in the United Kingdom.

Section 5 of the 1989 Act also makes it an offence for journalists or editors to publish information where they know it to be protected by the Act and have cause to believe that publication would be damaging to the national interest. The Act does not allow any defence of acting in the public interest: unauthorised disclosure, and in some cases publication, of protected information is a criminal offence even though it may expose criminal activities, corruption or serious government malpractice. The absence of such a public interest defence is a particular cause for concern, even though there was no such defence in the old Act of 1911, but it may be that scrutiny in the courts and the common sense of juries will tend to keep a check on any abuse of the 1989 provisions. Only one prosecution has occurred so far.

Unauthorised disclosure of government information outside the areas specified in the Official Secrets Act 1989 is not a criminal offence, but it may well expose the culprit to internal disciplinary procedures. The government may also use the civil law to obtain injunctions against publication or to claim damages.

"D Notices"

The "D Notice" system is an informal system which acts as a restraint on press coverage of sensitive defence and security topics. The notices are issued by the Defence, Press and Broadcasting Committee, a body composed of officials from government departments concerned with national security and representatives of broadcasting organisations and the press. The Committee gives guidance on the publication of material which is sensitive on national security grounds, and from time to time issues notices warning that publication of certain stories may be harmful to national security. The system lacks legal force: the

Committee cannot prevent publication and prior clearance from the Committee is no defence to prosecution under the Official Secrets Acts.

Further information

Organisations specialising in the right to free speech are:

- Article 19
  33 Islington High Street
  London N1 9LH
  tel: 0171 278 9292

- Campaign for Press and Broadcasting Freedom
  8 Cynthia Street
  London N1 9JF
  tel: 0171 278 4430

Chapter 11

Access to Information

Gerry McCormack

The main justification for giving someone access to information held by others is that informed citizens are the basic ideal upon which a free and democratic society is premised. But there are more specific grounds as well. A person may want to check the accuracy of information held about him or her. There is the fear that if government is allowed to operate in secrecy it will abuse the powers entrusted to it and its officials will become corrupt. Allow people access to official information and they will be able to participate more effectively in law-making and administration.

In this chapter, the way the law *restricts* and *confers* access to information is examined. The final section argues the need for a Freedom of Information Act and considers the system of voluntary disclosure of information introduced by the last government under the Citizens' Charter initiative.

Laws restricting access

Broadly speaking, there are seven ways in which the law in Northern Ireland may *restrict* access to information. Three of these - the rules on contempt of court, disclosure of official secrets and "D notices" - have already been discussed in Chapter 10.

Contracts

There may be a contract in existence, one of whose terms prevents a contracting party from disclosing information to a non-contracting party. This is common in employment contracts, which often prohibit employees from revealing information acquired during the course of their employment. It also exists in contracts between banks and account holders.

Breach of confidence

In certain circumstances the law imposes an obligation not to disclose information received in confidence. It is generally necessary that the recipient has expressly or impliedly acknowledged the obligation, but he or she will not be held to it if the information is already in the public domain. This defence was upheld in a 1978 case where John Lennon tried unsuccessfully to prevent the *News of the World* from publishing an article by his former wife about their married life. Lord Denning said that the relationship of the parties had ceased to be their private affair. Similar arguments prevailed in the "Spycatcher" case, where the House of Lords concluded that publication of Peter Wright's memoirs in Britain could not be prevented because they had already been published and much publicised throughout the world.

A second possible defence to an action for breach of confidence is the public interest. The courts take this to mean that no-one can be prevented from disclosing information which indicates the commission of a crime. If a journalist wishes to reveal details of misconduct confided to him or her by someone involved in the misconduct, he or she cannot be prevented from doing so (see *British Steel Corp. v Granada Television Ltd*, 1980). The European Court of Human Rights has recently held that in other situations the UK's law on disclosure of sources is a violation of the right to free speech enshrined in the European Convention on Human Rights (*Goodwin v UK*, 1996).

Privacy

There is no general right to privacy in the law of Northern Ireland. Various Private Members' Bills have been put forward to create the right on a UK basis, but none of these has yet been enacted by Parliament. However the law relating to trespass, nuisance, defamation and malicious falsehood does provide a degree of protection. For instance, where a private detective posing as a post office engineer obtains entry to a building and places a bugging device in a telephone receiver, this would be trespass to land as well as trespass to goods. The persons in possession of the land and telephone could sue for compensation. The damages awarded would be increased in cases of insolent or oppressive behaviour ("aggravated" and "exemplary" damages). But it has been held that an owner of land does not possess all of the air above the land, so he or she cannot sue an aerial photographer who flies over the land to take pictures of it. Constant overhead surveillance might constitute what the law terms a nuisance or even an assault, as would the making of persistent telephone calls to a person's home or office (*R v Ireland*, 1997). The law relating to malicious falsehood proved of assistance to an actor whose privacy had been infringed in *Kaye v Robertson* (1990) (see Chapter 10).

As regards invasions of privacy by the press, it may be that the only effective remedy is a complaint to the Press Complaints Commission (see too Chapter 10). This Commission has an independent chair and 15 other members, but of these only five are not drawn from the press or the media in general. Anyone may complain to the Commission about an invasion of privacy, whether personally affected or not. The Commission may censure a newspaper or journalist, but it has no power to fine or to award compensation. While newspapers are expected to publish an adverse adjudication, they are not legally compelled to do so. A complainant retains his or her right to pursue legal action.

Where it is alleged that a TV or radio broadcast has infringed a person's privacy there is an opportunity of making a complaint to the Broadcasting Standards Commission (see too Chapter 10). This consists of at least three members and was established under the Broadcasting Act 1996. If it considers that there has been an unwarranted invasion of privacy, the Commission may require the broadcasting body to publish an apology in, *e.g.,* the *Radio Times* or to broadcast a summary of the complaint and the Commission's findings.

Telephone tapping and tampering with mail

In the *Malone* case an English court confirmed that a person had no right not to have his or her telephone tapped by state authorities. There was nothing to make the practice unlawful, therefore it had to be tolerated. Mr. Malone then took his case to Strasbourg, where the European Court of Human Rights decided in 1984 that the United Kingdom's law was in breach of Article 8 of the European Convention on Human Rights (*Malone v UK,* 1984). Article 8 guarantees the right to respect for everyone's private and family life, home and correspondence. The Court said that the United Kingdom's law did not indicate with sufficient clarity the scope and manner of exercise of the relevant discretion conferred on the public authorities.

The Interception of Communications Act 1985 was passed in order to comply with the European Court's judgment in the *Malone* case. It is now an offence for anyone to intercept communications sent by post or by means of a public communications system. The offence is committed, however, only where the interception is intentional and intention may be difficult to prove in a particular case. For instance, in 1992 there was no prosecution when details of a private telephone conversation allegedly involving the Princess of Wales were published. Moreover, interception remains permissible if it is consented to (*e.g.* when someone wishes to trace offensive telephone calls) or if it is carried out under a warrant issued by the Secretary of State, who must not issue one unless he or she considers that the warrant is necessary:

- in the interests of national security;
- for the purpose of preventing or detecting serious crime; or
- for the purpose of safeguarding the economic well-being of the United Kingdom.

The Prime Minister appoints a Commissioner to supervise the issuing of the warrant and there is a tribunal to investigate complaints. If the tribunal finds that the Act has been violated it must inform the complainant and the Prime Minister and it may cancel the warrant, order the intercepted material to be destroyed and direct compensation to be paid. If the tribunal finds no violation of the Act, the complainant is told this but not whether interception has in fact been carried out. There is therefore still no absolute right to know whether your telephone is being tapped and no figures have been released on the number of taps authorised in Northern Ireland.

The 1985 Act does not deal with surveillance by electronic bugging devices. The use of such devices is not of itself a crime, though physically placing an electronic bug may give rise to a civil action for trespass. In any event, more sophisticated modern devices are capable of listening in on conversations from a considerable distance.

Laws conferring access

Data Protection Act 1984

This Act was passed in order to comply with a Council of Europe Convention of 1981. It compels users of data to register with the Data Protection Registry, non-registration being a criminal offence. The Registrar can issue enforcement or de-registration notices against registered users who violate the Act's data protection principles. To check whether these principles are being maintained the Registrar has powers of entry and inspection. There is a Data Protection Tribunal to hear appeals against decisions taken by the Registrar.

A user of data is defined by the Act as a person who "controls the contents and use of the data" which are part of a collection processed or intended to be processed by that person or by someone on his or her behalf.

The core of the Act is the part giving "data subjects" the right of access to stored data. Upon request in writing (for which a charge of up to £10 can be made) a data user must within 40 days state whether he or she has any personal data relating to the person making the request and must supply that person with a copy of such data. The data subject must be an identifiable living person, not a company. If damage or distress is caused as a result of an inaccurate entry, compensation is payable by the data user unless he or she can prove that such care was taken as was reasonably required in all the circumstances to ensure the accuracy of the data at the time. A court can order inaccurate data to be rectified, erased or supplemented.

Exemptions

Three important matters are exempt from registration:
- personal data required for the purpose of safeguarding national security;
- payroll and accounting data;
- data held for domestic or club purposes.

Matters exempt from the subject access provisions are:
- the three items already listed;
- personal data held for the prevention or detection of crime;
- personal data held for the assessment or collection of any tax or duty;
- personal data relating to the physical or mental health of the subject;
- data held subject to legal professional privilege or for the making of judicial appointments;
- data held in confidence for statistical or research purposes.

Data protection principles

The data protection principles which all data users must adhere to are laid out in Schedule 1 of the 1984 Act.

- The information to be contained in personal data must be obtained and processed fairly and lawfully.
- The personal data must be held only for one or more specified and lawful purposes.
- Personal data held must not be used or disclosed in any manner incompatible with the purpose(s) for which it is held.
- Personal data held must be adequate, relevant and not excessive in relation to the purpose for which it is held.
- Personal data must be accurate and, where necessary, kept up to date.
- Personal data must not be kept for longer than is necessary.
- An individual is entitled at reasonable intervals and without undue delay or expense to be informed by any data user whether he or she holds personal data about that individual, and to have access to any such data.
- An individual is entitled, where appropriate, to have personal data corrected or erased.
- Computer bureaux must take appropriate security measures against unauthorised access to or alteration, disclosure, loss or destruction of personal data.

Non-computerised personal files

The Data Protection Act does not at present apply to data kept elsewhere than on computer. Such non-computerised files are often very detailed. Before the end of 1998, however, the UK will have to implement a 1995 European Union Directive which greatly extends the protection granted to people mentioned on non-computerised files. In England, the Access to Personal Files Act 1987 went some way towards plugging the gap in the present law. It gave power to the Home Secretary to make regulations conferring on people a right of access to information about themselves on local authority records. To date regulations have been made covering housing, social work and education records. The Act does not, however, permit access to employment records, government benefit and immigration records, or bank, building society and credit records. Similarly, the Access to Medical Reports Act 1988 provided a very limited right of access to non-computerised medical records. The rights conferred by these two Acts were eventually extended to Northern Ireland by the Access to Personal Files and Medical Reports (NI) Order 1991. The comparable Access to Health Records Act 1990 has been extended to Northern Ireland by the Access to Health Records (NI) Order 1993.

Company and land records

The Companies (NI) Order 1986 requires companies incorporated in Northern Ireland to supply certain information to the Companies Registry. This may then be examined by members of the public on payment of a fee. The companies must also disclose certain facts and figures in their annual reports (and in any prospectuses issued prior to the issue of shares to the public).

The Land Registration Act (NI) 1970 provides for the registration of the ownership of property in the Land Registry, details of which may be consulted by the public. This scheme applies principally to rural property. The Registration of Deeds Act (NI) 1970 provides for the registration of "memorials" (*i.e.* shortened versions of certain documents of title to land), a scheme which particularly covers urban property and which again allows for public access.

Registration of births, deaths and marriages

The registration of births and deaths is provided for under the Births and Deaths Registration (NI) Order 1976. Article 34 requires the Registrar General to keep an index for each register and this is open for inspection by the public. Any individual may obtain a certified copy of an entry in the register upon payment of a fee.

The picture regarding marriages is similar. All marriages, with the exception of Roman Catholic marriages, are governed by sections 68-71 of the Marriages (Ireland) Act 1844, which permit searches in the registers. Much the same effect is achieved for Roman Catholic marriages by section 19 of the Registration of Marriages (Ireland) Act 1863, as amended.

Local authority records

Section 23 of the Local Government Act (NI) 1972 requires meetings of a local authority to be open to the public, a right of access which extends to the Fire Authority of Northern Ireland but not to Education and Library Boards or to Health and Social Services Boards. A copy of the agenda at local authority meetings must be supplied on request to any newspaper. The right to inspect the minutes covers all such meetings held during the preceding six years (Local Government Act (NI) 1972, s. 100C).

The 1972 Act permits a council to pass a resolution excluding the public from a meeting whenever publicity would be prejudicial to the public interest:

- by reason of the confidential nature of the business to be transacted; or

- for such special reasons as may be specified; one such special reason may be the need to receive advice from a non-council source in private.

There is also a power to exclude disorderly or misbehaving members of the public and to ban photographs or recordings (s. 27). In England, the right of access is greater in that it extends to meetings of committees and sub-committees within the local council (see the Local Government (Access to Information) Act 1985).

Public records

Public records relating mainly to Northern Ireland are stored at the Public Records Office (NI), which was established under an Act of Parliament in 1923. By section 3, records are to be delivered to the office 20 years after their making. Access to members of the public is possible 30 years after a document has been made, but this period may be extended in three situations:

- if the papers are exceptionally sensitive, their disclosure being contrary to the public interest on security or other grounds;

- if the documents contain information supplied in confidence, the disclosure of which might constitute a breach of faith; or

- if the documents contain information about individuals, the disclosure of which would cause distress or danger to living persons or their descendants.

Discovery of documents

After a court action has been started the parties to it can be compelled to disclose the existence and contents of certain documents, a process known as "discovery". For county court actions, discovery is regulated by Order 15 of the County Court Rules (NI) 1981; for High Court actions the relevant provision is Order 24 of the Rules of the Supreme Court (NI) 1980, as amended. A court order for discovery is required only if the parties do not volunteer the information themselves. A court would need to be convinced that production of the documents in question is necessary for disposing fairly of the case or for saving costs.

Generally speaking, there is no power to order discovery against someone who is not a party to the proceedings. The correct procedure is to call that person as a witness to give oral testimony. But the House of Lords held in *Norwich Pharmacal Co. v Customs and Excise Commissioners* (1974) that, where a person through no fault of his or her own gets mixed up in another person's wrongdoing, he or she may incur no personal liability in law but is under a duty to assist the victim of the wrongdoing by giving him or her full information. In a further decision, *British Steel Corp. v Granada Television Ltd* (1980), the House of Lords stressed that an applicant's interest in obtaining information so as to detect and punish wrongdoing must be shown obviously to outweigh the public interest in protecting the source and ensuring the free flow of information to the media. Moreover, no order can be issued against a stranger who is completely uninvolved in the suspected wrongdoing.

A further important law is the Administration of Justice Act 1970. Section 31 permits what is called "pre-trial" discovery: a person who is likely to be a party to legal proceedings concerning injury or death can apply for an order of discovery against another likely party. The disclosure of documents might then enable the applicant to discover whether he or she has a case worth starting in the courts. Section 32 of the 1970 Act enables a claimant in a personal injury or fatal accident case to obtain discovery of, for instance, medical records. This provision is to be generously interpreted in the plaintiff's favour (see *O'Sullivan v Herdmans Ltd*, 1987).

Limitations to obtaining discovery

There are two important limitations to the right to obtain discovery of documents:

- the claim of legal professional privilege protects all confidential communications between a client and his or her lawyer, as well as some confidential communications between either of these people and a third party;
- public interest privilege allows the minister who is at the head of a relevant government department to contend that disclosure of the documents in question would be injurious to the public interest, either because of their contents or because of the class of documents to which they belong. In recent years the courts have made it clear that if a public interest claim is asserted by the government the judges can inspect the documents to see whether in fact the public interest does lie in their being kept secret. This point was also made

clear by Sir Richard Scott in his inquiry into the Matrix Churchill "Arms to Iraq" affair in 1996.

The need for a Freedom of Information Act

As can be seen, there is a mishmash of legislation providing a right of access to information in limited circumstances. There is no general law conferring such a right, as there is in other countries. Sweden has the longest established system of access, dating back to the Constitution of 1766. But the American experience is the one most often referred to. In 1946 the Administrative Procedure Act was passed there to establish a right of access to government records, but only in relation to proceedings taking place before an administrative body. A more far-reaching Freedom of Information Act was passed in 1966 and it has given rise to a great deal of litigation. Canada, Australia and New Zealand each enacted a Freedom of Information Act in 1982.

A number of schemes have been proposed in the United Kingdom for affording the public a right of access to government-held information. A Green Paper in 1979 concluded that a major step forward would be the production of a Code of Practice to guide ministers in reacting to requests for information. Mr. David Steel put forward a Private Members' Bill in 1984, but it failed to gain enough Parliamentary support. The Bill would have established an Information Commissioner to exercise investigatory powers and to order access to be granted. Appeals would have gone to an Information Appeal Tribunal. Various other private members' bills have been introduced to secure freedom of information legislation but none of them obtained the necessary support.

The last Conservative government refused to heed calls for the introduction of comprehensive statutory freedom of information legislation. It did, however, introduce greater voluntary disclosure of information under the Citizens' Charter initiative, which extends to Northern Ireland. Moreover, the Code of Practice on Access to Government Information, originally published in 1994, includes five commitments to:

- supply facts and analysis with major policy decisions,
- open up internal guidelines about departments' dealings with the public,
- supply reasons with administrative decisions,
- provide information under the Citizens' Charter about public services, what they cost, targets, performance, complaints and redress, and

* respond to requests for information.

All Northern Ireland departments and their agencies are covered by this Code, as are many other public bodies. To obtain the information it is necessary to write to the appropriate department, agency or body explaining what information is required. While particular files or documents do not have to be specified it pays to be as precise as possible. The Code of Practice suggests that you should receive a reply within 20 days. It also says that a great deal of information will be provided free of charge, especially where it is necessary to explain:

* benefits, grants and entitlements,
* the standards and performance of services,
* the reasons for administrative decisions made in your case,
* the way in which you may exercise rights to appeal or complain about a decision; or
* regulatory requirements bearing on your business.

There may be a charge if the information requested does not come within one of these categories and causes additional work. Charging schemes vary and so the relevant department or agency must be contacted for details. If you are dissatisfied with the outcome of a request for information the matter should be taken up in the first instance with the person to whom the request was made and if that proves unsuccessful then generally speaking with the chief of the relevant department. In the case of the Department of Finance and Personnel it is the Permanent Secretary of the Department at Rosepark House, Upper Newtownards Road, Belfast BT4 3NR.

It should be noted that even under the Code of Practice there are extensive categories of official information which remain confidential. These exemptions come under no less than 15 heads. Category 2 refers to internal discussion and advice, which is explained as meaning information whose disclosure would harm the frankness and candour of internal discussion. With such wide-ranging exemptions official bodies still have substantial scope to withhold information. It is suggested that the need for a specific statutory right of access to official information has not disappeared.

Unfortunately, however, a Freedom of Information Bill is not among the measures brought forward by the new Labour government in the first session of this Parliament. This is particularly disappointing given Prime Minister Tony Blair's personal commitment to a Freedom of Information Act. Mr. Blair has been quoted as saying that a Freedom of Information

Act would signal "a culture change that would make a dramatic difference to the way that Britain is governed...It is part of bringing our politics up to date, of letting politics catch up with the aspirations of people and delivering not just more open, but more effective and efficient government for the future." A White Paper on the subject is due to be published within the next two or three months.

Further information

For more details on people's rights to freedom of information contact:

- Campaign for Freedom of Information
  Suite 102
  16 Baldwin's Gardens
  London EC1N 7RJ
  tel: 0171 831 7477

Chapter 12

Religious Discrimination

Stephen Livingstone

Discrimination on grounds of religion or political belief has been a central civil liberties issue in Northern Ireland's history. From the beginnings of the Northern Ireland state a public commitment was given to preventing religious discrimination, in that section 5(1) of the Government of Ireland Act 1920 provided that the Parliament of Northern Ireland could not:

> *give a preference, privilege or advantage, or impose any disability or disadvantage, on account of religious belief.*

However, expressing a commitment to the absence of discrimination is one thing, devising the mechanisms to eradicate it is another. By the 1960s the civil rights movement and a number of studies, notably the government-appointed Cameron Commission, had established the existence of significant discrimination in housing and employment. Most legislative action to counter this has been in the area of employment but there have been some anti-discrimination measures in other fields too.

Complaints of employment discrimination

If people feel they have not been selected for an interview, job or promotion because of their religion or political views, they will succeed in a claim of discrimination if they can prove a number of points:

- that they have been the victim of either *direct* or *indirect* discrimination;
- that the discrimination was carried out by a "relevant body";
- that the discrimination related to a "relevant matter"; and

- that the discrimination is not protected by any of the exceptions in the legislation.

Direct discrimination

The legislation defines direct discrimination as occurring where a relevant body treats a person less favourably than other persons would be treated on grounds of religion or political opinion (s.16(2) of the Fair Employment (NI) Act 1976, as amended by s.49 of the 1989 Act). This is probably what most people think of when they consider what discrimination is, namely deliberately refusing a job or promotion to someone because he or she is a Catholic or Protestant. However, direct discrimination is not limited to such malicious or deliberate action: an employer will still be liable even if the discrimination is applied out of concern for the person, or the views of others. In the case of *Neilly v Mullaghboy Private Nursing Home* (1991) the employer was found to have discriminated where she dismissed a cook from her nursing home job because the residents of the home said they did not want a Catholic cook from the Irish Republic. This was discrimination even though the employer did not share the residents' views. Employers will also be liable under this head of discrimination if they fail to protect employees from sectarian harassment, whether by other workers or customers, where they are aware of such harassment (and arguably where they reasonably ought to be aware of it).

Direct discrimination also occurs where decisions are based on generalised assumptions about people of a particular religion or political opinion, *e.g.* where a brewery refuses to employ a member of the Free Presbyterian Church because of an assumption that the abstentionist policy practised by that church would mean that its members would not be loyal and enthusiastic brewery employees. The employer would need to establish that the attitudes of that particular applicant would not be likely to make him or her a good employee. The fact that the definition states that less favourable treatment need only be based on "grounds of religion or political opinion" means that discrimination occurs whenever religion or political opinion becomes one factor in the decision. It would therefore be discrimination to dismiss an employee because his wife was a Catholic, even though the employee was not. The Fair Employment Tribunal has indicated that the term "political opinion" is not limited to opinions about the constitutional position of Northern Ireland (see *McKay v NIPSA,* 1994).

The number of cases in which religion is explicitly given as a reason for a decision is likely to be small. However, a person may feel that, though he or she has been refused a job or promotion on grounds that do not obviously involve religion or politics, the "real" reason for the decision was his or her religion or political opinions. The courts have recognised that deciding claims of discrimination will often involve making inferences and attempting to unearth facts not immediately available. A number of things may help a person claiming direct discrimination to bring these facts into the open:

- Where an application is made to the Fair Employment Tribunal (discussed below) the rules on "discovery" of documents applicable to county court actions will apply (see page 188). The Tribunal has indicated that even confidential documents relating to interviews and selections can be discovered where it is in the public interest that they be available for the applicant's case. In addition, the applicant may serve a prescribed form on those alleged to be discriminating which contains questions about their reasons for doing any act or about any other relevant matter. The replies can be used in evidence in any tribunal hearing. If the alleged discriminator fails to reply within a reasonable time, or if the tribunal finds the reply to be evasive, it may draw whatever inferences it considers just and equitable.

- The courts and the Tribunal have indicated that a *prima facie* case of discrimination will exist where a better qualified person of a different religion is not shortlisted, appointed or promoted. At this point the employer is called upon to explain the non-discriminatory reasons why this person was not shortlisted etc. (*Fair Employment Agency v Craigavon Borough Council*, 1980). Indeed, in *Department of the Environment v Fair Employment Agency* (1989) the Northern Ireland Court of Appeal indicated that this inference could be drawn where the applicants were equally qualified. Other cases show that, if the reasons the employer puts forward to explain the different treatment of the person complaining from that of someone of a different religion are vague or subjective, the Tribunal is entitled to conclude that the "real" reason was discrimination. In one case the Tribunal was satisfied there was discrimination when a better qualified person was passed over for a job and there was no evidence as to what criteria were adopted in short-listing and making appointments. The Tribunal decisions to date indicate that an employer's case will be greatly weakened if he or she has failed to adhere to the Fair Employment Commission's Code of Practice (see page 209). Failure to use objective criteria, train interviewers, retain notes or remove the display of sectarian emblems have all been referred to by the Fair Employment Tribunal as factors which have been taken into account in the process of drawing inferences. In general, compliance with the Code of Practice is regarded by the Tribunal as central to determining whether discrimination has occurred or not. In one case it stated "for this Code is the employer's sword in the affirmative action road to equality of opportunity and the employer's shield when he is attacked for alleged discrimination".

Indirect discrimination

This occurs where one of the "relevant bodies applies a condition or requirement" equally to all applicants or employees but where the "proportion of persons" of a particular religious belief or political opinion who "can comply" with this condition or requirement is "considerably smaller" than those not of that belief or opinion. The condition or requirement must be to the detriment of the person complaining of discrimination because he or she cannot comply with it and the person or body applying the condition or requirement "cannot show [it] to be justifiable irrespective of the religious belief or political opinion of the person to whom it is applied".

What this rather convoluted formulation means is that employers may be liable for discrimination where their employment decisions are based on criteria which may have nothing to do with religion or political opinion but whose effect is to reduce substantially the number of members of a particular religious or political group who could be considered for the employment in question. If the use of such criteria does have this effect the employer will be liable for discrimination unless he or she is able to show that the criteria are important for the job in question.

Examples of indirect discrimination are:

- an employer requiring all employees to live in East Belfast;
- recruiting all employees from a particular youth club which is run by the Catholic church;
- recruiting on the recommendation of current employees where the current workforce is overwhelmingly of one religion;
- promoting only people with particular qualifications which are generally unavailable to people from one community, or promoting only people with a certain length of service where members of a

particular religious group are under-represented among those with that length of service.

This notion of indirect discrimination was introduced into Northern Ireland's fair employment law for the first time by the Fair Employment (NI) Act 1989. However, it has been employed for some time in sex discrimination law throughout the United Kingdom and in race discrimination law in Great Britain. Its use there has given rise to certain areas of doubt:

- The first of these concerns the use of the phrase "condition or requirement". The Northern Ireland Court of Appeal in *Hall(Robert) and Others v Shorts Missile Systems* (1997) endorsed the view that the condition or requirement in question had to be a "must", *i.e.* that a person would be entitled to the job etc only if he or she complied with it.

- The second issue is the reference to "can comply". This appears to mean "can comply in practice", so it would not be a valid argument for an employer to say that Catholics could comply with a requirement that employees must live in East Belfast.

- Thirdly, the proportion in question must be "considerably smaller". There is no clear indication as to what proportion is sufficient. In an English case the Employment Appeal Tribunal indicated that 95.3% of men in the economically active population who are not in receipt of an occupational pension is a considerably smaller proportion than the 99.4 % of women who are similarly situated. In the *McCausland* case (1992) the Fair Employment Tribunal stated that a difference of 2% of Protestants compared with 1.5% of Catholics being able to be appointed via an internal civil service trawl was *not* "considerably smaller". There is also little law on the question of what "pool" of employees or potential employees is relevant for comparison. It seems that one looks to the pool of people from the complainant's community who are qualified for the job in question on all the criteria the employer uses, apart from those challenged as indirectly discriminatory. Thus, if the job is a relatively low skill one, the pool might be the entire Protestant or Catholic population. If it requires high skill, the pool might be Protestant or Catholic workers with a particular qualification (where the requirement of that qualification is not itself being challenged as discriminatory).

- The fourth issue is what employers must show if they argue that a condition or requirement is "justifiable". The Fair Employment Tribunal has adopted the approach developed in the race discrimination context. This indicates that there has to be an "objective balance between the discriminatory effect of the condition or requirement and the reasonable needs of the party who applies the condition" (*Hampson v Department of Education and Science*, 1989). These reasonable needs may include economic or administrative needs. This suggests that it is not enough for an employer to produce just any reason, but nor must the employer prove that the condition or requirement was necessary for performance of the job. The Tribunal must carry out a balancing test.

"Relevant bodies"

Employers are the main body against whom claims of discrimination may be brought. But five other bodies are mentioned in the Fair Employment Acts. These are:

- persons with statutory power to select employees for others;
- employment agencies (at least as regards acts done as an employment agency);
- vocational organisations;
- persons providing training services; and
- persons with power to confer qualifications which might facilitate employment; in *Bone v Department of the Environment for NI* (1993) the Court of Appeal indicated that the term "qualification" was limited to a status conferred on someone relating only to their work or trade, and which was either necessary for the work or trade or an advantage in that work or trade; therefore a pilot's licence would appear to be a qualification but not planning permission for a property developer or a bank loan for a business.

Employers are prohibited from discriminating against not only applicants for employment but also those they already employ, including "contract workers" supplied by someone else.

"Relevant matters"

Complaints may be made in respect of:

- refusal of a job or promotion;
- dismissal or redundancy arrangements;
- the terms on which employment is offered;
- "the arrangements made for determining employment" (which includes shortlisting, interview procedures, and application forms);
- "access to benefits"; and

- being "subjected to any other detriment"; the courts have indicated that someone will be subject to a "detriment" if a "reasonable worker would or might take the view that they had been disadvantaged" (*De Souza v Automobile Association*, 1986).

The Fair Employment (NI) Act 1976 (as amended) gives the Fair Employment Commission (FEC) power to seek "injunctions" (*i.e.* prohibitions) against advertisements which indicate an intention to discriminate directly against someone.

Under section 16(3) of the 1976 Act it is unlawful to discriminate against anyone because he or she is or has been involved in proceedings under the Act, either as complainant or witness ("victimisation"). It will not be unlawful, however, where the allegations in question are false and not made in good faith.

Exemptions

There are three general exemptions from unlawful discrimination.
- section 41 of the 1976 Act exempts acts done to comply with a statutory requirement passed before the 1976 Act came into force;
- section 42 of the 1976 Act indicates that where the Secretary of State issues a certificate indicating that an act was done for the purpose of safeguarding national security, public safety or public order it is exempt from challenge as discriminatory; the FET has made it clear, however, that even where a certificate has been issued it can examine aspects of the employment not covered by it; the legality of these section 42 certificates is currently being tested in a case pending before the European Court of Human Rights (*Tinnelly & Sons and McElduff v UK*).
- section 57(3) of the 1976 Act states that discrimination on the ground of a person's political opinion will not be unlawful where that opinion includes approval or acceptance of the use of violence for political ends connected with Northern Ireland.

There are also specific exemptions for particular jobs:
- employment or occupation as a minister or priest;
- employment for the purposes of a private household;
- employment as a teacher in a school;
- actions by employers may in addition be exempt if they are taken as one of the *affirmative action* provisions provided for in the Fair Employment Acts; these are discussed below (see page 205).

The Fair Employment Tribunal

If someone feels that he or she has been the victim of direct or indirect discrimination an application should be made within three months to the Fair Employment Tribunal. The Tribunal will send a copy of the application to the Labour Relations Agency, which is under a duty, if requested by both the applicant and the body being complained against, to try to achieve a settlement without the application being heard by the Tribunal. The Agency can also intervene of its own accord if, after considering the application, it feels it could achieve a settlement with a reasonable chance of success.

If a Labour Relations Agency settlement is not attempted, or if it proves unsuccessful, the application will be heard by the Fair Employment Tribunal. Currently there is an average of two years between the issuing of proceedings and a case being heard by the Tribunal. The FET is organised along the same lines as an industrial tribunal and the President of the industrial tribunals is also President of the Fair Employment Tribunal. The applicant may represent himself or herself in person before the Tribunal or may be represented by a lawyer, but legal aid is unavailable. The applicant may, however, apply to the Fair Employment Commission both for initial advice on making an application and for free representation before the Tribunal (see page 210). The Commission has a discretion to grant assistance in representation where it feels that the case raises an issue of principle or is too complex for the applicant to deal with unaided or where any other special circumstances are present.

The Tribunal hearings will normally take place in public but the Tribunal can sit in private to hear certain categories of evidence. These include:

- evidence which the Tribunal feels it may be against the interests of national security or public order to be heard in public;
- evidence which consists of information given in confidence;
- information which might cause substantial injury to the undertaking which employs the person giving it; and
- evidence which would create a substantial risk of exposing someone to physical attack or sectarian harassment.

Remedies

If the claim of discrimination is accepted by the Tribunal, various remedies are available. The Tribunal may:

- make a declaration of the parties' rights;
- recommend that the discriminating party should take specified action within a prescribed period to eliminate the effects of the discrimination; in one case the Tribunal ordered the employer to put up a sign to the effect that the applicant had been discriminated against; or
- award damages; awards may include compensation for injured feelings, or aggravated damages where a person has been treated in an especially arrogant or callous manner; in the case of *Duffy v EHSSB* (1991) both categories were invoked and a total of £25,000 was awarded; in this case the Tribunal also awarded exemplary damages, but the Court of Appeal has subsequently decided that these are punitive and not within the scope of the legislation (*O'Gara v Limivady BC*, 1995); in *McConnell v Police Authority for Northern Ireland* (1997) the Court of Appeal said aggravated damages should not be awarded on top of compensation for injury to feelings.

Since 1995 there has been no upper limit on the total compensation the Tribunal may award in respect of any one complaint (Fair Employment (Amendment) (NI) Order 1995). However no damages will be available for unintentional indirect discrimination. If the Tribunal makes a recommendation and the discriminating party fails to comply within a reasonable period, the Tribunal may subsequently make an award of damages if it did not do so before, or increase the damages awarded. An appeal on a point of law can be made against any aspect of the Tribunal's decision to the Court of Appeal.

Actions to ensure equality of opportunity

The measures already explained are all targeted at preventing employers and other relevant bodies from using discriminatory criteria in respect of jobs, promotions, benefits and qualifications. However, they are of limited effectiveness, as they begin to "bite" only when employers receive applications for jobs, promotions, etc. In Northern Ireland, for a variety of historical reasons, the perception has grown that certain jobs are essentially reserved for one religion and that there is little point in people from another religion bothering to apply for them. Hence applications are not forthcoming from the under-represented group and substantial imbalances in workforces remain. Anti-discrimination provisions are unlikely alone to achieve the aim of the legislation that employment, qualifications and promotions are genuinely open to all, regardless of religion or political opinion. For this reason the legislation contains other measures aimed at ensuring "equality of opportunity" and "fair participation".

The definition of "equality of opportunity" is given in section 20 of the 1989 Act. This states that a person has equality of opportunity with a person of any other religious belief if he or she has:

> *in any [employment] circumstances the same opportunity...as that other person has or would have in those...circumstances, due allowance being made for any material difference in their suitability.*

This definition is similar to that previously contained in section 3 of the Fair Employment (NI) Act 1976. The Standing Advisory Commission on Human Rights has observed that the Fair Employment Agency (the body replaced by the Fair Employment Commission) interpreted section 3 to mean that equality of opportunity was denied if practices adopted by employers operated to exclude members of a community under-represented in the workforce or discouraged applications from that community. Such practices include those now described as "indirect discrimination", *e.g.* word-of-mouth recruiting. But the Agency's interpretation seemed to go further. It included practices, such as displaying sectarian symbols at workplaces or advertising only in newspapers not generally read by the under-represented community, which had the effect of discouraging applications from that community.

On some occasions the Agency also recommended the taking of positive steps to remedy past under-representation, such as setting goals and timetables for minority representation in the workforce or establishing training programmes targeted at the under-represented community. There remained some doubt as to whether recommending positive steps, as opposed to recommending the removal of barriers to recruitment, was within the definition of equality of opportunity. Some ambiguity about the scope of the concept remains. However the 1989 Act also introduced a new term, "fair participation", which employers can in some circumstances be required by the Fair Employment Commission to attain. "Fair participation" is not defined in the legislation, but the Code of Practice issued by the Department of Economic Development indicates that what is fair depends on the circumstances and that:

> *employers should be making sustained efforts to promote [fair participation] through affirmative action measures and, if appropriate, the setting of goals and timetables. It does not mean that every job, occupation or position in every undertaking in Northern*

Ireland must reflect the proportionate distribution of Protestants and Roman Catholics in the province.

What this appears to be aiming at is that if the employer is or should be aware (through monitoring) of significant under-representation of one community in the workforce, and is not taking steps to counteract this, a failure to ensure fair participation exists.

The legislation does not place employers under a specific duty to ensure equality of opportunity or fair participation but does give the Fair Employment Commission powers to require action where an employer is failing to ensure either. It also places a number of other specific duties on employers which are designed to assist the ensuring of equality of opportunity.

Monitoring

The Fair Employment (NI) Act 1989 now requires all employers with a workforce of more than 10 employees, to register with the Fair Employment Commission. Failure to register exposes an employer to a fine not exceeding £2,000. Any new employer taking over a registered concern must apply within one month to the Commission to change the registration. To any proceedings in respect of non-registration there is a statutory defence of having a reasonable excuse for failing to make an application.

The Department of Economic Development (DED) has power to certify a body as a public authority in a number of specified circumstances - a Westminster or Northern Ireland Department, a body created by statutory provision or "a person appearing to the Department to exercise functions of a public nature". Lists of bodies already certified can be found in the Fair Employment (Specification of Public Authorities) Order (NI) 1989. Although public authorities are exempt from registration requirements, they are not exempt from the requirements placed on registered concerns to provide information.

Registered employers (and public authorities) are required to monitor the composition of their workforce by religion. As the Code of Practice states, such monitoring is less concerned with a person's religious beliefs than with ascertaining his or her "community background", Protestant or Catholic. The exact information which the employer has to collect and the methods by which it is to be collected are spelt out in the Fair Employment (Monitoring) Regulations (NI) 1989. Guidance for employers is also provided in the Code of Practice (see page 209).

To ascertain a person's community background an employer can use one of three "principal methods". These are:
- asking what primary school the employee attended;
- asking for all the schools the employee attended; or
- directly asking which community employees perceive themselves as belonging to.

The DED has published a schools list, "The Classification of Schools for Monitoring Purposes", which is to be used along with questions about schools attended to classify an employee's community background.

If none of the three principal methods establish to which community an employee belongs, an employer can fall back on the "residuary method". This allows an employer to use a variety of information about an employee or applicant, including his or her name, membership of clubs or societies and sporting or leisure pursuits, to determine to what community he or she belongs. Employers must inform employees which community they have been classified as belonging to. After being so informed, employees have seven days to challenge what they see as inaccuracies.

Registered concerns (and public authorities) are required to submit a monitoring return each year to the Fair Employment Commission on the composition of their workforce. The information must be broken down by sex and job category. Employers of over 250 people, and public authorities, are also required to produce monitoring returns (similar to those for employees) regarding applications for employment and to retain these for three years. Failure to produce a monitoring return without reasonable excuse exposes an employer to a fine of up to £2,000, while sending in a monitoring return which is not prepared in accordance with the regulations can lead to a fine of up to £10,000. Employees or anyone else who provides false information, knowing it will be used for a monitoring return, also commit an offence.

Information provided for the purposes of monitoring is confidential and anyone who discloses it is guilty of an offence and liable to a fine up to £2,000. There are exceptions for disclosure which is necessary for legal proceedings, disclosure to the Fair Employment Commission and disclosure to someone else in the business or public authority whose duties reasonably require such information.

Periodic reviews

Employers are required to carry out reviews of workforce composition at no more than three year intervals after registration. These are directed at discovering whether members of each community have fair participation in the workplace. If the employer determines that they do not then the employer should determine what affirmative action, if any, would be appropriate. Affirmative action may include the setting of goals and timetables regarding the composition of the workforce and applicants.

General affirmative action measures

Section 58 of the 1989 Act defines affirmative action as "action designed to secure fair participation in employment by members of the Protestant or Roman Catholic community in Northern Ireland". This may include:

• abandonment of practices which discourage participation;
• adoption of practices which encourage participation.

Modifying or abandoning restrictive practices means dealing with the kinds of things that the provisions on indirect discrimination are aimed at, e.g. looking at the educational qualifications normally set for a job and deciding whether these are really necessary for that job and whether they are likely to have a discriminatory effect. It could include considering the means by which jobs are advertised or abandoning informal methods of recruitment, such as by word-of-mouth.

As regards measures to encourage participation, the basic rule is that an employer can do anything which does not itself turn out to constitute either direct or indirect discrimination (unless it is specifically exempted as discussed below). Thus, an employer cannot, under the guise of an affirmative action programme, set aside a certain percentage of jobs for members of a particular religious group. The provisions do not allow for "quotas" or for "preferential hiring". However, an employer may establish a target and timetable for improving the participation of a certain section of the community in the workforce, or carry out a monitoring scheme even where this is not required by the legislation.

Specifically exempted affirmative action

The legislation specifically exempts certain actions from challenge as directly or indirectly discriminatory if taken as part of an affirmative action programme. These are:

• provision of training facilities;
• redundancy; and

• encouraging applications from an under-represented community.

Provision of training facilities

The first of these is provided for in section 37A of the 1976 Act. This exempts the provision of training facilities in a particular place or to a particular class of people, provided that the class is not a "class framed by reference to religious belief or political opinion". Unfortunately, the legislation is not a model of clarity here. It does not allow the provision of training only to members of a particular religious group, unlike the affirmative action provision in article 48 of the Sex Discrimination (NI) Order 1976, which allows the setting up of "women only" or "men only" training schemes in specified circumstances. But it is not clear whether, provided that an employer does not expressly refer to religion or political opinion in establishing criteria for training, a training scheme will still be immune from challenge.

If this *is* the position then an employer who wished to offer training specifically to Catholic staff, and discovered that the secretarial staff were all Catholic, would be protected by the legislation if training were offered only to the secretarial staff. On another interpretation such action would be unlawful as the criteria for training, although not expressly referring to religion, had been chosen with religion in mind; it would have been "framed by reference to religious belief". Of these two interpretations it seems that the former has been accepted as correct by the Court of Appeal in *Hall (Robert) and Others v Shorts Missile Systems* (1997). There the Court upheld Shorts' decision to alter redundancy selection systems in order to prevent dismissals having a disproportionate effect on recently hired Catholic workers.

A further problem for employers is how this provision relates to sex discrimination law. For instance, some of the criteria which employers might use in selecting people for training could indirectly discriminate against women by being based on age, years of employment or full-time status in the organisation. Schedule 2 of the 1989 Act amends the Sex Discrimination (NI) Order 1976 to ensure that training schemes for men or women only will not be challengeable under fair employment law by reason that they indirectly discriminate against a particular religious group, but there is no comparable exemption from the requirements of sex discrimination law.

Redundancy

A second exempt form of affirmative action, contained in section 37B of the 1976 Act, is any affirmative action practice adopted with regard to redundancy. The comments made above about the interpretation of "by reference to religious or political opinion" in section 37A apply here too. In the *Robert Hall* case (see above) a majority of the Court of Appeal appeared to take the view that such a policy would not amount to unfair dismissal of such employees even where it had not been agreed with trade unions.

Encouraging applications from the under-represented community

A final exempt form of affirmative action, contained in section 37C of the 1976 Act, are measures taken to encourage applications from an under-represented community for employment or training. This permits employers to strengthen contacts with minority schools with a view to encouraging applicants, or to advertise primarily (or perhaps even exclusively) in one sector of the press. It would seem lawful for employers to advertise the fact that they have set goals and timetables for minority representation in their workforce as a means of encouraging minority applicants to apply. What the section would not seem to permit is "encouraging applications" by actually discriminating in favour of the under-represented community when selecting people for employment or training. However, if merely having a "preference" for people from a particular locality or with particular qualifications or experience (even where this is not shown to be job-related and is compliable with by a substantially smaller section of one community) is not indirectly discriminatory (assuming that a "preference" would not be a "condition or requirement") then it would appear to be lawful to advertise such a preference as part of an affirmative action programme.

FEC directed affirmative action

The above discussion concerns circumstances where an employer voluntarily adopts an affirmative action plan. In some circumstances the Fair Employment Commission may impose an affirmative action plan on an employer. Section 12 of the 1989 Act empowers the FEC to issue directions to employers if, after a formal investigation (see page 210), the Commission concludes that an employer is not affording equality of opportunity and is unable to secure an undertaking from the employer that it will take steps to ensure equality of opportunity. Such directions may include the setting of goals and timetables.

If the directions have not been complied with "within such period as the Commission considers reasonable" the FEC can apply to the Fair Employment Tribunal (FET) for an enforcement order. If the FET upholds the FEC application it may make an order setting out what steps should be taken to give effect to the directions and specifying that the employer must report what action has been taken to the FET within a certain time. Failure to comply with any part of this order renders the employer liable to pay a fine to the DED of up to £30,000. Employers have a right of appeal to the FET at the time the FEC's directions are issued, on the grounds that they are already affording equality of opportunity or that the directions are inappropriate. A right to appeal to the Court of Appeal on a point of law exists regarding any of the FET's decisions.

The FEC also has power to make recommendations of affirmative action where an employer's review discloses that members of a particular community are not enjoying or are not likely to continue enjoying fair participation in employment. However, it does not appear that the recommendations are themselves legally enforceable.

Contract compliance

The term "contract compliance" is borrowed from American experience of government contracting. There, however, it works as an incentive system whereby government grants and contracts are made more available for those with affirmative action programmes. The Northern Irish provisions are more like a penalty scheme, where grants and contracts may be lost for proven failure to afford equality of opportunity.

The provisions deal with limitations on the award of public grants and contracts. These are significant in that over 40% of private sector concerns in Northern Ireland are in receipt of some form of public funds. The Act indicates that public authority contracts and government financial assistance should be denied to "unqualified people". There are four circumstances in which a concern can become unqualified:

- after conviction of an offence relating to failing to register;
- after conviction for failing to rectify the register when a new employer has taken over the concern;
- after conviction of an offence relating to failure to return a monitoring return; and

- as a result of receiving a penalty after failing to comply with a Tribunal order to enforce an employer's undertaking or FEC directions.

Where any of these conditions is satisfied, the FEC may issue a notice stating that such a person is unqualified and the FEC can take all reasonable steps to bring this to the attention of public authorities. Employers have rights of appeal against this notice to the FEC, thence to the FET and eventually to the Court of Appeal on a point of law. Public authorities are disbarred from entering into contracts with or accepting tenders from unqualified persons. Northern Ireland government departments may also refuse to pay any grant or discretionary assistance to unqualified persons. The FEC has enforcement powers by injunction from the High Court if it feels that a public authority is likely to breach its duty not to give contracts to disqualified persons, but no such powers exist in respect of government grants.

The Secretary of State may exempt contracts if he or she certifies that the work is necessary or desirable for the purposes of safeguarding national security, public safety or public order. A Northern Ireland department may also exempt a contract if it certifies that the work could not otherwise be done without disproportionate expense.

The Fair Employment Commission

The role of the Fair Employment Commission is central to the fair employment legislation. Some of its powers and functions have been highlighted in earlier parts of this chapter but others have not yet been mentioned. The address of the Commission is:

- Andras House, 60 Great Victoria Street, Belfast BT2 79B (tel: 01232-240020).

Information

In general the FEC has an educational role in relation to the legislation. It is empowered to provide training courses, hold conferences, undertake research, disseminate information and establish services for giving advice on equality of opportunity. It is also specifically required to recommend affirmative action when appropriate and to maintain a Code of Practice for the promotion of equality of opportunity. Although failure to observe the Code's requirements does not of itself render anyone liable to proceedings, it is clear that the Fair

Employment Tribunal relies heavily on the fact of compliance or non-compliance with the Code when determining whether an employer's action amounts to unlawful discrimination. The current version of the Code remains that first produced in December 1989 by the DED.

Assistance with complaints

Any person complaining of unlawful discrimination is entitled to advice from the Commission unless the complaint is frivolous. The Commission is also empowered to give assistance, including legal representation, to any complainant where the case raises an issue of principle or its complexity makes it unreasonable to expect the complainant to deal with it unaided.

Investigation

Under section 11 of the 1989 Act, the FEC may conduct an investigation for the purpose of establishing whether a body is affording equality of opportunity. Before beginning an investigation the FEC must serve a notice on those it intends to investigate, indicating the scope and purpose of the investigation. The investigation must take place in private and those investigated must have an opportunity to comment on the matters referred to in the notice. The Commission has the same powers as the High Court as regards the compelling of witnesses and the production of documents. Any obstruction without reasonable excuse of the Commission's investigation can be referred to the High Court, which can deal with it as though the offence had been committed in relation to that Court.

Monitoring

The Commission must maintain a register of employers containing the names and addresses of all concerns which qualify. All registered concerns are required to serve a monitoring return on the Commission, which is under a general duty not to disclose any information from which the religious belief of any individual could be discovered.

Enforcement

The Commission has a variety of powers concerning enforcement:
- The FEC has the ability to secure undertakings and to obtain directions when, having carried out a formal investigation, it

concludes that a concern is not affording equality of opportunity. Any undertakings obtained or directions issued may be subsequently enforced by an application to the Fair Employment Tribunal.

- The FEC may ensure that concerns carry out monitoring and reviews of employment practice satisfactorily (see pages 203-205). Again there is power to seek enforceable undertakings or issue directions if this is not done.
- The Commission has enforcement powers in respect of access to public grants and contracts (see page 208). It is under an obligation to publicise the names of those concerns ineligible for public contracts and may seek injunctions to prevent public authorities from entering into contracts with unauthorised concerns.
- The Commission has enforcement powers in respect of discriminatory advertisements. It is empowered to seek an injunction to restrain publication of any advert which indicates an intention directly to discriminate against anyone on the grounds of his or her religious belief or political opinion.

Other provisions against discrimination

Northern Ireland Constitution Act 1973

By section 19(1) of the Northern Ireland Constitution Act 1973, acts by government and public bodies which are discriminatory on political or religious grounds are made unlawful and actionable in the courts. Even Orders in Council can be challenged under this heading. Only a small number of cases have so far invoked the Act, perhaps because it is generally assumed that "discrimination" in the Act refers only to "direct discrimination". In *In re R (A Minor)* (1997) a juvenile detained in the Rathgael training school alleged that he should have been detained in a less Protestant-dominated location, but his claim failed.

PAFT and TSN

In recent years the government has adopted measures to ensure that all government decision-making takes account of equality concerns. These measures do not currently have legal force. The Policy Appraisal and Fair Treatment Guidelines (PAFT) were adopted in 1994 and require that all government departments and public bodies take account of their policies on a broad range of social groups to ensure equality of opportunity and equity of treatment. Their impact thus goes beyond issues of religious discrimination to include different treatment on grounds of gender, disability or sexual orientation. Targeting Social Need (TSN) is a policy which is designed to ensure that resources are targeted at disadvantaged groups within the community.

Standing Advisory Commission on Human Rights

The 1973 Act also established the Standing Advisory Commission on Human Rights, which has the function of advising the Secretary of State for Northern Ireland on the adequacy and effectiveness of the law preventing discrimination on the grounds of religious belief or political opinion. The address of the Commission is:

• Temple Court, 39 North Street, Belfast BT1 1NA (tel: 01232-243987).

The Ombudsman

As explained in Chapter 2, the function of the Ombudsman is to deal with complaints from members of the public who claim to have suffered injustice by reason of "maladministration" by those bodies which fall within his or her jurisdiction. Maladministration includes discrimination and since the fair employment legislation largely covers issues of employment discrimination the Ombudsman restricts his or her attention to cases falling outside the remit of the FEC (*e.g.* cases where a national security certificate has been issued, or complaints of discrimination in the provision of public services).

The Employment Equality Review

The Standing Advisory Commission on Human Rights published a comprehensive review of the fair employment legislation in June 1997. Amongst the most important of the recommendations contained in this review are that:

• the meaning of affirmative action should be broadened, in particular so as to encompass measures aimed at helping the long-term unemployed;

• the concept of indirect discrimination should be widened and damages should be available to applicants even if the employer had no intention to discriminate in these circumstances;

- the Fair Employment Tribunal should be empowered to award exemplary damages in appropriate cases; and
- the PAFT Guidelines (see page 211) should be placed on a statutory basis.

It remains to be seen whether, and with what speed, the government will implement these recommendations.

Chapter 13

Sex Discrimination

Beverley Jones

Legislation to eliminate discrimination between the sexes was introduced into Northern Ireland in the mid-1970s. It followed developments in Great Britain, which were in turn influenced by the American civil liberties movement of the 1960s. In addition, the United Kingdom was seeking membership of the European Union and the Treaty of Accession required the introduction of equal pay for equal work between men and women.

European Union law and Northern Ireland law

European Union law plays a crucial role in the interpretation of the domestic legislation governing equal treatment between men and women in Northern Ireland. It takes precedence over conflicting provisions in the domestic laws of member states. It is interpreted and enforced by the European Court of Justice in Luxembourg by way of cases brought before it either by the EU's Commission or through references from the national courts of member states.

Article 119 of the Treaty of Rome 1957 (which created the Community now known as the Union) requires equal pay for men and women engaged in equal work. "Equal pay" means:

- pay for the same work at piece rates must be calculated on the basis of the same unit of measurement, and
- pay for work at time rates must be the same for the same job.

In 1975 the Equal Pay Directive (75/117/EEC) further defined the concept as meaning:

for the same work or for work to which equal value is attributed, the elimination of all discrimination on grounds of sex with regard to all aspects and conditions of remuneration. In particular, where a job classification system is used for determining pay it must be based on the same criteria for both men and women and so drawn up as to exclude any discrimination on grounds of sex.

In 1976, another Directive (76/207/EEC) was passed aimed at achieving equality in respect of access to employment, vocational training, promotion and other working conditions. Similar Directives have been passed concerning social security, occupational pension schemes and the protection of self-employed women and spouses who work for the self-employed during pregnancy and motherhood. In 1994, a Directive (92/85/EEC) was implemented setting out minimum standards for the protection of pregnant and breast-feeding workers.

The Equal Pay Act (NI) 1970 was amended by the Sex Discrimination (NI) Order 1976 and both pieces of legislation came into effect in July 1976. The two laws are supposed to be read as an "harmonious code", though such a reading is difficult since their language is different and they cover mutually exclusive areas. The equal pay legislation, which was further amended in 1984, governs only sex discrimination which arises in terms and conditions of individual contracts of employment concerning pay. The Sex Discrimination (NI) Order 1976, as amended by recent Orders, was intended to eliminate discrimination in other aspects of employment. In addition, the Order has provisions outlawing discrimination on the grounds of sex in the field of education and in the provision of goods, facilities and services to the public.

The equal pay legislation

Between 1976 and 1984 a woman (or a man) was entitled to equal pay only where she was employed on "like work" with, or work rated as equivalent to, that done by a colleague of the opposite sex. In the case of *Commission of the European Communities v UK* (1982), the European Court of Justice held that the Equal Pay Act (NI) 1970 did not comply with the requirements of Article 119 nor with the Equal Pay Directive since there was no provision enabling a woman doing work of *equal value* to a man undertaking a different job to claim equal pay. The government was held to be in breach of its European obligations and was required to introduce amending legislation.

The Equal Pay (Amendment) Regulations (NI) 1984 provide a statutory right for women undertaking work of equal value with men to claim equal pay. However, the procedure for such a claim is complex, costly and lengthy.

Making an equal value claim

Claiming is regulated by the Industrial Tribunal (Constitution and Rules of Procedure) Regulations (NI) 1996. First, at a preliminary hearing the tribunal considers whether it is reasonable to compare the applicant's job with the male job with which she wishes it to be compared. It is the applicant who chooses the comparator, who must work either at the same place or for the same employer at a different place but under the same terms and conditions. The tribunal will also consider at this stage whether the claim should be dealt with as a "like work" or "rated as equivalent" claim. The European Court of Justice has confirmed that equal value means *at least* equal value (*Murphy v Bord Telecom Eireann,* 1988).

The fact that there are men doing the same work as an applicant, and who are paid the same, does not preclude an equal value claim with comparators engaged in different jobs (*Pickstone v Freeman's Mail Order Ltd,* 1988). It may, however, be relevant at a later stage of the proceedings when the employer is entitled to raise the defence that the difference in pay is due to a "genuine material factor" not based on sex. At the same time, where the employer is alleging that the jobs being compared are the subject of a job evaluation scheme, the tribunal will consider whether such a scheme is "analytical" and whether it is tainted with sex discrimination. An analytical scheme is one which compares jobs under headings such as skill, effort, responsibility and decision-making, rather than making whole job comparisons. In the case of *Bromley v H & J Quick Ltd* (1988), the Court of Appeal in England set out guidelines for the requirements which must be met if the scheme is to preclude an equal value claim. In *McAuley and Others v EHSSB* (1990) the Court of Appeal of Northern Ireland held that the job evaluation scheme which applied to all health service ancillary workers in Great Britain could not preclude an equal value claim in Northern Ireland, because the scheme had never been applied to Northern Ireland.

Once the tribunal is satisfied that the claim is reasonable and has excluded the application of a job evaluation scheme, the matter may be referred to an independent expert who prepares a report on whether the jobs compared are of equal value. There is a small panel of independent experts who are appointed by the Labour Relations Agency in Northern Ireland specifically for this purpose. Under the Equal Pay (Amendment)

Regulations (NI) 1996 there is no longer any *obligation* to refer equal value claims to an independent expert.

At this point the employer may raise any matters which he or she believes constitute "a genuine material factor" defence. The House of Lords in *Rainey v Greater Glasgow Health Board* (1987) held that a difference in pay which was objectively justifiable would defeat a claim for equal pay. At a European level, in *Von Hartz v Bilka Kaufhaus GmbH* (1986) the court in Luxembourg has confirmed the need for objectivity in justifying differential access to pay and benefits. The tribunal can accept, reject or adjourn consideration of the "genuine material factor" defence. If the defence is accepted, the claim fails. If it is rejected or adjourned, the independent expert prepares a report for the tribunal. The average time for the preparation of reports is approximately two years, even though the original Regulations contemplated a much shorter period (seven weeks). The 1996 Regulations allow for progress reports to be provided by independent experts with a view to reducing delays.

Once the report is completed the tribunal is reconvened. If the tribunal decides to admit it as evidence, the facts on which it is based cannot be disputed. If the report is not admitted as evidence, the tribunal must appoint a second expert to prepare a report. A tribunal can accept or reject an expert's findings and the parties themselves are entitled to call their own expert evidence to refute the independent expert's report. In practice this is a hard task, though not impossible.

In the case of *Hayward v Cammell Laird Shipbuilders Ltd* (1988), the employer argued that, even though the applicant did work which was of equal value to that of her male comparators, she was not entitled to an increase in pay because her overall terms of employment were no less satisfactory than those of the men, since she enjoyed access to pension rights and sick pay which they did not. The House of Lords ruled that she was nevertheless entitled to the increase in pay, as she could compare a specific less favourable term of her contract with a similar term contained in the males' contracts. The court ruled that it was not required to consider the value of the overall package of terms and conditions enjoyed by the applicant and her male colleagues. In 1991 the European Court of Justice in Luxembourg upheld this approach in *Barber v Guardian Royal Exchange Assurance Group* and in the *Danfoss* (1989) and *Royal Copenhagen A/S* (1995) cases, which both set out an employer's obligation to ensure "transparency" in pay structures.

If the "genuine material factor" defence fails, the applicant will be entitled to an equality clause in her contract of employment. She will then be entitled to equal pay, which can be back-dated for up to two years. The case of *Levez v T H Jennings Ltd* (1997) is currently challenging the limit on back pay through the European Court of Justice.

Difficulties with the legislation

It is arguable that the current legislation still fails to provide women with the machinery necessary to obtain proper redress. Commentators have argued that the legislation does not comply with European law in a number of important respects. The processing of cases remains inordinately lengthy, despite 12 years of the operation of the legislation. Without expert advice and legal representation throughout, it is unlikely that any claim will succeed. Absolute bars to claims, under the job evaluation and genuine material factor provisions, may contravene individual rights of review.

Given the substantial differentials in pay between men and women, employers have every reason to seek to defeat equal pay claims, particularly where industries employ predominantly female workers. It remains unclear what genuine material factors can defeat a claim. In *Fleming & Others v Shorts plc* (1991) it was argued unsuccessfully by the company that the separate collective bargaining structure justified the pay differential between men and women. The tribunal found that this merely explained why there was sex discrimination. The issue of separate collective bargaining as a defence to equal value claims was considered by the Luxembourg Court in *Enderby v Frenchay Health Authority and the Secretary of State* (1993) and it has endorsed the approach adopted in *Fleming*. In turn *Enderby* was endorsed by the Northern Ireland Court of Appeal in *BRS Ltd v Loughran* (1997).There are instances of employers changing the duties of applicants or comparators in order to circumvent the law, as well as threats of dismissal or redundancy if claims are pursued.

The Confederation of British Industry has called for the repeal of the legislation arguing that it places too heavy a burden on industry. There is, however, little evidence of employers reviewing their pay structures to ensure implementation of the principle of equal pay. Indeed, many employers are adopting a policy of doing nothing until faced with a claim. In 1996 the European Commission published its Code of Practice in this area and it remains to be seen what status tribunals will give to this Code in future equal pay claims. Despite all the difficulties with the equal value procedures the Equal Opportunities Commission for Northern

Ireland (see page 226) continues to receive a growing number of equal pay complaints.

The sex discrimination legislation

The Sex Discrimination (NI) Order 1976, as amended, provides limited protection against unequal treatment of men and women in the fields of employment, education and the provision of goods, facilities and services to the public. There are a number of important exclusions which restrict the scope of the legislation, but unlike the equal pay legislation the Order contains definitions of what constitutes discrimination. In addition, the Order sets up the Equal Opportunities Commission for Northern Ireland (the EOC). The legislation speaks only of discrimination on the basis of sex or marriage, but tribunals and courts – including the European Court of Justice – have recently extended protection to persons discriminated against on the basis of their transsexuality *(P v S and Cornwall County Council,* 1996) or homosexuality (*Grant v South West Trains Ltd,* 1997: pending before the ECJ).

While the terms are not specifically used, two forms of discrimination are defined in the 1976 Order: "direct" and "indirect".

Direct discrimination

Direct discrimination means treating an individual less favourably than a person of the opposite sex (and, at work, a married person less favourably than a single person). For example, if girls have to obtain higher marks than boys to secure a grammar school place then a *prima facie* case of unlawful discrimination arises, under the education provisions of the Order. Unless it can be shown that the reason for the less favourable treatment is unrelated to the sex of the children, it will be unlawful. The motive for the treatment is irrelevant, even if it is intended for perceived good reasons (*In re EOC for Northern Ireland,* 1988). It is for the tribunal or court to determine whether the reason provided for the less favourable treatment is not based on sex. In the case of *Wallace v South Eastern Education and Library Board* (1980), the Northern Ireland Court of Appeal recognised that there was rarely clear evidence of sex discrimination and that unless a tribunal or court were able to draw an inference of unlawful discrimination from the circumstances of the complaint the purpose of the legislation would be largely defeated.

Indirect discrimination

Indirect discrimination is the application of a requirement with which a considerably smaller proportion of one sex than the other (and, in employment cases, married as opposed to single people) can comply. For example, a height requirement of five feet six inches excludes more women than men and so unless the requirement is justifiable it will amount to unlawful discrimination.

Proving indirect discrimination is difficult. The applicant must first establish that there is a requirement which constitutes a barrier. The courts have generally interpreted this liberally, though in a race discrimination case in England the Court of Appeal held that the requirement must constitute an "absolute bar" (*Perera v Civil Service Commission*, 1983). This judgment fails to appreciate that many conditions which appear to be optional operate as barriers in practice. Fortunately, Court of Appeal judgments in England are not binding in Northern Ireland and it is to be hoped that the Northern Ireland courts will not follow the narrow approach adopted in *Perera*. It appears that the European Court takes a less technical approach to the issue (see the *Bilka* case, page 217 above).

Whilst the legislation does not stipulate the need to prove statistically that the condition has an adverse impact on one sex, courts have generally required such evidence, which may be difficult to obtain. In *NE Education and Library Board v Briggs* (1990) the Northern Ireland Court of Appeal held, however, that a tribunal is entitled to conclude adverse impact, without statistical evidence, from its own knowledge of the position of men and women generally. Once the adverse impact has been proved, the onus shifts to the employer to justify it. In the *Bilka* case (see page 217) the European Court laid down the definitive test for justifiability. The condition must be both necessary and proportionate to achieve the required objective without sex discrimination. Finally, the complainant is required to show that the requirement has operated to his or her detriment before it will be held unlawful.

The unwieldy definition of indirect discrimination was noted in the judgment of the European Court of Justice in the equal pay case of *Enderby* (1993) (see page 218). The European approach to the elimination of discrimination is result-orientated and the aim should be to remove barriers to equality of opportunity rather than erect complex technical hurdles preventing change.

Victimisation

The legislation defines and prohibits victimisation. It aims to protect a person from being less favourably treated because he or she has asserted a right under the equality laws. In a race relations case before the Employment Appeal Tribunal in England (*Aziz v Trinity Street Taxis Ltd*, 1988) it was held that the appellant had failed to show victimisation since he had produced no evidence to suggest that he would have been treated any differently had he complained under other legislation.

However, in a fair employment case, the Northern Ireland Court of Appeal appeared to reject the approach in *Aziz*, holding in *NHSSB v FEC* (1994) that a complainant did not have to prove that the victimisation was solely or predominantly due to the earlier complaint.

Sex discrimination in education

Articles 24-29 of the 1976 Order make it unlawful for a body responsible for the provision of education to discriminate against girls or boys. This applies to both schools and the Education and Library Boards, but the Order does not cite the Department of Education as a "body responsible". The reason for this appears to be that the Department is expected to ensure that schools and Boards do not offend the legislation. *In re EOC for Northern Ireland and Others* (1988) the Department marked "11 plus" papers, adjusting the scores for boys and girls differentially. It then separated the sexes, taking the top 27% of boys and the top 27% of girls as eligible for free grammar school places. The effect of this practice was to exclude some girls with better marks than some boys from free places. The High Court held that the practice constituted unlawful discrimination and that the Boards had contravened the Order by implementing the Department's decision. The Department itself was found to have contravened article 40 of the Order, which prohibits the issuing of unlawful instructions.

It should be noted, however, that the Order contains special exemptions for single sex schools.

Provision of goods, facilities and services

Article 30 of the 1976 Order requires that goods, facilities and services must be available to both sexes "in the same manner and on the same terms as are normal in relation to men". Whilst there are no definitions of "goods", "facilities" or "services" in the Order, access to loan facilities and service in a public bar have been held to fall within these provisions, but in *R v Entry Clearance Officer, Bombay, ex parte Amin* (1983), the House of Lords held that the provision of vouchers allowing entry into the United Kingdom did not constitute a "facility" under the English equivalent to article 30 in Northern Ireland's law.

The Court also held in *Ex parte Amin* that the section applies only to "market-place activities", *i.e.* activities which can be undertaken by a private individual. To a large extent this appears to exclude the state from liability for discrimination and to prevent scrutiny of the operation of government policies in the areas of social security and taxation. However, European law can in some instances provide protection from state discrimination. The failure to pay invalid care allowance to a married woman who gave up work to nurse an infirm relative owing to discriminatory assumptions made by the Department of Health and Social Security was found to be contrary to the European Social Security Directive in *Drake v Chief Adjudication Officer* (1985). This case led to many married women becoming eligible for the benefit.

Another exemption which limits the scope of article 30 is that governing private clubs. Under this, women are often denied equal access to sporting facilities, and the denial can extend to the use of public facilities, such as at golf clubs. In *Bateson v YMCA* (1980) the Northern Ireland High Court held that a temporary day membership card, which allowed access to a snooker table, did not make the facility a private club, so to deny women access to it amounted to unlawful discrimination.

Sex discrimination in employment

The 1976 Order makes it unlawful for employers to discriminate in the selection of employees and in the treatment of their workforce. This covers training and promotion opportunities, benefits, facilities, services, dismissals or "any other detriment" (art. 8).

Only if there is a "genuine occupational qualification" is it lawful for an employer to seek specifically to employ a man (or woman), or to consider one sex only for training or promotion (art.10). In some circumstances, however, employers and training bodies can provide under-represented groups with the skills necessary for work which they may not have done traditionally (arts. 17, 48 and 49). Courses can be run in companies trying to encourage applications for particular posts where there have been few or no women (or men) in the previous 12 months. Training bodies can provide courses limited to one sex or to persons who may have been away from employment because of domestic responsibilities.

Firms employing less than six employees, and private households, used to be excluded from the 1976 Order. But in the case of *Commission of the European Communities v UK* (1983), the European Court of Justice held that these exclusions were unjustified. It did, however, recognise that there might be instances when an employer could seek a person of a particular sex for employment in a private household. The Sex Discrimination (NI) Order 1988 (which parallels a 1986 Act in Great Britain) implemented the European Court's ruling.

Sexual harassment

"Sexual harassment" is now recognised as behaviour which can amount to unlawful discrimination. It encompasses unwelcome sexual advances and sexually explicit comments as well as physical assault. An industrial tribunal in Belfast upheld the first claim in the United Kingdom in the case of *M v Crescent Garage Ltd* (1982). Subsequently, in *Porcelli v Strathclyde Regional Council* (1984) the House of Lords established conclusively that a campaign of unpleasant and lewd comments by the applicant's male work colleagues, which resulted in her seeking a transfer, constituted unlawful sex discrimination. The fact that the behaviour was not sexually motivated was not considered relevant, since the complainant was subjected to treatment to which a man would not have been subjected. Same-sex harassment may also be unlawful if it is gender-specific. However, bullying, when not related to sex, does not appear to be prohibited by the Order.

Pregnancy

Employers are allowed to provide preferential treatment for women in connection with pregnancy and maternity but the Order provides no specific protection against *less* favourable treatment on these grounds. Because the legislation compares like with like in determining "less favourable" treatment, an early claim of unlawful discrimination on the ground of pregnancy failed (*Turley v Allders Department Stores Ltd*, 1980). As a man could not become pregnant, said this decision, the failure to promote, or the dismissal of, a pregnant woman was not unlawful. An industrial tribunal in Northern Ireland was the first in the UK to disagree with this interpretation. In *Jordan v Northern Ireland Electricity Service* (1984) the tribunal, appreciating the inadequacy of the Order in dealing with one of the fundamental grounds for discrimination against women, held that the reason for the failure of the employer to promote Mrs Jordan was that she was pregnant and that this amounted to sex discrimination. The tribunal did not address the question of the need for a comparison. In England the approach to such claims has been, generally, to compare pregnant women with sick men in order to bring the claim within the scope of the Order.

By contrast, tribunal decisions in Northern Ireland continued to develop an interpretation of the Order construing unfavourable treatment on the grounds of pregnancy as unlawful discrimination without the need for a comparison (*Donley v Gallagher Ltd*, 1987; *McQuade v The Lobster Pot*, 1989). In the *Dekker* and *Hertz* cases (1991) two decisions of the European Court adopted the approach taken by the industrial tribunals in Northern Ireland. The House of Lords in *Webb v EMO Air Cargo (UK) Ltd (No.2)* (1995) finally accepted that there was no need for a male comparison in order to provide protection from pregnancy discrimination. Indeed the Employment Rights (NI) Order 1996, consolidating employment rights, has implemented protection from dismissal on grounds of pregnancy (see Chapter 19). However there remain outstanding concerns about the adequacy of protection in national legislation against pregnancy discrimination despite the European pregnant and breast-feeding workers' Directive of 1994.

One issue which has been clarified is that the failure to pay a woman full pay during maternity leave does not amount to unlawful discrimination. The decision of the European Court of Justice in *Gillespie and Others v Northern Health and Social Services Board* (1996) held that a maternity allowance should be "adequate". Provided such allowance is no less favourable than statutory sickness benefits, it would meet the test of adequacy. However, failure to pay a woman her pay rise during pregnancy *was* held to be discriminatory.

Retirement and pensions

Matters relating to "death or retirement" fall outside the scope of the 1976 Order. However, in the case of *Marshall v Southampton and S W Hampshire Area Health Authority* (1986) the European Court held that, whilst discrimination in the state pension age was lawful, the domestic legislation could not preclude protection against *dismissal* at different ages for men and women, even though they were based on the age at which people became entitled to the state pension. Though the Sex Discrimination (NI) Order 1988 limits the scope of this exclusion, successful challenges to the exclusion, which commenced with *Barber v Guardian Royal Exchange Assurance Group* (1990) continue. However, governments of the member states of the EU have taken steps to limit the impact of the *Barber* case by passing a Protocol to the Treaty of Rome precluding redress for discrimination prior to the *Barber* judgment.

Thousands of cases concerning discrimination in pension benefits for part-time workers have been lodged before tribunals in Great Britain and Northern Ireland. Many part-time workers were excluded from pension benefits and they are seeking to protect pensions by claiming previous years' benefits. These claims raise complex issues about the extent of retrospective pay, calculations of contributions and time limits. A number of references have been made to the European Court of Justice, including one from a Belfast tribunal, *Magorrian and Others v EHSSB* (1996), and a consolidated case from a Birmingham tribunal, *Preston and Others v Wolverhampton Health Care NHS Trust & Others* (1996). It will take some time before the implications of *Marshall, Bilka* and *Barber* are fully addressed.

Collective agreements

In *Commission of the European Communities v UK* (1983), the failure to provide a remedy against discrimination appearing in non-binding collective agreements between unions and employers was found to be contrary to European law. The government argued unsuccessfully that, since the agreements were legally unenforceable, there was no necessity to provide a remedy. It was held that, irrespective of the legal effect of these agreements, they did in fact regulate working conditions and industrial relations. The 1988 Order makes void any term of a contract of employment which arises from discrimination in a collective agreement, but does not provide a mechanism to challenge the actual agreement.

National security certificates

Until 1988 there could be no consideration of matters covered by the 1976 Order whenever a certificate asserting that a question of national security had been issued by the Secretary of State. In *Johnston v Chief Constable of the Royal Ulster Constabulary* (1986), the applicant was one of 39 female reservists in the RUC whose three-year contracts of employment were not renewed, whilst those of male colleagues were. When the women challenged the decision, the Secretary of State issued a national security certificate. The case was referred to the European Court of Justice, which held that the failure to provide in Northern Irish law for judicial review of the national security certificate was a breach of

European law. The Sex Discrimination (Amendment) (NI) Order 1988 implemented the Court's ruling. This issue has also arisen in relation to religious discrimination (see Chapter 12).

Protective legislation

Article 52 of the 1976 Order allows for the retention of many discriminatory pieces of legislation on grounds of health and safety. Much of the discriminatory protective legislation was in fact repealed early in 1990.

Remedies

In a claim of sex discrimination an industrial tribunal can issue a declaration that the employer has unlawfully discriminated against the applicant. It can also recommend that the employer should reduce the effect of the discrimination on the applicant. Finally, the tribunal can award unlimited compensation

However, there are no injunctive powers (*i.e.* orders to do or not do something) and this means that the remedies of the court are often inappropriate, especially in sexual harassment cases. In addition, the powers of the tribunal to recommend means of redressing the impact of discrimination are very limited.

The Equal Opportunities Commission for Northern Ireland

The EOC was set up by the 1976 Order to work towards the elimination of discrimination, promote equality of opportunity between men and women and keep the relevant legislation under review. To carry out this remit the Commission was given powers to undertake research, initiate educational campaigns and enforce the legislation.

Its statutory enforcement powers are three-fold:

- it can, in certain circumstances, assist individual complainants to pursue legal cases (art.75); this has formed the bulk of the Commission's enforcement work since its establishment;
- it can undertake formal investigations where it believes that there may be widespread discrimination (art.58); the complex provisions and the lack of resources required for these investigations have meant that only a few have been completed during the Commission's existence; and

- in very limited circumstances the Commission is empowered to take legal action in its own name (arts. 38-42).

A radical change in the powers of the Commission is required if it is to have the necessary tools to combat discrimination. It should be given wider investigative powers together with greater scope to pursue legal actions. Since discrimination affects groups of people, class or representative actions are the necessary weapons to combat unlawful behaviour.

Conclusion

A comprehensive piece of legislation on sex discrimination and equal pay is urgently needed. It should require positive action by employers and state institutions, as the mere prohibition of discrimination is insufficient to secure equality.

The failure of the state to provide a comprehensive system of child-care facilities, combined with the complex provisions which fail to offer proper protection for pregnant working women, mean that the burden of domestic responsibilities continues to rest upon women's shoulders. Stereotypical attitudes persist. Equal pay will not be won until sex segregation in employment is removed and women have equal representation in higher managerial grades. Strengthening the law to provide a coherent enforceable set of rights manifests the commitment of the state towards the principle and practice of equality. Its importance is in setting the standard to be followed by society.

Chapter 14

Race Discrimination

Ciaran White

International law

International law prohibits racial discrimination in Article 26 of the
UN's International Covenant on Civil and Political Rights (1966).
Neither Article 2(2) of the International Covenant on Economic, Social
and Cultural Rights (1966) nor the European Convention on Human
Rights (1950) prohibits racial discrimination in so many words, but they
do require states to guarantee that the rights protected by those treaties
will be exercised without discrimination based on race. However, the
most significant international legal treaty dealing with racial
discrimination is the UN's Convention on the Elimination of All Forms of
Racial Discrimination (1965). This obliges the UK to pursue, by all
appropriate means, and without delay, a policy of eliminating racial
discrimination in all its forms and to promote understanding amongst all
races. The government's success in meeting these obligations is
examined, on a periodic basis, by the Committee on the Elimination of
Racial Discrimination. This Committee's criticism of the UK for failing to
enact anti-racism legislation for Northern Ireland was instrumental in
securing the enactment of the Race Relations (NI) Order 1997.

The 1997 Order

The Race Relations (NI) Order 1997 Order is very similar to the
Race Relations Act 1976 (the applicable legislation in Great Britain),
though there are some key differences which will be noted where
appropriate. The legislation outlaws racial discrimination in the
workplace, in education, in the availability of goods, facilities and

services, and in the disposal and management of premises. It also provides a mechanism for victims of discrimination to obtain redress, as well as establishing the Commission for Racial Equality for Northern Ireland (CRE(NI)).

As with all anti-discrimination legislation, there are important concepts which require explanation in order to appreciate the manner in which the legislation operates (see too Chapters 12 and 13).

Direct discrimination

The courts have formulated a very simple test to act as a guide in establishing whether direct discrimination has taken place: "Would the complainant have received the same treatment from the defendant but for his or her [race]?" (*James v Eastleigh Borough Council*, 1990). Motives or intentions are irrelevant: if an employer refuses to employ a person because he or she fears that that person will be harmed by other racist employees, that still amounts to unlawful discrimination, notwithstanding the fact that it is done with the best of intentions. "Race" need not be the only ground on which a decision was made. It will still be unlawful if race was an important factor in the decision, even though other considerations also influenced it (*Owens and Briggs v James*, 1982).

Because discrimination occurs where, on racial grounds, a person treats another less favourably than he or she treats, or would treat, other persons, the victim need not suffer less favourable treatment because of his or her own racial origins. A person who is dismissed because he or she refuses to comply with management's instructions to expel black youths from the workplace, for example, will be a victim of racial discrimination despite the fact that he is white (*Showboat Entertainment Centre v Owens*, 1984). Similarly, in *R v CRE, ex parte Westminster City Council* (1984) the High Court found that discrimination occurred when the Council, under pressure from an all-white workforce, refused to employ a black man in its refuse collection section.

Indirect discrimination

Indirect discrimination occurs where conditions or requirements are imposed which, while superficially free from racial bias, operate in a disproportionately disadvantageous way upon persons of a particular racial group. The definition of indirect discrimination, in article 3(b) of the 1997 Order, has four elements:

• a requirement or condition is applied equally to all,

- the proportion of persons from the same racial group as the alleged victim who can comply with the requirement or condition is considerably smaller than the proportion of persons not belonging to that racial group,
- the requirement or condition cannot be shown to be justifiable, and
- the requirement or condition operates to the detriment of the alleged victim because he or she cannot comply with it.

Some examples will help to explain the term. A refusal to employ a person because he or she is of ethnic minority origin would be direct discrimination, whereas a refusal to employ someone because he or she was not born in Northern Ireland would amount to indirect discrimination. This is because a significantly smaller proportion of persons of minority ethnic origin could comply with such a requirement. Charging "overseas" students significantly higher fees than "home" students has been deemed by the House of Lords to be indirect discrimination (*Orphanos v Queen Mary College,* 1985), though such fees are now justified by legislation (Education (Fees and Awards) Act 1983).

The adverse effect of the requirement or condition does not amount to unlawful discrimination if it can be shown to be justified. In deciding this the courts will balance the degree of discrimination against the need for the requirement. In *Hampson v Department of Education and Science* (1990) a judge said that "justifiable" requires an objective balance between the discriminatory effect of the conditions and the reasonable needs of the party who is applying the condition". The difficulty with this test, however, is that it appears to equate "justifiable" with "reasonable", rather than with "necessary" or "extremely important". Nevertheless the statement has since been approved by the House of Lords in *Webb v EMO Air Cargo (UK) Ltd (No. 2)* (1995). An example of a justifiable condition can be found in *Panesar v Nestlé Co. Ltd* (1980), where employees in a confectionery factory were prohibited from wearing beards for hygiene reasons. This condition was not a discriminatory one even though it impacted adversely on Sikhs, because it was a justifiable requirement in the context of that business.

Racial groups and racial grounds

As we have seen, discrimination on racial grounds, or against racial groups, is unlawful. However, what are "racial grounds" and how does one ascertain what is a "racial group"? "Racial grounds" are defined, in article 5(1), as meaning colour, race, nationality, or ethnic or national origins and a racial group is one composed of persons defined by reference to any of these grounds. It has been left to the courts to provide further guidance on defining what groups are protected by the legislation. This was done by the House of Lords in *Mandla v Dowell Lee* (1983). In that case a young Sikh boy, who wished to attend a private school, was denied admission on the basis that he could not comply with the school policy on uniforms, because he wore a turban over his unshorn hair, in accordance with the tenets of his religion. Religious discrimination legislation does not apply in Great Britain and his complaint was that he had suffered racial discrimination. It was thus vital to establish whether Sikhs were an ethnic group protected by the legislation. Lord Fraser set out what he considered were the criteria to judge whether a group was an ethnic one. There are two essential criteria which a group must possess:

- a long-shared history, of which the group is conscious as distinguishing it from other groups, and the memory of which it keeps alive;
- a cultural tradition of its own, including family and social customs and manners, often but not necessarily associated with religious observance.

There is also a range of non-essential criteria. Compliance with these is not crucial, but it does serve to reinforce the view that the group is an ethnic one. They are:
- a common geographical origin or descent from a small number of common ancestors;
- a common language not necessarily peculiar to that group;
- a common literature peculiar to that group;
- a common religion, different from that of neighbouring groups or from the general community surrounding it;
- being a minority, or being an oppressed, or dominant group, within a larger community.

In *Mandla v Dowell Lee* (1983) Sikhs were considered to be an ethnic group and the requirement regarding school uniforms was therefore held to be indirectly discriminatory. As a result a number of legislative amendments had to be made to accommodate Sikhs. One of these makes Sikhs exempt from the requirement to wear safety helmets on construction sites (art. 13 of the Employment (Miscellaneous Provisions) (NI) Order 1990).

Jews have also been considered an ethnic group (*Seide v Gillette Industries Ltd*, 1980), as have English Romanies (*CRE v Dutton*, 1989) and Welsh people (*Griffiths v Reading University Students' Union*, 1997). However, Rastafarians do not qualify *(Crown Suppliers (PSA) v Dawkins,* 1991). A significant difference between the English Act and the Northern Ireland Order is that, in article 5(2)(a) of the 1997 Order, Travellers are specifically included as an ethnic group protected by the legislation. They are defined as:

> *the community of people commonly so called who are defined (both by themselves and by others) as people with a shared history, culture and traditions including, historically, a nomadic way of life on the island of Ireland.*

Because of the existence of the Fair Employment (NI) Acts 1976-89, the Race Relations (NI) Order specifically withholds protection from groups defined by reference to religious belief or political opinion. This means that Catholics and Protestants, for example, will not be in a position to use the 1997 Order where they allege discrimination on the basis of their religious identities. Instead they must bring a complaint under the fair employment legislation, if possible. However, if they can prove that the discrimination was on the basis of their "Irishness" or "Britishness", they may be protected by the 1997 Order.

Segregation

Segregating persons on racial grounds is "less favourable treatment" (art. 3(3)) and therefore always amounts to direct discrimination. This ensures that those of a racist mentality cannot escape the effect of the legislation by arguing, for example, that they have provided facilities of an identical, but segregated, nature for different racial or ethnic groups and that therefore no group has been less favourably treated. Thus, if an employer has separate toilets for Asian and white employees this will amount to unlawful racial segregation.

Victimisation

Victimisation occurs where a person is subject to less favourable treatment because he or she has:
- brought a case under the 1997 Order,
- given evidence or information in connection with a case brought by someone else,

- alleged that a person has contravened the Order, or
- done anything under the legislation.

Victimisation occurs where the victim is treated less favourably merely because the discriminator believes, or suspects, that the victim has done, or intends to do, any of these acts (art. 4). However, in two cases the victimisation provisions in England have been narrowly interpreted, presenting difficulties for future complainants. In *Kirby v Manpower Services Commission* (1980), an employee in a Job Centre was transferred to less desirable work after he reported incidents of alleged racial discrimination on the part of employers to the local Community Relations Council. His employers considered his actions to amount to a breach of confidence and justified his transfer on that basis. The industrial tribunal considered that the transfer did not amount to victimisation because any employee disclosing confidential information would have been treated in this way. In *Aziz v Trinity Street Taxis Ltd* (1988) an Asian taxi driver, who felt that he was unfairly discriminated against in the fee he was being charged by the organisation to operate another taxi, made a complaint to an industrial tribunal. In the course of the proceedings it was disclosed that Mr Aziz had secretly recorded conversations with other members of the organisation to support his claim. He was subsequently expelled from the organisation. His complaint of victimisation failed because the Court of Appeal accepted the organisation's assertion that it had expelled Mr Aziz because he had breached the trust of the other members of the organisation. The victimisation provisions therefore protect a person only if the action taken against him or her follows because it is known, or believed, that he or she has made use of the Order and not because of some other reason.

Employment

Discrimination in the recruitment of new employees or in the treatment of existing employees is outlawed. There is no limit to the size of firm, company or organisation to which the legislation applies. Trade unions and employers organisations may not discriminate when considering applications for membership or when affording members access to benefits, facilities or services. Bodies which confer qualifications which are necessary to allow persons to engage in a particular trade or profession are also covered by the Order. Those involved in vocational training which would equip a person for employment are prohibited from discriminating in the terms on which it provides access to that training or to the facilities concerned with that training. Partnerships are also included within the ambit of the legislation, so that partners may not discriminate when selecting a new partner, when setting the remuneration for an existing partner or when treating existing partners. Barristers may not discriminate when choosing a "pupil" *(i.e.* trainee barrister) and it is also unlawful for any person to discriminate when instructing a barrister. Recruitment to the police must also be conducted in accordance with the legislation.

The legislation extends protection to contract workers, so that a builder who has a contract with NIE, for example, which pays considerably more than other work which he is contracted to do, is guilty of discrimination where he denies an Indian man the opportunity to work on that contract.

If it is a "genuine occupational qualification" (GOQ) that a person be of a particular ethnic group then an employer will have an effective defence (art.8). This means that if it can be demonstrated that it is a bona fide requirement that the post-holder be of a certain ethnic origin, it is not unlawful discrimination to prefer such a person. This exception applies only in respect of certain prescribed occupations where such a person is required for reasons of authenticity. These occupations are:

- dramatic performances or other entertainments,
- modelling as an artist's or photographer's model, and
- working in a place where food and drink are provided to and consumed by the public.

The defence also applies where a person is needed to provide personal services promoting the welfare of a particular group and these services can most effectively be provided by a person of that racial group. Employing a Chinese person, therefore, to act as a health visitor to the Chinese community is unlawful provided that a person of that ethnic origin is best placed to deliver those services to the Chinese community. However, an employer cannot avail of this defence where he or she has employees of the racial group in question who are capable of carrying out the relevant duties, whom it would be reasonable to employ on those duties and whose numbers are sufficient to meet the employer's likely requirements without undue inconvenience (art.8(4)).

Employers are liable for acts of discrimination committed by employees in the course of their employment, whether or not done with the employer's knowledge or approval (art.32(1)). They do have a defence if they can prove that they took such steps as were "reasonably practicable" to prevent the employee from either doing a particular act or doing similar acts (art.32(5)). If the employer does avail of this defence (e.g. because he or she has provided anti-racism training) then the only other option open to the victim is to bring proceedings against the employee alone. However, the employee is often unlikely to be in a position to afford to pay damages.

Affirmative action measures

Positive discrimination - e.g. preferring a black person to a white person for a vacant position because black persons are under-represented in the "work-force" - is unlawful. It could be lawful only if it were a "genuine occupational qualification" (see above) that the person be of Afro-Caribbean origin. But although the legislation does not authorise positive discrimination, it does allow for what are generally termed "affirmative measures". These provide exemptions from the Order where access to training facilities is provided for, or encouragement directed at, members of a particular racial group only. They apply, however, only where that group has "special needs" or where there has in the past 12 months been an under-representation of persons from that group in a particular sector of the workforce. English language instruction may be a "special need".

Education

Discrimination by either public or private educational establishments in relation to an application for admission to a school, college or university, or in the treatment of existing pupils in those establishments, is prohibited by article 18 of the 1997 Order. This prohibition applies to all levels of education, from primary to tertiary. Education and Library Boards and the Council for Catholic Maintained Schools (CCMS) are under a further duty not to discriminate (art.19). There is also a general duty on public sector educational establishments to "secure that facilities for education, and any ancillary benefits or services are provided without racial discrimination" (art.20). This general duty therefore should persuade educational establishments to "equality-proof" their provision.

The enforcement of provisions relating to education is slightly different from that for other provisions. For instance, the Department of Education (DENI) can intervene to issue directions to an educational establishment or authority which has failed to observe article 18, 19 or 20 (art.21). An individual's right to bring a complaint to a county court where the discrimination is related to an admission decision, the treatment of a pupil or the discharge by an Education and Library Board, or the CCMS, of its statutory duties, is not affected. However, the general duty on the public sector of education to ensure that facilities for education are provided without racial discrimination can be enforced only by DENI (art.21). If the Department refuses to enforce it, an individual might be able to obtain a judicial review of that refusal.

The duty of education authorities to comply with parental preference about the school at which they wish their child to be educated (see Chapter 18) is not limited by the racial discrimination legislation. In *R v Cleveland County Council, ex parte CRE* (1990) the Court of Appeal had to interpret the relationship between these two laws. A mother wished to have her daughter (who was of mixed English and African descent) moved from a primary school with nearly all Asian pupils, to one that was predominantly white. The request was made because the mother feared her child would learn Pakistani at the expense of English. The court concluded that the local education authority had not committed an unlawful act in acceding to the mother's request.

Goods, facilities and services

Goods, facilities and services made available to the public, or to a section of it, whether for payment or not, cannot be provided or made available in a discriminatory manner. The legislation helpfully provides examples of what amounts to "facilities" and "services". These are:

- access to public places,
- availability of accommodation in hotels, boarding houses or similar establishments,
- facilities by way of banking or insurance for grants, loans, credit or finance,
- entertainment, recreation or refreshment facilities,
- education facilities, transport or travel services,
- services provided by a profession or trade, or by a local or public authority.

The services of a "local or public authority" are not further defined. However, the courts in Great Britain have had occasion to interpret this part of the equivalent legislation there. In *R v CRE, ex parte Hillingdon London Borough Council* (1982) it was accepted that housing provision is a service for the purposes of this provision, though housing allocation by a public authority is also covered by the provisions relating to premises (see below). Presumably health and social services provision would similarly be categorised as a "service", but the courts have yet to consider this matter.

A major limitation on the applicability of the provision resulted from a House of Lords decision in *R v Entry Clearance Officer, Bombay, ex parte Amin* (1983), where their Lordships decided that a refusal by an immigration officer in Bombay to issue a special voucher to an Indian woman to enable her to settle in the UK, on the ground that a woman could not be a head of household, was not a service provided by a public authority. "Goods, facilities and services" was to be construed as applying to acts which were at least similar to acts which could be done by private persons and the Entry Clearance Officer was not providing a service but performing the duty of controlling would-be immigrants. This suggested that there was a range of governmental activities that would not be covered by anti-racism legislation and that government could discriminate with impunity in those areas. As a result of this case an amendment was made to the 1976 Act (by s.5 of the Housing and Planning Act 1986) ensuring that the 1976 Act applies to the planning process in Britain. An equivalent provision is not included in the 1997 Order, so it is unclear whether planning is a service of a public authority for the purposes of the law in Northern Ireland.

The scope of this provision was further confused by *Savjani v Inland Revenue Commissioners* (1981), where the Court of Appeal held that the IRC, in complying with their duty to collect tax, also provided a service for the purposes of the Race Relations Act because they determined the manner in which a person demonstrated that he or she was entitled to tax relief. Mr Savjani had therefore suffered discrimination because he was required to produce a full birth certificate for his child before obtaining relief, whereas non-Indians were required to produce only a short birth certificate. The CRE in Britain has argued that an appropriate amendment should be made to the race relations legislation to ensure that it applies to all governmental activities.

Clubs

Most private clubs are now covered by the race relations legislation. Associations with more than 25 members may not discriminate in admitting a person as a member or in allowing him or her to avail of any of the benefits offered to members. But some clubs remain exempt. Associations whose main object is "to enable the benefits of membership to be enjoyed by persons of a particular racial group, defined otherwise than by reference to colour" are not subject to the legislation. Thus a

Zimbabwean Students Association, for instance, although restricting membership to one racial group, would not be guilty of discrimination because non-Zimbabweans are not permitted to join. However, such an association would be guilty of discrimination if it refused to admit white Zimbabweans.

Premises

Landlords, estate agents, rental agencies and anyone selling, letting or in any way disposing of premises in Northern Ireland, may not discriminate on racial grounds (art.22). This prohibition extends to both the public and private sectors. Private individuals selling their homes escape the effects of the legislation only if they do not use the services of an estate agent and do not publish adverts indicating that the property is for sale. Otherwise, refusing to sell property to a minority ethnic person would amount to discrimination, as would charging a higher price. Where premises are "small" and the person selling or renting the property or a near relative (*e.g.* spouse, parent, child or grandchild) continues to live in the residential accommodation, sharing it with the other persons, then the legislation will not apply. "Small premises" are those where (a) the residential accommodation comprises no more than two other households and (b) the premises cannot accommodate more than six persons, excluding the relevant occupier and his or her near relatives.

Exemptions

There are a number of circumstances where the 1997 Order is deemed not to apply. These are briefly set out here:

- Any action carried out in accordance with legislation is not covered by the Order (art.40(1)).
- An act of discrimination based on a person's nationality, place of residence or length of residence inside or outside the United Kingdom is not unlawful if it is done to comply with any arrangement approved, or condition imposed, by a minister or government department (art.40(2)).
- Acts which are done for the purpose of safeguarding national security, or protecting public safety or public order, are not unlawful (art.41). This exemption is wider than that found in the 1976 Act. In that statute only acts deemed to safeguard national security are exempt.

- Sports associations or competition organisers are not guilty of discrimination where nationality, place of birth, or length of residence requirements are imposed in order to determine whether a person is eligible to represent some area or to compete in any sporting competition.

The duty on district councils

Every district council is under a duty to "make appropriate arrangements with a view to securing that its various functions are carried out with due regard to the need to (a) eliminate unlawful racial discrimination and (b) promote equality of opportunity, and good relations, between persons of different racial groups" (art. 67).

This is a duty to be pro-active about eliminating racial discrimination and in that sense is similar to, though more extensive than, the general duty on public sector education establishments found in article 20. It differs from almost all of the provisions examined so far in that, whereas they prevent unlawful discrimination, this duty obliges councils to consider how they might go about eliminating it, and how they might promote good relations. On the other hand, given that district councils in Northern Ireland are responsible for a narrower range of activity than their counterparts in Britain, this duty is not as significant an innovation in Northern Irish law as it might have been.

The equivalent duty in the 1976 Act – section 71 - has been interpreted by the courts in a number of cases. In *Wheeler v Leicester City Council* (1985) the Council had imposed a ban on Leicester City Rugby Football Club prohibiting it from using council property. It had done this because three club members had played on the English Rugby Football Union's 1984 tour of South Africa. The council defended its action on the basis that it was acting in accordance with its duty to promote good race relations having regard to the significant number of persons of Asian or Afro-Caribbean ethnic origin in its area. The House of Lords considered the ban unreasonable and that the club was being punished though it had done no wrong.

The Order allows local authorities to adopt a limited "contract compliance" policy (*i.e.* ensuring that contractors are "fair" employers before awarding them contracts) when exercising their contractual powers (Sched. 2, para.6). Generally they must not have regard to "non-commercial matters" when awarding contracts. Matters which are "non-commercial" include:

- political interests of contractors, directors, partners or employees,

- financial support by contractors of any institutions to or from which the council gives or gets support, and
- the country of origin of supplies, or the locations in any country of the business interests of the contractors.

Local authorities are, however, permitted to ask questions, which will be approved by the Department of Economic Development, seeking information or undertakings relating to workforce matters, provided these matters are "reasonably necessary" to secure compliance with article 67.

Criminal justice

One element of anti-racism legislation applicable in Great Britain has not been extended to Northern Ireland. Under section 95(1) of the Criminal Justice Act 1991 the Secretary of State is required to publish on an annual basis such information as he or she considers expedient for the purpose of, amongst other things:

facilitating the performance by ... persons [engaged in the administration of criminal justice] of their duty to avoid discriminating against any person on the ground of race or sex or any other improper ground.

Nowhere is this duty explicitly stated, but it is clearly implied. The courts, however, are not subject to the Race Relations (NI) Order and the police are subject to the Order only when recruiting. However, racial harassment by a police officer would amount to a disciplinary offence, and a complaint can be made to the Chief Constable or to the Independent Commission for Police Complaints (see Chapter 6).

The Commission for Racial Equality (NI)

The 1997 Order creates the Commission for Racial Equality for Northern Ireland (CRE(NI)), which must have between five and seven commissioners, and which is obviously the equivalent body to the CRE in Great Britain. Its functions are to:

- work towards the elimination of discrimination,
- promote equality of opportunity and good relations between persons of different racial groups generally, and
- keep the legislation under review and submit proposals for amending it.

The Order provides the Commission with a range of powers to fulfil these statutory duties. It may therefore provide financial or other assistance to organisations concerned with "the promotion of equality of opportunity, and good relations, between persons of different racial groups" (art.43) or it may undertake, or commission, research or educational activities (art.44). The Commission is also empowered to issue Codes of Practice about a range of different topics:

- elimination of discrimination in employment,
- promotion of equality of opportunity in employment between different racial groups,
- elimination of discrimination in the field of housing, and
- the promotion of equality of opportunity in housing between persons of different racial groups.

Failure to adhere to any provision of the Codes is not itself an unlawful act but, in any cases taken under the Order, a failure to comply with them could be used as evidence in the court or tribunal.

Higher profile activity will include assisting complainants to bring proceedings under the Order (see below). The Commission may grant assistance if it thinks fit to do so:

- on the ground that the application raises a question of principle;
- on the ground that it is unreasonable, having regard to the complexity of the case, to the applicant's position in relation to the respondent or any other person involved, or to any other matter, to expect the applicant to deal with the case unaided; or
- by reason of any other special consideration.

Assistance can range from giving advice to arranging for the complainant to be legally represented.

Formal investigations

One of the more important powers available to the Commission is the ability to conduct a "formal investigation" (art.46). These are conducted in relation to particular firms, companies or organisations in order to ascertain whether equality of opportunity operates in particular workplaces and spheres of life or because it is suspected that unlawful acts of discrimination are being perpetrated. They may be initiated by the Commission or by the Department of Economic Development. Before commencing a formal investigation the CRE must draw up terms of reference and give general notice of the investigation, unless it is confined to "named persons" (*i.e.* a specific individual or firm), in which case notice is given to those persons only.

Before embarking on a "named person investigation" the CRE must have a belief, however tenuous, that the named person has been guilty of performing a discriminatory act and that belief must be stated in the proposed terms of reference (*In re Prestige Group plc,* 1984). An opportunity must be given to the named person to challenge the proposed investigation of the act in question, and this has become known as the "preliminary inquiry". Because of article 48(2)(b) the Commission can, in named person investigations only, require the disclosure of documents and the attendance of persons to give oral testimony, without needing the permission of the DED. However, the difficulty the Commission faces is that, at the preliminary inquiry stage, it cannot exercise these subpoena powers because the investigation does not in fact begin until the preliminary inquiry is concluded and the Commission confirms that it will proceed. If during the course of a named person investigation the CRE is satisfied that a person has committed an unlawful act of discrimination, or is responsible for a discriminatory practice, a discriminatory advert or inducing or instructing others to discriminate, it may issue a "non-discrimination" notice (see below). These unlawful acts are explained before dealing further with non-discrimination notices.

General investigations are more exploratory in nature and may relate, for example, to a particular industry in a locality. They can be commenced without a belief that a particular discriminatory act has taken place, but no person, firm or organisation can be mentioned in the terms of reference. The power to require disclosure of documents and attendance of persons cannot be exercised in regard to general investigation without the permission of the DED (art.48(1)). Failure to comply allows the CRE to obtain an order from a county court directing compliance, and failure to obey a county court order can be treated as contempt of court (art. 48(4) and (5)).

The report of a formal investigation can make recommendations to any person "with a view to promoting equality of opportunity between persons of different racial groups as well as recommending amendments to the legislation to DED. If the investigation is initiated by the CRE, the report must be published or made available for inspection. If the investigation is requested by the DED, the report is not to be published, unless the CRE is requested to do so by the Department (art. 49).

Non-discrimination notice

A non-discrimination notice prohibits the person to whom it applies from doing any of the specified acts again and, if necessary, requires that the Commission be notified of consequential alterations to any existing practices or arrangements. However, a non-discrimination notice cannot be served until the person named in it has been given the opportunity to make oral or written representations within 28 days. A right of appeal against a non-discrimination notice lies to an industrial tribunal, if the matter involved concerns employment matters, or to a county court if the matter relates to the provision of goods, facilities, services or premises.

Enforcement

Enforcement of the 1997 Order is carried out chiefly in industrial tribunals and the county courts. The enforcement provisions are broadly divisible into two types - those that relate to enforcement by individuals and those that relate to enforcement by the CRE.

Complaints by individuals about discrimination in employment must be made to an industrial tribunal within three months of the alleged discriminatory incident. Where individuals consider that they have been victims of discrimination in the provision of goods, facilities or services, or the disposal or management of premises, these allegations must be made to a county court within six months of the alleged discriminatory act. A county court or tribunal does have a discretion to accept complaints outside these time limits if "in all the circumstances of the case" it considers it "just and equitable" to do so.

Where the complaint is one of racial discrimination relating to an admission decision made by an educational establishment, the treatment of existing pupils or the performance of statutory duties by Education and Library Boards, or the CCMS, then a slightly different procedure applies. Before a case can be initiated the Department of Education must be notified of the complaint. It has up to two months to consider the allegation, though it may if it wishes waive this period if it does not require further time to consider the matter. Once this period has elapsed the victim then has six months within which to make the complaint.

There are a number of options open to an industrial tribunal if it finds the allegation of discrimination proven (art.53). It may:

• make a declaration as to the legal rights of the parties,

- make an order requiring the respondent to pay such compensation to the victim as would be obtainable in a county court, or
- recommend that the respondent take, within a specified period, action which would reduce or eliminate the adverse effect of the act of discrimination; a failure to comply with such a recommendation allows the tribunal at a later stage to award damages or to increase the amount already awarded.

Successful complainants in a county court can be awarded damages, which may include an amount for injured feelings. However, no damages are available for indirect discrimination if the service provider can show that discrimination was not intended by the imposition of the condition or requirement in question.

The Commission alone has enforcement powers in relation to a number of specific activities, namely discriminatory advertisements and pressurising or instructing others to discriminate. If it considers that either of these events has occurred, it may bring proceedings to have it confirmed that the alleged discriminatory act occurred (art.60). If the matter relates to employment, the Commission's application is made to the industrial tribunal; in all other matters applications are made to a county court. In situations where the Commission fears that similar acts of unlawful discrimination are likely to be performed, it may apply to a county court for an injunction to restrain such activity (art.60(4)).

Undertakings not to discriminate in the future

Sometimes the Commission may not need to resort to the tribunal or county court or initiate a named person investigation to deal with unlawful discriminatory acts, discriminatory practices, discriminatory adverts, or instructions or inducements to discriminate. It is allowed to accept binding undertakings from someone who has committed any one of these breaches of the Order that he or she will not do so in the future. The undertaking may commit that person to:

- do, or refrain from doing, certain acts,
- institute certain practices or arrangements, or
- change existing practices or arrangements.

The undertaking must be in writing and agreed between that person and the Commission. Failure to comply with the terms of the undertaking allows the Commission to apply to a county court for a decision on whether there has been failure to comply.

Persistent discrimination

The Commission is given a special power to deal with discriminators who appear to be continuing to perform unlawful acts of discrimination even though they have been censured in the past for similar behaviour. If within five years of the issuing of a non-discrimination notice or a finding of unlawful discrimination by a tribunal or a county court, the CRE believes that a discriminator will carry out further acts of discrimination or is responsible for "discriminatory practices" contrary to article 28, it can apply to a county court for an injunction restraining him or her from doing so (art.59).

For further information on race discrimination contact:

- Commission for Racial Equality (NI)
  Scottish Legal House
  65-67 Chichester Street
  Belfast BT1 4JT (tel: 01232-315996)

- Chinese Welfare Association
  133-135 University Street
  Belfast BT7 1HQ (tel: 01232-288277)

- Multi-Cultural Resource Centre
  12 Upper Crescent
  Belfast BT7 1NT (tel: 01232-244639)

- Northern Ireland Council for Ethnic Minorities
  73 Botanic Avenue
  Belfast BT7 1JL (tel: 01232-238645)

- Northern Ireland Council for Ethnic Equality
  c/o Bryson House
  28 Bedford Street
  Belfast BT2 7FE (tel: 01232-325825)

- Northern Ireland Council for Travelling People
  30 University Street
  Belfast BT7 1FZ (tel: 01232-237372)

Chapter 15

Rights of Disabled People

Christine Bell

In its 1992 study entitled "The Prevalence of Disability in Northern Ireland", the Policy, Planning and Research Unit of the Northern Ireland Office found that 17.4% of the adult population is disabled, a figure which is 20% higher than corresponding statistics in Great Britain. A further report by the Unit in 1997 indicated that almost 60% of disabled adults have net earnings of less than £100 per week, that 75% of them are unable to work, and that almost 25% could not go out of their house or garden on their own. It also emphasised the high cost to disabled people of disability-related aids and the financial difficulties faced by parents of disabled children.

International human rights instruments make it clear that not only are disabled persons entitled to exercise all the civil, political, economic, social and cultural rights embodied in these and other instruments, they are also entitled to exercise them on an equal basis with other persons. Despite this, the Disability Discrimination Act 1995, which applies in an amended version to Northern Ireland, was the first British statute to address discrimination against disabled people. The Act has been criticised by disabled people and activists for some serious flaws, but at least it provides a starting point for addressing discrimination and can be used by disabled persons to assert some rights. The experience of anti-discrimination legislation in other areas such as religion, political belief, race and sex, has been that strategic test cases and continued lobbying can help to strengthen anti-discrimination provisions.

The Disability Discrimination Act 1995 aims to make it unlawful to discriminate against disabled persons in connection with:

• employment;

• the provision of goods, facilities and services.

This chapter deals with the Act's key provisions on these matters and provides some guidance on how they relate to other existing provisions dealing with disability.

Finding the law

The Disability Discrimination Act 1995 covers all of the United Kingdom. To find out how it applies in Northern Ireland, the Act must be read together with the Northern Ireland modifications as set out in Schedule 8 to the Act. The Act provides for regulations expanding and explaining some of its key provisions, to be made by different government departments. Four such sets of regulations have been published already:

• the Disability Discrimination (Meaning of Disability) Regulations (NI) 1996,
• the Disability Discrimination (Employment) Regulations (NI) 1996,
• the Disability Discrimination (Sub-leases and Sub-tenancies) Regulations (NI) 1996, and
• the Disability Discrimination (Services and Premises) Regulations (NI) 1996.

The Act also provides that Codes of Practice can be issued. There is at present a Code of Practice governing the employment provisions, and a Code of Practice covering Rights of Access to Goods, Facilities, Services and Premises. Finally, as provided for by the Act, guidance on the definition of disability has been issued by the Department of Economic Development in a booklet entitled "Guidance on Matters to be Taken into Account in Determining Questions Relating to the Definition of Disability". Neither the codes nor the guidance impose legal obligations, but they are admissible before an industrial tribunal or court when they seem relevant to a case. They are all available from The Stationery Office Bookshop, 16 Arthur Street, Belfast BT1 4GD. An information pack containing explanatory booklets dealing with the Act's different provisions can be obtained by calling: 0345 622 633 or 0345 622 644.

The definition of disability

Unlike sex, race and fair employment discrimination legislation, where definitions of sex, race, religion and political belief have been left to industrial and fair employment tribunals (see Chapters 12 to 14), "disability" is specifically defined by the 1995 Act. According to the Act, a person is disabled if he or she has:

- a physical or mental impairment which has a substantial and long-term adverse effect on his or her ability to carry out normal day-to-day activities.

There are therefore three aspects to this definition.

Physical or mental impairment

The term "physical impairment" is not explained by the Act, but, the Code of Practice indicates that it includes impairments of senses such as sight and hearing. A supplementary Schedule to the Act explains that a "mental impairment" includes "an impairment resulting from or consisting of a mental illness only if the illness is a clinically well-recognised illness." The Code of Practice explains that this means that an illness must be recognised by a respected body of medical opinion. The Disability Regulations published under the Act specifically exclude certain mental states which might otherwise be considered to be illnesses. These are:

- addiction to or dependency on alcohol, nicotine, or any other substance (other than as a result of the substance being medically prescribed),
- seasonal allergic rihinitis (*e.g.* hayfever), except where it aggravates the effect of another impairment,
- tendency to set fires,
- tendency to steal,
- tendency to physical or sexual abuse of other persons,
- exhibitionism, and
- voyeurism.

Adverse affect

The impairment must adversely affect the individual's ability to carry out normal day-to-day activities. Schedule 1 to the Act provides that an impairment is to be taken to affect the ability of a person to carry out normal day-to-day activities only if it affects one of the following:

- mobility,
- manual dexterity,
- physical co-ordination,
- continence,
- ability to lift, carry or otherwise move everyday objects,
- speech, hearing or eyesight,
- memory or ability to concentrate, learn or understand, or
- perception of the risk of physical danger.

This list is exhaustive, although regulations may provide, greater or fewer categories in the future. The impairment can count as a disability even if medical treatment alleviates the effect, except in the case of poor eyesight corrected by glasses or contact lenses. Severe disfigurements are covered by the Act without the person having to demonstrate an adverse effect on his or her ability to carry out normal day-to-day activities. Progressive illnesses such as muscular dystrophy and human immunodeficiency virus (HIV), which are likely to have a substantial adverse effect in the future, count as disabilities from the first moment when the condition leads to an impairment which has *some* effect on the ability to carry out normal day-to-day activities, even though this effect is not yet *substantial*.

Substantial and long-term

The adverse effect must be substantial and long term. The Code of Practice explains that a "substantial" effect is "more than a minor or trivial effect". However, the precise scope of the term is likely to be contested in tribunals. "Long-term effects" includes a period of at least 12 months, or which is likely to last 12 months, or likely to last the rest of the person's life. If an impairment ceases to have a substantial effect, it is to be treated as a continuing impairment if it is likely to recur. It is also worth noting that the definition of "disability" includes those who have had a disability in the past.

One confusing aspect of the definition of the term "disability" is that it does not replace the previous definitions of disability or "handicap" contained in prior legislation. The one exception to this concerns the definition of disability contained in the Disabled Persons (Employment) Act (NI) 1945, which provided for a quota employment scheme. This is largely repealed by the 1995 Act and persons who were registered as disabled under the 1945 Act are to be automatically treated as falling within the term "disabled" under the new legislation for a period of three years from 2 December 1996 (the date when the employment provisions came into force). After this time these persons, if they want to bring a discrimination case, will have to establish themselves as disabled under the definition in the 1995 Act.

Employment

The Act applies to all employers who employ 20 or more persons within Northern Ireland and the rest of the United Kingdom. It outlaws three types of discrimination with respect to employment:

- discrimination with regard to recruitment, employment terms, opportunities for promotion, transfer, training, dismissal, or any other opportunity or benefit,
- failure to comply with a duty to make reasonable adjustments, and
- victimisation.

Discrimination and obtaining or keeping employment

Discrimination occurs where an employer:

- for a reason which relates to the disabled person's disability, treats him or her less favourably than he or she treats or would treat others to whom that reason does not or would not apply, and
- the employer cannot show that the treatment in question is justified.

Treatment is justified if the reason for it is both material to the circumstances of the particular case and substantial. The Code of Practice explains that this means that "the reason has to relate to the individual circumstances in question and not just be trivial or minor". For example, if a blind person who is not employed for computer work because of a general assumption that blind people cannot operate computers, this would be unjustified because it is based on a general assumption (that blind people cannot operate computers) rather than on a reason which is material to the particular circumstances. As this is a generalised assumption, it would not be a material reason as it is not related to the *particular circumstances*.

Reasonable adjustments

Discrimination also occurs where an employer fails to comply with a duty to make reasonable adjustments to accommodate the disabled person, and the employer cannot show that failure to comply with that duty is justified. Section 6 of the Act imposes a duty on employers to "take such steps as it is reasonable, in all the circumstances of the case, for him [or her] to have to take" to prevent any arrangements made by the employer or any physical feature of the premises occupied by the employer, from placing the disabled person concerned "at a substantial disadvantage in comparison with persons who are not disabled". The Act sets out examples of such adjustments, which include:

- making alterations to the premises,
- allocating some of the disabled person's duties to another person,
- altering work hours,
- allowing absences for rehabilitation, assessment or treatment, and
- acquiring or modifying equipment, instructions, reference manuals, procedures for testing or assessment.

These adjustments have to be made only where the disadvantage suffered is "substantial". As an example of insubstantial disadvantage the Code of Practice refers to a situation where a particular doorway cannot be negotiated by an employee using a wheelchair but there is an easy alternative route to the same destination.

In determining whether it is "reasonable" to expect an employer to take a modifying step, the following factors are relevant:

- the extent to which taking the step would prevent the effect in question,
- the extent to which it is practicable for the employer to take the step,
- the financial and other costs which would be incurred by the employer in taking the step and the extent to which taking it would disrupt any of his or her activities,
- the extent of the employer's financial and other resources, and
- the availability to the employer of financial or other assistance with respect to taking the step.

There is a link between these first two types of discrimination. Where an employer fails (without justification) to make the reasonable adjustment required, then the employer cannot justify less favourable treatment unless it could have been justified even if the adjustment had been made. In practical terms, this rather complicated legal mechanism means that an unjustified failure to make a reasonable adjustment to alleviate a barrier to a disabled applicant cannot amount to an "excuse" for not employing the disabled person. The Code gives the example of an employee who uses a wheelchair and is not promoted, solely because the work station for the higher post is inaccessible to wheelchairs, though it could readily be made so by rearrangement of the furniture. If the furniture had been rearranged, the reason for refusing promotion would not have applied. The refusal of promotion would not therefore be justified. Special provisions apply where the premises needing modification are leased rather than owned by the employer or organisation against which discrimination is alleged.

Victimisation

The Act also prohibits victimisation of anyone who has taken action under the Act. This is capable of protecting a non-disabled person, such as someone who gives testimony in a case brought under the Act.

Positive action

The Act protects only disabled persons and (apart from the victimisation provision) does not protect non-disabled persons. Therefore additional positive action which employers may choose to take to favour disabled persons is protected from a claim of discrimination by a non-disabled person. Also, the Act specifically protects charitable work or training provided for the benefit of disabled persons defined as a group by their disability.

Advertisements

A discriminatory advertisement is not of itself unlawful but can help prove an employment discrimination case. In race, sex and religious discrimination legislation, discriminatory advertisements are themselves unlawful. The Act provides that where a job advertisement has suggested that disability discrimination will take place, the tribunal should assume (unless the contrary is shown) that the reason for refusing to offer employment to the disabled person was related to the complainant's disability.

Contract work and discrimination by trade organisations

The Act also prohibits discrimination against disabled persons in relation to contract work and discrimination by trade organisations (such as trade unions and professional associations). The trade organisation provisions are largely similar to those for employment generally, outlawing discrimination and providing a duty to make reasonable adjustments.

Occupational pensions and insurance services

Section 17 of the 1995 Act states that every occupational pension scheme is deemed to include a rule of non-discrimination against disabled people. Similarly, by section 18, an insurer who has arrangements with an employer to provide benefits to employees in situations such as retirement or accident must make sure that there is no discrimination against disabled persons.

Enforcement

Where a person has a complaint of disability discrimination he or she may bring a case to an industrial tribunal, which may order that compensation be paid or require the employer to take action to reduce the adverse effect of the discrimination. The provisions of the Act cannot be excluded by employment contract provisions. As with sex and religious or political belief discrimination legislation, there is provision for conciliation through the Labour Relations Agency.

Other laws relating to disability and employment

Many of the employment provisions of the Disabled Persons (Employment) Act (NI) 1945 were repealed by the 1995 Act. Still remaining, however, are the sheltered employment provisions of section 15 of the 1945 Act, which give the Department of Economic Development the power to provide employment for registered disabled people whose disability is such that they could not otherwise find employment in the open market. The Department exercises this power in several ways. First, it funds the "Employment Support Scheme" (formerly known as the Sheltered Placement Scheme). This enables employers to employ severely disabled people at a reduced rate, which is broadly equivalent to their capacity for employment. For instance, if the disabled person's capacity is assessed at 50%, the employer has to pay only 50% of the usual wages for the job. The remaining portion of the wages is made up by one of three sponsoring organisations, Ulster Sheltered Employment Ltd, Disability Action and the Industrial Therapy Organisation. Second, the Department also funds one sheltered workshop based in Belfast and managed by Ulster Sheltered Employment Ltd. Finally, the DED runs the Job Introduction Scheme, which offers a weekly premium to employers who provide a trial period of six weeks employment to disabled people. Details on the Employment Support Scheme can be obtained from the Disablement Employment Advisor at the local offices of the Training and Employment Agency.

Goods, facilities and services

Part III of the 1995 Act makes it unlawful for a provider of services to discriminate against a disabled person:

- in refusing to provide, or deliberately not providing, any service which he or she provides or is prepared to provide to members of the public;
- in the standard of service which is provided to the disabled person or the manner in which it is provided to him or her; or
- in the terms on which a service is provided to the disabled person.

As with employment, it is also unlawful discrimination to fail to comply with any duty imposed on the provider by the Act, in circumstances in which the effect of that failure is to make it impossible or unreasonably difficult for the disabled person to make use of any such service. Victimisation amounts to discrimination in this context too.

The definition of provision of services is a wide one. It includes the provision of *any* goods or facilities, and a person is a provider of services if he or she is concerned with the provision, in the United Kingdom, of services to the public or to a section of the public, whether for payment or not. The Act gives examples, including:

- access to and any use of a place where members of the public are permitted to enter;
- access to and use of the means of communication;
- access to and use of information services;

- accommodation in a hotel, boarding house or other similar establishment;
- facilities by way of banking or insurance or for grants, loans, credit or finance;
- facilities for entertainment, recreation or refreshment;
- facilities provided by employment agencies; and
- the services of any profession or trade, or any local or other public authority.

There are separate rules for transport providers (see page 261). The Act does not cover private clubs and associations. A club will usually be considered private if it has strict conditions regulating membership.

The definition of "discrimination" is similar to that in the employment part of the Act. A provider of services therefore discriminates against a disabled person if:

- for a reason which relates to the disabled person's disability, he or she treats the disabled person less favourably than he or she treats or would treat others to whom that reason does not or would not apply, and
- he or she cannot show that the treatment in question is justified.

However, the definition of what constitutes "justification" is different in the case of goods and services in several important respects, which seem to make the discrimination easier to justify. In the case of goods and services, treatment is justified only if:

- in the opinion of the provider of services, one or more of the conditions listed in the Act is or are satisfied, and
- it is reasonable, in all the circumstances of the case, for the provider to hold that opinion.

The conditions are:

- that the treatment is necessary in order not to endanger the health or safety of any person (including the disabled person in question);
- that the disabled person is incapable of entering into an enforceable agreement, or of giving an informed consent, and for that reason the treatment is reasonable in that case;

- where a disabled person is refused services, that the treatment is necessary because the provider of services would otherwise be unable to provide the service to members of the public;
- where services are provided to the disabled person at a different standard or on different terms, that the treatment is necessary in order for the provider of services to be able to provide the service to the disabled person or to other members of the public; or
- where the service is provided to the disabled person on different terms, that this difference reflects the greater cost to the provider of services in providing the service to the disabled person.

As in the case of employment, a duty is imposed on providers of goods and services to make reasonable adjustments where they have "a practice, policy or procedure which makes it impossible or unreasonably difficult for disabled persons to make use of a service." In such a case it is a duty "to take such steps as is reasonable, in all the circumstances of the case, for [the provider] to have to take in order to change that practice, policy or procedure so that it no longer has that effect". These steps may include changing a physical feature of a building, or providing a way of avoiding it, or an alternative method of making the service in question available, or providing audio tape or a sign language interpreter. This duty, however, is not yet in force: it is to be introduced gradually over the next 10 years. Furthermore, the duty will be a limited one: a maximum cost is to be set down by regulations and the duty to make modifications is limited as it does not require the provider of goods and services to exceed this cost. As with the employment provisions, there are special provisions for the duty to modify buildings held on a lease.

Even when it is fully operational this part of the Act is likely to be difficult to enforce for several reasons. First, the mechanism for determining what amounts to a justification for discrimination is very complicated to understand, and is likely to require both expert advice and litigation to clarify how it will work in practice. This in turn means that providers of goods and services are unlikely to perceive clear obligations which they need to abide by. Second, it introduces a subjective test to the question of what amounts to "justification", whereby something can be justified if in the opinion of the provider (the alleged discriminator) it is justified, provided that that opinion is reasonable. The Act provides for a Code of Practice to be issued to give practical guidance for service providers. This Code has been prepared by the newly established Northern Ireland Disability Council (see page

264) and is issued by the Department of Health and Social Services for Northern Ireland.

Housing and disposal of premises

Part III of the 1995 Act also prohibits discrimination relating to letting or selling land or property, although landlords and members of their immediate family who let out rooms to six or fewer people in their own homes are not affected by these provisions. Discrimination is defined as before, and occurs when a person:

- offers less favourable terms to a disabled person,
- refuses to sell or let to a disabled person,
- treats a disabled person differently on lists, such as those of council housing departments, accommodation bureaux and estate agents,
- offers different facilities to a disabled person,
- refuses a disabled person access,
- evicts a disabled person, or
- refuses to give people consent to sub-let to a disabled person.

Practical examples of such discrimination would be property owners or landlords who charge a disabled person a higher price for property, more rent than other tenants, or a higher deposit against damages.

As with the provisions on employment and goods and services, different treatment of disabled people from other people may be justifiable and hence not amount to unlawful discrimination. It may be justifiable:

- on health and safety grounds,
- if allowing access to a facility to a disabled person would stop others from using it,
- if giving a disabled person different access to the facility is necessary to allow others to gain access, or
- if the disabled person is not capable of entering into a legally enforceable agreement or of giving informed consent.

While these provisions aim to prohibit discrimination against disabled persons, they do not require people selling or letting land or property to disabled people to alter the premises in order to make them more accessible. In order to achieve independent living a disabled person must have access not just to housing, but to housing suited to his or her specific needs. There are other provisions which address the question of accessibility, albeit inadequately.

Public sector housing

In Northern Ireland public sector housing is provided and administered by the Northern Ireland Housing Executive ("the Executive") (see Chapter 20). The Executive attempts to meet the needs of disabled people in two ways. First, under the Chronically Sick and Disabled Persons (NI) Act 1978, section 3, the Executive, when proposing a new building scheme, is under a duty to have regard to the needs of the chronically sick or disabled and to distinguish which houses in the proposed scheme are suitable for their needs. This is a general duty only. The disabled person has no right to insist on the provision of public sector housing which is specially adapted to his or her needs.

Second, all applications for public sector housing are subject to the Executive's Housing Selection Scheme (as approved by the Department of the Environment under art. 22 of the Housing (NI) Order 1981). Applicants for housing are placed in order of priority on the basis of their particular needs (recently Housing Association waiting lists were merged with those of the Executive). Top priority, *i.e.* A1 grouping, can be awarded where the applicant or a member of his or her family is in hospital or another institution from which he or she cannot be discharged due to lack of suitable housing. Priority A2 grouping can be awarded where an applicant or a member of his or her family has special health or welfare needs and requires to be re-housed in more suitable accommodation, thus remaining in the community.

Private sector

The biggest obstacle to a disabled person wishing either to purchase or to rent private property is that it will generally not be adapted to his or her special needs. The Executive facilitates some adaptation work in the private sector through grants issued under the Housing (NI) Order 1992. In addition to the standard renovation grant, there are two types of grants which make specific provision for disabled people.

Disabled facilities grant

By virtue of article 52(3) of the Housing (NI) Order 1992 a mandatory disabled facilities grant is available for work which will:

- provide access to, within or around the disabled person's dwelling,
- facilitate the preparation and cooking of food by the disabled occupant,
- improve or install a suitable heating system, or
- make it easier for the disabled occupant to use a source of power, light or heat.

A discretionary grant may also be available where the purpose of the work is to make the dwelling suitable for the accommodation, welfare or employment of disabled applicants (art. 52(4)).

Grants will be awarded only where the work is necessary and appropriate to meet the needs of the disabled occupant and provided it is reasonable and practical to carry out the work, having regard to the age and condition of the dwelling or building (art. 52(1)). Applications can be made by either owner-occupiers or tenants. However, disabled facilities grants are means-tested. Depending upon his or her income, the applicant may be required to contribute to the cost of the adaptations. Moreover, multiple means tests will be applied if there is another person living in the dwelling who has an interest in it. This means that that person's income will also be taken into account in determining the amount of the grant.

Grants are available for the cost of both materials and labour but are subject to a maximum award of £20,000.

Minor works grant

Minor works grants are discretionary (art. 69). They are available for the same type of adaptations as disabled facilities grants but are subject to a maximum of £1,000. Applicants for minor works grants must be in receipt of income support, family credit, housing benefit or disability working allowance.

Persons who would like further details about these grants should contact:

- The Northern Ireland Housing Executive
  Home Improvement Service
  32-36 Victoria Street
  Belfast BT2 7BA
  tel: 01232- 317000

Homelessness

The provisions of the Housing (NI) Order 1988 are considered in full in Chapter 20. It is worth noting that if the applicant is mentally or physically disabled or normally resides with someone in those categories, he or she will be defined as being in "priority need", one of the conditions for establishing A1 status under the Order.

Enforcement

A discrimination claim in the areas of goods, services and property can be enforced as civil proceedings as if they were tort claims. In Northern Ireland they are brought in a county court. The obligations cannot be excluded by contract.

Other legislation relating to access

In addition to the 1995 Act's provisions relating to modification, which may force employers to address access provisions or face a discrimination suit, the Chronically Sick and Disabled Persons (NI) Act 1978, sections 4 and 8 (as amended), place an obligation on anyone undertaking the provision of a building to which the public will have access or which is intended for use as a university, school, office or factory, to make "appropriate provision" for the needs of persons with disabilities as regards means of access, parking and sanitary conveniences. "Appropriate provision" is defined in Part R of the Buildings Regulations (NI) 1990. These make general design recommendations regarding parking spaces, approach to the building, door widths and floor and wall surfaces. The legislation is, however, limited. First, it applies only to the types of buildings specified above. Second, it applies only to new buildings or to existing buildings which are undergoing substantial structural changes. And third, although the regulations are, in theory, legally binding, they are worded so generally as to be largely unenforceable in practice.

By virtue of article 6 of the Planning (NI) Order 1991, the Department of the Environment, when granting planning permission, is required to draw the attention of the applicant to the Buildings Regulations. However, planning permission will not be refused for failure to comply with the regulations and it is not a criminal offence to construct a building which contravenes the regulations.

The regulations made under the Disability Discrimination Act 1995 provide that it is never reasonable to require an employer to take steps in relation to a disabled person to the extent that this would involve altering any physical characteristic which complied with the above Building Regulations. Thus, in the case of "overlap", the Building Regulations are to apply.

Public transport

Part V of the 1995 Act relates to public transport. These provisions are not yet in force, and no date for their introduction has yet been specified.

Taxis: The Act allows the Department of the Environment to make regulations providing for accessibility of taxis for disabled persons generally and the use of wheelchairs specifically. These may address the size of door openings, the floor area of passenger compartments, the amount of headroom in the passenger compartment, and the fitting of restraining devices to ensure the stability of wheelchairs. The Act requires drivers of accessible taxis to help disabled people in and out of their taxis and with their luggage, and to carry guide and hearing dogs free of charge. Taxi drivers who cannot comply on medical grounds will be exempt. Otherwise, drivers who fail to comply will be guilty of an offence.

Public service vehicles: The Act allows the Department of the Environment to make regulations governing access to coaches and buses to ensure that disabled persons can get on and off these vehicles and travel in safety and reasonable comfort. Regulations can be made only after consultation with such representative organisations as the Department thinks fit.

Trains: The Act allows the Department of the Environment to make regulations ensuring that all trains operated by Northern Ireland Railways are accessible to disabled persons.

Private transport

Private transport is not covered by the 1995 Act but it is worth noting that there are various statutory provisions aimed specifically at the disabled user of private transport.

Driving licences

Disabled people receiving the mobility component of disability living allowance may apply for a provisional driving licence at 16 years of age, instead of the minimum age of 17 years specified for able-bodied people (the Motor Vehicles (Driving Licences) Regulations (NI) 1989). However, a person may not be granted a driving licence if he or she is suffering from certain diseases or physical disabilities (art. 6 of the Road Traffic (NI) Order 1981). These include:

- epilepsy,
- liability to sudden attacks of disabling giddiness or fainting, and
- eyesight falling below a prescribed standard.

In addition, a licence will be refused if the applicant suffers from any disease or disability which would be likely to cause his or her driving to be a source of danger to the public.

If a person is aware that he or she is suffering from a relevant disease or disability, written notice must be given to the Department of the Environment. Failure to do so amounts to a criminal offence.

If a person suffers from a relevant disease or disability which is not prescribed, he or she is entitled to ask for a driving test to establish if driving would be a source of danger to the public (art. 6(2)(b) of the Road Traffic (NI) Order 1981). If the applicant passes the test, and is not otherwise disqualified, he or she may not be refused a licence solely on health grounds. However, if the test proves his or her fitness to drive vehicles only of a particular construction or design only, any licence granted must be limited to such vehicles.

A person who suffers from epilepsy will not be refused a licence if he or she can satisfy certain conditions which establish that his or her condition is appropriately controlled (art. 6(2)(d) of the Road Traffic (NI) Order 1981).

The orange badge scheme

The Department of the Environment issues badges to be displayed on motor vehicles used by disabled people (Chronically Sick and Disabled Persons (NI) Act 1978, s. 14). The conditions of entitlement to an orange badge are set down in the Disabled Persons (Badges for Motor Vehicles) Regulations (NI) 1979. In order to qualify for an orange badge, the disabled person must be a person who:

- uses a motor vehicle supplied by the DHSS or is getting a grant towards the running of a car;
- uses a motor vehicle which is exempt from vehicle excise duty;
- is registered blind;
- is dependent upon the use of a wheelchair outside the home;
- has an amputation or absence of a limb which causes considerable difficulty in walking;
- suffers from defects of the spine or of the central nervous system or other motor defect which makes control of the lower limbs difficult; or
- has some other permanent and substantial disability which causes considerable difficulty in walking.

The advantage of having an orange badge is that badge holders are exempt from certain car parking restrictions. The Scheme allows a vehicle displaying an orange badge and driven by a disabled person, or in which a disabled person is a passenger, to park:

- without charge or time limit at parking meters;
- without time limit where waiting is allowed for only limited periods; and
- for a maximum of two hours where parking restrictions indicated by yellow lines are in force.

It is a criminal offence for a person to display an orange badge if he or she has no entitlement to it. It is also an offence for a person not entitled to a badge to use a parking space reserved for a disabled person's vehicle.

Badges can be obtained from the Roads Service Division of the Department of the Environment. They have offices throughout Northern Ireland: look under Roads Service in the business and services section of the telephone book.

Vehicle excise duty

All vehicles on the road are liable to vehicle excise duty, better known as road tax. However, by virtue of section 4(1)(g) of the Vehicle Excise Act (NI) 1972, disabled people can in certain circumstances claim exemption from vehicle excise duty for one car. Application forms for an exemption certificate can be obtained from:

* The Regional Disablement Service
  Musgrave Park Hospital
  Stockman's Lane
  Belfast BT9 7JB
  tel: 01232-382255

The certificate can be used as proof of exemption when applying for a tax exemption disc from the Vehicle Licensing Centre in Coleraine.

Rate relief

Applications for exemption from rates on property used by disabled people can be made under the Rates (Amendment) (NI) Order 1979, article 5. This provides for relief on garages or parking spaces which accommodate a vehicle used by and required for meeting the needs of a disabled person. Application forms for rate relief can be obtained from any local Rates Office.

Disabled children

Further information on the rights of children who are disabled is provided in Chapters 17 and 18.

The Northern Ireland Disability Council

The Disability Discrimination Act 1995 established the Northern Ireland Disability Council to advise the government about eliminating and reducing discrimination against disabled people, and the operation of the Act, but not about employment. However the government has recently extended the remit of the Council to include employment. The Council has from 10 to 20 members, appointed by the Department of Health and Social Services for Northern Ireland. They represent a wide range of views and are appointed from among people who know about the needs of disabled people and people who have had a disability, or have experience of industry, business or the professions. At present there are 13 members of the Council. Its address is Room C4.8, Castle Buildings, Stormont, Belfast BT3 3PP (tel: 01232-520528).

Before the Council gives advice to the government, it must identify the costs and benefits associated with the implementation of its advice, and consult with other relevant bodies with an interest in the matter. The Council is also charged with preparing a Code of Practice on the goods, facilities and services aspects of the Act, and has in fact produced such a Code. The Northern Ireland Council has also undertaken social attitude research on disability, to be published shortly. A much criticised aspect of the Council has been that, unlike the Equal Opportunities Commission, the Fair Employment Commission or the Commission for Racial Equality, it cannot support or investigate individual complaints of discrimination against disabled persons. However, a recent government announcement made a commitment to establishing a Disability Commission which would have such power.

Mental disability

While the 1995 Act, as has been noted, covers both physical and mental disabilities, the civil liberties of mentally disabled persons are also affected by the Mental Health (NI) Order 1986. This Order applies to people who are suffering from a "mental disorder", which is defined to include mental illness, mental handicap and any other disorder or disability of the mind.

The Order makes provision in six major areas. They are as follows.

- Articles 4-11 of the Order specify the circumstances in which a person may be compulsorily admitted to hospital for an assessment of his or her mental health.
- Articles 12-15 specify the circumstances in which a person may be detained in hospital for treatment.
- Articles 18-26 provide for the appointment of a guardian.
- Articles 42-61 make provision for the remand, trial and detention of people suffering from a mental disorder who are involved in criminal proceedings or who are under sentence for a criminal offence.
- Articles 62-69 specify the circumstances in which a person suffering from a mental disorder may or may not be treated without his or her consent.

- Articles 97-109 provide for the management of the property and affairs of mental patients.

Any law which confers the power compulsorily to admit people to hospital, to detain them for medical treatment which they have not consented to, and to assume responsibility for the management of their affairs, must necessarily have serious civil liberties implications. The legislation is, not surprisingly, extensive and at times complex. A Code of Practice for use by doctors and administrators involved with mentally disordered people has been issued by the Department of Health and Social Services. Persons seeking information on the rights of the mentally disabled under the Mental Health Order should contact a solicitor or the Association for Mental Health:

- Association for Mental Health
  Information Unit
  80 University Street
  Belfast BT7 1HE
  tel: 01232-328474

Conclusion

The United Nations' Declaration of the Rights of Disabled Persons (1975) asserts the right of disabled people to be self-reliant, to live as they choose and to participate in social, creative and recreational activities within their communities. While the Disability Discrimination Act 1995 is a long way forward from the piecemeal and largely unenforceable legislation which preceded it, it is unlikely to enable disabled persons to achieve these objectives. Apart from the fact that it has nothing to say about the education needs of disabled people, the Act has three other major flaws.

The definition of disability

The definition of disability is purely medical in nature and thus fails to recognise the social and cultural factors which are present in disability and impairment. As a United Nations' report on disability points out, "persons may be treated as if they were disabled and subjected to many kinds of restrictions (occupational, social, educational, etc.) although from a clinical point of view they are not actually disabled." This may be the case, for example, with facial disfigurements. The clinical basis of the definition is not only inaccurate, but fails to capture the way in which society constructs the notion of "disability". It may therefore be used to justify discrimination rather than to challenge social conditions.

The definition of discrimination

Direct discrimination is outlawed, but unlike in the legislation on sex, race and religious or political discrimination, indirect discrimination is not. Furthermore, the disability discrimination definition of direct discrimination is significantly weaker, since direct discrimination can be justified in a broad range of prescribed circumstances.

The small business exemption

The exclusion of businesses with less than 20 persons from the Act's employment provisions greatly reduces its effectiveness in Northern Ireland, where over 90% of companies fall into this category.

The British government has recently responded to criticism by announcing that a task force on disability will be established to examine the effectiveness of the current legislation, and that in the meantime the outstanding provisions of the legislation will be implemented as soon as practicable.

Further information about disability discrimination can be obtained from:

- Disability Action
  Communications Unit
  2 Annadale Avenue
  Belfast BT7 3JR
  tel: 01232-491011

- Rights Now (Northern Ireland)
  83 Silverstream Avenue
  Belfast BT14 8GL
  tel: 01232-711625

- PHAB (Physically Handicapped and Able Bodied)
  25 Alexandra Gardens
  Belfast BT15 3LJ
  Phabline: tel: 01232-322690 (Belfast)
  01504-371030 (Derry)
  01622-245954 (Omagh)

- Mental Health Commission
  Elizabeth House
  116-118 Holywood Road
  Belfast BT4 1NY
  tel: 01232-651157

- National Schizophrenia Fellowship
  37/39 Queen Street
  Belfast BT1 6FB
  tel: 01232-248006

Chapter 16

Family and Sexual Matters

Brice Dickson and Madge Davison

Marriage and marriage breakdown

People are free to marry whomever they like (Article 12 of the European Convention on Human Rights), with the exception of close relatives. In Northern Ireland one has to be aged at least 16 and not to be in a "prohibited degree of relationship" with one's intended spouse; it is not legal, for instance, for a woman to marry the father of her divorced husband (unless this first husband, and his mother, have already died). The prohibited degrees of relationship are listed in the Family Law (Miscellaneous Provisions) (NI) Order 1984, article 18, as amended by the Family Law (NI) Order 1993.

The law governing the breakdown of marriages offers two remedies, "separation" and "divorce". Most of the rules on separation are to be found in the Domestic Proceedings (NI) Order 1980, while those on divorce are in the Matrimonial Causes (NI) Order 1978. A separation case will be dealt with in a summary way in a magistrates' court but a divorce must be heard either in a county court or the High Court. The High Court must be used if the case is a defended one.

Separation

In rare situations a spouse may wish to obtain an official decree of "judicial" separation rather than a decree of divorce. But what most people usually refer to as separation is a less formal status, namely where the spouses are living apart, often with one of them (usually the husband) paying money at regular intervals to the other. The wife obtains the *right* to such payments by applying to a magistrates' court for a "financial provision order", which might be for a lump sum or for periodical payments (known as "maintenance"). The law does not compel the spouses in such situations to live apart and indeed the legislation specifically allows for a case to be adjourned if, even though the spouses are already living apart, there is a reasonable possibility of a reconciliation. But if a financial provision order is granted and the parties then live together for a period exceeding six months, the order ceases to have effect.

The grounds for a financial provision order

There are two ways in which a financial provision order may be obtained. The first is by the agreement of both spouses. The second is by satisfying a court that one of the five grounds mentioned in the Domestic Proceedings (NI) Order 1980 has been fulfilled. These are:

- that the other spouse has failed to provide reasonable maintenance for the applicant;
- that the other spouse has failed to provide reasonable maintenance for any child of the family;
- that the other spouse has committed adultery;
- that the other spouse has behaved in such a way that the applicant cannot reasonably be expected to live with him or her; or
- that the other spouse has deserted the applicant.

An application must be brought to the court within a year of the conduct in question. The ground of unreasonable behaviour can include the following: practising sexual perversions, continually "nagging" or using obscene language, being a manic depressive, alcoholic or addicted to drugs, casting doubt on the paternity of children, doing DIY alterations which cause prolonged inconvenience, being convicted of criminal offences relevant to the family relationship, using violence on the spouse or children, and being hyper-critical of the other spouse.

Other factors taken into account

A resident magistrate has to consider the following points before making an order:

- the income, earning capacity, property and other financial resources of the parties now and in the foreseeable future;
- the financial needs, obligations and responsibilities of the parties;

- the standard of living enjoyed by the parties;
- the age of each party and the duration of the marriage;
- any physical or mental disability of the parties;
- the contribution made by each of the parties to the welfare of the family, including whether one of the parties looked after the home and cared for the family; and
- any other relevant matter, including the conduct of each of the parties.

If a case has been adjourned for a lengthy period, say for welfare reports on the children, it is possible to seek an interim order for maintenance in order to provide temporary financial relief.

Either party can apply to a magistrates' court for a variation of the original order on the ground that his or her means or circumstances have changed. An appeal against a decision can be made to a county court and from there to the High Court, but only on a difficult point of law.

Divorce

The Matrimonial Causes (NI) Order 1978 provides only one ground for divorce, namely irretrievable breakdown of marriage. The spouse who asks for a divorce is called the "petitioner"; the other spouse is called the "respondent". In order to show that irretrievable breakdown has occurred, a petitioner must prove one or more of the following:

- that the respondent has committed adultery;
- that the respondent has behaved in such a way that the petitioner cannot reasonably be expected to live with him or her;
- that the respondent has deserted the petitioner for a continuous period of at least two years;
- that the parties have lived apart for a continuous period of at least two years and that the respondent consents to a decree being granted; or
- that the parties have lived apart for a continuous period of at least five years.

With respect to adultery, it is only in rare cases that good evidence is available, so a spouse's admission to the adultery can be used against him or her in court. In cases of divorce by consent after two years of separation, it is necessary to satisfy the court that true consent exists: there must be no deceit or mistake as to any of the relevant information.

A person may not petition the court for divorce until the marriage has lasted for at least two years. A "decree *nisi*" is granted on the day of the hearing, with a "decree absolute" being granted six weeks later if there are no difficulties. Usually a petitioner for divorce will have to go into the witness box in court to give oral testimony. However, under article 15 of the Family Law (NI) Order 1993 this is no longer necessary if the divorce petition is based on two years' separation (with consent) or five years' separation (with or without consent).

Financial provision and divorce

Once a petition for divorce has been lodged, a court can make a variety of orders in relation to financial provision.

- *Maintenance pending suit*: the court can order either party to make periodical payments to the other in order to cover reasonable expenses arising between the beginning of the case and the time when the divorce is finally granted.
- *Financial provision after a decree*: the court can order a lump sum and/or periodical payments to be given to the spouse and/or the children of the family.
- *Property order after a decree:* the court can make an order regarding property belonging to the parties and this can include ordering a transfer of the matrimonial home.

Residence of, and contact with, children

The law on this matter has been reformed by the Children (NI) Order 1995, which was modelled on the Children Act 1989 for England and Wales. Amongst other changes the Order replaces custody and access orders with residence and contact orders. Under article 10 of the Order, in any family proceedings before a court where a question arises concerning the welfare of any child, the court may make one of the following orders:

- a *residence order*, settling the arrangements to be made concerning the person with whom a child is to live; where a residence order is made in favour of two or more persons who do not live together, the order may specify the periods during which the child is to live in the different households concerned (art.11(4)); the person in whose favour a residence order is made is given parental responsibility for the child (art.12);

- a *contact order*, requiring a person with whom a child lives, or is about to live, to allow the child to have contact with a person named in the order;
- a *specific issue order*, giving directions for deciding a specific question which has arisen, or may arise, in relation to any aspect of parental responsibility for a child;
- a *prohibited steps order*, requiring the consent of the court before a person takes a step specified in the order (*e.g.* taking the child abroad).

A person can apply for a residence or contact order if he or she is a party to a marriage (whether it is subsisting or not) and the child is a child of that family, or if the child has lived with him or her for at least three years (not necessarily consecutively) or if he or she has the consent of those who have parental responsibility for the child (art.10(5)). The court must have particular regard to (amongst other things) "any risk there might be of [the application] disrupting the child's life to such an extent that he [or she] would be harmed by it" (art.10(9)(c)).

Any of the above orders may be made subject to conditions (art.11(7)), but none of them (except a residence order) can be made with respect to a child who is in the care of an authority (art.9(1)) (see Chapter 17) and no order shall be made which is to have effect after the child has reached 16, "unless [the court] is satisfied that the circumstances of the case are exceptional" (art.9(6)). Under article 16 of the Order, if a court has power to make one of the above orders it may require an authority (*e.g.* a Health and Social Services Board) "to make a suitably qualified person available, to advise, assist and (where appropriate) befriend any person named in the order".

Child abduction

If a child is abducted from one country to another the legal position is in most countries the same. This is because it was settled by an international treaty agreed at The Hague in 1980. In the United Kingdom this treaty has been given the force of law by the Child Abduction and Custody Act 1985, the policy of which is that, generally speaking, a child should always be returned to the county where he or she habitually resided before being abducted. But the Act allows a court to refuse to order the child's return if it is satisfied that "there is a grave risk that his or her return would expose the child to physical or psychological harm or otherwise place the child in an intolerable situation" (Sched.1, art.13). This discretion was exercised by the Northern Ireland Court of Appeal in *Re K* (1997), a case where a Northern Irish mother had taken her two children from their home on a Greek island and refused to return them there.

Child support

Under the Child Support (NI) Orders 1991 and 1995, the Child Support Agency is able to ask single parents in receipt of social welfare benefits for the name of the other parent of their child. The Agency will then seek to recover money from that other parent. In return that parent may well apply for greater access to the child. If the first parent does not disclose the identity of the other parent, his or her welfare benefits may be reduced by up to 20%.

Domestic violence

One of the most important features of the Domestic Proceedings (NI) Order 1980 is the power it gives to magistrates to order protection for a spouse and children from a violent partner to a marriage or from a cohabitee. At present, two types of order can be made. In 1996 the government issued a proposal for a new Family Homes and Domestic Violence (NI) Order, but this will not become law until some time in 1998. It will provide for non-molestation and occupation orders and will allow a wider range of applicants to seek relief, including certain relatives living in the same household. Child abusers will be able to be removed from the home. For the time being, however, the law is as described below.

Personal protection order

To obtain this an applicant must satisfy the magistrate that the respondent has used or threatened to use violence against the applicant or a child of the family, and that an order is necessary for the protection of the applicant or child. Once obtained, the order restrains a spouse or cohabitee from "molesting" the applicant or child and prohibits the spouse or cohabitee from inciting, procuring or assisting another person to molest the applicant. It can be granted even if the applicant and the spouse or cohabitee are still living together.

Exclusion order

Very often a personal protection order is coupled with an exclusion order, which may operate in one or more of the following ways:

- giving the applicant exclusive use of the joint home;
- prohibiting the respondent from entering the home;
- requiring the respondent to permit the applicant to enter the home and have peaceful use and enjoyment of it;
- preventing the respondent from selling the home or surrendering a lease on it;
- ordering the respondent not to damage or interfere with any services in the home; or
- ordering the respondent not to remove any goods from the home and not to sell, damage or destroy any goods in it.

If the respondent damages, destroys or disposes of any goods in the home, the court can order him or her to repair, replace or restore these or to pay a sum of money instead. An exclusion order can also exclude the respondent from the street where the home is situated, but it must not interfere with the reasonable conduct of the respondent's life. It can exclude the respondent from specified premises other than the matrimonial home (or from their vicinity), provided the applicant or a child is living there, *e.g.* the applicant's parents' home, or a Women's Aid Refuge. In one case a magistrate was prepared to exclude a violent husband from the area between the matrimonial home and the nearest public telephone - to ensure that the wife could reach help unmolested. An exclusion order may last for up to six months and may be extended for any period not exceeding six months.

The power of arrest

A power of arrest is attached to every personal protection and exclusion order. The clerk of the court notifies the divisional commander of the RUC in the area where the applicant resides and where the excluded premises or areas are situated. A constable has power to arrest anyone whom he or she reasonably suspects of having breached an order by molesting the applicant or child, or by being in or attempting to enter the matrimonial home or other area specified in the order, or by damaging or interfering with any services or goods so specified. A constable may carry out the arrest without a warrant, using such force as is reasonable in the circumstances, and may if necessary enter the matrimonial home or other premises by force. Following his or her arrest, the person or cohabitee may be conditionally released or detained in custody until being brought before a court.

This is only a power of arrest, not a duty to arrest, so very often the exercise of the power rests on the judgment of a police constable. If no action is taken by the police the applicant can complain to the court about the breach of the order. Under the Family Law (NI) Order 1993 breach of an order is itself a criminal offence, punishable in a magistrates' court with a fine of up to £2,500 and three months' imprisonment.

"Emergency" orders

The Domestic Proceedings (NI) Order 1980 also contains provisions to cope with an emergency situation in relation to domestic violence. It is possible for an applicant to be before a magistrate within a few hours of an attack. A magistrate has power to order an interim personal protection or exclusion order if satisfied that there may be imminent danger of physical injury to the applicant or a child. The hearing of the application will be in private, but where a magistrate refuses to grant an interim order there can be no appeal. Interim orders do not take effect until the violent spouse or cohabitee is served with notice, and their effect is temporary, usually lasting for a period of five weeks or until the hearing for a full order. It is, however, possible to renew the interim order if the full hearing cannot take place within five weeks.

Problems in practice

There is no doubt that the powers in the 1980 Order, especially regarding exclusion orders, are extremely penal provisions. Whilst most magistrates view applicants fairly and sympathetically, often assisting them by ordering that service of the orders on the spouse or cohabitee be carried out by the RUC, this is not always the case. Among the difficulties experienced in practice are the following:

- a belief that "professional" men should not be excluded from their homes;
- an attitude against granting these orders if the parties are living in the same home;
- demanding medical evidence of the assaults;
- refusing the orders unless the spouse or cohabitee has been violent to the children as well as to the applicant;

- refusing the orders if the violent spouse or cohabitee has nowhere else to live; and
- refusing the orders if the magistrate considers that there is the slightest chance of a reconciliation.

If a magistrate voices any such reasons for refusing the orders there is nothing to stop the applicant in a suitable case from applying to the High Court for judicial review to have the magistrate's decision quashed (see Chapter 2). A magistrate sitting in these cases often hears evidence of criminal offences ranging from common assault to grievous bodily harm. At the moment, regrettably, he or she does not automatically have to refer the case to the Director of Public Prosecutions for criminal proceedings to be considered.

Abortion

The law on abortion in Northern Ireland is much more restrictive than in the rest of the United Kingdom. It stems both from statute law and from the law laid down by judges. The Abortion Act 1967 does not apply here. The main Act which does apply is the Offences Against the Person Act 1861, which makes it an offence for a woman unlawfully to procure a miscarriage on herself by using "noxious poisons", "things" or "instruments". The maximum penalty is life imprisonment. This is also the penalty if someone else performs an operation on a woman so as unlawfully to procure a miscarriage.

The use of the word "unlawfully" shows that some abortions are lawful. It has always been accepted that they are lawful in cases where they are necessary in order to save the life of the mother. In *R v Bourne* (1939) a gynaecologist in England was acquitted of carrying out an unlawful abortion on a 14-year-old girl who had been the victim of a multiple rape by soldiers. The judge said this was because the doctor had been of the opinion on reasonable grounds and with adequate knowledge that the probable consequences of continuing the pregnancy would have been to make the woman a physical or mental wreck. Although this view was queried by Lord Diplock in a 1981 case, it remains the law in Northern Ireland. Moreover, section 25 of the Criminal Justice Act (NI) 1945 specifically provides a defence to an abortionist if he or she acts in good faith for the purpose of preserving the life of the mother. In *Northern Health and Social Services Board v F and G* (1993), where a 14-year-old girl was 13 weeks pregnant and her parents were at odds on whether she should have an abortion, the judge declared that an abortion would not be unlawful but recognised that the girl would have to go to England to find a doctor willing to carry out the operation.

The law in practice

Naturally the medical profession in Northern Ireland is not happy that the law in this area is so unclear. Doctors receive little guidance from the Department of Health and Social Services and the medical teaching profession has had to draw up its own guidelines on the interpretation of the law for the benefit of medical students. The practice appears to be that abortions are performed in Northern Ireland only where there is a serious risk to health or life. More than half the women seeking abortions here are refused and abortions are performed only in the first three to five months of pregnancy. It remains uncertain whether there is any specific policy in relation to performing abortions on disabled foetuses. There is also no guarantee that an abortion would be performed if a woman became pregnant as a result of rape. If the medical profession refuses to perform an abortion on a woman in Northern Ireland, and she does not want to give birth, she is effectively faced with the choice of a trip to England or recourse to a back-street abortion here. If she does choose to give birth, there are agencies to counsel and help her (*e.g.* the Brook Advisory Centre and Life).

Sexual offences

Although the overall crime rate in Northern Ireland is lower than that in England and Wales, one category of crime which is committed at a higher rate in Northern Ireland is that of sexual offences. This has been the case for many decades. In 1996 there were 264 rapes recorded by the RUC.

In England and Wales the main legislation governing these offences is the Sexual Offences Act 1956, which was updated by the Sexual Offences (Amendment) Acts 1976 and 1992. In Northern Ireland some of the legislation is still Victorian in origin, being chiefly the Offences Against the Person Act 1861, the Criminal Law Amendment Act 1885 and the Vagrancy Act 1898. More recent laws include the Children and Young Persons Act (NI) 1968, the Sexual Offences (NI) Order 1978 and the Homosexual Offences (NI) Order 1982. The Northern Ireland Office is currently reviewing the law on sexual offences with a view to proposing new comprehensive legislation.

There are really three main types of sexual offence: rape, buggery and indecent assault. After discussing these, special consideration will be given to crimes involving incest, prostitution and indecency. Advice on some of the matters covered in this section can be obtained from either:

- Rape Crisis Centre (Belfast)
  PO Box 46,
  Belfast BT2 7AR,
  tel: 01232-249696

- Nexus,
  PO Box 220,
  Belfast BT1 7HP,
  tel: 01232-326803 or 01504-260566 (Derry).

Rape

By article 3(1) of the Sexual Offences (NI) Order 1978, a man commits rape if he has unlawful sexual intercourse with a woman who at the time of the intercourse does not consent to it and at that time he knows that she does not consent to the intercourse or he is reckless as to whether she consents to it.

"Sexual intercourse" here requires penetration of the woman's vagina by the man's penis, but nothing more. As regards the woman's consent, apparent consent is not real consent. Rape is therefore committed whenever the woman's "consent" is obtained by threats of personal violence, by fraud, or whenever the woman is so mentally vulnerable, or young, or drunk, that her knowledge and understanding are such that she is not in a position to decide whether to consent or to resist. The man is guilty of rape if he obtains the woman's consent by impersonating her husband (hardly a likely occurrence), but not if he merely pretends to be some other person. If a man's defence to a charge of rape is that he believed that the woman was consenting to sexual intercourse, the jury must consider whether there were reasonable grounds for such a belief. The test is therefore objective, not subjective.

In 1991 the judges in the House of Lords changed the ancient rule that a wife is always presumed to have consented to intercourse with her husband (*R v R*). A man can now be guilty of raping his wife, even if they are otherwise "happily" married. In England this change was confirmed by legislation (the Criminal Justice and Public Order Act 1994), but no such confirmation has yet occurred in Northern Ireland.

Young people

There is a rule laid down by the judges (though it has been changed in England and Wales) that a boy younger than 14 is incapable of committing rape or assault with intent to commit rape. But he can be convicted of aiding and abetting a rape or of indecent assault, as indeed can a woman.

In the case of females under 17, there can be no consent in law to sexual intercourse. The girl herself does not commit any offence by having intercourse (and may, *e.g.*, be prescribed contraceptives) but the male does, even if he has reasonable cause to believe that the girl is 17 or over. If the girl is over 14 and under 17, the man is liable to be sent to prison for up to two years, but the prosecution must be begun within 12 months of the commission of the offence. If the girl is under 14, the man can be sent to prison for life if intercourse takes place, or for up to two years if there was an attempt at intercourse (Criminal Law Amendment Act 1885, ss. 4 and 5). The age of consent for girls in England and Wales is 16, not 17 as in Northern Ireland.

Punishment and compensation

The maximum penalty for the crime of rape is life imprisonment (s. 48 of the Offences Against the Person Act 1861), while that for attempt to commit rape, or for assault with intent, is seven years' imprisonment (ss. 1 and 2 of the Attempted Rape, etc Act (NI) 1960). The Northern Ireland Court of Appeal has said that the starting point for rape in a contested case should be seven years' imprisonment, not five as in England and Wales (*R v McDonald and Others*, 1989).

A rape victim can begin a civil action against the rapist, though obviously this is worth doing only if he has assets out of which he can pay compensation to the victim. The action has to be begun within six years of the incident (or of the victim turning 18, if that is later). A court has no discretion to extend this period. If the victim is suing someone other than the abuser (*e.g.* a social worker) for not dealing with the complaint properly, he or she has three years in which to sue and a judge *can* extend this period. In addition, a rape victim who becomes pregnant as a result of the attack, and who decides to give birth to the child and keep it, is entitled to £5,000 compensation from the state (art. 9 of the Criminal Injuries (Compensation) (NI) Order 1988). In England and Wales ex gratia *(i.e.* discretionary) compensation to victims of child sex abuse is paid by the state even though the victim becomes aware of the effects of the abuse only in later life. But in Northern Ireland, supposedly because of pressure on public expenditure, no such compensation is paid.

Identification in sexual offence cases

On account of the sensitive nature of trials alleging rape and other sexual offences, special provisions have been introduced to protect both the alleged victim and the alleged offender. By article 6 of the Sexual Offences (NI) Order 1978, as amended by the Criminal Justice (NI) Order 1994, after a person has been officially accused of a sexual offence nothing which is likely to lead members of the public to identify a particular person as the complainant can be published or broadcast in Northern Ireland; the only exceptions to this are where a judge directs that the restriction should be lifted in the public interest or in order to induce persons who are vital to the accused's defence to come forward. Anyone who publishes information in breach of article 6 is liable to be fined up to £500.

It should be noted that anonymity attaches to the complainant only after a person has been officially accused. Until then, even though the matter may still be under investigation, the alleged victim's name (if he or she has not yet officially complained) may be revealed to the public. If the case does go to trial, however, every alleged rape victim has a right not to have to confront any question or evidence put forward by the defence about his or her sexual experience with someone other than the accused. This right can be overridden by the magistrate or judge only if he or she is satisfied that it would be unfair to the accused to refuse to allow the evidence to be submitted or the question to be asked. The victim, however, is not entitled to have her own legal representative in court.

The anonymity of the person accused of the sexual offence is *not* protected: the Criminal Justice (NI) Order 1994 changed the law on this point.

Buggery

Anal intercourse, whether between men or between a man and a woman, cannot amount to the crime of rape in Northern Ireland (in England male rape *is* recognised as a crime). In Northern Irish law the relevant provision is still section 61 of the Offences Against the Person Act 1861, which says that :

whosoever shall be convicted of the abominable crime of buggery, committed either with mankind, or with any animal, shall be liable to imprisonment for life.

By section 62 any attempt to commit buggery, or any assault with intent to commit it, is an offence carrying a sentence of up to 10 years' imprisonment. Consent is not a defence to a charge of buggery, so a husband can be convicted of committing the offence on his wife, or a cohabitee on his willing partner. But usually the defendant in these cases is a child abuser. In 1996, 58 offences of buggery were recorded by the RUC.

In England and Wales, but not in Northern Ireland, the Criminal Justice and Public Order Act 1994 decriminalised anal intercourse between consenting heterosexual couples. Following the 1981 decision in *Dudgeon v UK*, where the European Court of Human Rights held that the law in Northern Ireland making all male homosexual acts an offence was in violation of Article 8 of the European Convention on Human Rights, the government introduced the Homosexual Offences (NI) Order 1982. As explained below, this legalised certain categories of homosexual acts.

Indecent assault

Indecent assault is an assault or battery (*i.e.* threatened or actual physical contact) accompanied by circumstances of indecency. Merely touching somebody without his or her consent and in circumstances of indecency can constitute the offence. Even if consent has supposedly been given, this is no defence if the assault was of a kind to cause harm interfering with the victim's health or comfort, or if it was obtained by fraud. Most importantly, a female in Northern Ireland who is younger than 17 cannot give a valid consent. Nor, depending on the circumstances, may a person who is mentally vulnerable. The House of Lords has held that persons who indulge in sado-masochistic practices can still be guilty of indecent assault, even though the participants fully consent to what is done to them (*R v Brown*, 1992), and the European Court of Human Rights confirmed this decision (*Laskey, Jaggard and Brown v UK*, 1997).

Behaviour constituting indecent assault can range from a tap on the bottom to forced oral sex. Indeed, because the current legal definition of rape is so limited, many very serious acts can be prosecuted only as indecent assaults. Penetration of a woman's vagina by anything other than a penis is such an act. The definition of rape is limited for historical reasons: what was originally being protected was simply a woman's right not to be made pregnant unwillingly. Today the maximum penalty for indecent assault, whether committed against a man or a woman, is 10 years' imprisonment.   In 1996 there were 768 indecent assaults on females recorded by the RUC, and 223 on males.

Closely allied to the crime of indecent assault is the offence of indecent conduct towards a child (72 recorded offences in Northern Ireland in 1996).   This is governed by section 22 of the Children and Young Persons Act (NI) 1968, which provides that a person who commits an act of gross indecency with or towards a child under 14, or who incites a child under 14 to such an act with the accused or with another, is liable to be sent to prison for up to two years.

In England and Wales, by the Sexual Offences (Amendment) Act 1992, provisions on anonymity have been extended to cover not just rape cases but most other sexual offences too.   As yet there has been no comparable extension of the Sexual Offences (NI) Order 1978.

Incest

Incest is still governed in Northern Ireland by the Punishment of Incest Act 1908 (15 recorded offences in 1996). It can be committed by both males and females. Under section 1(1) of the 1908 Act a male is guilty of incest if he has sexual intercourse with a female who is, to his knowledge, his mother, sister, daughter or granddaughter. If the female is under 14 the maximum penalty is life imprisonment, otherwise the maximum is seven years' imprisonment. Attempts to commit incest carry a maximum sentence of two years' imprisonment. In all cases the consent of the female is immaterial.

Under section 2 of the 1908 Act a female commits incest if she is 16 or over and consents to have sexual intercourse with someone whom she knows to be her son, brother, father or grandfather. The maximum penalty is seven years' imprisonment, whatever the age of the male involved.   A girl under 16 who willingly has incestuous intercourse commits no offence. For the purposes of the crime of incest, the terms "brother" and "sister" include half-brother and half-sister and it does not matter whether the child or grandchild involved is born in lawful wedlock. All prosecutions require the consent of the Attorney-General for Northern Ireland and must be held in private.

In Northern Ireland Court of Appeal follows the English Court of Appeal's guidelines on sentencing in incest cases (*R v Charters*, 1989). These suggest that incest with a girl over 16 should attract a sentence of up to three years' imprisonment, incest with a girl aged 13 to 16 should carry a sentence between three and five years, and incest with a girl under 13 should carry six or more years.

As regards the measures that can be taken to protect children from sexual abuse, the relevant legal provisions in Northern Ireland are primarily section 31 of the Children and Young Persons Act (NI) 1968 and article 65 of the Children (NI) Order 1995. Any person reasonably suspected of committing a sexual offence against a child can be arrested by police without a warrant (s.31) and the child can be removed by the police to safe accommodation in cases of emergency (art.65). The JP must first be satisfied that there is reasonable cause to suspect that the child or young person has been or is being assaulted, ill-treated or neglected in a manner likely to cause unnecessary suffering or injury to health. (See also Chapter 17, where emergency protection orders are explained).

Prostitution

It is not an offence for a woman or a man to "sell" his or her body for sex, but it is an offence to solicit custom, to assist in the management of a brothel or to live off the earnings of a prostitute. Prostitution, for this purpose, need not entail actual sexual intercourse; it is enough, in the words of one judge, if a woman "offers her body for purposes amounting to common lewdness for payment in return" (Darling J in *R v de Munck*, 1918).

In all towns in Northern Ireland it is an offence for a prostitute to loiter and importune "passengers" for the purpose of prostitution: see section 167 of the Belfast Improvement Act 1845, section 28 of the Town Police Clauses Act 1847 (for Belfast and Derry) and section 72 of the Towns Improvement (Ireland) Act 1854 (for other towns). The maximum penalty is a £200 fine. By section 1(1) of the Vagrancy Act 1898 - extended to what is now Northern Ireland in 1912 - it is an offence punishable by up to six months' imprisonment if a man:

- knowingly lives wholly or in part on the earnings of prostitution; or
- persistently in any public place solicits for immoral purposes; the judges have said that this offence cannot be committed by a man who kerb-crawls; the law was changed in England in 1985 but in Northern Ireland kerb-crawling remains, strictly speaking, a legal activity.

If a man is proved to be living with, or to be habitually in the company of, a prostitute, or is proved to have exercised control, direction or influence over the movements of a prostitute in such a manner as to show that he is aiding, abetting or compelling her prostitution, the burden of proof is then on him to show that he was not knowingly living on the earnings of prostitution (s. 1(3) of the Vagrancy Act 1898). The Criminal Law Amendment Act 1912 extended the scope of the earlier Act by permitting females to be convicted of aiding, abetting or compelling another woman's prostitution. Article 8 of the Homosexual Offences (NI) Order 1982 specifically criminalises men or women who live on the earnings of male prostitution, allowing a maximum penalty of seven years' imprisonment to be imposed.

The Criminal Law Amendment Act 1885 creates further offences in this area:

- section 2 makes it an offence to procure or attempt to procure any female to become a common prostitute and by section 3 the use of intimidation, fraud or drugs for these purposes is specifically criminalised;
- section 6 prohibits any person who is the owner, occupier or manager of premises from permitting "defilement" of girls under 17 on those premises;
- section 7 outlaws the abduction of women under 18 for the purpose of enabling them to have unlawful sexual intercourse with any man;
- section 8 makes it an offence for a person to detain any woman against her will in any premises so that she can have unlawful sexual intercourse with any man.

All of these offences under the 1885 Act carry a maximum prison sentence of two years. The offence under section 2 is one for which the police can arrest without a warrant.

Two more provisions affecting children should be noted here:

- Section 21 of the Children and Young Persons Act (NI) 1968 makes it an offence for any person who has the custody or care of a female under 17 to cause or encourage the commission of unlawful sexual intercourse with her or the commission of an indecent assault upon her. It can be enough if the accused person (who may be a man or a woman) has knowingly allowed the girl to consort with any person of known immoral character. The maximum penalty is two years' imprisonment.

- Section 23 of the 1968 Act makes it a crime punishable with six months' imprisonment and an unlimited fine to allow any child of at least four years of age to reside in or to frequent a brothel.

Indecency

There are some offences relating to sex which are designed to protect not particular victims but the general public. According to a leading legal textbook, under the ordinary common law (*i.e.* the law laid down by judges), "in general all open lewdness, grossly scandalous behaviour, and whatever openly outrages decency or is offensive and disgusting, or is injurious to public morals by tending to corrupt the mind and destroy the love of decency, morality and good order, is an offence indictable at common law" (Archbold, 1996 ed, page 2/369). It seems that the offence can be committed only in a public place (so that at least one other person may see it). In theory, there is no limit to the penalty that can be imposed but it must obviously be proportionate to the outrageousness of the act. Merely leaving notes in public places for young boys is not by itself indecent (*R v Rowley*, 1991), but exhibiting in a commercial art gallery earrings made out of human foetuses is (*R v Gibson*, 1990).

The judges have not yet confirmed that two or more persons can be convicted of conspiring to outrage public decency but they have said that there is an offence known as conspiracy to corrupt public morals (see *Knuller v DPP*, 1972). Another common law offence is that of exposing one's naked body in public. Very few prosecutions are brought these days for such a crime, though in theory "streaking", "mooning" and sun-bathing in the nude would qualify. A more common type of proceeding is the one brought under section 4(d) of the Vagrancy Act 1824 - extended to what is now Northern Ireland in 1871. This says that every man who wilfully, openly, lewdly and obscenely exposes his penis with intent to insult any female (*i.e.* a "flasher") is to be deemed "a rogue and vagabond". He can be sent to prison by a magistrate for up to three months.

District councils in Northern Ireland may make bylaws regulating certain acts of indecency and, except in Derry and Belfast, section 72 of the Towns Improvement (Ireland) Act 1854 provides that every person who commits any act contrary to public decency shall be liable to a fine not exceeding £200. More generally, it is an offence under section 9(1) of the Criminal Justice (Miscellaneous Provisions) Act (NI) 1968 - as amended by the Public Order (NI) Order 1987 - to behave indecently in any street, road, highway, other public place, any place to which the public have access, or any premises where intoxicating liquor is sold.

Homosexuality

Prior to the introduction of the Homosexual Offences (NI) Order 1982, acts of male homosexuality were illegal in Northern Ireland. Even the distribution of literature about homosexuality, or the provision of counselling, were criminalised through being labelled incitement or aiding and abetting. Although the law in England and Wales was altered by the Sexual Offences Act 1967, it was only after a judgment of the European Court of Human Rights in 1981 (*Dudgeon v UK*) that the government changed the law for Northern Ireland. Article 3 of the 1982 Order provides that it shall not be an offence for a man to commit buggery or gross indecency with another man provided that the act is done in private, that the two men consent and that they are each at least 21 years of age. By the Criminal Justice and Public Order Act 1994 this age limitation was brought down to 18 (s.145), and following a concession made by the UK government in a case before the European Commission of Human Rights (*Sutherland v UK*, 1997) there is to be a free vote in Parliament on reducing the age limit still further to 16. But these laws do not alter some well-established principles - such as that a person under 14 cannot be convicted of buggery, and that homosexuality between members of the armed forces, or between merchant seamen, is unlawful.

It remains an offence for a man to procure another man to commit a homosexual act with a third man, but it is not an offence for a man to procure the commission with himself by another man of such an act. Persistent public solicitation, however, is still outlawed by the Vagrancy Act 1898 - unless a magistrate or a jury were to hold that homosexuality is not an "immoral purpose", which in Northern Ireland is unlikely. A judge or jury is also entitled to hold that homosexual advances by one man on another are good grounds for the defence of provocation if the latter loses his self-control and kills the first man (the so-called "Portsmouth" defence).

The 1982 Order (as later amended) also revised the maximum sentences which may be imposed for illegal homosexual acts. If the intercourse is with a boy under 16, the maximum penalty is life imprisonment. If with a man 16 or over, but who did not consent, it is 10 years. If with a man 16 or over but under 21 who consented (and presuming the accused is over 21), it is five years. For other situations the maximum is two years' imprisonment.

There is no law which specifically prohibits lesbianism, certainly not if it is carried out by consenting adults. But the offence of indecent assault may be committed if one of the women involved has not properly given her consent.

The age of consent and responsibility

It has already been pointed out that, as far as the right to consent to sexual intercourse is concerned, the age limit for females in Northern Ireland is 17, whereas in England it is 16. There is no age limit for males, but a male under 18 cannot lawfully consent to any homosexual act. Once a person has reached the age of 16, he or she can consent to any surgical, medical or dental treatment without needing to obtain the agreement of his or her parents or guardian (Age of Majority Act (NI) 1969, s.4). It appears, moreover, that even a child who is under 16 can consent to such treatment if it is clear that he or she fully understands the nature of the treatment being proposed. This means that it is possible for girls under 16 to be prescribed contraceptive treatment, even though it is unlawful for a male to have sexual intercourse with a girl who is under 17 (see the *Gillick* case, 1985).

A person can get married at the age of 16 if the consent of his or her parents or guardians is obtained, though even when such consent is absent the marriage will still usually be valid in the eyes of the law. Once a person reaches 18, no consents at all are required.

As regards responsibility under the criminal law, in Northern Ireland a boy under 14 cannot be convicted of rape or of assault with intent to commit rape. No child who is over 9 and under 14 can be charged with any crime unless the prosecution can prove that he or she knew that what was being done was wrong (although the present government proposes to change this rule). In law, a "child" is a person who is aged 13 or less and a "young person" is someone aged 14 to 16; special rules have been laid down for processing such youngsters through the criminal courts, with "juvenile courts" (soon to be called youth courts) being set up to deal with most minor offences (see Chapter 17). There is a conclusive presumption in law that no child under the age of 10 can be guilty of any criminal offence (Children and Young Persons Act (NI) 1968, s. 69). When a youth court is exercising powers in welfare cases it is to be called a family proceedings court (Children (NI) Order 1995, art.164(4)).

Chapter 17

Children's Rights

Anne McKeown

This chapter deals with the rights of children to care and justice. Further information on the rights of children in other contexts is provided in Chapters 5, 16, and 18. The international standards most relevant to this chapter are the United Nations' Convention on the Rights of the Child 1989 (UNCRC), the United Nations' Standard Minimum Rules for the Administration of Juvenile Justice 1985 (known as the Beijing Rules) and the United Nations' Guidelines for the Prevention of Juvenile Delinquency (the "Riyadh" Guidelines) 1990.

The Children (NI) Order 1995

The general principles of the UNCRC are substantially reflected in the Children (NI) Order 1995 (the Order), the main legislation relating to the care of children in Northern Ireland. Brought into force in November 1996, the Order shifts the balance of rights and responsibilities between children, parents and social workers, in favour of partnership with parents and the participation of children in decision- making. It mirrors the Children Act 1989 in England and Wales. Judicial interpretations of that Act can be expected to be highly persuasive in Northern Ireland. The Department of Health and Social Services (DHSS, or the Department) has overall responsibility for implementing crucial aspects of the Order. There are four Health and Social Services Boards, each of which is responsible to the Department for services to children within its area.

The Health and Personal Social Services (NI) Order 1991, as amended in 1994, enabled the establishment of HSS Trusts. These are independent charitable companies limited by guarantee and the legislation allows them to undertake the statutory child care functions which are the responsibility of Boards. Boards purchase services from the Trusts and may stipulate conditions, but Trusts are entitled and expected to develop their own plans and priorities. In practice it is the Trusts which deliver all services to children. Although there is a local Trust delivering such services in every area of Northern Ireland, Boards may also purchase services from other sources.

Article 154 of the Order allows the DHSS to "conduct or promote research or investigations into any matter connected with the functions under this Order of the Department (and) authorities". Such research could reasonably be expected to inform the establishment, monitoring and review of policies within Board areas and the remedial action required to rectify any discrepancies which may arise.

Children in need

The Order extends the powers of Boards to prevent children being admitted to care and to support families which are caring for children "in need". Article 17 defines a child as "in need" if:

- he or she is unlikely to achieve or maintain a reasonable standard of health or development without the provision of services;
- his or her health or development is likely to be significantly impaired or further impaired, without the provision of such services; or
- he or she is disabled.

This definition is open to variable interpretation, particularly in relation to "a reasonable standard of health or development". Elsewhere in the Order the test of "significant harm" requires the comparison of a child's health or development with "that which could reasonably be expected of a similar child" (art.50(3)). If such comparisons were used to distinguish those "in need", this could exclude from the "in need" category children who are disadvantaged because of poverty, culture, ethnicity or lack of resources in a particular area. The Department and the Boards have agreed "operational indicators" of children in need but these are broad illustrative categories and are not definitive.

Duties of Boards in respect of children in need

Article 18 of the Order provides that:

It shall be the general duty of every authority...to safeguard and promote the welfare of children within its area who are in need, and...to promote the upbringing of such children by their families, by providing a range and level of personal social services appropriate to those children's needs.

Services may be provided to the child in need, his or her family, or any member of the family, "if the service is provided with a view to safeguarding and promoting the child's welfare" (art.18(3)). While assistance may be unconditional, authorities may charge for services, having regard to a family's ability to pay. People in receipt of income support, family credit or disability working allowance are exempt from such charges (art.18(9)). Services provided may include "giving assistance in kind or, in exceptional circumstances, in cash" (art.18(6)). This allows Boards (through Trusts) to provide emergency assistance to families. Items such as food, or the temporary loan of blankets and cookers, may be provided in conditions of fire, flood or social upheaval, or when necessary to prevent the need for children to be separated from their families and accommodated by the authority. The provision is not used in circumstances where an application for social security benefits, loans or grants would be appropriate.

To enable Boards to carry out their functions, specific powers and duties are set out in Schedule 2 of the Order. These include duties to take reasonable steps to identify the extent to which there are children in need within the authority's area, to publish information on services and to ensure this is received by those who might benefit from it. The authority must maintain a register of disabled children and provide services enabling them to lead lives which are as normal as possible. Services should prevent the neglect and abuse of children and authorities should take steps to reduce the need to bring criminal or care proceedings in relation to children. Advice, guidance, counselling and occupational, social, cultural or recreational activities may be provided through family centres or elsewhere. When providing day care facilities and encouraging people to act as foster parents, authorities should consider the racial groups to which children belong. In several instances, the Board must provide such services only to the extent it considers appropriate.

Day care, childminding and other services

Day care is defined (art.19(1)) as "any form of care or supervised activity provided for children during the day." Authorities *must* provide day care for children "in need" aged five or under who are not yet attending schools, and they *may* provide it for other such children not deemed "in need". Boards (through Trusts) are empowered to provide training, advice, guidance and counselling for day care workers, but are not obliged to do so (art.19(4)).

Authorities *must* provide care and supervised activities outside school hours and during school holidays for school children "in need" and *may* provide such facilities for any school child. Provision should take account of facilities maintained by others, including district councils or education and library boards.

The range of services provided by Trusts can include day nurseries, playgroups, out of school clubs, holiday schemes, parent and toddler groups, toy libraries, drop-in centres and play-buses. They may also resource community, voluntary and church schemes, such as parents' self-help groups. Bodies whose help is requested, such as education and library boards, are obliged to comply with the request if this is compatible with their own statutory duties. A Board, in conjunction with the appropriate district council and education and library boards, must review the total provision of day care, childminding and other services at least once every three years (art. 20).

Registration of childminding and day care services

Both childminders and persons wishing to provide day care must first register with the relevant Trust (art.118). This register is open to the public.

Schools, hospitals, children's homes and nursing homes are exempt from definitions of day care and childminding and are not required to register as such. Premises where day care is provided on less than six days in any year are also exempt from registration but the person providing care must still notify the relevant Trust in writing before the first occasion when the premises are to be used (art.121).

Article 119 defines a childminder as a person who looks after children under 12 years of age for reward, for more than two hours in any day. Exemptions from this definition include parents, relatives, people with parental responsibility, foster parents and nannies.

A person may be disqualified from being registered to provide childminding or day care services, because, for example, he or she has been convicted of a prescribed (e.g. violent or sexual) offence. No one disqualified from being registered can be employed, or have a financial or management interest, in the provision of day care without disclosing the disqualification to the authority and obtaining its written authorisation (art.122). A Board may refuse to register an applicant if that person or any person residing on the premises or employed or likely to be employed on the premises is not "fit to look after" or "be in the proximity of" children under the age of 12 (art.124).

Boards may impose such reasonable requirements on child- minders (art.125) and persons providing day care for young children (art.126) as they consider appropriate. Currently there is no requirement that such persons hold a relevant child care qualification. The conditions and requirements which do apply regarding maintenance of premises, food hygiene and so on are set out in the Children (NI) Order Regulations and Guidance, Volume 2. One set of Regulations exempts certain supervised activities from the requirement to register. These include "uniformed organisations and religious activities for children, leisure and recreational activities, extra-curricular activities occurring mainly in schools, activities designed to enhance a child's skills and attainments including dancing, sports related activities and education tuition".

Staff and volunteers

The DHSS has issued "Our Duty to Care", a set of guidelines on the recruitment, training and selection of all staff or volunteers who work with children. This followed a Social Services Inspectorate investigation, commissioned in November 1992, into the case of Martin Huston, a volunteer convicted of a series of sexual offences against children.

The DHSS has also extended the remit and use of the Pre-employment Consultancy Service (PECS), which had previously been established following the Kincora sex abuse scandal. PECS provides a vetting service said to "complement" standard recruitment procedures by giving prospective employers access to information thought to have a bearing on prospective employees' or volunteers' suitability. These checks are available to any organisation whenever the post (paid or unpaid) involves substantial access to children and the organisation's recruitment and selection procedures comply with the principles set out in "Our Duty to Care". The Children's Homes Regulations (NI) 1996 oblige certain childcare employers to notify the DHSS of any conduct suggesting that a person may not be suitable to work with children.

Any person aged 10 years or over may be vetted through PECS. The following information is provided:

- RUC details of convictions, cautions, and bindovers,
- names of people reported to the Health and Social Services Management Executive and believed to be a risk to children or thought to have abused them, and
- information drawn up by the Department for Education and Employment of people who are legally barred from working in schools - known as list 99.

As, this information can be exchanged, as long as it is accurate, because there is no right of privacy in Northern Ireland. While international standards provide that a person should have the right not to have damaging information unreasonably or arbitrarily distributed, the need to protect others can justify interference with this right. The best interests of the child must always be a primary consideration (UNCRC, art. 3).

There is uncertainty, however, regarding the standard of proof required for referrals to the DHSS of names thought to be a risk to children. Currently, appeals against names being added to the PECS list are made to the DHSS itself. Complaints regarding the maladministration of the process can be made in the normal way to the Ombudsman; complaints regarding the reasonableness of decisions can be judicially reviewed (see Chapter 2).

Investigation of abuse and neglect

Many professionals can be involved in the protection of children – social workers (*e.g.* in Trusts and in the NSPCC) the police, the probation service, medical practitioners, health visitors, nursing staff and teachers. Area Child Protection Committees have been established at Board level to monitor and review the child protection policies of the relevant agencies and oversee the work of Child Protection Panels (CPP), which operate at Trust level. The CPP's role is to implement policy and to facilitate multidisciplinary working to prevent, investigate and treat child abuse. In practice, both social workers and the police will have the key roles in dealing with more serious allegations of child abuse and neglect. The police will be concerned to investigate whether any offence has been committed, while the social workers will focus on the child's welfare and the family's capacity to provide care.

When a child discloses abuse to any professional, that person must report it immediately. Failure to do so may result in disciplinary action or, with the permission of the DPP, the person may be prosecuted for failure to report a crime (Criminal Law Act (NI) 1967, s.5). In circumstances where a Trust has reasonable cause to suspect that a child "is suffering or is likely to suffer significant harm", it has a duty to investigate (1995 Order, art.66). An assessment of the needs of the child and family should be undertaken. Where social workers have concerns about a child's welfare, they should first seek the voluntary co-operation of parents in making an assessment, and may provide services to help the family care for the child. "Harm" is defined as ill-treatment or impairment of health or development, compared with that which could reasonably be expected of a similar child (1995 Order, art. 50(3)). Health is defined as physical or mental health, and development as physical, intellectual, emotional, social or behavioural development. Ill-treatment includes forms which are not physical.

If there is an allegation that child abuse has occurred, a strategy discussion will normally be held between social workers and police within 24 hours of receiving the referral or discovering the facts. The "Protocol for Joint Investigation by Social Workers and Police Officers of Alleged and Suspected Cases of Child Abuse" will govern the investigation process. This can include joint interviews, the purpose of which is to make the investigation less distressing for the child. The RUC have established special Child Abuse and Rape Enquiry (CARE) Units to deal with cases of child abuse and sexual offences (see also Chapter 16).

Volume 6 of the 1995 Order's Guidance and Regulations states that within 15 days of a formal (social work) investigation being initiated, a child protection case conference should be held to decide whether there is sufficient concern to place the child's name on the Child Protection Register. While the Guidance says that information is shared on a need to know basis, all agencies in contact with the child may, initially, be invited to attend. If it is decided to place the child's name on the Register the case will be reviewed in six months' time. Family members, including the alleged abuser and the child under discussion, may also be invited to attend the whole or part of these case conferences. If the alleged abuser is not heard the case conference may be held to have acted unfairly and in breach of natural justice (*R v Norfolk County Council, ex parte M*, 1989). Decisions as to who attends are taken by the professionals and the child has no ability to prevent, delay or restrict the exchange of information between the agencies. On registration of a child, the case conference should set a time limit for the completion of a comprehensive assessment and an initial child protection plan. The child protection plan is a written agreement drawn up with parents and carers. It outlines the roles and expectations of agencies and carers with regard to the child's care and protection. A child may be "de-registered" by a child protection case conference if it is believed that circumstances have changed significantly and the child is no longer at risk. Chapter 11 describes any person's right of access to information held about him or her. In child care cases, a person's right to information may be restricted to prevent information being disclosed which could place the child at risk (*Re M (A Minor) (Disclosure of Material)*, 1990).

The child's evidence

If a child is interviewed jointly by a police officer from the CARE unit and a social worker, consideration will be given to whether he or she should have a parent, relative or friend present. The need for medical examination and for video recording of interviews will also be considered. Such recordings may be used in either civil or criminal court proceedings. There is no restriction under the hearsay rule on the admissibility of videos in family proceedings. The Children's Evidence (NI) Order 1995 has inserted new provisions into the Police and Criminal Evidence (NI) Order 1989 which allow a video recording of an interview with a child to be used as the child's evidence-in-chief in criminal proceedings, subject to certain conditions. A Memorandum of Good Practice has been issued by the Northern Ireland Office on how the video recording of these interviews should be conducted. This covers technical issues as well as legal and other matters, including the importance of keeping the child informed and gaining the child's agreement to the video recording.

The Children's Evidence (NI) Order 1995 allows for a notice of transfer to be issued by the DPP if satisfied that there is enough evidence to commit a defendant to trial. This enables the case to be heard by the Crown Court without a preliminary hearing in a magistrates' court. There is no appeal against a notice of transfer. At trial, the child's evidence and/or cross-examination may be through a television link so that the child does not have to see the alleged abuser while giving evidence. Currently, if a child is to be compensated for injuries caused, he or she must make application within three years of his or her eightecnth birthday (Criminal Injuries (Compensation) (NI) Order 1988, art. 9).

The employment of children

The employment of children is now mainly regulated by articles 133-148 of the Children (NI) Order 1995. In general, no child under the age of 13 can be employed at all, and no child who is 13 or older can work before 7.00 am or after 7.00 pm or for more than two hours on any one school-day (art.135). Nor can a child be employed in street-trading or in any occupation likely to be injurious to his or her health or education. But children *can* be licensed by an education and library board to take part in a public performance or (if 13 or older) to train for performances even of a dangerous nature.

An officer of an education and library board, or a police officer, can be granted a warrant to enter premises to make inquiries concerning a child if there is reasonable cause to believe the regulations are being contravened. Any person employing a child in contravention of the law (or any parent allowing it) can be fined up to £1,000, while any child engaged in street-trading can be fined up to £200 (art.148).

Children and the civil courts

Article 164(4) of the Children (NI) Order 1995 provides that a juvenile court "sitting for the purpose of exercising any jurisdiction covered by or under (the) Order may be known as a family proceedings court." The Children and Young Persons Act (NI) 1968 continues to apply in respect of the constitution of these courts.

Under the Children (Allocation of Proceedings) Order (NI) 1996, seven family proceedings courts have been established, one in each county court division. It is intended that, by limiting the number of venues, these specialist courts will develop a degree of expertise and experience. Applications will normally begin in the family proceedings court unless:

(a) other proceedings are pending in the High Court or the county court in relation to the child, or,

(b) such other proceedings having commenced, the court has become concerned about a child's welfare and has directed social services to undertake an investigation into a child's circumstances to establish whether it is appropriate to make a care or supervision order (art. 56). In these circumstances that application will be made either to the original court or any other court to which it is allocated by the original court.

Applications may also be transferred from the family proceedings court to a specialist county court (known as a Care Centre) if the proceedings are exceptionally grave, important or complex. Applications may then be transferred from the Care Centre to the High Court if the issues are considered appropriate for determination in the High Court and it would be in the best interests of the child. Any proceedings which have been transferred may be returned to the original court if the transfer criterion no longer applies.

Appeals from a family proceedings court will be to a Care Centre, which for the purposes of the appeal will sit without lay assessors. Where cases have already been transferred to the Care Centre, decisions of that court may be appealed to the High Court, and so on in the normal way.

Court orders and child protection

Child's welfare paramount

Article 3 of the Children (NI) Order 1995 requires a court determining any question relating to a child's upbringing to regard the child's welfare as the "paramount consideration". The article provides the court with what has become known as a "welfare checklist". This includes consideration of the child's ascertainable wishes and feelings, his or her physical, emotional and educational needs, the likely effect on the child of any change in circumstances, his or her age, sex, background and other relevant characteristics, the capacity of the child's parents to meet his or her needs, and any harm the child has suffered or is at risk of suffering. The court must also have "regard to the general principle that any delay in determining the question is likely to prejudice the welfare of the child" (art. 3(2)) and so must "draw up a timetable with a view to determining (any) question without delay" (art.11(1)(a)). The direction that the court "shall not make (any order) unless it considers that to do so would be better for the child than making no order at all" (art. 3(5)) establishes a presumption of non-intervention.

Assessment and protection orders

In some situations social workers will be able to ensure the child's safety by persuading the alleged abuser to leave the home. Schedule 2, paragraph 6 of the 1995 Order empowers the Trusts to provide alternative accommodation for an alleged abuser. Alternatively the "non-accused" parent may apply for a personal protection or exclusion order (see Chapter 16).

Trust and NSPCC social workers (art.49) may apply for a child assessment order (CAO) (art.62) in circumstances where there is insufficient information to be sure that a child is suffering significant harm, but where parents will not co-operate to allow an assessment to be made. Such an order has a maximum duration of seven days and the court directs the type and nature of the assessment to be carried out. A child of sufficient understanding may, however, refuse to undergo any medical, psychiatric or other assessment. The child will remain at home, separated from parents only if necessary to comply with court directions, e.g. for the duration of medical or other interviews.

If a court, hearing an application for a CAO, becomes satisfied that there are grounds to make an emergency protection order (EPO), it must make this order instead. Any person, moreover, may apply directly to the court for an EPO (art. 63). In certain circumstances (*e.g.* at weekends or at night) an EPO may be issued by a resident magistrate or member of the juvenile court panel sitting alone (Sched. 7). The court will make an EPO if satisfied that there is reasonable cause to believe that the child is likely to suffer significant harm if he or she is not removed from the situation (*e.g.* the family home) or does not remain in the situation (*e.g.* in hospital recovering from an injury). EPOs last for up to eight days and can be extended for a further seven days. Certain people, including the child and his or her parents, may apply for the discharge of an EPO after a period of 72 hours (art. 64), but no appeal can be made against court decisions to make, extend or discharge an EPO (*Essex County Council v F*, 1993). An EPO grants parental responsibility to the applicant whilst it is in force. This allows the applicant to take whatever action is necessary to safeguard the child's welfare and comply with DHSS requirements.

In practice it will usually be Trust or NSPCC social workers who apply for EPOs. Although such orders allow for the removal of a child from the family home, the applicant is still required to ensure the child has reasonable contact with parents, anyone else who has parental responsibility for him or her, and others, such as people he or she was living with before the order was made. However, the court may restrict such contact if it considers this appropriate (art. 63(6)) and may direct that medical, psychiatric and other assessments be made, subject to the right of a child of sufficient understanding to refuse to submit to examination or assessment. The police have powers to take children into police protection for up to 72 hours where a child might otherwise suffer significant harm (art. 65). They may also assist in searching premises for a child in need of emergency protection, if the court issues a warrant to this effect (art. 67).

If there continue to be concerns regarding children subject to CAOs, EPOs or police protection then application may be made by the Trust or NSPCC for a care or supervision order (see below). Alternatively, where concerns about a child's health or development relate to specific matters rather than the parents' general capacity to provide care or control, social workers may seek leave of the court to apply for an article 8 order, if the child is under 16 years. Article 8 prohibits the making of residence or contact orders in favour of a Trust but a "specific issue order" or a "prohibited steps order" can be obtained (see also Chapter 16). A specific issue order could be made if, for example, a child needs treatment, such as a blood transfusion, where parents refuse to consent or cannot be contacted. A prohibited steps order can be made to prevent parents from doing something which could prejudice the child's health or development. Even if social workers apply for a care or supervision order, the court has power to make an article 8 order of its own motion (art.10(1)(b)) if it believes that this would be the most appropriate course of action.

Care and supervision orders

Where a Trust or the NSPCC apply to the court for a care or supervision order, the court has power to make either order irrespective of the preferred option of the applicant (art.50(6)). Decisions to make either order may be made only if the court is satisfied that the child is suffering or likely to suffer significant harm which is attributable to a lack of parental care or to the child being beyond parental control (art.50(2)). The harm the child is experiencing must be current or likely to occur in the future. Events which have happened in the past are relevant to the extent that they might influence present or future conduct.

To ensure that the court's decisions are based on the known facts, the rule that parties to litigation may obtain an expert's report which remains privileged unless the party wishes to rely on it may be overridden in children's cases. All relevant reports should be disclosed. This applies to the Trust (*see R v Hampshire County Council, ex parte K*, 1990) and to all other parties in care proceedings (see *Oxfordshire County Council v M*, 1994).

The court may make interim care or supervision orders if satisfied that there are reasonable grounds for believing that the grounds for making a full order exist (art.57(2)). The maximum period of an interim order is, in the first instance, eight weeks. Subsequent orders may be made for maximum periods of four weeks (art.57(4)).

Supervision orders have an effect for a period of one year and may be extended up to three years (Sched. 3, para. 6). The order can include directions as to psychiatric and medical treatment, with the child's consent. The supervisor may require the child to live at a specified place, and to participate in activities. He or she should "advise, assist and befriend the supervised child" (art. 54).

The effect of a care order (art.52) is to give the designated authority parental responsibility for the child, who must be received into its care. The Trust has power to limit the extent to which any person may exercise his or her parental responsibility for the child, if this is reasonable for the purposes of promoting the child's welfare. Children in care should normally be allowed contact with parents, guardians and others with whom they resided prior to the order being made. Trusts can apply to the court for permission to refuse contact with any person (art. 53) and may refuse contact itself in any case, on an emergency basis, provided the refusal does not last for more than seven days. Parties to care proceedings are invited to comment on arrangements for contact before a care order is made.

No care or supervision order may be made with respect to a child who has reached the age of 17 (or 16, in the case of a child who is married (art. 50(4)). Any care or supervision order may be discharged by the court on application of the child or person who has parental responsibility for him or her or the authority designated by the order (art. 58). Where a care order is discharged the court has power to substitute a supervision order, if it wishes to do so.

Guardians *ad litem*

In almost all of the above cases, the court will appoint a guardian *ad litem* who will be "under a duty to safeguard the interests of the child" (art. 60). To ensure the independence of the guardian *ad litem*, a new agency has been established known as the Guardian Ad Litem Agency, and it has a panel of guardians who are qualified, experienced social workers. Once appointed, a guardian's role is to investigate all the circumstances of the case and make a report to the court to assist it to consider the child's welfare and to take decisions in the best interests of the child. The guardian will consult parents and others as necessary. He or she will also examine the Trust plans for the child and may make recommendations in respect of these. He or she has a right of access to and copies of any records relevant to the Trust or NSPCC's contact with the child and may present any part of any record as evidence in court (art. 61). Where the guardian believes that acquiescing to the child's wishes is not in his or her best interests, both the child's view and the guardian's should be reported to the court.

The guardian will appoint a solicitor to act for the child if the court has not already done so and where the child is not of sufficient understanding the guardian will instruct the solicitor on the child's behalf. Article 60 empowers the court to appoint a solicitor for any child whether or not a guardian *ad litem* is appointed, provided a child of sufficient understanding wishes to instruct a solicitor and/or this appears to the court to be in the child's best interests. Solicitors should act on the instructions of a child of sufficient understanding in the normal way. There is no definition in the Order of "sufficient understanding". The principle has, however, been tested in relation to medical decisions. A child of 16 years can consent to medical or other treatment without the consent of a parent or guardian (Age of Majority Act (NI) 1969, s.4). A younger child may do so if he or she fully understands the nature and implications of the proposed treatment (*Gillick* v *West Norfolk and Wisbech AHA, 1985*). However, a younger child who refuses life-saving treatment may be given such treatment if the High Court in its inherent jurisdiction or anyone with parental responsibility for the child consents to it (*In re W, 1992*).

Accommodation for children

A Trust *must* provide accommodation for children in need whenever the person caring for them is prevented from doing so for whatever reason (art. 21(1)(c)) and *may* provide accommodation for any child if it considers that this would safeguard or promote his or her welfare. The Trust should ascertain the child's views, if he or she is able to express them. The Trust does not acquire parental responsibility by providing accommodation. While the child's daily care has been delegated to the Trust (art. 5(8)), it cannot take major decisions or continue to care for the child without the consent of a person with parental responsibility. In emergencies, where such persons cannot be contacted or do not consent, *e.g.* to medical treatment, the Trust may seek leave to apply for an article 8 order (see Chapter 16).

Any child found lost or abandoned may also be provided with accommodation (art. 21(1)(b)), and so an emergency protection order need not be acquired unless the child is also believed to be at risk of significant harm. A person who has reached the age of 16, but is under 21, may be accommodated by a Trust if his or her welfare "is likely to be seriously prejudiced if it does not provide" such accommodation (art. 21(3)). When a person of this age group agrees to be accommodated, the Trust need not discharge him or her at the request of a person with parental responsibility (art. 22(5)).

Children's homes

The Children (NI) Order Regulations and Guidance, volume 4 "Residential Care", govern the care of children admitted to Trust, voluntary or privately run children's homes. All voluntary and privately run homes must be registered. These children's homes, and those run by Trusts, will be inspected by officers of the Board's Registration and Inspection Unit. Registration of voluntary or privately run children's homes may be subject to such conditions as the authority thinks fit (arts. 81 and 97) and will be reviewed annually (arts. 86 and 102). Appeals against decisions of the authority on matters relating to registration can be made to a Registered Homes Tribunal. A person who has been disqualified from fostering a child privately cannot be involved in the management of, or employed in, or have a financial interest in, a voluntary or privately run home without disclosing this to the Trust and obtaining its written permission to do so (arts. 78 and 94).

The Guidance requires children's homes to be adequately staffed to meet the aims and objectives of the Unit, having regard to the age, sex and characteristics of the children. No child should be placed in a home before other options such as family placements are considered and all children admitted to care must have a written care plan. Care planning should aim to promote the child's welfare in consultation with the child and family, having regard to their wishes and feelings. Each child's case should be reviewed within two weeks of the child being admitted to care, reviewed again not more than three months later and thereafter every six months (Review of Children's Cases Regulations (NI) 1996, reg. 3). If the child is accommodated for only short periods (not more than four weeks in any single period or more than 90 days in any 12 month period) then the review will take place within 3 months of the beginning of the first short period, and six monthly thereafter while the case continues.

Reviews take the form of meetings which the child, the family and relevant professionals are invited to attend. Children can make their views known in writing, on tape or by other means. A child's religious, linguistic, cultural and ethnic background must be taken into account in making plans for the child to meet his or her needs.

In maintaining good order and discipline, staff should promote the participation of children in decision-making and take account of the child's age, understanding and competence. The Guidance states that formal (non physical) sanctions should be used sparingly and, if administered, recorded in a separate log book. Sanctions specifically excluded by the regulations include corporal punishment, deprivation of food and drink, restriction or refusal of visits or communications, requiring a child to wear distinctive or inappropriate clothing, withholding medication, intentional deprivation of sleep, and intimate physical searches. Staff may refuse a child permission to go out, or require a child to pay for or contribute to the repair or replacement of any items stolen or damaged.

Holding a child is permitted. For example, leading a child away from destructive or disruptive behaviour by the hand, arm or by means of an arm around his or her shoulder. Holding is distinguished from physical restraint by the degree of force used. Holding would discourage, restraint would prevent an action. Physical restraint is permitted by the Children's Homes Regulations (NI) 1996 (reg. 8) to the extent that it is "action immediately necessary to prevent injury to any person or serious damage to property" (see also Criminal Law Act (NI) 1967, s. 3 regarding use of reasonable force). Afterwards the child should be counselled on why restraint was necessary and be given an opportunity to put his or her side of the story. The residential social worker's line manager should discuss the incident with him or her within 24 hours and a full report should be prepared within 48 hours. The child should also be interviewed by someone not directly connected to the home in question, for example the field social worker. The frequency with which physical control is used should be monitored.

Responsible authorities (Trusts, voluntary organisations, and privately run children's homes) are required to have a procedure for considering representations, including complaints, about children's services and to publicise these. The complainant can be the child, a person with parental responsibility or any person considered to have sufficient interest in the welfare of the child. The complaint may be written or oral. Where problems are unresolved, the complaints procedure should be initiated, an investigation should take place and the complainant should be notified of the outcome of the investigation.

Secure accommodation

Article 44 of the 1995 Order and the Children (Secure Accommodation) Regulations (NI) 1996 provide the statutory framework for the restriction of the liberty of children in care.

A child should not be kept in secure accommodation unless he or she "has a history of absconding and is likely to abscond from any other...accommodation" and, if absconding, "is likely to suffer significant harm" or to injure him or herself or other persons if kept in other accommodation (art. 44). A child should not continue to have his or her liberty restricted once the criteria cease to apply. The protection of others is, however, considered a valid reason for the continued use of secure accommodation. (art. 26 (5) and *In re M (A Minor)(Secure Accommodation Order)*, 1995).

No child under the age of 13 years may be placed in secure accommodation without the prior approval of the DHSS. Before seeking such approval, Trusts should first discuss the case with the Social Services Inspectorate. Regulation 6 sets a maximum period of 72 hours, either consecutively or in aggregate in any period of 28 days, for the restriction of a child's liberty without court authority, unless the 72 hour period expires late on a Saturday, a Sunday or public holiday. In this instance the period will be treated as if it did not expire until 12 noon on the next working day. The maximum period a court may authorise a child to be kept in secure accommodation is three months in the first instance, although on subsequent applications the court may authorise secure accommodation for six months at a time.

No court may exercise its powers to restrict a child's liberty unless the child is legally represented in court, except where a child who has been informed of the right to legal aid, and given the opportunity to do so, has refused or failed to apply (art. 44(7)). A guardian *ad litem* should be appointed, unless the court does not consider this necessary to protect the welfare of the child. Article 166 makes provision for appeals against court decisions to authorise or refuse to authorise restriction of a child's liberty. The Trust must also appoint three persons to review the placement within one month of its commencement and thereafter at three monthly intervals.

The child's care should also be reviewed in the normal way in accordance with article 45. Trusts providing secure accommodation must keep records of occasions when the child is locked up alone in any room other than during usual bedtime hours. Secure accommodation is inspected by the Board's Registration and Inspection Unit and the DHSS oversees these Units through the Social Services Inspectorate.

Aftercare, advice and assistance

Article 35 of the 1995 Order empowers Trusts to provide advice and assistance to persons who were in various forms of care at any time after reaching their sixteenth birthday and who are still under 21 years. A young person who qualifies for assistance may have been looked after by a Trust, a voluntary organisation, or a registered children's home. Young people who were accommodated for a consecutive period of at least three months by an education and library board, a residential care home, a hospital, any other prescribed accommodation or who were privately fostered also qualify, even if the period of three months began before the child reached the age of 16 (art.35 (3)). The Trust *must* provide assistance to young people if they were looked after by the Trust or a voluntary organisation and *may* provide it if the young people were accommodated in the other circumstances described (art.35(4)). The conditions are that the young person must ask the Trust for help of a kind it can give. The Trust must be satisfied that the person needs such help and that the agency or person previously caring for him or her cannot give it. Assistance can be in kind or, in exceptional circumstances, cash.

The Trust can make payments and give grants in relation to the young person's employment and education. It can continue to make a contribution or grant for a course of education or training even if the person reaches the age of 21 before the course is completed. Young people have a right to make complaints in relation to the aftercare provided to them (art.37).

While voluntary organisations and privately run homes do not have a statutory duty to provide after care, they must prepare the young person for the time when he or she ceases to be accommodated by them (arts. 76 (1)(c) and 92 (1)(c) respectively).

Children with a disability

All of the provisions already mentioned in this chapter apply to disabled children as they do to others and should be suitable to their needs. A child is defined as disabled if he or she is "blind, deaf, or dumb or suffering from mental disorder of any kind or substantially and permanently handicapped by illness, injury or congenital deformity or such other disability as may be prescribed" (art.2(2): see Mental Health (NI) Order 1986, art. 3 for the definition of mental disorder). While Trusts must keep a register of disabled children, this is designed to help planning and monitoring services. Parents do not have to agree to their child being registered and provision of services is not dependent upon it. Publications relating to services for children with a disability should take account of the needs of people with communication difficulties.

Some children with a disability will have their needs assessed under the Chronically Sick and Disabled Persons (NI) Act 1978, the Education and Libraries (NI) Order 1986, the Disabled Persons (NI) Act 1989 or other legislation, and Trusts need not make a separate assessment to meet their obligations under the 1995 Order.

Trusts have a duty to ensure that the welfare of children being provided with accommodation in a hospital (art.174), a school (art. 176), private hospital, residential care or nursing home (art. 175) or by an education and library board (art.177) is being adequately safeguarded and promoted. Trusts should be notified if the child has been or is intended to be accommodated in such facilities for a period of at least three months.

Article 175 empowers a person authorised by the Trust to enter any residential care home, nursing home or private hospital within the Trust's area for the purpose of ensuring that the child's welfare is safeguarded. There are no such powers in respect of education and library board establishments.

Children and criminal justice

The main statute governing the treatment of juveniles in the criminal justice system is the Children and Young Persons Act (NI) 1968 (CYPA, or the Act). The criminal law relating to children is, however, undergoing considerable change at present. The Criminal Justice (NI) Order 1996 (CJO), which applies to children as well as adults, is expected to be fully implemented during 1998 and this chapter has been written as if the Order is current law. Furthermore, a new proposal has been issued specifically aimed at young people: the Criminal Justice (Children) (NI) Order (CJCO). This will largely replace the Children and Young Persons Act and reference will be made where appropriate to the changes which it proposes.

The age of criminal responsibility is 10 years. The 1968 Act distinguishes between a child (a person under the age of 14) and a young person (a person who is 14, 15 or 16) (s.180). In the proposed CJCO a child will mean "a person who is under the age of 18". Specific references to the 1968 Act, therefore, relate to children under 17, while references to the proposal relate to children under 18.

The juvenile court

Cases in Northern Ireland's juvenile courts are heard by a panel of three members, one of whom must be female. The panel consists of two lay members and a legally qualified resident magistrate as chairperson. The two lay members must attend an approved training course. They are selected from lists drawn up by the Lord Chancellor (whose functions are carried out by the Northern Ireland Court Service). Decisions are taken by a majority of the members.

Section 48 of the CYPA 1968 obliges the court to "have regard to the welfare" of children brought before it. This is a lower standard than that set for family proceedings (see page 298). The proposed CJCO includes an additional principle that courts should have regard to the fact that "any delay in dealing with the child is likely to prejudice the child's welfare". The proposal will establish a new youth court (art.27 re-enacts and amends s. 63 of the 1968 Act) which will be composed in the same way as the juvenile court but also deal with 17-year-olds.

Parents do not have party status but they may be required to attend court proceedings and can be given the opportunity to give evidence, call witnesses, or make a statement. Proceedings are in private, with only a limited number of people entitled to attend. It is an offence to publish or broadcast information which identifies or is likely to lead to the identification of a child or young person concerned in court proceedings, unless the Secretary of State dispenses with these restrictions in the interests of justice. The court may direct the exclusion from the court of all those not directly involved in proceedings, if the child's evidence relates to matters of an indecent or immoral nature.

To date, children under the age of 14 have been afforded some limited protection against a finding of guilt by the doctrine of *doli incapax* (the presumption that they do not know right from wrong). The current government is proposing to abolish this presumption.

Arrest and detention

Section 49 of the CYPA 1968 ensures that children are detained separately from adults in police stations and the proposed CJCO says that girls must be under the care of a woman. The powers of the RUC and army to stop, search, arrest, and question children aged 10 and over are described in Chapters 3, 4 and 5. Children are subject to both ordinary and emergency law in virtually the same way as adults. Children aged 14 and over can have negative inferences drawn from their failure to give evidence in court. However, article 58 of the PACE (NI) Order 1989 amends section 52 of the CYPA 1968 to give children in police detention an additional right to have a person responsible for their welfare informed as soon as practicable that they have been arrested and why and where they are detained. Social services and the probation service may also be informed if the child is in care, or a supervision or probation order is in force. Article 10 of the proposed CJCO will re-enact section 52.

Both EPA and PACE Codes of Practice provide that a child should be cautioned and informed of his or her rights in the presence of an appropriate adult. This person may be a parent, guardian, relative, social worker or any responsible person over 18 who is not a police officer or employed by the Police Authority. The role of the appropriate adult is to advise and assist the child, ensure that he or she understands the questions, is fairly treated and that there is no oppression. He or she may consult privately with the child at any time or may contact a solicitor on the child's behalf, but he or she does not have the right to maintain confidentiality if the child gives him or her information which might assist the police. Under the proposed CJCO, 17-year-olds will become entitled to have an appropriate adult present during questioning.

Once there is sufficient evidence to charge the child, questioning should cease. The child will be released on bail if he or she, or his or her parent or guardian, enter into a recognisance (with or without sureties) except if the charge is one of homicide or other grave crime or if the child's release would "defeat the ends of justice". Under the proposed CJCO bail will be refused to a child arrested under warrant, or to a child under 14 arrested without a warrant, only if he or she was arrested for a serious offence or if detention is believed necessary to protect the public.

The court may also grant the defendant bail and bind him or her over to reappear (Magistrates' Courts (NI) Order 1981, art.127) or remand him or her in custody (CYPA, s.51). In exceptional circumstances, children aged 16 and younger may be bailed to their parents but provided with accommodation in a children's home, with the consent of the relevant Trust. Seventeen-year-olds may be accommodated in a bail hostel if the court would otherwise be unwilling to agree to bail. This option has tended to be used only in a limited number of cases. In practice bail hostels are run by voluntary sector organisations such as Extern, Dismas House and Thompson House. They are funded by the Probation Board of Northern Ireland and are also used for other probation clients such as ex-prisoners.

A juvenile may be remanded for the purposes of obtaining further information (CYPA, s.67). The Act requires the juvenile to be brought before the court every five weeks, while the proposed CJCO will require the child to appear before the court every two weeks. Children who are not released on bail may be held in a remand home or Young Offenders' Centre.

Cautioning, diversion and crime prevention

Informal warnings and formal police cautions can be an effective means of avoiding the need to process offenders through the courts. For this reason they are usually a preferred option for both children and parents. A caution is given only on an admission of guilt, possibly without legal advice and may be cited later as evidence of a criminal record. The cautioning system has been criticised by the House of Commons' Select Committee on Home Affairs as operating inconsistently and even arbitrarily. It has recommended that statutory regulations should be introduced to standardise procedures.

The RUC Juvenile Liaison Scheme deals with offenders largely outside the formal criminal justice system. Its purpose is to divert young people away from re-offending. Juvenile Liaison Officers work with probation service, social services, education, and voluntary bodies on Juvenile Liaison "Bureaux" (JLB). Bureaux may make recommendations regarding the appropriateness of any child being given a warning, advice, or an official caution. These recommendations are not binding and prosecutions may proceed if this is believed to be in the public interest. There are currently seven Bureaux, covering 11 police sub-divisions, but it is proposed to extend the coverage throughout Northern Ireland over the next two years. Diversionary and support schemes are being developed to prevent crime and divert children from committing offences. These may be accessed directly, through the above mentioned agencies, and/or via the JLB. Services range from individual counselling to family therapy, domestic violence programmes, anti-drug misuse strategies, Youth Support Schemes (such as the Belfast-based Eastside and Westside Projects), community safety schemes, and the safer streets projects. There have been attempts to tackle sectarian attitudes through the "Fair Play Project" and some pioneering work is beginning through the "New Careers Project", jointly sponsored by the Probation Board of Northern Ireland and the University of Ulster. A number of ex-offenders are training as detached youth workers to work with young people who are at high risk of offending.

Pre-sentencing reports

Magistrates and juvenile courts have power to adjourn a case after a finding of guilt and before sentence for the purpose of "enabling enquiries to be made or of determining the most suitable method of dealing with the case" (Magistrates' Courts (NI) Order 1981, art. 50). A pre-sentence report (PSR), also known as a social enquiry report, regarding the circumstances of any child may be provided by a probation officer or a social worker (Criminal Justice (NI) Order 1996, art. 2). Probation officers are assigned to one or more court districts and have a statutory responsibility to provide reports to the criminal courts if required (Probation Board (NI) Order 1982, art.14A, inserted by Sched. 5 to the Criminal Justice (NI) Order 1996).

Under the CJO 1996, article 9, such reports must be obtained by the court before it makes a probation order (if it is to include special conditions), a community services order, or combination of these two orders, or a supervision order (if it is to include special requirements).

While a court may decide that a PSR is unnecessary, it must give its reasons in open court. Where a PSR is not obtained, an appeal court should obtain one or explain why it is unnecessary. Similarly, a PSR should usually be obtained if a custodial sentence is to be passed. This must always be done in respect of a child under 17, unless the court has information available from a previous report.

PSRs should provide information on the child's home circumstances, physical and mental health, and "character". They will also include an examination of the child's history of offending and should, where possible, identify the causes of the behaviour, the potential for family support, any risk factors and mitigation, and the anticipated impact of the various sentencing options on the child. It is Probation Board policy that PSRs are shared with the defendant and/or the defendant's family before the court hearing, and any recommendations explained. The Criminal Justice (NI) Order 1996, article 34, obliges courts, other than juvenile courts, to give a copy of the probation officer's report to the offender or his or her legal representative. If the offender is under 17 years of age and is not legally represented, a copy of the report must be given to his or her parents or guardian.

Non-custodial disposals

Juvenile and magistrates courts may not use the words "conviction" and "sentence" in relation to children and young people found guilty of an offence. Instead they must talk of a "finding of guilt" and "disposal". The types of non-custodial disposals available include the following.

(a) *Absolute or conditional discharge.* An absolute discharge means that the child is unconditionally released and has no further liability for the offence for which he or she was found guilty. A conditional discharge has the same effect except that the child must commit no further offence for a specified period, not exceeding three years.
Before making either of these orders, the court must be satisfied that it is "inexpedient to inflict punishment", having regard to the nature of the offence and the character of the offender (CJO, art. 4). If a person commits an offence within the period of conditional discharge, the original court or a Crown Court may deal with the offender as if he or she had just been convicted (CJO, art.5). Ancillary orders for costs, compensation, restitution or disqualification from driving may be made with an absolute or conditional discharge. Parents of a child under 14, who is conditionally discharged, may be required to enter into a recognisance for the good behaviour of the child. If the offender is 14 or over, but under the age of 17, either the child or his or her parents may be required to enter into a recognisance (CJO, art. 7). `

(b) *Recognisance or binding over*. This is an undertaking to the court that the offender will be of good behaviour for a specified period and that a specified sum will be paid to the court if he or she breaches that undertaking. The recognisance operates like a suspended fine and is similar in effect to a conditional discharge. The maximum period for which a person may be "bound over" to keep the peace in this way is two years. The court may order the parents of a child under 17 to enter into a recognisance as security for the good behaviour of the child "in addition to or in lieu of any other order" (CYPA, s.76 (2)).

(c) *A fine*. This is a financial penalty on an offender. A court dealing with a juvenile has power to fine his or her parent or guardian. The court must order the fine to be paid by the parents if the offender is under 14 and may do so in any case (CYPA 1968, s.76(1)). A fine may be combined with a period of detention or imprisonment but not with a probation order (CJO, art.11). The ultimate sanction for default is imprisonment.

In the proposed CJCO, article 35 re-anacts and amends section 76 of the 1968 Act to place a duty on the parent or guardian to pay fines imposed on children under 16 and allows the court to impose this in respect of older children. Guardian is defined as any person who has care of the child including Trusts (art.2). Before fixing a fine to be imposed on an offender a court must take account of his or her financial circumstances as well as the seriousness of the offence (CJO, art. 29 and Sched.3). To this end, a financial circumstances order may be made obliging the offender to provide the court with the relevant information (CJO, art.30).

(d) *A probation order*. This order can be made in respect of anyone over the age of criminal responsibility, provided the sentence is not fixed by law (CJO, art.10(1)). It requires the person convicted of an offence to be placed under the supervision of a probation officer for a period of not less than six months, nor more than three years. Its purposes are to secure the rehabilitation of the offender, to prevent or reduce offending behaviour, and to protect the public.

Before making a probation order the court must obtain the consent of offenders aged 14 years or over, having explained in ordinary language the reasons for making the order, the effect of it, and the consequences of any failure to comply with its requirements. The probationer (*i.e.* the offender), the probation officer, and any institution where he or she is required to reside or to attend will be given a copy of the probation order.

Schedule 1 to the CJO 1996 allows additional conditions to be included in a probation order. These are:

- that the probationer reside at a specified place for a specified period;
- that he or she attend such Probation Board approved place as the probation officer may direct, to participate in activities (for not more than 60 days in total);
- that he or she attend a day centre for not more than 60 days;
- that he or she receive medical treatment for a mental condition which requires and is susceptible to treatment. Treatment may be as an in-patient or an out-patient, in a specified place or places, but the nature of the treatment may not be specified in the order; (any one subject to a probation order with treatment conditions may refuse any surgical, electrical or other treatment if it appears reasonable having regard to all the circumstances);
- that he or she receive treatment for alcohol or drug dependency which is believed to have contributed to the offence and which requires and is susceptible to treatment. Treatment may again be as an in-patient or out-patient in a named hospital and be changed with the consent of the probationer and notified in writing to the probation officer.

Amendments to the requirements of a probation order may be made on the application of the probationer or the probation officer to the court. A probation order may not be reduced, but it can be discharged or extended (to the maximum of three years). The court has power to substitute a conditional discharge for the remainder of a probation period when an order has been discharged (CJO, art. 12) (see also Combination Orders and Custody Probation Orders below).

(e) *A community service order* (CSO*).* Anyone aged 16 or over may, with his or her consent, be subject to a CSO for an offence punishable with imprisonment or detention providing the offence is not one for which the punishment is fixed by law. The offender is required to undertake a period of unpaid community work for not less than 40 and not more than 240 hours (art. 13), within 12 months of the making of the order. This period may be extended on application to the court. Where a CSO is made for two or more offences, the hours of work may run concurrently or consecutively, provided that the total hours worked does not exceed the maximum of 240.

(f) *A combination order* (CJO art.15). Offenders aged 16 or over may be subject to a combination order if convicted of an offence punishable with imprisonment or detention (unless punishment is fixed by law). The order comprises a probation order *and* a CSO. In this instance the probation order must be for not less than 12 months and not more than three years. The CSO hours worked must be not less than 40 hours and not more than 100 hours. The reason for giving the order must be stated in court and explained to the offender in ordinary language.

(g) *A supervision order.* Children aged 10 to 13 who are found guilty of an offence punishable in the case of an adult with imprisonment can be made the subject of a supervision order (CYPA, s.74 (1)(c)). The child may be supervised by either a social worker or a probation officer. The maximum period of the order is three years and the effect is similar to that of a probation order. It can include requirements as to residence and treatment for a period of not more than 12 months (see CYPA, Sched.3). The social worker or probation officer must visit, advise, and befriend the child while he or she is subject to the order (CYPA, s. 82). There is no provision under the proposed CJCO for the new Youth Court to make a supervision order.

(h) *An attendance centre order.* Children under 17 who are found guilty of an offence punishable in the case of adult with imprisonment, or in breach of a probation order, may be made subject to an attendance centre order. The child will attend for the designated period, which will not be less than 12 hours (unless, given his or her age and circumstances this seems unreasonable) and not more than 24 hours (CYPA, s.135). The centre provides various educational and other activities and its purpose is diversionary.

(i) *Deferment of sentence.* Any magistrates' or Crown Court may defer passing sentence, for up to six months, for the purpose of enabling the court to have regard to the offender's conduct after conviction, providing the offender consents. However, if in the meantime he or she commits any further offence and is convicted, the court may then pass sentence before the expiration of the period of deferment. A Magistrate may not exercise this power where the Crown Court deferred passing a sentence, and the Crown court may not pass a sentence which could not be passed by a magistrates' court, if this court made the deferment (CJO, art.3).

(j) *A suspended sentence.* This disposal differs from a conditional discharge in that there is a specific term of detention, in a Young Offenders' Centre, not exceeding two years, which may be activated on the commission of a further offence (Treatment of Offenders Act (NI) 1968, s. 18, as amended by CJO, art.23). Such a sentence should not be passed unless detention would be appropriate without the power to suspend the sentence. The operational period of the suspension may be between one and three years. The sentence may be passed with a fine or compensation order. If a further (imprisonable) offence is committed the court can order the original sentence to take effect, substitute a lesser term which is to take effect, extend the operational period (to expire not later than three years from the date of the suspension), or make no order. This last option is available only if the court is of the opinion that making an order would be unjust in the circumstances (Treatment of Offenders Act (NI) 1968, s. 19).

Breaches of community orders

If a person is in breach of a "community order" (*i.e.* (d) to (h) above), a juvenile or magistrates' court may:

- impose a fine not exceeding £1,000;
- make a community service order (subject to conditions for making the order outlined above); or
- make an attendance centre order (if the child is under 17).

However, the court may instead decide to revoke the original order and deal with the offender as if he or she had just been convicted, choosing any of the original options open to it. A further offence is not itself a breach of a community order.

Custodial sentences and remands

Remand homes

A child or young person may be remanded by the police (CYPA, s. 50(2)) or a court (s.51(1)) to await trial in a remand home and can be sentenced to detention there for up to one month (CYPA, s.74(3)), or six months if convicted of a terrorism-related offence (EPA 1996, s.14). CYPA, s.132 allows for the provision and inspection of remand homes. In selecting the home to which a child is to be committed, regard must be paid to his or her religion. Children detained in or being conveyed to and from a remand home are deemed in legal custody. Assisting escapes or harbouring a person who escapes is an offence (CYPA, s.133). In practice all training schools (see below) are also remand homes and there are no separate "Remand Home" rules. In the proposed CJCO it is intended to repeal these provisions. Children not released will be brought to a Juvenile Offenders' Centre (JOC) and will appear before a magistrate within 36 hours.

Training schools/Juvenile Offender Centres

Courts have power to commit a child or young person to a training school if he or she is found guilty of an offence punishable in the case of an adult with imprisonment (CYPA, s.74(1)(a)). The training school order lasts between six months and two years or until the young person becomes 19, whichever is the earlier (CYPA, s.87, as amended by the Treatment of Offenders (NI) Order 1989, art.6). He or she may be released on licence following the minimum period of six months, at the school manager's discretion (CYPA, Sched. 5, para. 8 as amended). The licence may be revoked at any time.

In placing a child in a training school, the court must have regard to his or her religious persuasion. Traditionally the voluntary sector schools – St Patrick's Training School for boys and St Joseph's Training School for girls – have catered for Catholic children, while the statutory sector school, Rathgael, has catered for boys and girls of Protestant and other religions. In 1995, the Northern Ireland Office restricted the number of places available in St Patrick's to 19, and subsequently Catholic boys were placed in Rathgael. A parent or guardian may apply to have a child moved to a different school, but only if a place is available (see *Re Fisher*, 1996). In *In re R (A Minor)*

(1997) a youth alleged that, as a Catholic, his detention in Rathgael was unlawful discrimination, but his claim failed. The proposed CJCO repeals the obligation to consider religious persuasion in placing a child.

The NIO has power to classify training schools by age, religion or other characteristics (CYPA, s.139). Currently the three schools mentioned above are classified as "open" and a fourth school, Lisnevin, as "closed." Lisnevin provides secure custody for Catholic and Protestant boys. No similar provision exists for girls. The Act makes no mention of secure custody, but section 140 deals with prevention of escapes. Any child who escapes from training school may be arrested without warrant by a police constable, or any person authorised by the managers of the school. A person acting on the instructions of the manager to prevent escapes has "all the powers, protection and privileges of a constable" (CYPA, Sched. 5 para. 15).

The training school system operates on the assumption that any training school, or part of a training school can be made secure on the instructions of the manager to prevent escapes. The validity of this assumption has never been tested in court. Both St. Patrick's and Rathgael have units operating semi-secure provision, despite being "open" schools. In practice, however, the open schools operate very different regimes from that in Lisnevin. This institution conforms to the specifications of a Grade C prison, with a central panopticon. Children wear school issue clothes and footwear. They are regularly searched, are locked in and visits to and from family are restricted and supervised. The open schools are domestically designed, less austere and visits to and from family and community are not restricted in the same way.

CYPA, Schedule 5, para. 12, empowers the Northern Ireland Office to order the transfer of a child from one school to another at any time. The proposed CJCO will re-enact these powers. Currently children may be transferred from the "open" schools to Lisnevin with the agreement of a semi-independent admissions panel. The child has no legal representation and the system may, therefore, infringe articles 37 and 40 of the United Nations Convention on the Rights of the Child and rules 14 and 15 of the Beijing Rules.

The Training School Rules (NI) 1952 are the regulations governing the operation of all training schools. They are out of print and out of date, dealing with matters such as the (now illegal) administration of corporal punishment. In practice NIO directives control the main aspects of operational policy in the schools, but these are not available to the public. The proposed CJCO should lead to the introduction of publicly accessible regulations for the administration of these institutions.

A person released from training school is under the supervision of the managers of the school for three years or until the age of 21 (whichever is earlier). A person under supervision, aged 19 years or less, may be recalled to the school for up to 6 months, if this is believed to be in his or her best interests (CYPA, s.89).

The proposed CJCO replaces training school orders with Juvenile Offender Centre orders, though 17-year-olds will continue to be detained in Young Offenders' Centres. The new order will endure for six months unless the court specifies that it must be for longer; it will in any case, not exceed 2 years and will comprise a period of detention in a JOC followed by a period of supervision by a probation officer. The child will be in custody for one half of the period of the order. The length of time the child spends in custody will be reduced by any period spent on remand in relation to the case.

If a juvenile breaches a JOC order, he or she will be liable on conviction to 30 days in a JOC (with no reduction in the period of supervision) or a fine not exceeding £200 if under 14 or £1,000 if older. The managers of a JOC will have parental responsibility for detained children but are not included in the definition of guardians and will not, therefore, be subject to fines in the same way as Trusts may be.

There is an Independent Representative Scheme in place to allow young people in training schools or Young Offenders' Centres to complain to an independent person about their treatment. The Scheme is run by the Northern Ireland Association for the Care and Resettlement of Offenders and funded by the NIO. It has no statutory basis and is dependent on the voluntary co-operation of the manager of the institution concerned. The local Ombudsman has no remit to deal with complaints regarding maladministration.

Young Offenders' Centre

Male offenders aged 17-21 years can be committed by court to the Young Offenders' Centre (YOC) Hydebank, Belfast, but females are committed to the Young Persons Wing at Maghaberry Prison, Lisburn. The management and regulations of both the Young Offenders' Centre and the Prisons are contained in the Prison and Young Offender Centre Rules (NI) 1994. The Treatment of Offenders (NI) Order 1989, article 7, restricts the use of YOCs to persons not less than 16 years and not more than 21 years. The maximum term of imprisonment is four years.

A 16-year-old may be sent to a YOC only if the court certifies that he or she is so "unruly or depraved in character that no other method of dealing with him or her is appropriate" (CYPA, s. 72(3)). However, the Treatment of Offenders Act (NI) 1968, section 2, as amended, allows the Secretary of State to transfer to a YOC young people not less that 14 years of age in certain circumstances. A 15-year-old may also be ordered to be detained in a YOC if:

(a) he or she has absconded from a training school and, with the consent of the Secretary of State, is brought before a juvenile court (CYPA, s.140),

(b) he or she has been guilty of serious misconduct at the school (CYPA, Sched.5, para 11(1)(b)), or

(c) he or she is so seriously unruly or subversive that his or her removal is necessary for maintaining school discipline.

The proposed CJCO will repeal the CYPA provisions allowing for 15-year-olds to be transferred transfer from a training school to a YOC.

The Secretary of State may direct that a person under 21 years be transferred from the YOC to prison if a Visiting Committee reports him or her to be "incorrigible" or a "bad influence" on other inmates (Treatment of Offenders Act (NI) 1968, s.7(1)(b)). The young person can serve the remainder of his or her term in prison.

Custody probation orders

Custody probation orders may be considered by the court, when a sentence of 12 months or more would be justified. The court may direct that the person should serve a custodial sentence, reduced by the time the court believes should be taken into account because the offender will also be supervised by a probation officer on his or her release. The period of supervision will be not less than 12 months nor more than three years (Criminal Justice (NI) Order 1996, art.24).

Restrictions on custodial sentences

Article 19 of the Criminal Justice (NI) Order 1996 restricts the use of custody to crimes which the court regards as so serious as to justify custody or, in the case of violent or sexual crimes, where custody is necessary to protect the public. The court must state its reasons for giving a custodial sentence unless the offender refuses to consent to a community sentence.

Sexual offences

On sentencing a person in respect of any sexual offence, the courts are empowered to direct that, instead of early discharge through remission, the person must be under the supervision of a probation officer for the whole of the sentence period following release from YOC or prison (Criminal Justice (NI) Order 1996, art. 26).

Grave crimes

Children convicted of any offence, punishable in the case of an adult with 14 years in prison or more (CYPA, s.73 (2)) or 5 years or more in the case of a terrorism-related offence (EPA 1996, s.14(1)), may be detained for a specified period in such place and under such conditions as the Secretary of State may direct. Children (under 18) convicted of offences carrying a life sentence may be detained during the pleasure of the Secretary of State (known as SOSPs) (CYPA, s. 73(1)). These provisions will be re-enacted in article 45 of the proposed CJCO.

Section 73 also allows the Secretary of State to release an offender on licence under such conditions as he or she may direct. The licence may be varied or revoked at any time. This will be re-enacted in article 46 of the proposed CJCO.

Conclusion

The introduction of the Criminal Justice (NI) Order 1996 and the proposals in the CJCO will in many respects bring the juvenile system more into line with the Beijing Rules and UNCRC. However, there will continue to be certain aspects of the criminal justice system which do not meet these international standards, such as the indeterminate nature of SOSP sentences, the lack of legal representation for children transferred between training schools and Juvenile Offender Centres, the failure to address actual and potential inequality of treatment on the basis of gender and religion, the low age of criminal responsibility, and the failure to include the best interests principle to underpin the deliberations of courts or agencies working to rehabilitate children who offend.

For further information on children's rights contact the Children's Law Centre, 101 University Street, Belfast BT7 1HP tel: 01232-245704.

Chapter 18

Education Rights

Chris Moffat

This chapter describes some of the rights which parents and their children have while the children are of compulsory school age. The main focus is on the fairness of the compulsory systems of education, thus it does not cover pre-school or tertiary education. The key legislation concerning primary and secondary education in schools is:
- the Education and Libraries (NI) Order 1986 (the 1986 Order),
- the Education Reform (NI) Order 1989 (the 1989 Order),
- the Education and Libraries (NI) Order 1993 (the 1993 Order),
- the Education (NI) Order 1996 (the 1996 Order), and
- the Education (NI) Order 1997 (the 1997 Order).

The right to education

The right to education is recognised in the Universal Declaration of Human Rights (1948) and in other international conventions. The United Nations' Convention on the Rights of the Child (1989) defines education as, amongst other things, the development of:
- the child's personality, talents and mental and physical abilities to their fullest potential;
- respect for human rights and fundamental freedoms;
- respect for the child's parents, for his or her own cultural identity, language and values, for the national values of the country in which the child is living and the country from which he or she may originate, and for civilisations different from his or her own; and
- the preparation of the child for responsible life in a free society, in a spirit of understanding, peace, tolerance, equality of sexes,

friendship among all peoples, ethnic, national or religious groups and persons of indigenous origins and respect for the natural environment.

Where education is administered compulsorily, however, other issues of rights arise. For instance, Article 12 of the Convention recognises that children have the right to have their views on their own education taken into account, the view of the child being given due weight in accordance with the age and maturity of the child.

Rights and duties of parents

The European Convention on Human Rights (in Protocol 1) says that, "No person shall be denied the right to education. In the exercise of any functions which it assumes in relation to education and to teaching, the state shall respect the right of parents to ensure such education and teaching in conformity with their own religious and philosophical convictions". The UK has ratified this protocol, but with a reservation limiting it to "measures compatible with the provision of efficient instruction and the avoidance of unreasonable public expenditure".

The 1986 Order provides that pupils should be educated according to the wishes of their parents, so long as this is "compatible with the provision of efficient instruction and training and the avoidance of unreasonable public expenditure" (art.44). There is, however, no agreed definition of "unreasonable public expenditure" or of how parents' wishes should be ascertained. The courts have generally been reluctant to intervene.

Parents have a duty to make sure that their children of compulsory school age (4-16 years) receive "sufficient full-time education suitable to their age, ability and aptitude, and any special educational needs they have, either by regular attendance at school or otherwise" (art. 45). "Parent" includes a guardian and every person who has actual custody of a child or young person.

Children are of compulsory school age between 4 and 16 years. The relevant date for determining the lower and upper limits of compulsory school age is 1 July:

* children whose fourth birthday occurs before 1 July are of compulsory school age from the following September (however children with later birthdays may enrol in primary schools if there are surplus places);

- children whose 16th birthday occurs before 1 July reach the upper limit of compulsory school age at the end of their current school year (1989 Order, art.156).

There is therefore provision for seven years of primary education and five years of secondary education, though over half of pupils stay on at school for a further two years to complete seven years of secondary schooling.

Parents can educate their children otherwise than at school, *e.g.* at home, but the arrangements must be approved by the Department of Education and the local Area Board must be satisfied that they are "suitable for the child's age, ability and aptitude, and any special educational needs he or she has" and that attendance is regular.

Educational provision

Most schools in Northern Ireland are grant-aided and pupils receive their statutory education entirely, or almost, free of charge. All grant-aided schools are managed by boards of governors with broadly similar statutory duties but with different management and funding structures which reflect their denominational or community origins. There is a high degree of social and communal segregation in pupil enrolment between different school types (except in "integrated schools") which is unparalleled in any other region of Western Europe. Over 90 per cent of Catholic pupils attend Catholic schools and 99 percent of non-Catholics attend state schools. Secondary education is selective at an early age; pupils go to either grammar or secondary school at 11 years according to the result of a competitive transfer exam taken during the last year of primary school.

Types of schools

Controlled schools

Controlled schools are provided and managed by Education and Library Boards (Area Boards or ELBs). They comprise 65 nursery, 461 primary, 78 secondary and 18 grammar schools as well as special schools. Their boards of governors include Area Board representatives and representatives of the original owners, usually Protestant churches, known as transferors. Controlled schools are meant to be non denominational "state" schools, but in practice the majority of pupils are Protestant.

Catholic maintained schools

Voluntary Catholic maintained schools are provided by the Roman Catholic denominational authorities. They include 26 nursery, 434 primary and 78 secondary schools. Boards of governors include trustees appointed (since 1989) by the Council for Catholic Maintained Schools (CCMS) and representatives of the Area Board or the Department of Education. No pupil may be refused admission to a voluntary maintained school on religious grounds, but the schools are intended primarily for Catholic pupils.

Voluntary grammar schools

There are 54 voluntary grammar schools, including 23 with prep (*i.e.* preparatory) departments, provided and managed by various trusts, Catholic or Protestant denominational foundations or religious orders. These schools select pupils on the basis of academic ability and are permitted to charge all pupils an annual capital fee of up to £80. Most voluntary grammar schools include representatives of trustees from one or other of the main denominational authorities on their boards of governors.

Grant-maintained integrated and controlled integrated schools

There are currently 19 primary and 9 secondary integrated schools. The 1989 Order requires that the "management and ethos of (integrated) schools is such as is likely to attract reasonable numbers of both Protestant and Roman Catholic pupils" (art.66(2)). As a matter of principle the schools seek to maintain at least a 40:60 balance between the two main denominational traditions amongst teaching staff and governors as well as pupils, although there is no statutory duty to do so. Denominational authorities are not represented as of right on governing bodies except in controlled integrated schools.

New grant maintained integrated schools may be established but they must raise their capital privately or voluntarily and operate independently until recognised by the Department of Education, when they become eligible for full recurrent funding and capital expenditure (where approved). Existing schools may also seek grant-maintained integrated or controlled integrated status (see page 348).

Irish medium schools

There are 10 Irish medium primary schools and two secondary schools; half are in the voluntary maintained sector (including one in the Catholic maintained sector) and half are independent, though funded on a temporary basis by Making Belfast Work or the European Peace and Reconciliation Programme. The boards of governors of grant-aided Irish medium schools are appointed by trustees and include Area Board representation.

Independent schools

A few (18) independent schools provide full-time education for pupils of compulsory school age. They are not grant-aided or required to comply with Education Orders except with respect to registration with the Department and the maintenance of minimum requirements as to premises, accommodation and efficient and suitable instruction having regard to the ages, sexes and abilities of the pupils.

Special schools

There are a number of schools for children with special educational needs which cannot be catered for within "ordinary schools". There are also special educational units within ordinary schools and hospital schools for children with particular types of disability which create severe learning difficulties.

Educational access

Open enrolment

Parents have the right to state their preference (in order of priority) for the school(s) they would like their child to attend (1997 Order, art. 9). The first and each subsequent preference is taken as a separate application for admission; if it is refused, the next preference is considered separately, and so on. Parents may choose any grant aided school in any board area.

There are detailed statutory rules about when schools may admit or refuse admission. The Department of Education determines each school's enrolment number (total school enrolment) and admissions number (maximum first year intake) largely on the basis of the physical capacity of the school. Schools may not exceed their enrolment and admissions numbers in any school year for the relevant age group except to admit a child with a statement of special educational needs or school attendance order or to comply with a direction of an Appeals Tribunal or the Department of Education.

Schools must draw up admissions criteria to be applied in selecting pupils where the school is oversubscribed. If under-subscribed it must admit all the children who apply. If it is oversubscribed it must apply its admissions criteria to allocate places and not admit any pupil above its admissions number. The only other circumstances in which schools may refuse admission are explained below.

Area Boards must publish details of arrangements for parents to express their choice of school, arrangements for the admission of pupils to each school, each school's admissions criteria and arrangements for appealing admission decisions.

Nursery schools

Nursery admissions are not controlled by legislation but policies are co-ordinated and published by Area Boards. Nursery provision in Northern Ireland (for children from three to the lower limit of compulsory school age) is substantially below that in the rest of the United Kingdom. Around one-sixth of Northern Ireland's three to four year olds attend nursery schools or nursery departments of primary schools. Shortage of places in a number of areas means that many places are part-time. Some children may be enrolled in reception or primary 1 classes where places exist.

Primary schools

Grant-aided primary schools must admit children of compulsory school age up to their enrolment and admissions number. Where they are oversubscribed they must apply their admissions criteria to select pupils up to the number of vacant places. A child who is below compulsory school age or who is not in the age group in which the majority of children are normally admitted to the school may be refused admission where this would "prejudice the efficient use of resources" (1997 Order, art. 13(5)).

Primary schools' admission criteria must:

- provide for admission of all children resident in Northern Ireland at the time of their proposed admission before any non-resident child;

- give the order of priority in which pupils shall be admitted if the school is oversubscribed;
- give priority to children who will have obtained compulsory school age at the time of the proposed admission;
- not select pupils by reference to ability, aptitude or performance in a test or examination held by, or on behalf of, the board of governors;
- apply admissions criteria to pupils of compulsory and below compulsory school age, including those who are already enrolled in an "approved" nursery class at the school.

Parents may appeal to an Appeal Tribunal against a decision to refuse admission if they think the school did not apply, or did not correctly apply, its admission criteria (see page 331).

Access to secondary schools

In most areas post-primary schooling is selective, with between 25 and 45 per cent of all places located in grammar schools. These are the only schools which may select pupils according to "ability", apart from a handful of non-grammar schools which may select a proportion of pupils in this way. A small number of areas operate a non-selective or delayed selection system, but there is no statutory definition of a "comprehensive" school. Pupils in these areas should take part in selection tests if they want to go to a grammar school in another area or at a later stage.

Non-grammar secondary schools are not permitted to use ability or aptitude as admissions criteria and must accept all the pupils who meet their admissions criteria regardless of ability.

Selection tests (the "11 plus")

The Department conducts an examination (1986 Order, art.110) to determine pupils' suitability for grammar schools, though it claims that there is no "pass mark" which can guarantee a grammar school place. Two sets of transfer tests in English, maths and science are set and marked by the Northern Ireland Council for Curriculum, Examinations and Assessment to assess pupils' academic ability.

Unless parents notify the Department through their principal on the appropriate form, their child will be regarded as participating in the selection test. Under the present arrangements under-age pupils may take the tests if the principal of the primary school they attend confirms that it is in "the best interests of the child". Over-age pupils may take them in some circumstances, with the Department's prior approval. A pupil with a statement of special educational needs is not intended to take part.

If a child's availability for, or performance in, the test is adversely affected by illness or other factors, parents must ensure the principal notifies the Department immediately enclosing any supporting evidence, *e.g.* a doctor's certificate or test supervisor's report. Marks are not adjusted for illness during the test, but a supplementary test may be taken.

Parents should get in touch with the principal of the secondary school(s) they have nominated if their child's performance has been affected. The school must take into account certified medical or other problems which may have affected performance in any tests.

Parents who are dissatisfied with decisions taken on the basis of any transfer test can complain. Arguably the test is unfair: there is considerable evidence to suggest that it is not a good predictor of ability, and that it discriminates against children from working class backgrounds and favours those who can pay for extra coaching. However, there is no obvious legal basis for challenging the test.

Transfer arrangements and secondary school admission

Both secondary non-grammar and grammar schools must admit children of compulsory school age up to their enrolment and admissions number; where they are oversubscribed they must apply their admissions criteria and not exceed the number of vacant places. This applies whether an application is for admission at the beginning of the first term of the school year or at some other time. A child who otherwise meets the criteria but is not in the age group in which the majority of children are normally admitted may be refused admission where this would "prejudice the efficient use of resources" (1997 Order, art.13(5)).

Grant-aided grammar schools have a right to refuse admission on two additional grounds even where there are vacant places:

(a) a child who at the normal transfer time otherwise meets the selection criteria may be refused if the school is of the opinion that it would be "detrimental to the educational interests of the child and it has obtained the approval of the Department to refuse admission" (1997 Order, art. 14(3)),

(b) a child may be refused at the beginning of the first term or when the majority of children of that age are admitted where the school is of the opinion that "the academic ability of the child is not of a standard equivalent to that of the pupils with whom he or she would be taught at the school" (art 14(5) or 14 (7)(a)).

Admission criteria

Under the Secondary Schools (Admissions Criteria) Regulations (NI) 1997, admission criteria must provide:

*   for admission of all children resident in Northern Ireland at the time of their proposed admission before any non-resident child;
*   for the order of priority for the admission of pupils where a school is over subscribed;
*   that where a grammar school uses the results in the transfer procedure tests it must admit day pupils with grade A before pupils with any other grade, and those with grade B1 before those with grades B2, B3, C1, C2 or D, etc; this need not apply to boarding pupils, so long as the number does not exceed the 1990 figure; and
*   that medical or other problems which may have affected a child's test performance must be taken into account where supported by a medical certificate or other appropriate documentary evidence.

Admission criteria must *not* include:

*   the fact that the school was the parent's first preference or a higher preference than any other school;
*   provision for selecting pupils by reference to ability or aptitude except in the case of a grammar school or a school which has been permitted to select some of its pupils by ability or aptitude;
*   performance in any test other than the "11 plus" or a special test set by an Area Board or the Department (*e.g.* for a pupil who has lived abroad);
*   the outcome of any assessment in Key Stage 2 (*i.e.* at age 11); and
*   in the case of selection for grammar schools between pupils who have the same transfer test grade, information provided by the primary school principal about the pupil's classroom performance.

Other criteria

Schools may apply any other admission criteria, provided they are legal (*e.g.* gender in the case of single sex schools) and not specifically proscribed in the regulations, and provided the views of the Area Board, or of the Council for Catholic Maintained Schools in the case of Catholic maintained schools, are considered.

Religious denomination may not be used as an admissions criterion if it would contravene section 19 of the Northern Ireland Constitution Act 1973 which prohibits religious discrimination by government departments or their agents. However, because of the way criteria are defined, religious denomination (apart from parental preference) may indirectly affect admissions. Examples of admissions criteria which are currently accepted by the Department of Education include: priority to pupils with family or ancestral links with the school; children of school employees; residence in a parish or other specified area; contributory or traditionally linked primary schools; behavioural report from previous school; distance from school; support for the aims of the school; equal balance of Protestant and Catholic pupils (in an integrated school). In the case of admission to grammar schools, ability as measured by performance in the transfer test has effectively become the sole admissions criterion except where "special circumstances" apply.

Once published, criteria must be applied in an unambiguous and procedurally fair way. There is no legal requirement that they be otherwise fair or even relevant (*In re Moore*, 1996). The whole area is extremely complex and arguably some criteria may be open to legal challenge. One group of parents argued that a secondary school's admissions criteria which favoured rural schools prejudiced the admission chances of pupils in a nearby urban estate (*In re Moore,* 1996). Their case was rejected at the Court of Appeal; but other cases could be more successful.

Appeal Tribunals

Parents who are dissatisfied with the refusal of a school to admit their child may appeal to an Appeal Tribunal (1997 Order, art. 15) but only on the grounds that the school did not apply, or incorrectly applied, its admissions criteria and the child would otherwise have been admitted to the school. Appeals cannot be made against a refusal to admit on the grounds of "admission prejudicial to the efficient use of resources" (art.13(5) or 13(7)), or "detrimental to the educational interests of the child" (art.14(3)) or "prejudicial to academic standards of grammar schools" (art.14(5) or 14(7)(a)). This does not preclude parents from seeking a judicial review on these grounds if they are aggrieved by a decision (see below).

Appeals must be made in writing to the Tribunal. Parents must be given an opportunity to appear and to make written and oral representations on their own behalf. No new information may be considered in an appeal. The decision of the Tribunal may be by consensus or by simple majority vote. If it finds in favour of the appeal, it must direct the board of governors of the school to admit the child even if this means the school will exceed its admissions and enrolment number.

Judicial review

Parents who are dissatisfied with the decision of an Appeal Tribunal, or who believe that a school's admissions criteria are not in accordance with the regulations, may seek a judicial review in the High Court (see Chapter 2). Generally this can reverse a decision of a Tribunal only if it can be shown that the Tribunal considered inappropriate (or did not consider appropriate) evidence or that no reasonable authority could have made the decision in question. Even if a judicial review finds in favour of a complainant it may reverse an Appeal Tribunal decision only if a proper application of the criteria would actually have resulted in admission. An important consideration for potential appellants is that only cases brought in the name of the child (rather than a parent) at the Appeal Tribunal are eligible for legal aid in any subsequent judicial review.

Children with special educational needs

Around one-fifth of all school children are considered to have special educational needs and to require special educational provision at some time during their lives. They include not only children with physical or mental disabilities but those who for various reasons are not able to develop at the same rate as other children. All schools have responsibilities for children with special educational needs, but a distinction is made between those who have a statement of special educational needs, for whom Area Boards have a particular responsibility, and others without a statement.

The duty of Boards

Under the 1996 Order, Area Boards must identify any registered pupil at a grant-aided school or child between the age of two and four years in their area who may have special educational needs. It must determine the "special educational provision which any learning difficulty the child has, calls for" (art.13). A health and social service authority which knows of such a child below compulsory school age must inform the child's parents and notify the appropriate Area Education Board (art.14). For a child under two the Area Board must first obtain the parents' consent before proceeding with an assessment. (art. 21).

Under article 3 of the 1996 Order , a child has "special educational needs" if he or she has "a learning difficulty which calls for special educational provision to be made for him or her." In turn, a child has a "learning difficulty" if he or she:

(a) has significantly greater difficulty in learning than the majority of children of his or her age, or

(b) has a disability which prevents or hinders him or her from making use of educational facilities of a kind generally provided at ordinary schools for children of his or her age.

A learning difficulty does not exist solely because the language in which the child will be taught is different from the one which at any time has been spoken in his or her home.

Special educational provision

An Area Board must make special educational provision for pupils who have a statement of special educational needs. The main ground for making a statement is that a child's special educational needs cannot reasonably be provided within the resources of a normal school. But no matter how severe a child's disability may be, parents can choose to have their child educated in an ordinary school, provided the Board agrees that it is compatible with:

"(i) the child receiving the special education provision which his or her learning difficulty calls for,

(ii) the provision of efficient education for the children with whom he or she will be educated, and

(iii) the efficient use of resources." (art.7(2)(b))

The child must be allowed to take part in the activities of the school "together with the other children" provided that the three conditions in article 7(2)(b) are met, and that it is "reasonably practicable".

A Board may also provide for special educational provision (a) in an institution outside Northern Ireland if it is one "which specialises in providing for children with special needs" or (b) in Northern Ireland otherwise than in a grant-aided school if the interests of the child require it and the arrangements are compatible with the efficient use of resources (art.10). It may pay fees and any reasonable maintenance and travelling expenses of the child and any person accompanying him or her and in certain circumstances may pay for special educational provision at an independent school or institution other than a school in Northern Ireland (art.11).

Referral, assessment and statements

The decision to make a statement is the most important educational decision for a child with special educational needs. Concerned parents can make a formal request for their child's educational needs to be assessed. Assessment should be carried out within six months unless the Board thinks it is not necessary. Assessment must be done in the proper way within a specified time. Parents have the right to be consulted at all stages. The Board may take medical, psychological and educational advice and consult the child's school principal and teacher. Parents may be present at an examination connected with the assessment of their child and in some cases must be present.

A Board does not have to make a statement of a child's special educational needs (art. 16). It may decide that no special provision is required (art. 17). If parents are dissatisfied with the decision they can appeal to a Special Educational Needs Tribunal. These now operate under the Special Educational Needs Tribunal Regulations (NI) 1997.

Provision for statemented children

A "statement" is a legally binding document which sets out what special educational needs a child has and the provision a Board intends to make to meet those needs, including the type of school or other institution. Parents must be allowed to comment on a preliminary draft of the statement and must be shown all the formal advice and evidence used to reach a decision.

Once a statement has been made, it is the responsibility of the Area Board to ensure that the board of governors of any school in which the child is placed makes the necessary special educational provision. Statements must be reviewed every 12 months. The parent may request another grant-aided school to be substituted.

Provision for non-statemented children

Only a small minority of children with special educational needs are statemented, so the provision for the remainder is of considerable importance to the parents concerned. School budgets include an element specifically for the provision for special educational needs and boards of governors must publish a special educational needs policy report on such matters in its annual report.

Where a child with non-statemented special educational needs attends an ordinary school, the school must use its best endeavours to ensure that:

(a) the special educational provision which his or her learning difficulty calls for is made;

(b) those needs are made known to all who are likely to teach him or her; and

(c) the teachers in the school are aware of the importance of identifying and providing for...pupils who have special educational needs (art. 8(1)(2)).

A Code of Practice (currently in draft form) sets out in detail the arrangements for non-statemented pupils with special educational needs. It provides for a Special Educational Needs Co-ordinator (SENCo) in each school to take responsibility for co-ordinating provision. Parents should be fully consulted. The SENCo should produce an "individual education plan" for each child in question. Depending on the nature and severity of the child's learning difficulty there are statutory provisions for the suspension or modification of the Northern Ireland curriculum and assessment procedures (see below).

Most of the arrangements for non-statemented children do not have the force of law and their parents have no right to appeal to the Special Educational Needs Tribunal. They may nevertheless be able to seek redress by making a formal request that their child's educational needs be assessed. They have a right to appeal to the Tribunal if refused. The value of the assessment process will be to gather sufficient information on the nature of the child's difficulties and to clarify their concerns about shortcomings in the provision made by the school. If parents feel the school has acted illegally, unfairly or unreasonably they may seek a judicial review.

For further information contact the your local Area Board or Disability Action, 2 Annadale Avenue, Belfast BT7 3JR (tel: 01232-491011)

The curriculum

The 1989 Order lays down a minimum legally required curriculum for every registered pupil of compulsory school age in every grant-aided primary and secondary school. Boards of governors and principals of every school have a duty to provide "a balanced and broadly based curriculum which:

(a) promotes the spiritual, moral, cultural, intellectual and physical development of pupils, and thereby

(b) prepares them for the opportunities, responsibilities and experiences of adult life" (art.4(2)).

The curriculum must include provision for religious education and for "areas of study" made up of "contributory subjects", some of which are compulsorily assessed. The areas of study must include the following:

- English
- Mathematics
- Science and Technology (science only at primary level)
- Environment and Society
- Creative and Expressive Studies
- Language Studies (in second level schools only, except in Irish medium schools).

For the purposes of the curriculum the child's school year is divided into four Key Stages (KS): KS 1 for the first four years of primary school; KS 2 for the last three years of primary school; KS 3 for the first three years of secondary school; and KS 4 for the last two years of compulsory schooling. The curriculum for each listed contributory subject must cover the "attainment targets" (what pupils are expected to know) and the "programmes of study" (what is required to be taught) and each pupil must be assessed at the end of each Key Stage. The curriculum is drawn up by the Northern Ireland Council for Curriculum, Examinations and Assessment.

Schools are also required to promote "wholly or mainly through the teaching of contributory subjects and religious education, the attainment of objectives in the following educational themes: Information

Technology; Education for Mutual Understanding; Cultural Heritage; Health Education; Economic Awareness and Careers Education (secondary schools only)" (1989 Order, art.8).

The Department can make other regulations concerning the curriculum, timetable and suitability of any study materials or resources used in a school. Schools must enter pupils for approved public examinations unless there are educational reasons for not doing so, and should in any case inform parents as soon as it has made a decision on such matters (1989 Order, art.136). Courses leading to external qualifications (*e.g.* business certificates) are permitted only if approved by the Department of Education (1989 Order, art. 9).

School records and reports

All grant-aided schools must keep and provide to parents information about pupils' achievements. Each year on 30 June or as soon as reasonably practicable, they must provide brief particulars of achievements in any subject or activity which forms part of his or her curriculum, the level of attainment in any statutorily assessed compulsory contributory subject and the result of any public examination for which he or she was prepared by the school, and, where the pupil was exempted from any part of a programme of study in that school year, a statement to that effect.

Schools must also provide or send to the pupils' parents on request, by 30 June or not later than 30 September, the summative record of the achievements of the pupil where he or she is leaving school at the end of Key Stage 2 and of each pupil finishing Key Stage 4 or leaving school in the sixth form.

Access to records

Individual pupils' assessments must not be made available to persons or bodies other than the parents concerned and the Department, except in specified circumstances.

Parents and pupils over 16 years have a right to see any "formative record" ("formal record of a pupil's academic attainments, his or her other skills, talents and abilities and his or her educational progress") after a request in writing to the school. If a parent or pupil regards it as inaccurate and gives notice in writing, he or she may amend or correct it. The written notice of complaint must be appended to the record and subsequently treated it as part of it. A complaint about a refusal to disclose or amend records should be lodged with the board of governors.

If a pupil moves to, or is under consideration for admission to another school, the formative record and any notices attached must be made available. Reports requested by an educational welfare officer, social worker, probation officer, prospective employer or college, do not require schools to disclose any of the following information regarding a pupil:

- details about home circumstances or religious denomination;
- the results of an individual pupil's attainment assessments;
- reports for the purposes of juvenile or magistrates' courts;
- statements of special educational needs;
- educational records covered by the Data Protection Act 1984 (see Chapter 11);
- information which in the opinion of "holders" would harm the physical, mental or emotional condition of the pupil or any other person to whom it relates;
- the contents of references to potential employers, universities or colleges or other national bodies concerned with student admissions.

Pupils with special educational needs

A pupil with a statement of special educational needs may be exempted from the statutory curriculum and assessment. Where a pupil has special educational needs but is not statemented, the principal of a school may require, or parents can ask, that the curriculum be modified or not applied. This may arise where a pupil is suffering from a temporary condition affecting his or her learning or where the pupil needs to be assessed by the Area Board with a view to a statement of educational needs being made or amended.

In either case the principal may direct that for an "operative period" (not more than six months) the curriculum, assessment procedures and educational themes may be modified or not applied. The principal must tell the governors and the pupil's parents and say what provision is being made for the pupil's education during the operative period. At the end of that period the principal must either restore full delivery of the curriculum or arrange for the pupil's special educational needs to be assessed.

Parents can ask the principal, to revoke or vary a direction currently in force but only once during an "operative period". Where parents are concerned about the situation, they may appeal to the board of governors of the school. The board may confirm the action or direct the principal to take such action as it considers appropriate and notify the parents in writing.

If parents are still not satisfied they can appeal to the Curriculum Complaints Tribunal (see below) or, if their child has a statement of special educational needs, to the Special Educational Needs Tribunal under article 18 of the 1996 Order.

Religious education

All schools, including special schools, must provide for both religious education and collective worship. This must be so arranged that: "(a) the school shall be open to pupils of all religious denominations for instruction other than religious education, and (b) no pupil shall be excluded directly or indirectly from the other advantages which the school affords" (1986 Order, art.21(4)). Ministers of religion of any denomination must be given reasonable access to pupils in order to give religious education, provided parents do not object. Parents can ask that the child be excused from any religion education classes and collective worship and if necessary withdrawn from school for reasonable periods. This request must be complied with (1986 Order, art.21(5)).

Religious education must be "in accordance with any core syllabus specified by the Department of Education". This "core syllabus" is one prepared in consultation with the four main churches in Northern Ireland. In addition, in controlled schools (other than controlled integrated schools) religious education must be undenominational, i.e. it must be "based upon the Holy Scriptures according to some authoritative version thereof but excluding instruction as to any tenet distinctive of any particular religious denomination"; and collective worship must "not be distinctive of any particular religious denomination" (1986 Order, art. 21(2)).

Voluntary grammar, Catholic maintained and integrated schools may determine their own provision for religious education and collective worship including, where appropriate, denominational instruction.

The Curriculum Complaints Tribunal

If parents are concerned about the way a school is discharging its duties in relation to the curriculum or assessment, religious education or collective worship, access to information or any related matter, they can apply in writing to the Curriculum Complaints Tribunal giving the grounds for their complaint (1989 Order, art.33). If the Tribunal upholds the complaint in whole or in part it may require the school to remedy the matter. If the school fails to comply with the notice the Tribunal may refer the matter to the Department.

Treatment at school

Absence

Schools must keep a register of pupils attending and must inform the Area Board if a pupil does not attend regularly and has no reasonable excuse including the following:

- sickness or other unavoidable cause (medical certificate required);
- there are no arrangements for transporting the child to the nearest "suitable school" and he or she is under 11 years of age and lives more than two miles away, or over 11 years and lives more than three miles away (or transport arrangements have been made but the child still has to walk these distances);
- the child is employed on work experience; or
- the parent can prove that he or she is engaged in a trade or business which requires him or her to travel and the child has attended school as regularly as the trade or business permitted and for at least 100 days during the last 12 months (1986 Order, art.48).

School attendance orders

If a child is not registered as a pupil at a school, the Area Board must be satisfied that the child is receiving suitable, *i.e.* efficient, full time education. However, there is no statutory procedure for determining what is suitable apart from failure to register at a school. In this case a Board can serve a written notice requiring the parents to satisfy them within 14 days that the child is receiving suitable education. The Board may send an education welfare officer to the child's home to investigate. If the parents cannot satisfy the board and it is believed to be "expedient that the child should attend school", the Board must:

- give advance notice to the parents of its intention to serve an order and of the school or schools it intends to specify in the order, then

- serve a "school attendance order" on the parents requiring the pupil to become a registered pupil at a school named in the order.

Parents may within the time limit of the notice (a further 14 days) apply for the child to be admitted to another school (whether a grant-aided school or an independent school). For a pupil with a statement of special educational needs, the school should be the school specified in the statement (1996 Order, art 27).

A school attendance order must continue in force, unless amended by the Board, for as long as the child is of compulsory school age or until the child would normally leave the school specified in the order. Parents may apply for the order to be revoked if arrangements have been made for suitable education otherwise than at school. Parents who are refused can appeal to the Department of Education. They should seek legal advice or get in touch with their local Citizens' Advice Bureau.

Education supervision orders

Where a child is a registered pupil at a school but does not attend regularly (or is the subject of a school attendance order which is not being complied with), the Area Board can seek an education supervision order at the family proceedings court (Children (NI) Order 1995, art.55). If an education supervision order is made, the effect is to transfer the duty and rights of the parents to secure the child's education to the Board.

Parents have a duty to comply with any directions given in an educational supervision order. An education supervisor is appointed and has a duty to advise, assist and befriend the child and to give directions to the child and his or her parents in such a way as will, in the opinion of the supervisor, secure that he or she is properly educated. Before giving directions the supervisor must, in so far as is reasonably practicable, "ascertain the wishes and feelings of the child and his or her parents including their wishes about where the child is to be educated" and "give due consideration, having regard to the child's age and understanding," to such wishes. Directions might include requiring the parents to escort the child to school or keeping the supervisor informed of any change of the child's address (especially in the case of an older child who might abscond from home). Unless they can show that they took all reasonable steps to comply with a direction or that the direction was unreasonable, parents who fail to comply are guilty of an offence.

An education supervision order is initially made for one year. It may be extended provided this is done three months prior to the date of expiry. Further extensions may not exceed three years.

The child, his or her parents or the Area Board may apply to the court to discharge the order if it is established that he or she is receiving a suitable education. A Board or education supervisor may apply for a discharge of the order if it is believed that it has failed. In this event the court may direct social services to investigate the child's circumstances. This may mean that a care order, which removes the child from the care of his or her parents, will be sought. In all such cases parents should seek legal advice or get in touch with their local Citizens' Advice Bureau (see also Chapters 16 and 17).

Discipline

The 1989 Order provides, in article 134, that the scheme of management for each grant-aided school must include a written statement of measures for promoting discipline. This should be available to parents.

Northern Ireland has to comply with the European Convention on Human Rights, under which corporal punishment in state schools is deemed to be inhuman or degrading treatment. Under the Education (Corporal Punishment) (NI) Order 1987 teachers have the same obligations towards pupils in their charge as any careful parent would have, including the power to administer any punishment which is reasonable in the circumstances, but not to inflict corporal punishment. (Independent schools are an exception: corporal punishment is still permitted so long as it is not "inhuman or degrading").

Parents have a right to be told of the reason for any punishment. If they feel that their child has been unjustly or unreasonably punished, they should write to the chief education officer of the Area Board or, in the case of a maintained, voluntary or grant-maintained integrated school, the chairperson of the governors, setting out their complaint in writing and seek legal advice from an advice centre or their local Citizens' Advice Bureau.

Suspension

Each Area Board, the governors of voluntary and integrated schools and the CCMS must have a scheme to be followed in relation to the suspension or expulsion of pupils.

An initial period of suspension should not exceed five school days in any one school term and a pupil should not be suspended for more than 15 days in any school term (Schools (Suspension and Expulsion of Pupils) Regulations (NI) 1995). Parents must be notified immediately and told of the period of the suspension: pupils cannot just be sent home. Parents must be requested to meet the principal to discuss the matter. The Area Board, the chairperson of the board of governors, and, in the case of a Catholic maintained school, the local diocesan office of CCMS must also be informed.

If parents are asked to give undertakings about their child's future conduct, these should be put in writing to avoid any misunderstanding. If they are not satisfied with the way the matter has been dealt with, they should ask for it to be reviewed. In the case of a controlled school, they should write to the chief education officer of the Area Board, in the case of a Catholic maintained school, to the director of the CCMS, or in the case of a voluntary school, to the chair of the board of governors.

Expulsion

Expulsion is meant to be a measure of last resort and to involve all parties, including parents, in deciding the most appropriate alternative educational provision for the pupil. A pupil may be expelled from school only after serving a period of suspension and only after consultation about the matter has taken place between the principal, the parents and, as appropriate, the chief executive of the Area Board, the board of governors or the director of the CCMS. They must consider the future education of the pupil at their meeting. A parent's refusal to take part in consultations cannot prevent a pupil being expelled.

If the expulsion or alternative arrangements are felt to be unreasonable, parents can appeal to an Appeals Tribunal (1993 Order, art.49).Written notice of the right to appeal must be given to the parents immediately by the principal, together with the time limit for appealing and where the appeal may be lodged.

The final responsibility for providing education for an expelled pupil lies with his or her parent, although the Area Board can assist. Where a pupil has been expelled from, or refused admission to, a school, the Area Board has the power to direct another specified grant-aided school within a reasonable distance from the child's home to admit the child, provided it is not one from which he or she has already been suspended or expelled.

Financial considerations

Charges

Grant-aided primary, secondary and special schools may not charge fees or ask parents to pay for or supply any books, instruments, equipment or transport required by the Northern Ireland curriculum or an approved public examination syllabus. With parental consent, they are entitled to charge for:

- education and transport in connection with "optional extras", *i.e.* additional music, sports or academic subjects which are not compulsory contributory subjects;
- entry fees for non-required public examinations;
- board and lodging for residential field trips (for parents on family credit or income support, costs can be remitted).

Grant-aided schools may ask for voluntary contributions from parents to school funds, provided it is clear that there is no obligation on parents to contribute and that pupils will not be treated differently according to whether or not their parents have done so (1989 Order, art.130).

Transport

An Area Board must make the arrangements it considers necessary for the provision of transport to facilitate the attendance of pupils at a grant-aided school. In the past such transport has been provided free as part of government policy on open enrolment. Boards have generally paid the reasonable travelling expenses of pupils either by providing free bus or train passes or petrol expenses for parents who drive their children to school.

From September 1997 free transport has been restricted to pupils attending special schools, those with special educational needs and those who are unable to gain a place at a "suitable" school or further education college within statutory walking distance from their home, i.e. more than two miles from the nearest "suitable" school for a primary pupil, or more than three miles from the nearest "suitable" secondary or grammar school from which an offer of a place has been received, for a post-primary pupil. "Suitable" provides for linguistic and religious preference where such alternatives are available. Parents who are dissatisfied with the decision of a board with regard to their child may be able to seek a judicial review. They should contact their local CAB or other legal advice centre.

Means-tested benefits

School uniforms and P.E. kit grants

Area Boards may give assistance towards the cost of school uniform and P.E. kit for special and post-primary school pupils if parents are on income support or income-related jobseeker's allowance. Students in further education are eligible only for the P.E. kit grant. A separate application on a form obtained from Board offices has to be made for each child each year.

Education maintenance allowance

Educational maintenance allowance is a mandatory means-tested benefit to assist with the cost of remaining at school beyond the minimum compulsory school leaving age (16 years). The amount is graduated according to the parents' joint disposable income, so long as it is below a very basic level (£7,262 in 1996/97). A separate application must be made for each child each year. Once a grant has been approved, it is usually paid in arrears, in two half-yearly instalments, at the end of February and the end of August, subject to satisfactory school attendance.

School meals

All grant-aided schools must provide school meals. Pupils (including nursery pupils) whose parents receive income support or income-related jobseeker's allowance are entitled to free meals. Children of parents on family credit receive instead a cash payment, though this does not generally cover the equivalent meals charge. An application form must be completed and sent to Board headquarters as soon as entitlement arises, as free meals cannot be provided until confirmation is received.

Grants towards boarding fees

A Board can make a grant towards the cost of boarding where it is satisfied that: "education suitable to [the pupil's] age, ability and aptitude and any special educational needs he or she may have cannot be provided otherwise than by the provision of board and lodging at a particular grant-aided school" (1989 Order, art.135). The grant is means tested. Parents should apply to their Area Board for details.

Who runs education?

The Department of Education

The Department of Education has a duty to "promote the education of the people of Northern Ireland" and controls all aspects of education. Apart from specific powers under the Education Orders (which the Department itself has drafted) it determines educational policy through its control of educational expenditure and its administrative relationship (backed by the power to give directions) with the Area Boards, the trustees and governors of voluntary schools and other statutory bodies such as the Northern Ireland Curriculum Council and the Council for Catholic Maintained Schools. It may "give directions as to the exercise of any power conferred or the performance of any duty imposed on that authority by the Education Orders" (1986 Order, art.101, as amended by 1989 Order, art.158). The Department is not directly answerable to any democratic forum apart from periodic scrutiny by House of Commons select committees.

Area Boards

There are currently five Area Education and Library Boards made up of members nominated from amongst the councillors of the district councils in the Board's area (40%), representatives of the transferors of controlled schools and trustees of Catholic maintained schools in the area together with other educational and libraries representatives.

Area Boards employ teachers in the controlled sector and are responsible for the maintenance of all controlled schools as well as other schools (where requested by the managers and trustees) in their area. Maintenance includes preparing financial schemes for the allocation of "budget shares", organising admissions arrangements and co-ordinating a range of services including special education, appeals and complaints tribunals, school meals, curriculum support, transport, etc.

Area Boards also have a general role in planning educational provision in their area, although the Department of Education has the major say in any changes in provision. They publish proposals whenever it is proposed to establish a new school, make a significant change, or have an existing school recognised as grant-aided (1986 Order, art.14) and relay comments or objections from the public to the Department. But there is no other provision for any form of public inquiry or for consultation over other forms of educational provision, such as special education, nursery schools or integrated education, and little evidence that parents' views or interests are systematically taken into account.

The Council for Catholic Maintained Schools (CCMS)

The CCMS was created under the 1989 Order as a statutory intermediate tier of management for primary and secondary Catholic maintained schools. The Council consists of the Northern Bishops of the Roman Catholic Church in Ireland and their representatives, together with persons appointed by the Department of Education and parents and teachers nominated by the five Catholic diocesan education committees. The Council appoints and employs teachers, promotes the planning of provision of Catholic maintained schools and provides support to Catholic maintained school trustees and Boards of Governors as well as protecting the ethos of Catholic schools. Its address is: 160 High Street, Holywood, Co Down BT18 9HT (tel: 01232-424255).

Transferors Representatives' Council

There is no statutory body for transferors, *i.e.* the representatives of trustees of former Church of Ireland, Presbyterian or Methodist schools which were transferred to the state. The Tranferors Representatives' Council is a voluntary body which supports and advises transferors who are school governors. Its address is: The Education Centre at St Nicholas, Cadogan Park, Belfast BT9 6HG (tel: 01232-682946).

Northern Ireland Council for Integrated Education

NICIE is a voluntary body which represents integrated schools and promotes and encourages the development of integrated education. The 1989 Order provided for the development of integrated schools and imposed a duty on the Department of Education to "encourage and facilitate the development of integrated education" (art. 64(1)). NICIE supports parents in establishing and securing voluntary funding for proposed integrated schools until they are recognised by the Department of Education. Approval is currently conditional on there being no suitable local alternative and on the school achieving a minimum first form intake (100 pupils for secondary schools, 25 pupils for primary) and a minimum of 30 per cent from the minority community in the area served by the school.

NICIE may also advise and support existing schools which seek to acquire either grant-maintained, integrated or controlled integrated status. The initial procedure for recognition requires a majority of existing parents voting in favour. The Department of Education must be satisfied that the school has a minimum 10 per cent intake from the minority community in the year before approval is granted and reasonable prospects of achieving at least a 70:30 religious balance. It is not clear how many "transformations" will result in genuinely integrated schools. The address of the Council is: 10 Lower Crescent, Belfast BT7 1NR (tel: 01232-236200).

Irish medium education

The Department's current strategy is for Irish medium education to be provided mainly in streams in Anglophone Catholic schools, although the Irish language community has reservations about the effect of this on language acquisition. Irish medium primary schools must demonstrate a potential to achieve an enrolment of 100 before the Department will grant funding. Some grant-aided and independent Irish medium primary and secondary schools and pre-school playgroups are affiliated to Gaeloiliuint, a voluntary organisation grant-aided by the European Union Programme for Peace and Reconciliation to develop Irish medium education. Independent Irish medium schools have also been funded on an interim basis by the same programme. Gaeloiliuint's address is: 216 Bothar na bhFal/Falls Road, Beal Feirste/Belfast, BT12 6AT (tel: 01232-239303).

Parents and school management

Recent legislation has considerably expanded the responsibilities of boards of governors of all grant-aided schools. Apart from the specific duties already discussed, they are responsible for financial management, day-to-day maintenance and upkeep of school premises and equipment, as well as the deployment and (except in controlled and Catholic maintained schools) employment of teachers, health and safety and the provision of required information. They also have a wide range of new communal obligations, including statutory responsibility to report on:

- the curriculum of the school, the educational provision for pupils and syllabuses followed, and the educational achievements of pupils (1989 Order, art.31);
- arrangements for the admission of pupils with special educational needs for whom a statement is not maintained, the steps taken to prevent them from being treated less favourably than other pupils and the facilities provided to assist them to access the school (1996 Order, art.8);
- steps taken "to develop or strengthen the school's links with the community and, in particular, to promote ... Education for Mutual Understanding (1989 Order, art.125).

The government has published a parents' charter of rights and responsibilities and has said that it wants parents to play an active part in education. But there are only a limited number of ways of influencing how decisions are taken. Schools must hold an annual parents' meeting, where parents may put forward their views on the school (1989 Order, art.126). Parents can request copies of the minutes of school governors' meetings and, subject to confidentiality and permission (which cannot be unreasonably be withheld), attend a meeting.

Parent governors are elected once every four years by other parents in a secret ballot at the annual parents' meeting. Parents may also be asked to serve as a nominee of trustees or transferors. Boards of governors are composed as follows:

	Cont. prim./ sec.	Cont. gram./ nursery	Catholic maintained prim./sec.	Vol. grammar	"Grant maintained" Catholic or grammar **	Grant maintained integrated	Cont. integrated prim./sec.
Nominated by:							
Transferors or trustees	4	-	6*	6*	4*	-	2
Foundation governors	-	-	-	-	-	3*	-
Area Boards	2	3	2	2	2	-	2
Dept.of Education	-	2	-		1	2	-
Elected by:							
Parents	2	2	1	1	1	2	2
Teachers	1	1	1	1	1	1	1
TOTAL	9	8	10	10	9	8	7

NB   * includes a parent of a pupil at the school
       ** A new voluntary management agreement under the 1993 Order which permits full capital funding to voluntary schools but entails a reduction in the trustees' overall majority of the board of governors.

Educational policy and pluralism

The current law relating to education in Northern Ireland poses a significant difficulty in securing full educational rights for all. As with the UK legislation from which it is derived, it is supposed to respect parents' religious and philosophical beliefs and to accommodate pupils of different religious and other backgrounds in a non-discriminatory way, but it is open to question whether the legislation in Northern Ireland achieves this.

Progress has been made in dealing with discrimination in the treatment of pupils attending Catholic schools in comparison with those attending other schools, but there has been less progress in promoting religious and philosophical freedom in school structures. And although the government has now accepted some responsibility for facilitating integrated education there is still no coherent policy for achieving it.

In many areas of Northern Ireland, parental choice is still effectively only choice to the extent that it permits a preference between alternative publicly-funded single-denomination schools. Efforts have been made through statutory educational schemes to promote the idea of respect for diversity and pluralism in schools, but there are statutory ambiguities in all sectors, including state and voluntary grammar schools, which reinforce the segregated demominational character of the mainstream system. For instance, all schools are exempt from fair employment legislation. There is thus no requirement to demonstrate cultural diversity and fairness in teaching appointments and promotions or in the authority structure of the school. Exemption may be appropriate in specific circumstances where the maintenance of the character of a denominational or multi-demoninational school demonstrably requires the appointment of a practising member of a religious group, but a universal exemption from fair employment rules in all schools must inevitably undermine efforts to educate for diversity.

Likewise, ambiguities about the status of denominational representation in schools generally and in intermediate tiers of denominational management and administration, about schools admission policies and about the statutory basis for denominational instruction in state schools, all have the effect of obscuring how far educational choice is limited to a question of denominational preference. The result has been that segregation in educational structures has become increasingly self-reinforcing and parents' rights to choose non-denominational or multi-denominational schools have been further restricted.

This lack of progress in fostering pluralism in existing structures has strengthened the argument that government has a duty to make proper provision for alternative non-segregated or multi-denominational state-funded education. Article 2 of Protocol 1 of the ECHR gives parents the right to "ensure education and teaching in conformity with their own religious and philosophical convictions", subject to a UK reservation limiting its obligation to "measures compatible with the provision of efficient instruction and the avoidance of unreasonable public expenditure". A similar formulation in article 44 of the Education (NI) Order 1986 has generally been interpreted as simply prohibiting discrimination against individuals who choose, on religious or philosophical grounds, to "opt out". But in the special circumstances of Northern Ireland, it is arguable that "opting out", whether by not attending certain school classes or activities or by withdrawing completely on grounds of conscience, is an inadequate alternative. The government has a duty to provide for greater diversity, either by protecting the non-denominational character of state schools or, if necessary, by giving greater support to a system of multi-denominational or integrated education.

The current policy of restricting the promotion of integrated schools by encouraging the "transformation" of existing schools rather than, as in the past, funding new integrated schools established by parents, does not provide choice in a non-discriminatory way. In practice, even if there is a successful ballot of parents at a segregated school in favour of transformation to integration, there is only a limited probability that a genuinely integrated school will result.

It is not clear whether, in the absence of a more democratic method of ascertaining parental wishes in the choice of school, this situation constitutes a breach of the principle of parental rights to a "ensure education and teaching in conformity with their own religious and philosophical convictions". What *is* clear is that the unwillingness of the government to deal effectively with extreme educational segregation is a failure of its duty to use its full powers to promote the educational diversity which can foster "respect for human rights and fundamental freedoms" (UN Convention on the Rights of the Child, Art.29).

Chapter 19

Employment Rights

Richard Steele

There has been extensive legal intervention in employment relations in Northern Ireland for many years. For convenience, the resulting laws, whether made by Parliament or by judges, can be divided into two categories. This chapter covers both, though the main focus is on the first.

- *Individual employment law* is concerned with the rights and obligations flowing from the terms of the contract between an employee and an employer. In recent years employees have been given the protection of a "floor" of employment rights, which can be improved upon by negotiation with an employer. To gain protection of most individual employment rights, qualifying periods of employment are required and, generally, the rights increase with length of service.
- *Collective employment law* is primarily concerned with the regulation of the bargaining relationships between trade unions and employers or employers' associations.

For an account of employment law with particular reference to religious or political belief, gender, disability or ethnic origin, see Chapters 12-15 respectively.

Employment law and the legal system

The introduction of substantial employment rights for employees has also resulted in the creation of specialised judicial bodies:

- The *industrial tribunals* are established under the Industrial Tribunals (NI) Order 1996. They comprise three persons: a legally qualified chairperson and two lay representatives, one chosen from a panel nominated by the Confederation of British Industry (CBI), the other from a panel nominated by the Northern Ireland Committee of the Irish Congress of Trade Unions (NIC/ICTU). Industrial tribunals deal mainly with individual employment matters such as unfair dismissal, redundancy, trade union rights, maternity rights and sex discrimination. They are intended to provide cheap, quick and informal methods of hearing complaints, but in many cases, due to the complexity of the legislation, the reality is different. Legal aid is not available for tribunal hearings but it is possible to utilise the "green form" scheme, whereby subsidised advice and assistance can be obtained from a solicitor in advance of a hearing. Appeals are available on a point of law to the Court of Appeal.

- The *Fair Employment Tribunal*, created by the Fair Employment (NI) Act 1989, hears complaints of discrimination on grounds of religious belief or political opinion (see Chapter 12) and is constituted in the same way as industrial tribunals.
- The *Industrial Court* is established by the Industrial Relations (NI) Order 1992 and acts as an arbitration body. It is composed of a legally qualified President and two lay members, one chosen from a panel nominated by the CBI and the other from a panel nominated by NIC/ICTU. It also has statutory responsibilities in relation to disclosure of information for collective bargaining purposes.

The relevant government department responsible for employment legislation and manpower policy is the Department of Economic Development (DED), but responsibility for certain employment functions has been devolved to various statutory bodies:

- The *Labour Relations Agency* (LRA), now established by the Industrial Relations (NI) Order 1992, has the duty to promote the improvement of industrial relations, in particular by attempting to settle trade disputes. It mainly provides advisory, conciliation, mediation and arbitration services.
- The *Health and Safety Agency* (HSA) was established by the Health and Safety at Work (NI) Order 1978. It reviews health, safety and welfare in connection with work and the control of dangerous substances and makes recommendations to the appropriate government departments. It is with those departments and the district councils that responsibility for the enforcement of safety laws rests.

- The post of *Certification Officer* was established by the Industrial Relations (NI) Order 1992. The Certification Officer has duties in respect of trade unions and employers' associations.
- The *Commissioner for the Rights of Trade Union Members* is now established by the Trade Union and Labour Relations (NI) Order 1995. The Commissioner may give advice and assistance to a trade union member when taking certain legal proceedings against a trade union.
- The *Commissioner for Protection Against Unlawful Industrial Action* was established by the Trade Union and Labour Relations (NI) Order 1995. An individual deprived of goods and services because of unlawfully organised industrial action may apply to the Commissioner for the grant of assistance to take proceedings against a trade union.
- The roles of four other statutory bodies - the *Fair Employment Commission*, the *Equal Opportunities Commission, the Northern Ireland Disability Council* and the *Commission for Racial Equality* are described in Chapters 12 to 15 respectively.

Contracts of employment

The great majority of employment rights which can be adjudicated upon by an industrial tribunal are limited to employees. An employee is defined by article 2 of the Trade Union and Labour Relations (NI) Order 1995 as an individual who has entered into or works under a contract of employment.

The basis of an employment relationship is the law of contract. A contract is formed when an employer makes a job offer to a potential employee and that offer is accepted. The terms of the contract define the rights and duties of both parties. These terms are normally a mixture of express, implied, statutory and incorporated terms.

- *Express terms*, which may be written or oral, are those actually agreed by the employer and employee.
- *Implied terms* may exist by the operation of custom and practice in an industry or be terms necessary to make the contract of employment work.
- *Statutory terms* are those implied into a contract by an Act of Parliament, such as equal pay legislation.
- *Incorporated terms* are those agreed by collective bargaining between a trade union and an employer and incorporated into the

contracts of employment of each employee covered by the collective agreement.

The courts have held that certain implied terms are basic to every contract of employment. The most important of these are:

- that an employee will obey all lawful and reasonable orders, take reasonable care in his or her work, not wilfully disrupt the employer's business and be honest; and
- that an employer will pay agreed wages, take reasonable care for the employee's safety and health, not require an employee to do illegal acts and not act in a manner likely to destroy the relationship of trust or confidence.

Written statements of terms

By Part III of the Employment Rights (NI) Order 1996 an employer must provide employees with a written statement of certain major terms of the contract of employment. This written statement is not itself the contract of employment but it may amount to much the same thing by being the only or best evidence of it, especially if the employee has signed a copy. The written statement must include the following:

- the names of the employer and employee;
- the date the employment began, and whether any previous employment counts as continuous employment with the present employer and, if so, when it began;
- the job title or a brief description of the work for which the employee is employed;
- the scale or rate of pay;
- the intervals at which wages are to be paid;
- the hours of work and normal working hours;
- the place of work;
- entitlement to holidays, holiday pay and accrued holiday pay on termination of employment.

In addition, the employee must be given the following information either in the principal statement or by reference to another document:

- terms and conditions relating to sickness or injury;
- terms and conditions relating to pensions and pension schemes;
- notice entitlement;

- where the employment is temporary, the period for which it is expected to continue, or, if it is for a fixed term, the date it is to end; and
- any collective agreements affecting terms and conditions of employment.

The statement of particulars must also provide details of disciplinary procedures (if the employer employs 20 or more employees) and details of grievance procedures. Additional information must be given where the employee is to work outside the United Kingdom for more than one month. If there are no particulars to be entered under any of the above headings, this must be stated.

Where there is a change to any of the terms about which particulars must be entered, the employer must give the employee written notification of the change.

An employee can complain to an industrial tribunal if:

- the employer has failed to provide a written statement;
- the written statement provided is incomplete; or
- there is a dispute as to the actual terms of the written statement.

An industrial tribunal may make a declaration specifying the particulars which should have been included or amending particulars which have been incorrectly set out. However, where an employer is in default no compensation may be awarded.

Breach of contract

Where there is a breach of the contract of employment proceedings may be brought in the ordinary courts (i.e. the country courts or High Court) for sums due under the contract and for damages. The courts may also grant declarations and injunctions. In addition, an employee can seek damages at an industrial tribunal for breach of his or her contract of employment or for a sum due under that contract if the claim arises or is outstanding on the termination of employment. An employer can also claim against an employee where the employee has claimed against him or her. A tribunal may award a maximum of £25,000 to be paid in respect of a contract claim.

Itemised pay statements

Under Part III of the Employment Rights (NI) Order 1996 employees must be given an itemised pay statement every time they are paid. The statement must specify the gross and net wages payable, the amounts of any fixed or variable deductions and, where parts of the net wage are paid in different ways, the amount and method of each part payment. If there are several fixed deductions, an employer, instead of listing each separately, can give a standing statement of fixed deductions, which must be renewed at least every 12 months.

If an employee does not get an itemised pay statement or disputes the content of the statement, he or she can complain to an industrial tribunal for a decision as to what should be included in the statement. If unnotified deductions have been made, the tribunal can order the employer to repay the amounts so deducted in the 13 weeks prior to the claim.

Deductions from wages

Part IV of the Employment Rights (NI) Order 1996 provides that an employer must not make any deduction from the wages of any worker, or receive payments from the worker, unless the deduction or payment is authorised by statute or by a relevant provision in the worker's contract, or agreed in writing in advance by the worker.

The legislation gives special protection to workers in retail employment. Where an employer makes deductions from a retail worker's wages on a pay day on account of cash shortages or stock deficiencies, the total amount deducted must not exceed one-tenth of the gross wages payable on that pay day. If, however, the cash shortage or stock deficiency is sufficiently large, the deductions can be spread over a number of pay days. In relation to the final instalment of wages the one-tenth limit does not apply.

A worker may complain to an industrial tribunal about excessive wage deductions, provided he or she does so within three months of the deduction being made.

Guarantee payments

Part V of the Employment Rights (NI) Order 1996 provides that employees who have been employed for one month or more may be entitled to certain guarantee payments from their employer if they are laid off or put on short-time working. However, an employee will lose the right to payment if he or she refuses an offer of suitable alternative employment, if there is no work because of a trade dispute involving the employer or an associated employer, or if the employee does not comply with the reasonable requirement of the employer to be available for work. The right to guarantee payments is currently limited to a maximum of £14.10 a day and will be paid for up to five days in any three-month period. An employee who does not receive the appropriate payment can apply to an industrial tribunal within three months.

Payment when suspended on medical grounds

There are certain types of employment in Northern Ireland, such as work with lead, paint and chemicals, which are covered by health and safety regulations allowing an employee to be suspended for medical reasons. A list of these regulations can be found in Part VIII of the Employment Rights (NI) Order 1996. The Order provides that an employee who has been suspended under these regulations and who has been continuously employed for one month or more is entitled to receive a normal week's pay for a maximum of 26 weeks. However, an employee will not be entitled to such payment if he or she is incapable of work due to illness or disablement, unreasonably refuses an offer from the employer of suitable alternative work, or does not comply with the reasonable requirements of the employer to be available for work.

Money owed on an employer's insolvency

An employee who is owed money by an insolvent employer can claim as a preferential creditor for unpaid wages up to a maximum of £800, for amounts owed in respect of a guarantee payment, payment during medical suspension, payment for time off work on union duties or to look for other work during redundancy notice, and for a "protective" award (see page 369). In addition, an employee can apply to the Department of Economic Development for payment out of the National Insurance Fund of certain sums owed by the insolvent employer. Under Part XIV of the Employment Rights (NI) Order 1996 the following can be claimed from the Department:

- arrears of pay up to a maximum of £210 per week for up to 8 weeks;
- holiday pay to which the employee became entitled during the previous 12 months, up to a maximum of £210 per week;
- statutory minimum notice pay up to a maximum of £210 per week;
- a basic award of compensation for unfair dismissal;

• repayment of apprenticeship fees.

When the Department makes such a payment to an employee, it can then seek to recover the debt from the insolvent employer. An employee who has applied to the Department can complain to an industrial tribunal within three months if the Department has not made the payment or if the payment is less than the amount entitled.

Victimisation

The Employment Rights (NI) Order 1996 entitles employees not to be subjected to a detriment on grounds of union membership or activities, on health and safety grounds, as trustees of occupational pension schemes or as employee representatives. The right not to suffer a detriment may be enforced by a complaint to an individual tribunal.

Trade union membership and activities

A certain degree of protection and some enforceable rights have been given to employees concerning trade union membership.

Dismissal

Article 136 of the Employment Rights (NI) Order 1996 provides that an employee can complain of unfair dismissal if he or she is dismissed:
• for being, or proposing to become, a member of an independent trade union (*i.e.*, one which is not under the control of an employer or an employer's organisation);
• for taking part at "an appropriate time" in the activities of an independent trade union; an "appropriate time" means time which is either outside working hours or during working hours if the employer has given consent; or
• for non-membership of a trade union.

The right not to be dismissed for trade union membership or activities applies to all employees and no period of continuous employment is required. In addition, a special interim procedure can be used to hear the case and there may be entitlement to a special award of compensation.

Victimisation

An employee who has not been dismissed but who has been victimised for trade union membership or activity or for non-membership of a trade union can also complain to an industrial tribunal within three months.

Time off work for trade union duties and activities

Under article 92 of the Employment Rights (NI) Order 1996 an employee who is an official of an independent trade union recognised by the employer is entitled to reasonable time off work with normal pay to carry out duties concerned with industrial relations between the employer and the employees, or to attend industrial relations training courses which are relevant to those duties and approved by NIC/ICTU or by the employee's union. Guidance about time off for union duties is contained in a Code of Practice issued by the Labour Relations Agency. Article 93 also provides that an employee who is a member of an independent trade union recognised by the employer is entitled to reasonable time off work, without pay, to take part in trade union activities, though this does not extend to time off for activities involving industrial action.

Maternity rights

Ante-natal care

Articles 83-85 of the Employment Rights (NI) Order 1996 provide that an employee who is pregnant has the right not to be unreasonably refused time off work with pay to enable her to receive ante-natal care.

Maternity leave

Part IX of the Employment Rights (NI) Order 1996 establishes a right to 14 weeks' maternity leave for all employees regardless of length of service or hours of work. The maternity leave period can commence, at the earliest, 11 weeks before the expected week of childbirth. It will *automatically* commence if the woman is absent from work due to pregnancy or childbirth during the 6 weeks prior to the expected week of the birth. Women have the right to return to their original job at the end of the period.

The legislation prescribes three notification requirements. First, a woman wishing to exercise her maternity leave rights must give written notice of her pregnancy and the expected week of childbirth at least 21 days before the maternity leave period begins. Second, she must give 21 days' notice (or as soon as is reasonably practicable thereafter) of the date on which she intends her leave to begin. Finally, if she wishes to return to work before the end of the 14-week period, she must give seven days' notice of her intended date of return.

During the maternity leave period all existing terms and conditions of employment (other than remuneration) must be maintained. In addition, an employee entitled to maternity leave must not work or be permitted to work by her employer during the period of two weeks beginning with the date of her confinement.

Risk assessment

The Management of Health and Safety at Work Regulations (NI) 1992 place specific obligations on employers to carry out a risk assessment of work undertaken by women of child-bearing age or a new or expectant mother where she may be exposed to any process, working condition or physical, chemical or biological agent which could give rise to risks to the health or safety of the woman or the baby. Where an employer is notified that a woman employee is pregnant, has given birth within the previous six months or is breast-feeding, the employer must again undertake a review of the current risk assessments for those tasks undertaken by the women to identify potential risks. Where the assessment identifies a potential risk, preventive or protective measures must be put in place and the employee informed of the contents of the assessment and the measures taken. If it is not possible to avoid the risk, the employer is required to alter the woman's working conditions, or if this is not practicable, to take action to find suitable alternative employment or to place the woman on paid leave for as long as is necessary to protect her safety or health or that of her baby.

Dismissal

Article 131 of the Employment Rights (NI) Order 1996 specifies that if a female employee is dismissed because she is pregnant, or because of any other reason connected with her pregnancy, she can complain to an industrial tribunal of unfair dismissal. No period of continuous employment is required. Dismissal in such circumstances will on the face of it be unfair. Dismissal of an employee on grounds of pregnancy may also constitute sex discrimination (see Chapter 13).

Right to return to work

Under Part IX of the Employment Rights (NI) Order 1996 greater rights to return to work following pregnancy are given to certain employees. A female employee who takes leave because of pregnancy has the right to return to her job within 29 weeks of the date of confinement and on terms and conditions as favourable as if she had not been absent. To have this automatic right to return she must have been employed for two years by the beginning of the eleventh week before confinement and must have notified her employer in writing at least three weeks before she stopped work that she intends to return to work.

The mother may be required to furnish written confirmation of her intention to return at any time after seven weeks following confinement. When she is able to resume her job she must give her employer three weeks' notice. An employer can delay the employee's return by up to four weeks if reasons are given. The employee can delay her return by up to four weeks if she is ill and produces a medical certificate or, if there is an interruption of work (*e.g.* due to industrial action), she can postpone the date of her return until two weeks after work resumes.

Even if the above notification procedures are followed, the right to return is subject to two exclusions:

- if it is not reasonably practicable to allow the woman to return to her original job, she may be offered alternative employment;
- if the firm employs less than six people, she need not be re-employed at all.

If the employee is not permitted by the employer to return to work, she can apply within three months to an industrial tribunal under the unfair dismissal provisions. Alternatively, if due to redundancy her job no longer exists and her employer cannot offer her a suitable alternative job, she is entitled to a redundancy payment and can apply to an industrial tribunal within six months. In both cases she will be considered to have been employed up to the date on which she intended to return to work.

Time off work

Time off for public duties

Article 78 of the Employment Rights (NI) Order 1996 entitles an employee to reasonable time off work without pay to perform certain public duties, *e.g.*, if the employee is a Justice of the Peace or a member of a district council, a Health and Social Services Board or an Education and Library Board.

Time off for occupational pension scheme trustees

Article 86 of the Employment Rights (NI) Order 1996 entitles an employee who is a trustee of an occupational pension scheme to paid time off work to perform his or her duties as a trustee or to undergo relevant training.

Time off for employee representatives

Article 89 of the Employment Rights (NI) Order 1996 entitles an employee who is an employee for the purposes of consultation on grounds of redundancy, transfer of an undertaking and health and safety at work, or who is standing for election to such a position, to paid time off work.

In the above circumstances where an employee is not afforded time off work a complaint can be made to an industrial tribunal. For further instances of where an employee can be allowed time off, see pages 361 and 370.

Health and safety at work

Health and safety standards in employment are regulated by both judge-made law and by a wide range of legislation. Under the judge-made law, employers have a general duty to take reasonable care for the safety and health of their employees. As regards legislation, in addition to specific health and safety provisions giving protection in, *e.g.*, factories and offices, employees receive health and safety protection under the Health and Safety at Work (NI) Order 1978.

General duties of employers

Article 4 of the 1978 Order specifies that it is the duty of every employer to ensure, so far as is reasonably practicable, the health, safety and welfare at work of all employees. This means, amongst other things, and as far as is reasonably practicable:

- providing plant and systems of work which are safe and without risks to health;
- ensuring safety in connection with the use, handling, storage and transport of articles and substances;
- providing such information, instruction, training and supervision as is necessary to ensure the health and safety at work of the employees.

An employer must prepare, and when appropriate revise, a written statement of general policy with respect to the health and safety at work of the employees and bring it and any revisions to the notice of the employees (unless there are fewer than six). The Health and Safety Agency has issued a guidance note entitled "Employers' policy statements for health and safety at work".

Risk assessment and prevention

The Management of Health and Safety at Work Regulations (NI) 1992 require employers to make a suitable and sufficient assessment of the risks to health and safety to which their employees, are exposed. Where there are five or more employees the findings of the assessment must be recorded as well as any group of employees found to be especially at risk. Employers must provide employees with appropriate health surveillance, having regard to the risks identified by the assessment. Employers must also make arrangements for the effective planning, organisation, control, monitoring and review of preventive and protective measures. To assist them undertake such measures employers must appoint competent persons with sufficient time and resources to fulfil their functions. They are required, in addition, to establish appropriate procedures to be followed in the event of serious and imminent danger to persons at work. Finally, employers must provide employees with comprehensible and relevant information on risks to their health, preventive and protective measures, procedures, the identity of competent persons who will implement the procedures and any risks notified to the employer by another employer who shares the work place.

Safety representatives

The Safety Representatives and Safety Committee Regulations (NI) 1979 require employers to recognise safety representatives appointed by recognised trade unions and to consult with them. An employer must establish a safety committee within three months if two or more safety representatives request it. The powers and duties of a safety representative are set out in the 1979 Regulations and are elaborated upon in two accompanying codes of practice. He or she can investigate potential hazards and dangerous occurrences at the work place, investigate complaints and make representations to the employer. To enable them to carry out their functions, safety representatives are entitled to such time off work with pay as is necessary.

In circumstances where employees are not represented by union-appointed safety representatives, the Health and Safety (Consultation with Employees) Regulations (NI) 1996 apply. The employer must consult either with the employees directly or with employee representatives on health and safety matters. The duties and powers given to such employees or their representatives are not as extensive as those given to union-appointed representatives.

Other duties

In addition to the general duties owed by an employer to the employees, the 1978 Order stipulates the duties of employers and the self-employed to non-employees, the duties of persons concerned with premises to persons other than their employees, and the duties of manufacturers as regards articles and substances for use at work. It is also the duty of every employee to take reasonable care for the health and safety of anyone who may be affected by the employee's acts or omissions at work. More recently, the health and safety legislation has placed additional duties on employees.

Enforcement

Enforcement of the health and safety legislation is the responsibility of various government departments and the district councils. The main enforcing body is the Health and Safety Inspectorate of the Department of Economic Development. This advises government bodies on the making of health and safety regulations and prepares and issues codes of practice on health and safety and approves codes made by others.

Failure of an employer to comply with safety legislation is normally a criminal offence. On conviction in a magistrates' court, penalties are by way of fines only. On conviction in the Crown Court, the penalty can be up to two years' imprisonment and an unlimited fine. In addition to their power to prosecute, enforcement officers have been given the right by articles 23-27 of the 1978 Order to:

* issue improvement notices requiring specified improvements to be carried out;
* issue prohibition notices forbidding employers from continuing specified activities if there is a risk of serious personal injury; and
* seize, and render harmless, any substance or article believed to be a cause of imminent danger or serious personal injury.

An employer can appeal to an industrial tribunal against the issuing of either an improvement notice or a prohibition notice.

Employment protection in health and safety cases

Articles 132 and 68 of the Employment Rights (NI) Order 1996 give protection against unfair dismissal and victimisation respectively to:

* employees appointed by the employer to undertake health and safety duties;
* safety representatives and members of a safety committee;
* other employees who bring safety issues to the attention of an employer;
* employees who leave their workplace in circumstances where they reasonably believe danger to be serious and imminent and which they could not reasonably be expected to avert; and
* employees who, in circumstances where they believe there to be a serious and imminent danger, take steps to protect themselves.

Termination of employment

An employment relationship can end in a number of ways. It may end by the mutual agreement of the parties, by the expiry of a fixed term contract or as a result of the employer's insolvency. Alternatively, it can be terminated at the request of either the employer or the employee. The law has given a degree of protection to employees on termination.

Minimum notice requirements

Part X of the Employment Rights (NI) Order 1996 lays down the following minimum periods of notice for every full-time employee who has been employed for at least one month (the periods can be extended by agreement):

- after one month, but less than two years: one week's notice;
- after two years: two weeks' notice; and
- one additional week for each year's work up to a maximum of 12 weeks' notice.

Written statements of reasons for dismissal

A dismissed employee who has been continuously employed for six months or more prior to the date of dismissal is entitled by article 124 of the Employment Rights (NI) Order 1996 to ask the employer for a written statement setting out the reasons for the dismissal. If the employer does not provide a statement, or if the particulars given are inadequate, the dismissed employee can apply to an industrial tribunal within three months. The tribunal can order the employer to pay the dismissed employee two weeks' wages, up to a maximum of £420.

Redundancy

The law takes two approaches to redundancy:

- it requires employers to inform and consult representatives of employees before redundancies are implemented;
- it provides for compensation to be paid to employees made redundant.

Consultation on redundancies

Part XIII of the Employment Rights (NI) Order 1996 provides that if an employer proposes to dismiss as redundant 20 or more employees at one establishment within a period of 90 days or less, the employer must consult all persons who are appropriate representatives of any of the employees who may be dismissed. Appropriate representatives of employees are employee representatives elected by them, representatives of independent trade unions recognised by the employer or, where there are both employee representatives and trade union representatives, the employer may choose with which group to consult.

Consultation must begin in good time and at least within the following timescale. If more than 100 employees are to be made redundant within 90 days, consultations must take place at least 90 days before the first dismissal. Otherwise consultation must take place at least 30 days before the first dismissal takes effect.

The consultation must include consultation about ways of avoiding dismissals, reducing the number of employees to be dismissed and mitigating the consequences of the dismissals. Moreover consultation must take place with a view to reaching agreement with the employee representatives.

The employer must disclose the following information in writing to trade union representatives:

- the reasons for the proposed dismissals;
- the numbers and descriptions of workers affected;
- the total number of employees of such description employed;
- the proposed method of selecting employees for dismissal;
- the proposed method of carrying out the dismissals; and
- the proposed method of calculating redundancy payments.

If an employer does not comply with the above requirements, a complaint can be made by the appropriate trade union to an industrial tribunal. If the tribunal upholds the complaint it may partly safeguard an employee's wages by making a "protective" award. This orders the employer to pay wages to redundant or potentially redundant employees for a specified period.

Individual redundancy payments

The intention of the redundancy provisions of the Employment Rights (NI) Order 1996 is to give a minimum level of compensation to employees dismissed for redundancy. The level of payment depends on the employee's age, pay and length of service. Compensation is for loss already suffered, not for any future loss. The provisions apply to employees who, since becoming 18, have at least two years' continuous employment with an employer or associated employer. If the facts are disputed, the employee must prove that he or she was dismissed and the employer must then show that the dismissal was not for redundancy.

By article 174, redundancy occurs where an employer ceases business or where there is surplus labour. Article 171 provides that dismissal occurs where the employer terminates the contract of employment with or without notice, or where a fixed-term contract expires without being renewed, or where an employee terminates the contract because of the employer's conduct – "constructive dismissal". If it is shown that the employee was not dismissed, there will be no entitlement to a redundancy payment.

Employees who have received notice of redundancy and who have worked continuously for two years or more are entitled under the provisions of article 41 of the Employment Rights (NI) Order 1996 to reasonable time off work to look for new employment or to make arrangements for training for future employment. During this period employees are entitled to be paid the appropriate hourly rate, up to a maximum of two days' pay.

The redundancy award

The size of the redundancy payment is dependent upon three factors: the amount of basic weekly pay (to a maximum of £210), the number of years' continuous employment (to a maximum of 20 years) and the age of the redundant person. A redundant employee is entitled to:

- half a week's pay for each year of employment between the ages of 18 and 21;
- one week's pay for each year of employment between the ages of 22 and 40;
- one and a half week's pay for each year of employment between the age of 41 and normal retirement age.

However, for each month that an employee's age exceeds 64 the redundancy payment will be reduced by one-twelfth. The maximum entitlement is £210 x 20 (number of years) x 1.5, *i.e.* £6,300.

Unfair dismissal

To bring an unfair dismissal claim an employee must normally have been continuously employed for two years before the termination of employment. However, under the Employment Rights (NI) Order 1996, no period of continuous employment is required in the following circumstances:

- where an employee is dismissed because she is pregnant or for any other reason conne Appendix Three -cted with her pregnancy (art. 131: see page 362);

- where the employee is dismissed for a health and safety reason (art. 132: see page 367);
- where the employee is dismissed for performing the functions of a trustee of an occupational pension scheme (art. 133);
- where an employee is dismissed for being an employee representative or being a candidate in an election to become an employee representative (art. 134);
- where the employee is dismissed for asserting a statutory right (art. 135);
- where the employee is dismissed for trade union membership or activity or for non-membership of a trade union (art.136: see page 360).

The dismissal of an employee or the selection for redundancy of an employee for one or more of the above reasons will be deemed to be unfair. A dismissal will also be unfair if there has been a contravention of the Transfer of Undertakings (Protection of Employment) Regulations 1981 (unless there was an economic, technical or organisational reason to justify the dismissal).

In addition, if an employee is dismissed instead of being suspended on medical grounds, the qualifying period is reduced from two years to one month.

A complaint of unfair dismissal must be made to a tribunal within three months of the termination of employment.

Dismissal

Article 129 of the Employment Rights (NI) Order 1996 provides that dismissal takes place where the contract of employment is terminated by the employer with or without notice, where a fixed-term contract expires without being renewed, or where the employee terminates the contract of employment because of the conduct of the employer. For there to be a "constructive" dismissal arising from an employee's resignation, the employer must have been guilty of a fundamental breach of the employment contract. If the employer contends that no dismissal took place, it is for the employee to satisfy an industrial tribunal that this is not the case.

Fair dismissal

Article 130 of the Employment Rights (NI) Order 1996 provides that some dismissals are automatically fair. It is for the employer to show that there was a fair reason for dismissal. When deciding whether this is so, an industrial tribunal will take no account of any pressure, such as industrial action, put on an employer to dismiss an employee. There will be a *fair dismissal* if:

- the employee is not capable of doing the job for which he or she was employed;
- the employee has not the qualifications necessary for the job;
- the employee's conduct warrants dismissal;
- the employee is redundant;
- the continued employment of the employee would contravene a duty or restriction imposed by law; or
- there is some other substantial reason to justify dismissal.

The employer's reasonableness

It is for the tribunal to decide whether the employer acted reasonably or unreasonably. There may have been a fair reason for dismissing an employee, but the employer may still have acted unreasonably. The standard applied by the tribunal is that of the reasonable employer. Tribunals have recognised that there exists a broad band of reasonable responses within which one employer might decide to dismiss while another might decide to impose a lesser penalty, such as a final written warning. The effect has been to make it more difficult for an employee to be successful in an unfair dismissal claim.

A decision on whether an employer acted reasonably is a question of fact for an industrial tribunal to decide. Only if it can be shown that no reasonable tribunal could have reached the same decision can a tribunal decision be successfully challenged on appeal. When considering the reasonableness of a dismissal tribunals take into account the Code of Practice issued by the Labour Relations Agency on "Disciplinary Practice and Procedures in Employment". This specifies certain features which should be an essential part of any disciplinary procedure, in particular that employees should know of complaints against them, be given an adequate opportunity to state their case and have the right to be accompanied by a trade union official or fellow employee at any disciplinary hearing. In addition, disciplinary action should not be taken until the complaint has been investigated carefully and an internal appeals procedure should be provided.

Remedies for unfair dismissal

Although the legislation lays primary emphasis on securing the reinstatement or re-engagement of the dismissed employee, there is no legal right for an employee to get his or her job back and in practice few awards of reinstatement or re-engagement are made. In the last analysis, if an employer sacks an employee and refuses re-employment, the only remedy available is monetary compensation.

Reinstatement takes effect as if an applicant has never been dismissed. This involves full restoration of pay and other benefits, including seniority and pension rights. *Re-engagement* occurs where the tribunal thinks that reinstatement is not practicable. It allows the employer to offer the employee another suitable job.

An *interim relief procedure* applies to an employee who is dismissed for trade union activity or for non-union membership. The employee must apply to an industrial tribunal within seven days of the dismissal. If the tribunal considers that the unfair dismissal application is likely to succeed, it may order reinstatement, re-engagement or the continuation of the contract of employment so that the employee can remain on full pay until the tribunal makes its final decision.

As regards *compensation*, two types of award can be made, although in certain cases an additional or special award is available. Compensation will be reduced if a tribunal decides that an employee contributed to the dismissal. An employee is also under a duty to make efforts to reduce the loss suffered.

A "basic" award compensates the employee for the loss of the job and is calculated in the same way as a redundancy award (see page 000). The basic award is subject to a maximum of £210 x 20 x 1.5, *i.e.* £6,300.

A "compensatory" award is made to compensate the employee for the actual loss suffered from the date of dismissal, up to a maximum of £11,300. The amount will be such as the tribunal considers just and equitable in all the circumstances. In practice, the calculation involves loss of earnings from the date of dismissal to the date of the tribunal hearing and future loss of earnings from the date of the tribunal hearing.

An "additional" award is made in two circumstances where an employer has failed to comply with a reinstatement or re-engagement order. First, in the case of a normal dismissal, an award of between 13 and 26 weeks' pay can be made. Second, where an employee has been dismissed for discrimination as defined by the Sex Discrimination (NI) Order 1976, the Fair Employment (NI) Acts 1976-89 or the Race Relations (NI) Order 1997, an award of between 26 and 52 weeks' pay can be made. The maximum weekly pay that can be taken into account in both situations is again £210.

The legislation provides for a "special" award of increased compensation to employees dismissed for trade union membership or activities, for non-membership of a trade union or for certain health and safety related dismissals. The minimum basic award is calculated in the normal way, but subject to a minimum of £2,770. On top of the basic and normal compensatory awards, a special award may also be made where the employee requests but does not obtain re-engagement or reinstatement. The award is 104 weeks' pay, subject to a minimum of £13,775 and a maximum of £27,500. If, however, a tribunal makes an award of re-engagement or reinstatement which is not complied with, then, unless the employer can show that it was not reasonably practicable to comply with the award, the special award is 156 weeks' pay, subject to a minimum of £20,600 but with no limit on the maximum.

Trade union law

A trade union is defined by article 3 of the Industrial Relations (NI) Order 1992 as an organisation which consists:
* of workers of one or more description and has as its principal purpose the regulation of relations between workers and employers or employers' associations; or
* wholly or mainly of an affiliated or constituent group of such organisations or their representatives.

The basis of a trade union's right to exist is the Industrial Relations (NI) Order 1992, and by article 3 of this Order they can sue and be sued in their own name. Even though a trade union is in law an "unincorporated association", any judgment, order or award may be enforced against it as if it were a public company.

The 1992 Order distinguishes between independent unions and others. A union is independent if it is not under the control of an employer or a group of employers and is not liable to interference arising out of the provision of financial or other support which tends towards such control. Only independent trade unions are accorded statutory rights concerning disclosure of information and consultation.

Their members are also given further rights concerning unfair dismissal and redundancy.

Trade union recognition

There is no general legal obligation requiring an employer to recognise a trade union. The decision to recognise and the extent to which recognition is afforded is a decision for an employer.

Collective bargaining and legal rights for unions

The normal method of negotiation between trade unions and employers or employers' associations is by way of collective bargaining. By Article 26 of the 1992 Order collective agreements are conclusively presumed not to have been intended by the parties to be legally enforceable, unless the agreement is in writing and contains a provision which states that the parties intended the agreement to be a legally enforceable contract. In practice, collective agreements are not enforceable. But certain terms of collective agreements, such as wage rates and holiday entitlement, are incorporated into an individual's contract of employment and can be agreed by an individual employee and his or her employer.

The 1992 Order says it is the duty of every employer, if requested to do so, to disclose information about his or her undertaking to the representatives of any trade union for the purposes of collective bargaining. A complaint of failure to disclose information can be referred to the LRA, which will attempt conciliation. If this fails, the matter may then be referred by the LRA to the Industrial Court, which may make a declaration stipulating a period within which disclosure is to be made. If the information is still not forthcoming, a further complaint may be made via the LRA to the Industrial Court, which may then order that the contracts of the employees specified in the claim should include the specified terms and conditions.

If an employer recognises an independent trade union for collective bargaining purposes, consultation must take place with such union representatives in advance of 20 or more redundancies or in advance of a transfer of an undertaking. Alternatively, an employer may consult with representatives of the employees (see page 368). In respect of health and safety the employer must recognise union-appointed safety representatives. Only in the absence of such representatives may an employer consult employees or their representative on health and safety matters (see page 366). Enforcement of a failure to consult is by way of complaint to an industrial tribunal.

Trade union administration

Part II of the Trade Union and Labour Relations (NI) Order 1995 concerns trade union administration and adds to the requirements placed on trade unions by Part II of the 1992 Order. Unions are required to compile and maintain a register of the names and addresses of their members. A union must inform its members and the Certification Officer about the conduct of its financial affairs. The Certification Officer has power to direct a trade union to produce documents relating to its financial affairs and to appoint inspectors to investigate the financial affairs of a union.

Trade union elections

Part III of the 1995 Order concerns trade union elections. It applies to trade unions with their head office located in Northern Ireland and they complement existing requirements placed on trade unions with their head office based in Great Britain. A trade union must ensure that every member of its executive committee has been elected to that position by secret postal ballot within the previous five years, although this provision does not apply to union employees who are within five years of retirement age. A union is required to appoint a qualified independent person to scrutinise the conduct of such elections by storing and distributing the voting papers and counting the votes cast. In a report, the scrutineer must state the number of voting papers distributed, the number returned, the number valid and invalid, votes cast and the name of the person appointed to oversee the ballot. Where it is contended that a trade union has not complied with the above requirements, an application may be made to the Certification Officer or to the High Court.

Rights of trade union members

Part IV of the 1995 Order concerns the rights of trade union members. Article 29 establishes a right of union members to a ballot before industrial action is taken. Where action is taken without the support of a ballot, a union member may apply to the High Court for an order.

Articles 31-34 establish a right not to be unjustifiably disciplined. Types of conduct in respect of which discipline is considered unjustifiable include:

- failure to participate in, or conduct indicating opposition to, industrial action;
- alleging that a union official has acted contrary to union rules or unlawfully; and
- seeking assistance or advice from the Certification Officer or the Commissioner for the Rights of Trade Union Members.

Union members who consider they have been unjustifiably disciplined may complain to an industrial tribunal for redress.

The Order provides that an employer may not deduct union subscriptions from a worker's wages under check-off arrangements unless the worker has authorised such deductions in writing within the previous three years. Where it is alleged that an employer has made an unauthorised deduction, a complaint may be made to a tribunal. Articles 38-41 establish the right of a union member, enforceable by a complaint to a tribunal, not to be unreasonably expelled from membership of a trade union.

Trade union political funds

Part V of the 1995 Order relates to the political funds of Northern Ireland trade unions. Similar provisions apply to unions with their head office located in Great Britain. It provides that union funds must not be used for political objectives unless approved by a secret ballot of union members, which is to be held at least every 10 years. Funds paid in furtherance of political objectives must be paid from a separate political fund. Union members who do not contribute to the political fund must not be disadvantaged and may complain to the Certification Officer if they consider this to be the case. The political objectives for which funds must be paid from the political fund are:

- the contribution to the funds of a political party;
- the provision of any service by a political party;
- the selection of a candidate for political office;
- the holding of any meeting by, or on behalf of, a political party; and

- the production, publication or distribution of any literature, document, film, sound recording or advertisement, the main purpose of which is to persuade people to vote for a political party.

A complaint may be made to the Certification Officer or to the High Court that a union has not conducted a ballot in accordance with the system approved by the Certification Officer.

A major difference exists between the position in Northern Ireland and that in Great Britain concerning trade union political funds. In Northern Ireland trade union members must *contract in* to the political levy rather than *contract out* as in Great Britain.

Industrial action

Part VIII of the 1995 Order consolidates and reforms the legal liability of trade unions and their members when engaged in industrial action. Article 97 provides that an act done by a person in contemplation of furtherance of a trade dispute shall be protected from certain liability in the law of tort. On the other hand, article 102 removes immunity from action in tort for secondary industrial action.

Articles 104-117 stipulate the balloting procedures that must be followed before lawful industrial action may be undertaken. Article 104 provides that a call by a trade union to take industrial action will not be protected unless the industrial action has the support of a ballot. A union must give seven days' written notice to the employer. The notice must state the union's intention to hold a ballot, specify the opening day of the ballot and describe the employees who will be called upon to vote. A sample of the voting paper must be provided three days before the opening of the ballot. Article 106 requires the union to appoint a qualified person to report on the conduct of the ballot, except where 50 or fewer members are entitled to vote. Article 108 provides that entitlement to vote must be given to those members who will be called upon to take industrial action.

The voting paper must contain a question which requires the person answering it to say by indicating "Yes" or "No" whether he or she is prepared to take part in a strike and/or a question whether he or she is prepared to take part in action short of a strike. In addition the following statement must appear, without qualification, on every voting paper: "If you take part in a strike or other industrial action, you may be in breach of your contract of employment". Every person entitled to vote must be allowed to vote without interference and be able to vote without incurring cost. Following the ballot, all persons entitled to vote and every relevant employer must be informed of the number of votes cast, the number answering "yes" and "no" and the number of spoiled voting papers. By virtue of article 117 a ballot ceases to be valid, for the purposes of lawful industrial action, at the end of the period of four weeks beginning with the date of the ballot.

In order for industrial action to be protected from certain tort claims, article 118 provides that the union must, not later than seven days before the industrial action is intended to start, give written notice to the employer of those employees whom the union envisages will take part in the action. The notice must indicate whether the action will be continuous or discontinuous, and state when the action is intended to start (if it is continuous) or the days on which it is intended to take place (if it is discontinuous).

Liability to pay compensation

A union may be held responsible for the actions of its officials (so-called "vicarious" liability). It is for the courts to decide whether a union is liable for the acts of its members or officials in respect of wrongs such as negligence or nuisance. In respect of the economic wrongs mentioned above, a union will be vicariously liable only for specified unlawful actions which are authorised or endorsed by a "responsible person", defined by article 21 of the Industrial Relations (NI) Order 1992 as:

- the principal executive committee;
- a person with the power to authorise such acts;
- the president or general secretary;
- any other employed official; or
- any committee of the union to which an employed official regularly reports.

However, the union will not be liable for acts authorised by the last two above if the rules of the union prevent that person or committee from authorising industrial action. Nor will the union be liable if the act has been repudiated by the first two above.

Where a union is found liable in court proceedings, the amount of damages which may be awarded is subject to certain upper limits specified by article 22 of the 1992 Order. These limits apply to all proceedings except those for negligence, nuisance or breach of duty relating to the use of property or resulting in personal injury. The limit on damages is dependent upon the membership of the union, ranging from £10,000 for membership up to 5,000 to £250,000 for membership above 100,000. For the purposes of calculating the number of members which a trade union has, members outside Northern Ireland are included. Damages may not be recovered from protected property such as political and provident funds belonging to a union or to an employers' association.

Picketing

There is no general right to picket. As with trade disputes, an immunity is conferred, this time by article 16 of the 1992 Order, which provides that it shall be lawful for a person to picket:

- at or near his or her own place of work, or
- if he or she is an official of a trade union, at or near the place of work of a member of that union whom he or she is accompanying and representing.

The picketing must be for the purpose of peacefully obtaining or communicating information, or peacefully persuading any person to work or abstain from working. In addition, if a person works at more than one place, or at a place where it is impracticable to picket, he or she is entitled to picket any premises of the employer from which he or she works or from which his or her work is administered.

Pickets can easily fall foul of both the criminal and civil law. For instance, they may be liable to criminal charges for obstruction of the highway or of the police, intimidation or contravention of the Public Order (NI) Order 1987 in respect of meetings and marches (see Chapter 9). They may also be liable to a civil action for trespass or nuisance.

Useful address:

- Commissioner for Rights of Trade Union Members
  Scottish Legal House
  65/67 Chichester Street
  Belfast BT1 4JT

Chapter 20

Housing Rights

Angela Hegarty

One of the major areas of contention in the past in Northern Ireland has been housing allocation. Since the establishment of the Northern Ireland Housing Executive in 1972 much of the controversy has subsided, but some problems remain, largely in relation to repairs and public funding. There are also problems in relation to the law, which, whilst it guarantees a number of rights, fails to protect individuals in some respects, most notably when they are homeless. The Council for the Homeless address is: 153 University Street, Belfast BT7 1HR (tel: 01232-246440). For an explanation of specific housing rights enjoyed by disabled persons, see Chapter 15. For an explanation of housing benefit, see Chapter 21.

The law distinguishes between different types of housing in Northern Ireland - the public rented sector, the private rented sector, and home owners. An occupant's rights and obligations are defined both by statute law and, if the occupant is a tenant, by the tenancy agreement or "lease".

A lease is essentially a contract between the landlord and the tenant agreeing, *e.g.*, how much rent the tenant must pay, who is responsible for repairs, and so on. A lease does not have to be in writing, but if it is then any dispute as to the lease's content will be easier to solve. In addition to whatever is agreed in the lease, the law lays down certain terms, *e.g.* that the tenant is allowed "quiet and peaceful enjoyment" of the property and is given a minimum period of notice to quit. Generally, in public sector housing a tenant will be given a written lease. In the private rented sector it is more common for leases to be merely oral.

Public rented sector housing

The main provider of public sector housing in Northern Ireland is the Northern Ireland Housing Executive (NIHE), which generally speaking performs the same functions as local authorities in Great Britain. It was set up and carries out its tasks under statute, which means that many of its decisions are judicially reviewable in the courts.

NIHE and registered housing association tenants enjoy certain special rights which are not necessarily enjoyed by private sector tenants. These relate, for instance, to security of tenure, the right to buy and rights to take in lodgers and sub-let.

Allocation

NIHE allocates accommodation according to priority. When a person applies to NIHE for accommodation he or she will be placed either on the Group A priority waiting list or on the Group B general waiting list. Within these groups an application will also be prioritised, *e.g.* a person may be classed as "emergency AI status". On the general waiting list (Group B) a person must have been resident in Northern Ireland for seven years and will be allocated points depending upon his or her current accommodation and family circumstances.

Tenancy agreements

Each NIHE tenant is given a standard form tenancy agreement which is a legal document setting out the terms and conditions of the occupation of the premises. A tenant is entitled to a copy of the tenancy agreement and a straightforward explanation of its terms (art. 38(3) of the Housing (NI) Order 1983). The most important terms of the agreement relate to payment of rent and rights and obligations in respect of repairs.

Rent

The tenancy agreement stipulates that the tenant agrees to pay all the rent owing. Any failure to do so results in NIHE trying to recover the amount as a debt or, in extreme cases, attempting to recover possession of the premises with a court order. Unlike privately rented accommodation there is no legal compulsion on NIHE to provide a tenant with a rent book, although in practice a giro book is usually supplied.

The obligation to pay rent is usually imposed only upon the tenant, *i.e.* the individual whose name appears on the tenancy agreement, and not upon his or her family. Where there is a joint tenancy the duty to pay is imposed upon all the tenants. Arrears of rent occur generally for the following reasons:

- Where there has been a mistake. If there is a mistake by the tenant, he or she is responsible for arrears in full and will have to come to an arrangement to pay. If there is a mistake by NIHE, any overcharging should in general be recoverable by the tenant while any undercharging cannot generally be recovered by NIHE.
- Where the tenant is unable or unwilling to pay. A tenant who cannot pay because of too little money or an emergency is best advised to start paying again at the first available opportunity, even if it is only part of the rent. He or she should seek advice on any extra benefit entitlement, *e.g.* housing benefit or family credit. This can sometimes be backdated, for up to 52 weeks, if good cause for a late claim can be shown (*e.g.* serious physical or mental illness). If possible a voluntary arrangement to pay off arrears should be entered into if any extra cash becomes available through benefits. If the tenant cannot come to such an arrangement, NIHE will use the following methods of recovery.

Recovery of arrears of rent

NIHE will first try to get a voluntary agreement with a tenant to repay the arrears, either by instalments or by a lump sum. If the tenant does not take up this option, NIHE may apply informal pressures such as refusing to grant a transfer or failing to carry out improvements. If these also have no effect, NIHE may turn to recovery through redirecting other financial sources such as grants, compensation benefits, etc.

Since the repeal of the Payments for Debt (Emergency Provisions) Act (NI) 1971 in 1991, the method for recovering arrears of rent from state benefits is as follows. There is a limit on deductions, but these must be made if a tenant is six weeks or more in arrears. If a benefit office agrees, deductions may be made after only four weeks, as this may be in the best interests of the claimant and his or her family. A tenant who gets income support, family credit or housing benefit can apply on grounds of hardship to NIHE's district manager to have no deductions made from redecoration or self-help repair allowances, but these are the only types of payment which qualify for such relief. NIHE may also deduct a limited amount per week from student grants. Where a tenant owing arrears is successful in a claim against NIHE, arrears can be deducted by NIHE before the money from the claim is handed over.

NIHE can also pursue debtors through the courts. Where the amount outstanding is a small one, NIHE can apply to the small claims court (part of the county court). More common however is the issue of a "process" in the local magistrates' court. Neither of these court actions can, however, lead to the repossession of the dwelling. In order to do this NIHE must apply to a county court for the grant of an "ejectment civil bill".

Levels of NIHE rents

NIHE fixes the level of its rents by totting up a points score for each dwelling based on its size, age and facilities and then multiplying the total by a figure set by the Department of the Environment every year. When the rent is increased NIHE notifies the tenant.

Where a tenant believes that an assessment is wrong he or she should write to the local district office of NIHE. If this is unsuccessful a further approach can be made to the Ombudsman (see Chapter 2), an application can be made to the High Court for judicial review of the rent or the tenant can wait to defend an action for arrears. In the latter two cases legal or other expert advice should be sought.

Repairs and improvements

The tenancy agreement in summary lays down that NIHE agrees to keep in repair the structure and exterior, to maintain anything in the dwelling which is its responsibility and to decorate the exterior every seven years. Anything which the tenant can remove is not NIHE's responsibility.

NIHE argues that its duty to repair arises only when its district manager has received written and specific notice from or on behalf of a tenant and after a reasonable period of time has elapsed. NIHE has indicated that it will respond to telephone calls in emergencies but believes that it is not legally obliged to do so. Local offices will prioritise repairs according to their urgency and set time limits within which the repair will be done. The standard of repair should be consistent with the age, character and prospective life of the house. In other words, expensive major restoration work to property due for redevelopment is unlikely, while minor holding repairs may be carried out.

The law has recently been amended to require NIHE to draft and implement a plan for certain types of repairs to be carried out within a specified time and for tenants to be compensated if the repairs are not carried out within that specified time (art. 31 of the Housing (NI) Order 1996).

If a property is damaged by flood, fire or other disaster, NIHE is not obliged to repair or restore it, but will normally do so unless the cost would be unreasonably high. NIHE is entitled to enter the building to do repairs but will only do so between 9am and 6pm after giving 24 hours' notice except in emergencies.

Recent changes to the law provide for the compensation of tenants who have made improvements to their homes (art.31 of the Housing (NI) Order 1996).

Security of tenure

If a tenant occupies a dwelling as his or her "only home" and the landlord is the NIHE or a registered housing association, the tenancy will, except in certain special circumstances, be a "secure tenancy". A secure tenant generally has the right to remain for as long as he or she wishes in the dwelling. Exceptions to this are set out in the Housing (NI) Order 1983. As well as having the right not to be evicted except by due process of law and after a valid notice to quit giving four week's notice has been served, the tenant can lose possession of the property only if the landlord body gets a court order (art. 27). Such an order for possession will be made only if one or more of 11 situations exist.

In the first six situations the court must think that an order for possession is reasonable, in the seventh there must be alternative accommodation available for the tenant, and in the remaining four both of these conditions must be present. The grounds for possession are as follows (art. 29):

- non-payment of rent or the breach of another obligation in the tenancy agreement;
- causing an annoyance to neighbours or using the premises for an illegal or immoral purpose;
- damaging or destroying any furniture provided, or failing to remove a lodger responsible for such damage or destruction;
- inducing the landlord to grant the tenancy by knowingly or recklessly making a false statement;
- failing to give up the premises while works are being carried out, even though the tenant knew this would be required;

- where a secure tenant has paid a fee in respect of an exchange of homes;
- where the landlord needs to do works of demolition or construction, all of which cannot be carried out in a reasonable time and for which possession is needed;
- where a house designed for a disabled person is now occupied by someone who is not disabled and is required again for a disabled person;
- where a registered housing association dwelling is usually let to a person who finds it difficult to have his or her housing needs met (other than for financial reasons) and the current occupant is not such a person;
- where the accommodation is for a person with special needs and the current occupant is a person who does not have those needs;
- where there is under-occupation of a house of which the tenancy was obtained through "statutory succession" by a member of the previous tenant's family (other than the spouse).

"Statutory succession" by a relative to a secure tenancy

If a secure tenant dies, the law provides for one succession by his or her nearest relative. Who this relative shall be is set out in article 26 of the Housing (NI) Order 1983. The right falls first to a husband or wife of the deceased, so long as he or she occupied the property as his or her principal home at the time of the tenant's death. For any other relatives, article 26 specifies residence for 12 months prior to the tenant's death and again the person must have lived in the property as his or her principal home. In practice the NIHE reduces the time requirement to six months.

There is only one succession allowed and, in cases of dispute, the NIHE may nominate who that person is to be. It must be an uncle, aunt, nephew, niece, child or "common law" husband or wife.

Transfer and exchange

NIHE allows a tenant to apply for a transfer. This is not a legal right but as it is provided for in the Executive's handbook it should be administered fairly and reasonably. Applications should be made to the Executive's local district office and will be considered for priority depending on whether the tenant has any rent arrears, though this barrier to transfer may be waived by the Executive if there are social and medical grounds and an arrangement is made to repay the arrears. The allocation of priority is on grounds similar to those discussed in connection with homelessness (see pages 389-391)

Exchanges of houses have been put on a statutory basis by article 32(A)(1) of the 1983 Order. This gives tenants the right to exchange, provided they have NIHE's written permission, which can be withheld only on very specific grounds.

The right to buy

The 1983 legislation on a tenant's right to buy has been repealed and replaced by provisions contained in the Housing (NI) Order 1992. The previous complicated home purchase scheme and NIHE's own voluntary purchase scheme have been replaced by a new House Sales Scheme issued by NIHE under article 96 of the 1992 Order. This scheme operates in much the same way as the previous arrangements, *e.g.* tenants will generally have a right to buy after three years.

Squatting in Housing Executive property

"Squatting" is a term commonly used to refer to entering and remaining in property without the permission of the occupier. In fact there are two elements to the conduct, entry and occupation, and both are criminal offences.

When a squatter or his or her dependents first enter a house they are trespassers who may be summarily evicted without a court order. The Criminal Justice (NI) Order 1986 confirmed that it was a criminal offence to enter property without the permission of the owner and in addition made it an offence to remain on the property after being asked to leave by the person lawfully entitled to possession. A resident magistrate (RM) can grant a possession order for the premises once a squatter has been convicted of an offence under the Order. If the squatter has used force or threatened violence then an offence has been committed under the Protection of the Person and Property Act (NI) 1969 and is punishable by a fine or imprisonment. In addition it is an offence to force entry and create an actual or possible breach of the peace (*e.g.* through barricading a building). Convictions of this kind are, however, rare.

The more recent Criminal Justice and Public Order Act 1994 creates a series of new criminal offences related to squatting. Most of these are imprisonable offences, but some are punishable by a fine. Crucially, these provisions also exempt residential occupiers, or people acting on their behalf, from legal provisions penalising the use of violence to secure immediate entry into premises in which there are squatters.

Whenever someone squats in NIHE property the following options are more likely to be used:

- A member of NIHE staff visits the property and encourages the squatters to leave. If they do not, a warning letter will be sent, giving the squatters seven days to vacate the premises and threatening legal action if they remain beyond that time. If they still refuse to go the matter is referred to NIHE solicitors to initiate a criminal prosecution or civil action. It is highly unlikely that squatters could successfully defend such an action.

- An action in the civil courts for possession of the premises, eviction of the squatter and sometimes even compensation for the unauthorised occupation (money known as "mesne profits") is usually begun by the issue of an "ejectment civil bill" in a county court, but may also be begun by issuing an "originating summons" in the Chancery Division of the High Court if the value of the property is significant. Where the premises concerned belong to NIHE, a registered housing association, a district council or the Crown, a possession order can be suspended for up to three months. Any judgment obtained can be enforced against the squatters by the Enforcement of Judgments Office (see Chapter 2).

Immediately after court proceedings NIHE will issue a "use and occupation" book with a covering letter making it clear that a tenancy is not being granted (*McCann v NIHE*, 1979). The squatters are then required to make periodic payments (as mesne profits, not rent, although in practice the two amounts are similar). The squatters remain trespassers and consequently have no right, for instance, to have the property repaired. They do, however, have some rights, in limited circumstances, in relation to injuries incurred on the property as a result of disrepair (see the Occupiers' Liability (NI) Order 1986).

NIHE officials are entitled to enter the property provided force is not used. A common tactic is to request that squatters come to the local NIHE office for an appointment. NIHE officials then enter the squat and secure it against the squatters' return, a course of action which is illegal if underhand.

Squatters are not protected by the illegal eviction and harassment provisions of the Rent (NI) Order 1978 (arts. 54-56) but a squatter who has been evicted may apply to NIHE as a person who is homeless.

The Housing Executive's duties to the homeless

For homeless people, or those threatened with immediate homelessness, there are two routes by which they may acquire "emergency A1 status" from NIHE. One route is the administrative scheme devised by the Executive itself; the other is the legal right available to some homeless persons created by the Housing (NI) Order 1988 and in operation since April 1989.

NIHE's administrative scheme

Under the Executive's own Housing Selection Scheme, a homeless person will normally get emergency A1 status if he or she is homeless due to:

- fire, flood, or other circumstances beyond the applicant's control;
- marital breakdown;
- successful court action by a landlord for the possession of a dwelling which the landlord may want to use for himself or herself or for a member of his or her family;
- the ending of a "tied" tenancy, *i.e.,* a tenancy which is let by an employer as part of a contract of employment (such as a farm labourer's cottage);
- being a serviceman moving to civilian life without accommodation, or the widow of a recently deceased serviceman losing married quarters;
- an exceptional need to sell the dwelling currently occupied; or
- other circumstances regarded by NIHE as exceptional, including situations where a person, through no fault of his or her own, has to reside in emergency accommodation or persistently change address in order to have accommodation.

Homelessness under the 1988 Order

Establishing a legal right to A1 status under the Housing (NI) Order 1988 requires the applicant to prove three points.

- That he or she is *in fact* homeless, having no place to live in Northern Ireland by virtue of ownership, a tenancy or an express or implied licence (*i.e.* a permission to be on property), or is *deemed* to be homeless because he or she cannot occupy a property with members of his or her family due to its physical condition or cost, or the applicant not being physically able to get into it, or there being a risk of violence from someone else living in it, or there being a threat of homelessness within the next 28 days through a court order for eviction.

• That he or she is "in priority need", *e.g.* is pregnant, over 60 years old or mentally or physically disabled (or normally resides with someone who is in one of these categories). Priority need also covers a young person (aged 16-21) who is at risk of sexual or financial exploitation, someone who has dependent children, or who is subject to domestic violence or to violence from outside the home, and a person who has a home which is rendered uninhabitable due to fire, flood or other unexpected disaster including illegal eviction.

• That he or she is not responsible for losing "settled" accommodation, when it was reasonable for him or her to continue to occupy that accommodation. This is the condition known as "intentionality". It applies whether the settled accommodation is in Northern Ireland or elsewhere. Behaviour by the spouse, partner or child of an applicant will not count against his or her application, unless it can be shown that there has been acquiescence in the act leading to the homelessness.

In reality, the majority of homeless people are excluded from the categories of people who are "in priority need". This is because they are single people, with no dependent children, aged between 21 and retirement age, and without any mental or physical disability, whose homelessness has not been a result of natural disaster or violence.

NIHE's duties under the 1988 Order

Those people who are both homeless and in priority need are entitled, as a minimum, to be provided by NIHE with suitable temporary accommodation for a reasonable period (up to 28 days) and to be given advice and assistance. They are also entitled to have their belongings stored, pending re-housing (art.13). NIHE is allowed to make a reasonable charge for this accommodation and storage. Even if the Executive finally decides that the applicant is intentionally homeless, these services have to be provided for a reasonable period thereafter in order to allow the applicant to find other accommodation (art. 10(3)). It is a criminal offence knowingly to make a false statement to the Executive intending to get accommodation as a result (art. 17).

A fully qualifying applicant will be made two suitable offers of accommodation (art. 12). If these are turned down, the applicant may be eventually housed from the ordinary housing waiting list, which is open only to persons who were born in Northern Ireland or who have resided here for the previous seven years. Someone coming directly from another EC country has no right to register on the list unless he or she also works in Northern Ireland.

In a recent House of Lords case, *Awua v Brent London Borough Council* (1995), the court took the view that the accommodation provided by the housing authority need only be "suitable" and not necessarily "permanent". The Housing Act 1996 (which does not as yet apply in Northern Ireland) amended this position slightly by requiring the authority to provide secure accommodation for a maximum of two years, after which the situation must be reviewed.

Challenging NIHE's decision

If NIHE, through its district office, refuses to grant A1 status to an applicant under the 1988 Order, the applicant is entitled to be told the reasons for this in writing (art. 9). The remedy for unsuccessful applicants is an appeal through NIHE's own appeals procedure, initially to the Regional Manager and then to the Director of Housing and Planning.

If NIHE makes a decision which is wrong in law, exceeds its powers or is unreasonable, perverse or absurd, the applicant may apply to the High Court for a judicial review of the decision (see Chapter 2), but NIHE has to have acted particularly badly for the High Court to grant a review. Even if successful, the matter may simply be returned to the Executive for reconsideration according to proper procedures, and this may not lead to a different conclusion from that reached earlier. Applicants should, however, always seek legal advice if refused housing by the NIHE. If temporary or permanent rehousing is not suitable, the applicant can also challenge this in court.

Grants

A new grants scheme was set up under the Housing (NI) Order 1992. Briefly, the new system applies a means test to applicants and distinguishes between mandatory grants (*i.e.* if the applicant satisfies all the criteria the grant must be awarded) and discretionary grants (where

NIHE may give financial assistance but is not required to). The new scheme recognises the following types of grants:

- renovation grants - aimed at making unfit properties fit;
- disabled facilities grants - for adaptation of fit properties for disabled residents (see also Chapter 15);
- replacement grants - to replace unfit isolated rural dwellings where renovation grants are inappropriate;
- minor works assistance - for carrying out minor works for specified target groups;
- repair grants - to carry out works required to be done by a statutory notice;
- common parts grants - to carry out repairs or improvements to the common parts of a building which contains more than one flat; and
- houses in multiple occupation grants - to bring unfit houses in multiple occupation up to the required standard.

NIHE have produced a series of leaflets on the grants system and these and further information can be obtained from any local NIHE grants office.

Private rented sector housing

Private tenants are those whose landlords are not NIHE or a registered housing association. There are three types of private tenancies - restricted, regulated and unprotected. It is essential to find out which type of tenancy is in question to be able to discover a tenant's rights to repair or to security of tenure and how much rent will have to be paid.

Restricted and regulated tenancies are protected tenancies under the Rent (NI) Order 1978. Most privately rented accommodation in Northern Ireland is "unprotected" by the Order. Unprotected tenants have only a few legal rights outside those agreed with the landlord in any written or verbal tenancy agreement. Such agreements do not have to be in writing if they are for under one year or from year to year. They can be entirely oral or partly oral and partly written. Tenancies will be private but not protected if the landlord is the Crown, a government department or an Industrial or Provident Society. If the lease is for more than 99 years or a "fee farm grant" the agreement will again fall outside the protection of the Rent Order. A fee farm grant is a very long lease (*e.g.* 999 years) subject to a "ground" rent; it is almost equivalent to full ownership.

Protected tenancies

A tenancy will *not* be protected if any of the following apply:

- the Net Annual Value (NAV) is over £140 (the NAV of any property can be checked at the local rates office);
- the property was built or converted after 6 November 1956;
- the landlord shares essential facilities with the tenant;
- the property has all reasonably necessary furniture, excluding cooking utensils, linen and crockery, unless a restricted rent certificate covers the dwelling or a public health notice has been served;
- the landlord provides food or services which are a substantial part of the rent, unless a restricted rent certificate covers the dwelling or a public health notice has been served; or
- the tenancy was not or cannot be presumed to have been rented out and controlled by the old Rent Restrictions Acts.

If the tenancy is protected the next step is to decide whether it is restricted or regulated. Telephoning the Rent Officer at Stormont (01232-763210) is a short cut to finding out. A tenancy is a regulated tenancy unless it is subject to a restricted rent certificate issued by a district council or unless, immediately before the commencement of the Rent (NI) Order 1978, the tenancy was controlled by the old Rent Restriction Acts and the NAV was under £60. A tenancy is also deemed to be restricted if a statutory nuisance notice has been issued by a district council. A landlord can apply to the council to convert a tenancy into a regulated tenancy if it comes up to a certain standard (set out in Sched. 3 of the 1978 Order).

Regulated tenancies are protected tenancies other than those which are restricted and they are obliged by law to meet certain standards. Since the introduction of the Housing (NI) Order 1992 the standards laid down in the Rent Order have been amended, with the result that a dwelling will meet the regulated tenancy standards if it is fit for human habitation.

Private tenants' rents

The levels of rent are differently controlled for restricted, regulated and unprotected tenants.

Restricted tenancies

The rents in restricted tenancies are fixed at what they were when the Rent (NI) Order 1978 came into force. They are usually just a few pounds per week. Tenants will often pay the rates also and these may now be more than the rent. A restricted rent can be increased only if the landlord applies to his or her district council in order to convert the tenancy into a regulated tenancy. There can be no review of the rent by the rent assessment committee. Any excess of rent paid by a tenant can be recovered by withholding future instalments (art. 23(2) of the Rent (NI) Order 1978).

Regulated tenancies

The rent of regulated tenants is supposed to be approximately equal to what NIHE would charge (art. 27(2)) and is regulated by the 1978 Order. The rent is fixed by applying to the Rent Office to have it registered and can be altered (apart from clerical errors) only by an order of the rent assessment committee or by the Department of Environment (art. 33). If a tenant applies to have the rent registered at a regulated rent, anything paid in excess of that rent during the previous two years can be recovered from the landlord (article 23(2)).

Unprotected tenancies

The rent charged in these tenancies is generally the amount the market will stand for the property, given its location, size, repair and facilities, but the amount will be affected by two factors:

- NIHE is authorised to restrict the amount of rent which can be paid through housing benefit . This restriction can be appealed to an independent housing benefit review board (see also Chapter 21). A tenant has to pay any excess which NIHE will not pay.
- The level of subsidy to home owners through mortgage interest tax relief means that it can be cheaper to buy rather than rent at the level a landlord may need to charge in order to make a profit.

All private tenants are entitled to a rent book (art. 38 of the 1978 Order) and failure to provide one by a landlord is a criminal offence.

Private tenants' rights to repairs

Restricted tenancies

Restricted tenants rarely have any repairing rights in their tenancy agreement. Usually the obligation to do repairs is on the tenant. Restricted tenants can normally only use the statutory nuisance and unfitness procedures described below. Withholding rent is not an option as the rent is so low.

Regulated tenancies

The landlord's duties to repair are laid down in articles 41 and 43-45 of the Rent (NI) Order 1978. He or she is responsible for the structure, the exterior (including paintwork), the supplies of electricity, gas and water and the interior, except for those obligations which article 42 imposes on the tenant. These latter include responsibility for fireplaces, tiles, all glass, tap washers and seals and any damage caused by the tenant or a lawful visitor. The tenant is also responsible for the interior decorative order.

If a landlord is in breach of his or her repairing duties by not carrying out the work after written or verbal notice has been given, a regulated tenant can do the following:

- Apply to the rent assessment committee to have the rent reduced (art. 31, as amended).
- Apply to the Environmental Health Department of the local district council for an inspection of the property. If the landlord has broken his or her repairing duties, the council will issue a certificate of disrepair (COD), listing the works required. If the landlord does not do the work, an order can be sought in a magistrates' court and ultimately a landlord may be fined. The council can also carry out the work itself if the landlord has not done it, and recover the cost from the landlord. If the council refuses to issue a COD, a tenant can appeal to a county court within 28 days (arts. 47 and 48).
- Ask the Environmental Health Department to inspect the premises to see if the disrepair is prejudicial to health or a nuisance (s. 110 of the Public Health (Ireland) Act 1878). The council may issue a notice forcing the landlord to bring the nuisance to an end. If the council does not issue a formal notice it may use an informal "seven day

notice" procedure.   In urgent cases where there is default by the landlord, a "nine day notice" will be issued if the ordinary procedure would lead to delay (art. 65(1) of the Pollution Control and Local Government (NI) Order 1978). Again the council can carry out the work and recover the costs.

• Inform NIHE that the house is unfit for habitation. A new set of unfitness criteria was introduced by the Housing (NI) Order 1992 and they relate to the following: standard of repair, structural stability, freedom from damp, natural lighting, ventilation, water supply, drainage and sanitary facilities, food preparation facilities and disposal of waste water.

Procedures if a house is unfit

If a house, or part of it, is deficient in one or more of the matters just mentioned so as to make it unsuitable for occupation, it is unfit. NIHE will first decide if the house can be made fit at reasonable expense. If it can, NIHE will issue a repairs notice forcing the owner to do the work in a specified time. Reasonable expense is based on whether the work can be carried out at a cost equal to or below 34 times the NAV of the property. The owner has a right of appeal, within 21 days of the issue of the notice, to a county court.   The owner may, however, offer an undertaking not to use the property for human habitation until it is made fit.

If the house cannot be made fit at reasonable expense, a "time and place meeting" is called by NIHE.   This meeting will involve the Executive, the local council's Environmental Health Department, the owner, and any mortgagee (such as a bank or building society). The owner may offer an undertaking to make the house fit and not to use it for human habitation until it is made fit. If this is the outcome a tenant cannot appeal.   If no undertaking is accepted, NIHE must issue a *demolition order,* unless this would affect adjacent buildings or the building is listed. If this is so, a *closing order* will be issued. The owner, or a tenant with more than one year to run on a lease, can appeal against a demolition order to a county court.

It is an offence to remain in the property beyond the date stipulated in a demolition order. Tenants should therefore try to make the best out of a bad situation by ensuring that they get "emergency A3 status" (which permits them to be re-housed by the Executive) and applying for compensation in respect of home-loss, disturbance and good maintenance.

It is not open to a regulated tenant to withhold rent to do repairs if there is no repairing duty on the landlord contained in the written tenancy agreement. A regulated tenant may, however, if taken to court for rent arrears, argue that any arrears should be set off against a failure by the landlord to do repairs. A tenant has no right simply to stop paying rent in protest at the lack of repair.

Unprotected tenancies

While unprotected tenants, like restricted tenants, cannot use the certificate of disrepair procedure and cannot apply to the rent assessment committee for a rent reduction, it may be possible for them to obtain assistance as follows. They should first of all look at the express terms of any written agreement, if one exists. This will set out, to some extent, the repairing rights and duties. In addition, the law generally implies the following terms into most agreements:

- that the tenant has the right to quiet enjoyment, *i.e.* not to be disturbed (s. 41 of the Landlord and Tenant (Amendment) Act (Ireland) 1860);
- that a furnished property is fit for occupation at the beginning of the tenancy;
- that the landlord is responsible for any common parts of which he or she retains control, such as stairways and halls; and
- if a property is rented out during the time it is being built, it should be built with proper materials and be fit for habitation on completion.

If the landlord knows or should know of disrepair, which is his or her obligation because of an express or implied term of the tenancy, and he or she has failed to carry out repair works, a tenant can take legal action for damages or a court order. Damages can include compensation for the reduction in value and enjoyment of the tenancy, inconvenience, annoyance, ill health and distress, and damage to the tenant's goods. If the amount of damages is small (*i.e.* under £1,000), it can be claimed in the small claims court. If the amount is larger, the matter will normally be dealt with by a full county court. Legal aid is available in this court but not in the small claims court, though the fees in the latter are very low.

An unprotected tenant may also withhold rent in order to cover the cost of doing the repairs, but should follow this specific procedure:

- the landlord should be twice notified of the disrepair by recorded letter, and given a reasonable time to deal with it; copies of the letters should be kept by the tenant;
- if the landlord does not comply, three estimates should be sought and the job given to the lowest tender;
- once the work has been done, an invoice should be forwarded to the landlord for payment;
- rent should be withheld to cover the cost if the landlord refuses to pay; if the cost is high, rent may be accumulated in advance and put in a separate bank, post office or credit union account.

Liability for defective premises

While only a tenant or a joint tenant can sue on the tenancy agreement, this limitation does not apply to claims for negligence, which can extend to friends, family and other guests. However, the basic rule is that a landlord is not liable for injuries arising from defects, whether visible or hidden, apart from any contractual obligations. But on to this principle are grafted the following exceptions:
- if a landlord was also the builder or designer he or she may be liable for a negligent act or omission causing forseeable injury or damage;
- if the injury was caused outside the tenanted property (*e.g.* on a staircase, walkway or lift), a landlord may be liable if the injury was forseeable; and
- under the Defective Premises (NI) Order 1975, any person carrying out works to a building, including conversions, should do the work in a professional manner using proper materials, so that it is fit for habitation when completed; this duty is owed to all future purchasers of the building and the 1975 Order also removes the legal immunity on a seller or landlord of property for any act or omission on the property before the sale or lease takes effect.

If a landlord tries to exclude liability for negligence from the tenancy agreement, this must be tested against the Unfair Contract Terms Act 1977, which requires the exemption clause to be reasonable (s. 2(2)). Liability for death or personal injury can never be avoided, by whatever means (s. 2(1)).

Private tenants' security of tenure

The following rights are enjoyed by all private tenants:

- a notice to quit, which need not be in writing, though it normally is, must be given at least four weeks in advance unless the tenancy agreement specifies a longer period (art. 62 of the Rent (NI) Order 1978);
- the tenant must not be harassed by any person with the intention of forcing the tenant to give up his or her home, or any part of it, or the exercise or any right (*e.g.* a right of way) or remedy (*e.g.* rights to repair); such harassment could amount to the serious offence of intimidation and should be reported to the police;
- the landlord must not unlawfully deprive a tenant of his or her house, or any part of it; this is also a criminal offence unless it was reasonable to believe that the tenant did not live there any more (art. 54(1) of the 1978 Order);
- evictions which do not follow the legal process of a notice to quit and proceedings in court are also unlawful (art. 56);
- tenants who have a written agreement can sue for damages if they are evicted or harassed; if they do not have a promise by the landlord of quiet enjoyment, this will be implied into the agreement unless it is actually excluded (s. 42 of the Landlord and Tenant (Amendment) Act (Ireland) 1860).

Protected tenancies

Both types of protected tenant enjoy the same security. They can be evicted only after a valid notice to quit has been served and an order obtained in a county court. The owner is therefore substantially restricted from regaining possession so long as the tenant uses the dwelling as his or her main residence.

Schedule 3 of the Rent (NI) Order 1978 specifies the circumstances a landlord must show to the court (unless he or she proves that there is suitable alternative accommodation available for the tenant) in order to recover possession. The court must also believe that it is reasonable to make an order. In six situations the court may, but does not have to, grant possession:

- the duty to pay rent or some other tenancy obligation has been broken by the tenant;
- there has been a nuisance or annoyance to others or use of the premises for immoral or illegal purposes;

- the tenant has allowed the premises to deteriorate or has actually damaged them;
- the tenant or sub-tenant has damaged furniture;
- the tenant has served a valid notice to quit, as a result of which the landlord has entered into a contract to sell and the court believes he or she would be seriously prejudiced if the sale did not go ahead; or
- the tenant has sub-let or given the property away by a formal transfer without the landlord's consent.

In eight further situations the court *must* grant possession:

- the tenancy is a service tenancy (let with a job) but the job has ended and the landlord wishes to rent the property to someone coming into his or her employment;
- the property is needed for the landlord's occupation or for a member of his or her close family, it was not bought after 1978, and great hardship would not be caused by granting possession rather than refusing it;
- the tenant has sub-let at a rent more than the maximum recoverable rent for restricted or regulated tenancies;
- the house is the main house on any agricultural land and the court believes the landlord intends to sell the land;
- the house was formerly occupied by the landlord and is required for his or her own use (provided the landlord informed the tenant before 1978 that the property might be recovered);
- the house has been bought for retirement, the owner has retired and died, and a family member who lived with him or her wishes to occupy it;
- the house is for a minister of religion, or a full-time lay missionary, and is the place from where he or she will perform his or her duties;
- a serviceman wishes to recover possession in order to live in the house and he or she was in the services when the house was bought and let out.

If a landlord misrepresents or conceals any facts to get back possession, the tenant may get compensation for resulting damage and loss (Rent (NI) Order 1978, art. 20).

The only other ways in which protected tenants can lose possession are:

- if there is a closing or demolition order on the premises (art. 45 of the Housing (NI) Order 1981); (if the house is only subject to an undertaking to make it fit, it can be reoccupied by a tenant again on the same terms and conditions as before); or

- if the landlord applies under article 69 of the Rent (NI) Order 1978 to a county court on the basis that a tenancy was misclassified as protected; possession proceedings can begin immediately if the landlord is successful.

Protected tenants can pass on their tenancies twice, after their death, to successors (known as "statutory tenants by succession"; see also page 386). The first successor will be the tenant's spouse, if he or she is residing in the house. Other family members must be living with the tenant permanently for over six months prior to the death, and not living there as a nurse or caretaker. If there is a dispute as to who should succeed, the Rent Order provides a specific preference order (Rent (NI) Order 1978, Sched. 1). There can be two or more joint statutory tenants, but the property will return to the landlord on the second statutory tenant's death.

A statutory tenant occupies property on exactly the same terms as the original tenant and the tenancy can be transferred during the lifetime of the statutory tenant so long as the landlord agrees and is a party to any agreement (art.17). The transfer must be voluntary and no money should change hands, except to pay for the statutory tenant's outgoings, or for any improvement he or she has made. If part of the premises are used for business purposes a sum can be paid for goodwill (art.18).

A court in matrimonial proceedings (separation, divorce, annulment or judicial separation) can transfer a protected or statutory tenancy (art. 6). The court can also direct adjustments to cover any liabilities or obligations arising before the transfer.

Unprotected tenancies

These tenants generally have little security. An unprotected tenant can remain in the property for any agreed period, but if he or she breaks the agreement (perhaps by non-payment of rent) the landlord need serve only a four week notice to quit (art.62) and then may take court proceedings. A landlord does not have to show any of the circumstances listed above for protected tenancies, nor show that suitable alternative accommodation is available. A tenant can ask for a "stay" (*i.e.* a delay) on the operation of the court order for a few weeks or months. Legal aid is not available for court representation.

The rights of home owners

Home owners are responsible for doing all repairs and, subject to building control and planning permission, can carry out any improvements or extension work to the home. An owner can remain in the property for whatever period he or she wishes, provided that any lender's payments are up-to-date, that the property is not vested by a government body and that it has not become unfit for habitation.

Paying for the house

There are two main payments: rates, payable to the Department of the Environment, and, if the purchase price of the property involved a loan, mortgage repayments to a building society or other lender.

Rates

Rates are a form of tax for local services. They are calculated by taking the Net Annual Value (NAV) of the property and multiplying that by the annual rate struck by the district council. If the occupier disagrees with a valuation, the matter can be taken up with the district valuer, then with the Commissioner for Valuation and ultimately with the Lands Tribunal.

Where the levels of rates are not contested they are generally payable by the occupier. An occupier on benefit, low wages or other very limited income may apply to NIHE for housing benefit to cover up to a maximum of 80% of the rates (see also Chapter 21). In suitable cases benefit can be backdated for up to 52 weeks, but the claimant must show good cause for submitting a late claim (*e.g.* serious illness or family stress). If rates are unpaid, the Rates Collection Agency will recover them by court action.

At present it seems unlikely that the council tax system which operates in England and Wales (formerly the poll tax system) will be introduced in Northern Ireland.

Mortgage repayments

These payments are the most important a home owner has to make. Failure to keep them up may result in the lender taking court proceedings to recover possession of the property. A mortgage is a legal device to allow a person to borrow money to buy property while using that property as security against any future failure by the borrower to repay.

A failure to make repayment allows a lender to approach the High Court to ask for that security. The court, however, has a discretion as to what should happen.

If a borrower on a mortgage is in arrears, for whatever reason, he or she should immediately contact the lender to make arrangements for getting through the crisis. Advice can be sought from a Citizens' Advice Bureau, Belfast Housing Aid or other advice agency. The following are some ideas to put to the lender:

- the borrower could ask to move to "interest only" payments; this is immediately possible if the mortgage is of the straight repayment variety and if it has an endowment policy attached this can be cashed in and used to pay the accumulated arrears;
- if eligible, the borrower could claim income support from the DHSS to enable the interest to be paid; income support is payable three months after the initial application, so the borrower should advise the lender of this gap and the reason for it;
- if the arrears are substantial, the borrower could suggest that the term of the mortgage should be lengthened (*e.g.* from 25 to 30 years), thereby slightly reducing the monthly repayments, or that the arrears should be "capitalised" (*i.e.* added to the sum originally borrowed);
- if the lender's branch office gives no satisfaction regarding proposals to reduce the arrears, the borrower could write to the head office.

If repossession proceedings are not defended, a court order will frequently be made giving the lender the right to immediate possession. Once the period allowed for appeal has passed (a few weeks), without the borrower leaving the premises, the lender can apply, after giving notice of intention to do so, to have the court order enforced by the Enforcement of Judgments Office. The lender might even at this stage respond to reasonable and realistic proposals for paying off the arrears, though the lender's legal costs will be added to the arrears then owing.

An owner who loses his or her home in this manner may be classified by NIHE as homeless (see pages 389-391), though may be considered "intentionally" so. A family member who has not participated or acquiesced in the failure to keep up payments (except a dependent child) may also apply as homeless and the intentionally homeless person can then be housed with him or her as a member of the family.

Repairing or improving the home

This is the owner's responsibility unless damage has occurred because of the negligence of another person, such as a neighbour or builder.

Otherwise an owner will have to finance any work out of savings, by borrowing, by grants from NIHE or perhaps by grants or loans from the DHSS social fund (see Chapter 21).

A bank or building society may lend money if the value of the property, less any existing loan (the "equity"), justifies it. It is always worth checking first whether the work would be covered by a grant. In certain cases this may pay for up to 90% of the work. Eligibility depends on the type of work and the value of the property.

The social fund administered by the DHSS can make grants of up to £400 for essential work to income support claimants who are also responsible for repairing their home. There is no strict entitlement to this, as the local office's funds may have run out and the Department has a wide discretion. It may instead offer a loan. Advice on the rate of repayments should then be taken. If the property is for some reason defective, the following points should be remembered.

- If the property had grant-aided work carried out to it and the defect relates to this work, the NIHE's approval of the work when paying out the grant is no guarantee that the work was carried out properly. The Executive may in certain circumstances be guilty of maladministration sufficient to found a complaint to the Ombudsman (see Chapter 2), but it is not legally liable to pay compensation to present or future owners.
- A surveyor instructed by a lender cannot generally escape liability for any negligent failure to recognise what should have been apparent if he or she had used reasonable care and skill.
- A property built after 1975 should be built in a professional manner with proper materials and be fit for habitation upon completion. A builder will be liable to anyone subsequently buying the property: article 3 of the Defective Premises (NI) Order 1975. There is a time limit on liability, namely six years after the owner (or tenant) knew or should have known of the defect.
- If a property has been bought from NIHE or a registered housing association and the Department of the Environment decides that it is defective because of its design or construction, the owner may apply to NIHE to reinstate the dwelling or in serious cases to buy it back.

Owners who have great difficulty in selling their homes by reason only of the "troubles" may benefit from the "SPED" (Special Purchase of Evacuated Dwellings) Scheme. This allows public purchase of a house which cannot be sold because of its location and closeness to civil disturbances or in cases of verifiable intimidation. If a house falls into this category the owner should enquire from a Citizens' Advice Bureau, a solicitor or Belfast Housing Aid as to whether he or she is eligible for help.

Planning rights

Planning in Northern Ireland is largely governed by the Planning (NI) Order 1991, which substantially amended the previous planning legislation, including the 1972 Order. Planning permission is required for any development of land and "development" is defined very widely in the legislation. Planning permission is also required for change of use, although only for "material" changes. Application for permission is made to the Department of the Environment for Northern Ireland (DOE) and must be in the prescribed form.

Vesting and compulsory purchase

The law governing vesting procedures is contained in the Planning (NI) Order 1991 and the Housing (NI) Order 1983, as amended.

Applications for vesting are usually made by NIHE in furtherance of its development powers, after an inspection, to the DOE, which also has the power to vest on its own behalf (art. 87 of the 1991 Order). Such applications are made under the Local Government (Compulsory Acquisition of Land) Regulations (NI) 1975, as amended by the 1991 Order. Where NIHE proposes to compulsorily purchase it must apply for a vesting order. The DOE considers the application and any objections made to it and may be required to hold a public inquiry, *e.g.* when the vesting application is in pursuance of a development scheme or is an acquisition for planning purposes under the Planning Orders.

Conduct of public inquiries

The chairperson of a public inquiry will be appointed by the Planning Appeals Commission (see below) if the vesting application is made under the Planning (NI) Orders and by the DOE if the application is made under the Housing (NI) Order 1983. Any person with an interest in the land and any other person allowed by the chairperson can appear in person or be heard through a representative. Case law has established that the rules of natural justice must be adhered to in the proceedings, *i.e.* no person may be a judge in his or her own case, there is a right to a fair hearing and those in charge of the inquiry must act fairly. After the conclusion of the inquiry the DOE may make a vesting order, notice of which must be published and served. Anyone who wishes to challenge the vesting order has one month from its publication in which to apply to the High Court to have the order suspended or overturned. A vesting order may be challenged only on certain grounds and an application to challenge such an order may be made only by someone with sufficient "standing", *i.e.* he or she must be a person who is sufficiently affected by the order.

Where no inquiry has been held, the DOE must serve notice of its decision on the applicant and consider his or her representations. There is no appeal mechanism but it is possible to apply to the High Court to have the decision judicially reviewed (see Chapter 2).

Compensation

Anyone who has an interest in the land vested has the right to be compensated for the loss of that interest, although the level of compensation will depend upon the kind of interest involved, *e.g.* a tenant will be entitled to less compensation than an owner. The rules relating to such compensation are contained in the Land Compensation (NI) Order 1982 and the Planning (NI) Order 1991. Furthermore, NIHE is obliged to rehouse persons displaced by a vesting order, as provided for by articles 40-41 of the Land Acquisition and Compensation (NI) Order 1973, as amended.

Planning Appeals

Appeals of routine planning decisions, *e.g.* refusals to grant planning permission, are heard by the Planning Appeals Commission. They are usually heard by one member of the Commission, who makes a report to the full Commission, and a decision is then taken. Details are available from:

- The Planning Appeals Commission
  107 Great Victoria Street
  Belfast BT2 7AG
  tel: 01232-244710

Chapter 21

Social Security Rights

Eileen Evason

Introduction

This chapter provides a very general overview of entitlement under the benefits system. As a preliminary to the discussion of provision for individual groups, three observations can be made.

First, although European law has had some effect at the margins via the Equal Treatment Directive, the UK government has been able, without difficulty, to substantially modify social security provision over the past 17 years. This has occurred despite, the popular perception that the payment of national insurance contributions produces some kind of contractual relationship between the individual and the state. In practice, national insurance benefits have been reduced in value, made less accessible or abolished altogether in much the same way as has occurred in other parts of the social security system. In essence, national insurance contributions are more appropriately regarded as a tax.

Second, benefits systems are not neutral. They reflect the contexts in which they operate and the priorities and perspectives which dominate policy as a whole at a given point in time. The social security system of the UK has been restructured over the past 17 years to ensure that it reflects and reinforces broader social, economic and labour market policies. In consequence, most of the changes made can be viewed as contributing to a very distinct agenda. There has been the general objective of cutting costs, though, as a result of the very high levels of unemployment over the past decade, expenditure has been held steady as a proportion of GDP rather than reduced. There has also been the objective of reducing and limiting the role of the state by shifting costs to others and by privatisation - "encouraging" individuals to make their own provision in the private market. Some alterations to the benefits system (the exclusion of unemployed 16-18 year olds from benefit and the introduction of the social fund) simply assume that other agencies - the family or charity - will fill the gap left by shrinking statutory provision. Explicit examples of cost-shifting include the 1994 revisions to statutory sick pay and the child support legislation (see below). The privatisation objective has been pursued explicitly in pension policy, through providing incentives to promote the development of personal pensions. A third key objective over the past decade has been to ensure that the benefits system in no way reduces, and indeed actively works to secure, willingness on the part of claimants to accept the terms and conditions of employment offered in a deregulated labour market.

Third, as a result of the amendments to benefits that have taken place, together with other policy changes, the balance within the social security system has shifted in recent years. In essence, social security systems may offer benefits in three main ways. Benefits may be on a contributory basis - that is, paid as of right without a means test if contribution and other conditions are fulfilled. Benefits may be universal - that is detached from contribution conditions but not dependent on means or income, *e.g.* child benefit. Thirdly, benefits may be payable only to those satisfying a test of means as well as other conditions which may be attached.

The Beveridge model of the 1940s, imperfectly executed as it was, envisaged national insurance as the centrepiece of provision with the role of the social security system being primarily to support those outside the labour market for one reason or another. In consequence of the strategy outlined above, however, support from the benefits system increasingly means reliance on means-tested benefits with all of the difficulties provision of this kind entails. There are the take up and poverty trap problems and a further difficulty is the way in which such provision deters effort and thrift. Additionally, means-tested benefits for those in poorly paid work in the labour market are of increasing significance in the drive to encourage the unemployed and lone parents to accept whatever employment is available. Indeed, for these groups policy discussions on the benefits system revolve purely and simply around the effectiveness of the structure in achieving this objective rather than on the extent to which provision meets need or prevents poverty. This, perhaps more than anything else, sums up the very fundamental changes that have occurred over the past 17 years and helps to explain why a set of provisions which may be thought to be primarily about assisting those in difficulty so frequently seems ill designed for this purpose.

Unemployed people

Provision for this group has been cut and amended on an ongoing basis since 1980, culminating in the introduction of the jobseeker's allowance (JSA) in October 1996 (see the Jobseeker's (NI) Order 1995). JSA replaced unemployment benefit - the national insurance benefit for the unemployed - and the means-tested assistance formerly available to the unemployed under the income support scheme (see below). JSA, in fact, consists of two benefits.

Contributory JSA

Receipt of this depends on claimants satisfying contribution conditions as well as meeting all of the tests outlined below. Put briefly, claimants must have actually paid class 1 contributions to the value of 25 times the lowest possible contribution in one of the two tax years preceding the year of the claim. Additionally, claimants must have paid or been credited with contributions to the value of 50 times the lowest possible contribution in both of the two tax years preceding the claim. These are exactly the same as the contribution conditions for unemployment benefit but satisfying them does not attract the same level of support.

Contributory JSA is payable only for six months, whereas unemployment benefit was payable for one year. Contributory JSA is payable at two rates, with claimants aged 18-25 being entitled, at the 1997-98 weekly rates to £38.90 and those aged 25 and over to £49.15. Unemployment benefit made no such distinction and the payment of varying amounts with no variation in contribution conditions is a significant change in practice. In line with unemployment benefit, no additions are payable for dependent children. However, whereas claimants of unemployment benefit received additions for adult dependents, i.e. partners with no or limited earnings, contributory JSA consists of an allowance for the claimant only. This represents a substantial cut and taken as a whole this benefit may be considered to be a very poor return for contributions paid. Finally, it should be noted that contributory JSA will be reduced pound for pound by any earnings from part-time work over £5 (there are some exceptions to this). The pound for pound deduction also applies to occupational or personal pensions of over £50 a week.

Income-based JSA

The inadequacy of contributory JSA means that many unemployed people will also need to claim this means-tested benefit at the outset of their claim. This is also the only source of support available when entitlement to contributory JSA is exhausted or where there is no entitlement in the first place because the claimant cannot meet the contributions conditions. The amount of benefit payable is assessed in the same way as for income support (see below). It should be noted that claimants with partners working 24 hours a week or more are excluded from this benefit regardless of the actual income of the couple.

Other conditions

For both contributory and income based JSA claimants must also comply with a number of other conditions. One is these is that they must not be working for more than 16 hours a week. There are four others.

a) Claimants must be capable of work

This is not a new provision but the new test of incapacity introduced for incapacity benefit in 1995 (see below) necessitates further consideration of it. Regulations provide that persons deemed capable of work for incapacity benefit *must* be accepted as such for JSA. The problem remains, however, that persons with very remote chances of securing employment are being decanted from incapacity benefit to JSA and, whilst some concessions are made to such persons, they may find it difficult to satisfy all of the conditions attached to this benefit.

b) Claimants must be available for employment

Claimants must be ready to take any job immediately unless, for example, they have caring responsibilities, in which case they must be available for work on 48 hours notice, or have been allowed a period of up to 13 weeks to look for work in their usual employment. It is important to emphasise that whether or not work is available, or is likely to be actually available, is irrelevant.

c) Claimants must be actively seeking work

Benefit is only payable for each week when claimants are actively seeking work and claimants can be required at any point to provide details of steps taken in the previous week to secure work. Steps include activities such as making written or oral applications for jobs and preparing a c.v. It would appear that two steps each week are sufficient to meet this condition.

d) Claimants must have a current jobseeker's agreement in force

The agreement sets out the steps the claimant will take to find work and is signed by both the claimant and a social security officer. If either decline to sign, no benefit is payable. Where claimants are unhappy with the contents of the agreement they can ask for it to be referred to an adjudication officer (AO) and, if they are still dissatisfied, to a different AO. From this point claimants may appeal to a social security appeals tribunal (SSAT) and, on a point of law, to a Social Security Commissioner. As claimants run the risk of losing benefit for significant periods if they enter into disputes over jobseeker's agreements the value of these procedures in practice is debatable and claimants have little real option but to agree to whatever the officer considers appropriate.

Sanctions

Claimants may be refused benefit for varying periods. They may lose JSA for between one and 26 weeks if it is decided that they lost their previous employment as a result of misconduct or leaving it without just cause. Claimants will also be sanctioned for two or four weeks if they fail to comply with a direction from an officer telling them to take some specific action to secure work or intended to enhance their chances of finding work. Claimants will be sanctioned for two or four weeks if they fail to take up a place on a training scheme and from one to 26 weeks if they fail to take up a job notified to them. Claimants can ask for these decisions to be reviewed and may appeal to an SSAT and, on a point of law, to a Social Security Commissioner. Sanctioned claimants on income-based JSA may apply for hardship payments. Where claimants are sanctioned the period for which this applies is deducted from the 26 week period of entitlement to contributory JSA. Sanctioned claimants may therefore find their entitlement to this is wiped out altogether despite the contributions they have paid.

Sickness and disability

Provision for these contingencies consists of a number of benefits which can be grouped into four main categories. First, some benefits (statutory sick pay (SSP), incapacity benefit, and severe disablement allowance (SDA)) have the function of providing a weekly income for persons incapable of work as a result of sickness or disability. Second, some benefits (attendance allowance and disability living allowance) are intended to provide assistance with the extra costs those with disabilities may incur. Third, the benefits system makes some provision for those suffering disability as a result of industrial injury. Fourth, there is some provision for informal carers - those, normally relatives, who give unpaid support to persons with disabilities in the community.

Statutory sick pay and incapacity benefit

Statutory sick pay is administered by employers. Prior to 1994 employers recovered the bulk of the cost incurred by deducting the amounts paid from their national insurance liability. This arrangement was in recognition of the fact that SSP was substituting for sickness benefit (now short term incapacity benefit) under the national insurance scheme. Now, however, the entire cost normally falls on the employer. This is clearly likely to make it more difficult for those with disabilities to secure work in the first place and employers may be reluctant to operate a provision whereby the state gives rights to individuals but makes no contribution to the resulting costs.

The 1997-98 weekly rate of SSP is £55.70. There are no additions for dependants. The benefit is payable for the first 28 weeks of sickness, after which claimants may transfer to incapacity benefit (see below). Employees may receive additional support depending on their contract of employment but as a basic minimum employees are entitled to SSP unless their earnings are below £62 a week or they are on contracts of under three months. It is not lawful for employers to employ people on a series of short term contracts to evade their liabilities. Cases of dispute can be referred to an AO of the Social Security Agency and claimants have a right of appeal to an SSAT. Employees not entitled to SSP should claim incapacity benefit.

Incapacity benefit replaced sickness and invalidity benefit in April 1995. In summary, the new arrangements deliver lower benefits which, in consequence of the new test of incapacity for work (see below), are more difficult to obtain. Receipt of incapacity benefit depends on claimants satisfying contribution conditions. Claimants must have actually paid class 1 or 2 contributions equal to 25 times the lowest possible contribution since joining the national insurance scheme and paid or been credited with 50 times this amount in each of the two tax years preceding the year of the claim. Persons incapable of work as a result of industrial injury were formerly exempt from these conditions but this concession was withdrawn in April 1995. Incapacity benefit consists of three elements.

- *Short term incapacity benefit.* This is payable for the first 28 weeks of sickness where there is no entitlement to SSP. The 1997-98 rate is £47.10. No additions are payable for dependent children and a significant saving has been made by the provisions which restrict the addition for an adult dependent (£29.15) to cases where the partner is over 60 or caring for dependent children.
- *Short term incapacity benefit at the higher rate.* Previously claimants transferred after 28 weeks of sickness to the broader and more adequate benefit for long term sickness - invalidity benefit. Now, after 28 weeks, unless they are terminally ill or on the highest rate of the care component of DLA (see below), claimants move on to another short term benefit which is payable for 24 weeks. Short term incapacity benefit at the higher rate consists (1997-98) of £57.70 for the claimant. The addition for an adult dependent (£29.15) is again payable only where the dependent is over 60 or caring for children. Additions for dependent children are, however, payable with this benefit, the current rate being £11.20 per child. Apart from the limited provision for adult dependents, further savings have been made by making this benefit taxable.
- *Long term incapacity benefit.* This is payable after one year. The 1997-98 rate is £62.45 for the claimant plus, if applicable, £37.35 for an adult dependent and £11.20 for each dependent child. This benefit differs from invalidity benefit which it replaced in a number of ways. No addition is payable from the state earnings related pension scheme. The age addition is payable only where incapacity occurs before the age of 45: £13.15 is payable where incapacity occurs before the age of 35 and £6.60 where the onset of incapacity occurred between the age of 35 and 44. Unlike invalidity benefit this benefit is taxable and it is payable only up to retirement age - 65 for men 60 for women.

The "own work" and "all work" tests of incapacity

For the first 28 weeks of incapacity the test of incapacity for work is whether claimants can do their normal job if they have an "own occupation" - that is a job they worked in for at least 16 hours a week for more than eight weeks in the 21 weeks preceding the claim. Persons without an "own occupation" must satisfy the "all work test". which also applies to all claimants after 28 weeks of incapacity unless they are in an exempt category. Those exempt include, for example, persons certified by the Benefits Agency Medical Services as suffering from a severe learning disability or severe mental illness.

The "all work" test differs from the previous arrangements in various ways. Formerly the test of incapacity related to actual work. Was there a job - regardless of its availability - that this person was fit to do? Consideration could also be given to the reasonableness of expecting the claimant to do such a job. By contrast, the "all work" test relates to functional capacity. Claimants complete questionnaires which cover a range of activities such as walking up and down stairs. For each activity there is a list of descriptors - statements which describe the varying extent to which people may be able to cope with the activity in question. The claimant is then examined by an examining medical officer - not his or her own GP - and this officer's report goes to an AO for a decision. In short, points are awarded on the basis of what the claimant can and cannot do. For example, being unable to walk up and down a flight of 12 stairs without holding on to something and taking a rest attracts seven points. Claimants are deemed to be incapable of work if they obtain 15 points from the physical disabilities list of activities or 10 points from the mental disabilities list or 15 from both combined with a minimum of six from the mental disabilities list.

The upshot of all of this is that it is quite possible for a person to have difficulties with a number of activities, which when taken together make it highly unlikely that he or she they could obtain and hold down any job, but which produce only 14 points so that the person is deemed capable of work. Claimants have a right of appeal to an SSAT and heavy use is being made of this to challenge the number of points awarded.

Severe disablement allowance

This benefit may be payable to those who are incapable of work but who cannot satisfy the contribution conditions for incapacity benefit. SDA is therefore an alternative to incapacity benefit therefore rather than an extra benefit, as is often thought. It is, moreover, extremely difficult to get. Receipt is conditional on the claimant having been incapable of work for 28 weeks and being 80% disabled by reference to the rates used for industrial injuries benefits. The 80% condition is deemed to be satisfied where claimants are on the top rate of the care component of the DLA (see below). Persons incapable of work before reaching their 20th birthday are exempt from the 80% test. Benefit is not payable to persons who are over the age of 64. The test of incapacity for work is the "all work" test (see above).

At the 1997-98 rates SDA consists of £37.75 for the claimant with £22.40 for an adult dependent and £11.20 for each dependent child. An addition depending on the age of onset of incapacity is also payable - £13.15 for those under 40, £8.30 for those between 40 and 49, and £4.15 for those between 50 and 59.

Industrial injuries benefits

There are no contribution conditions for these benefits but any accident which has occurred must have arisen out of, and in the course of, employment. In the case of disease the claimant can claim only if he or she has one of a list of prescribed diseases and has worked in a specified employment which has caused the disease. The case-law on this is extensive and, perhaps for this more than any other part of the benefits system, claimants wishing to appeal should contact a reputable advice centre if their trades union cannot assist.

For industrially injured claimants unable to work, SSP and incapacity benefits are payable on the same conditions as for other claimants. Additionally, disablement benefit is payable 15 weeks after the accident or onset of the disease regardless of whether the claimant is at work or not. The amount of disablement benefit, depends on the degree of disablement. In the majority of cases nothing will be paid if the condition is assessed at less than 14%. Otherwise weekly disablement benefit varies (in 1997-98) from £20.22 to £101.10. In addition, claimants may receive constant attendance allowance if their disablement is assessed at 100%, if they require constant attendance and if they claim within three months. Persons getting this allowance may also qualify for exceptionally severe disablement allowance.

A matter of considerable concern to the industrially injured - and others - relates to the provisions for the recovery of benefits where claimants are awarded compensation for personal injury. Under the provisions introduced in 1989, persons paying compensation are required to notify the DHSS of this. The DHSS then notifies the compensator of total benefit, up to a five year limit, paid in consequence of the accident or disease and this is deducted from the award, with the claimant receiving whatever is left. Only benefits claimed as a result of the accident or disease should be deducted. Awards of less than £2,500 are exempt, as are awards for accidents before 1989 and, in the case of disease, where the claim was made before this date. In consequence of these provisions claimants may find that they have gone through all of the strain of pursuing a claim for no gain whatsoever and with no allowance being made for the pain and stress they have experienced. These provisions have therefore been surrounded by considerable controversy and some amendments will be made to them for claims settled after October 1997. The part of the award for pain and suffering will be exempt from the deductions but the exclusion of awards below £2,500 will be abolished.

Attendance allowance

Attendance allowance is paid to those who are aged over 64 and so severely disabled (physically or mentally) that during the day they need frequent attention in connection with bodily functions or continual supervision in order to avoid danger to themselves or others, or during the night they require prolonged or repeated attention in connection with bodily functions or need someone else to be awake for prolonged periods "to watch over " them. At 1997-98 weekly rates, £49.50 is paid if care or supervision is needed day *and* night and £33.10 if the need is for the day *or* night. There are also residence conditions to be satisfied and benefit cannot be paid until the need has lasted for six months (except in the case of the terminally ill). Persons in hospital or other publicly provided accommodation lose their entitlement after four weeks.

This benefit is the subject of some confusion. It is normally paid to the person who needs care, not to the carer, and receipt hinges on the need for care or supervision rather than the existence of specified persons caring and the specific illness the person has. There are no contribution conditions and the means of the person are irrelevant. A major point to note is that attendance allowance is normally disregarded in the assessment of income support and housing benefit. It is therefore a real addition to resources.

Disability living allowance

DLA is for persons under 65 and replaced attendance allowance and mobility allowance in 1992. Because it is more generous than attendance allowance, provisions to assist the disabled now appear to discriminate on the basis of age. Those previously on attendance or mobility allowance have been transferred to DLA.

DLA consists of two components (care and mobility) and claimants may qualify for either or both. The care component is payable at three rates. The highest rate (£49.50 in 1997-98) is for persons requiring care or supervision both day *and* night. The middle rate (£33.10) is payable to those needing care or supervision day *or* night. The lower rate (£13.15) is payable to persons requiring care for a significant part of the day or unable to cook a main meal. Persons under 16 cannot qualify under the cooking condition.

The mobility component is payable at two rates to persons over the age of 5. The higher rate (£34.60 in 1997-98) is for persons unable or virtually unable to walk, persons who are both deaf and blind, the severely mentally impaired with severe behavioural problems, and double amputees. The lower rate (£13.15) is for those able to walk but requiring guidance or supervision.

Challenges to decisions on DLA can be made to a Disability Appeal Tribunal, and thereafter, on point of law to the Social Security Commissioner.

Invalid care allowance

Although it has been estimated that those people, normally women, who provide care for the sick and disabled in our society save the state roughly £20 billion per year, invalid care allowance represents the only significant recognition of the costs they incur and the service they provide. Benefit in 1997-98 amounts to £37.35 a week. Additions for dependents may be payable. The main conditions governing receipt are are that claimants must be under 65 when the claim is first made and caring for someone in receipt of attendance allowance or the middle or higher rate of the DLA care component, the task must take up 35 hours a week or more, and the claimant must not be gainfully employed (*i.e.* earning over £50 a week) or in full-time education (*i.e.* where class based or supervised study comes to 21 hours a week or over).

Prior to 1986, married women were excluded from receipt of this benefit, a restriction found to be contrary to the European Union's Equal

Treatment Directive. Whilst the removal of this discriminatory provision has helped some persons, the gains have not been as much as expected because of provisions governing the interaction between this and other benefits. Under the overlapping benefits regulations, invalid care allowance cannot be paid on top of another principal benefit, such as widowed mother's allowance. In addition, invalid care allowance cannot be paid under these regulations if the carer is a dependent of a person in receipt of any benefit which includes an addition for the carer as a dependent. Thus, a woman caring for a relative whilst her own husband is on invalidity benefit and claiming for her as a dependent will not be entitled to invalid care allowance. Finally ICA counts as a resource in the assessment of entitlement to means-tested benefits. Where ICA is deducted from income support or housing benefit, claimants are partially compensated, however, by the carers premium.

Lone parents

Approximately 25% of Northern Ireland families are now headed by lone parents, the overwhelming majority of these being women. With regard to lone parents generally, the benefits system distinguishes between men and women and deals differently with female lone parents depending on the cause of lone parenthood - the main division being between widows and the rest. Thus, there is no entitlement to any benefit for men who are widowed; if they are unable to work their only option is means-tested support. With regard to female lone parents, provision is made for widows but for all other female lone parents the main state benefit if they are unable to work is means-tested income support.

Provision for widows

Provision for widows now consists of three elements. Earnings do not affect entitlement to widows' benefits, though cohabitation or remarriage does. By virtue of the lowness of these benefits widows may still need to claim means-tested support.

- Widow's payment of £1,000 is normally payable to women under 60 whose husbands have paid the requisite national insurance contributions. This condition does not apply to those widowed through industrial accident or injury. Women over 59 may be entitled if the husband was not claiming a category A pension.
- Widows with dependent children will, if the husband's contribution record is satisfactory, receive the weekly widowed mother's

allowance, £62.45 per week in 1997-98, plus £9.90 for the eldest child and £11.20 for each other child. This is in addition to child benefit. It is payable immediately and for as long as there are dependent children.

- Widow's pension is payable only to women aged 45 or over and again there are contribution conditions. It can be paid immediately to a widow who has no dependent children and women receiving the widowed mother's allowance can, when they cease to be entitled to this, transfer to widow's pension, provided they are aged 45 or over. Less will be paid if the husband's contributions record is inadequate and women between the ages of 45 and 55 when they become entitled are awarded a proportion of the full basic rate.

Lone parents other than widows

For lone parents other than widows, the main options are child benefit and means-tested benefits. Until April 1997 lone parents not receiving additions for children via an insurance benefit could claim one parent benefit for the first or only child in addition to child benefit at the usual rates. From April 1997 child benefit and one parent benefit for the first or only child have been combined to form child benefit (lone parent rate), which is currently £17.10 per week. In April 1998 the special rate will be abolished for new claimants and lone parents will receive child benefit on the same basis as other families – currently £11.05 for first or eldest child and £9.00 for each other child. Lone parents not in employment (*i.e.* working less than 16 hours per week) can claim income support if their resources are below the prescribed levels.

Lone parents who are able to secure employment may also have their income increased via means-tested family credit and housing benefit (see below).

The major development with regard to lone parents in recent years has been the child support legislation of 1991 and the subsequent creation in 1993 of the Child Support Agency (the CSA) to assess, collect and enforce maintenance. The experience of other countries indicates that it is possible to introduce reforms in this area of social policy with public support. In the UK, however, the child support legislation has engendered almost as much hostility and controversy as the ill-fated poll tax. One reason for this may be that the main objective of the UK arrangements is to make the maximum savings possible for the benefits system.

The controversy has revolved around a number of points. First, the title of the White Paper which preceded the legislation - Children Come First – suggested that the intention was to make better provision for children. In practice, the legislation covers the maintenance of spouses as well as children, thus the focus is broader than that suggested. In addition, it was clear from the outset that large numbers of children would be no better off, as any additional maintenance obtained would be deducted pound for pound where the parent with care was on income support. A further point of concern relates to the impression given that the main target of the legislation was errant husbands making no contribution towards the support of their children. In practice, the pursuit of such fathers is time-consuming and may contribute little to meeting the targets for savings on benefits set for the Agency. Securing increased contributions from those already paying maintenance has therefore figured more largely in the activities of the CSA than was, perhaps, anticipated by the general public.

It was originally intended that the CSA would, in time, take over virtually all of the functions of the courts for all social classes with regard to maintenance. This is now unlikely to happen. The requirement to use the Agency extends only to lone parents claiming income support, family credit, disability working allowance and income-based jobseeker's allowance. Other lone parents not on these means-benefits may apply to the Agency to access its services, provided no court order is in force. Where there is a choice, there is a preference for voluntary agreements with a consent order from the courts rather than use of the CSA. This is hardly surprising as examples of harshness and incompetence on the part of the Agency have featured so prominently in the media.

Those in receipt of the benefits listed must co-operate with the Agency. Failure to do so - unless an exemption is granted – may result in the imposition of a benefit penalty. That is, the lone parent's benefit will be reduced at source via a RBD (Reduced Benefit Direction). For RBD's issued after 6 October 1996 the deduction is £19.66 a week. Exemption from co-operation may be awarded where the lone parent satisfies the Agency that there is a risk that he or she, or the children, would suffer harm or undue distress.

The formula

The formula for assessing the maintenance to be paid by absent parents is an on-going source of difficulty. In its original form the formula simply ignored previous arrangements - including clean break settlements in the courts. There was also concern over the failure to take sufficient account of the existence and needs of second families and variations in circumstances. Amending legislation in 1995 introduced the possibility of applications for departures from the formula, though these provisions will be used sparingly.

Briefly, the formula for calculating the liability of the absent parent involves five stages. The maintenance requirement is calculated first. This is the amount, based on income support rates, deemed necessary to support the parent with children. Next, the exempt income of the absent parent is calculated, i.e. the amount he or she is allowed for meeting living expenses. This is deducted from actual net income and the balance constitutes what is known as the assessable income. 50% of assessable income is deemed available to pay maintenance and additional payments will be levied if the 50% exceeds the maintenance requirement. Finally, further calculations have to be done as a result of the provisions to ensure that no absent parent pays more than 30% of net income by way of maintenance payments. Where absent parents have limited means there is nevertheless a minimum payment of £5.00 a week. Absent parents on income support or income-based jobseeker's allowance may have this set amount deducted from their benefit at source.

Completion of all of the procedures and calculations does not of course mean that lone parents are better off. The absence of any gain for those on income support has been noted. There are also the problems which may be encountered by women floated off income support as a result of the maintenance due. Such women lose their automatic benefits - most obviously, free school meals. Additionally, the absence of a maintenance guarantee - whereby the state underwrites the maintenance - means that women may be taken off income support, or have reduced entitlement to family credit, even though the maintenance is not being paid or paid irregularly. The record of the CSA on enforcement has been patchy and helps to explain the lack of sympathy for the Agency amongst those who might have been its strongest supporters - lone parents themselves.

Finally, it can be noted that there are rights to review with appeal to the child support appeal tribunal and, on a point of law, to a Child Support Commissioner.

Retired people

A central aim of the Pensions Act 1975 was that, as far as possible, everyone would be entitled to a basic pension plus an earnings-related pension either from their employer or from the state. Legislation in 1986, however, sought to reduce the commitment of the state and expand the role of the private market by reducing the adequacy of SERPS (the state earnings-related pension scheme) and encouraging membership of company pension schemes and greater reliance on personal pensions. The logic of this approach is clearly open to question in the light of the Maxwell scandal, the growing evidence of the inadequacies of safeguards for those in company pension schemes and the difficulties produced where advice on personal pensions owes more to considerations of profit and commission than to the needs of those advised. Whether the 1990s' pensions legislation will prevent such advice in the future is debatable.

- The current structure of pensions provision is as follows. All of these bits and pieces add up to less than might be expected, hence many pensioners have to rely on income support and housing benefit.
- Provided contribution conditions are fulfilled, a category A pension is payable (£62.45 per week). Payment of the pension is not conditional on retirement and there is no earnings rule. The full basic rate is payable only after contributions have been paid or credited for 90% of working life and it is a source of considerable surprise to many pensioners that their entitlement after 50 years of contributions is so little. The main reason for this is the decision in 1980 to uprate long term benefits in line only with *prices*. This has resulted in the basic category A pension falling steadily as a percentage of average wages. It is forecast that after 2,000 it will be under 10% and approaching the point where its abolition altogether will be feasible.
- Category B pensions (£37.35) are paid to married women relying for their entitlement on their husband's contributions. The category B pension is not payable until the husband claims his category A pension. Many married women now have some entitlement to a category A pension as well as the category B pension. Only one - the highest - can be paid however. Hence married women with entitlement in their own right to category A pension of less than £37.35 gain nothing from this.
- Category D pensions (£37.35 in 1997-98) are non-contributory and are paid to pensioners who are over 80 years of age and have no other pension or a pension below the category D level. Beyond the basic pension, claimants may be entitled to graduated retirement benefit under the 1961-75 state scheme. Normally, however, the amounts involved are trifling. Secondly, those retiring after April 1979 may have entitlement under SERPS introduced in 1975, except

for periods when they were in occupational pension schemes or personal pensions and contracted out of SERPs.

Means-tested benefits: income support

Because benefits available as of right are inadequate in many respects, income support, formerly called supplementary benefit, is of great importance. Income support assists those not in full-time (*i.e.* at least 16 hours per week) employment (and without partners in full-time employment), excluding the unemployed who claim JSA (see page 433). Persons with savings or assets of £8,000 or are or more also excluded. Benefit consists of the difference between resources (minus any "disregards" the claimant is entitled to) and the prescribed applicable amounts. Resources include earnings and most benefits paid to the claimant and his or her partner (excluding attendance allowance, DLA and housing benefit), plus tariff income on capital, *i.e.* savings between £3,000 and £8,000 are assumed to generate a weekly income of £1 for each block of £250. The applicable amounts consist of three elements.

- First, a basic personal allowance, £77.15 per week in 1997-98 for a married couple, £38.90 (if aged 18 to 25) or £49.15 for a single person, plus varying amounts for dependent children.
- Second, for certain categories of claimants set additions are made known as "premia".
- Third, help with some types of housing costs (notably mortgage interest payments) may be paid. For help with rent and rates, income support claimants must make a separate claim for housing benefit.

The scheme has given rise to a number of difficulties. To begin with, the basic allowance for single people under 26 is very low and certainly insufficient for them to live independently in the community. In addition, there is now no provision for increasing the weekly benefit of claimants with special needs (*e.g.* the cost of a special diet or extra heating). The premia which have been substituted for these provisions are not always sufficient to cover such special needs. Moreover, claimants who might previously have been able to claim help with such needs will not always happen to fall into a category attracting a premium. A further difficulty is that "single payments" (lump sums for exceptional items of expenditure) have been replaced by the social fund (see below).

Finally, a major source of current difficulty relates to the substantial cuts made recently in the assistance claimants may receive with mortgage payments. Unless claimants are in an exempt category, claimants with mortgages taken out after September 1995 receive no help for the first 39 weeks of the claim. Up to various limits, assistance with mortgage interest payments at a standard rate is payable after this. With regard to mortgages obtained before October 1995, claimants receive no help for the first eight weeks of the claim, 50% of the costs for the next 18 weeks and, 100% of such costs after this (again up to varying limits). The amount payable will be reduced if there are non-dependents in the household or costs are deemed unreasonable. In short, despite policies to encourage home ownership, owner occupiers may receive very little assistance, and are expected to take out insurance policies to meet their housing costs when their circumstances change and they have difficulty meeting their costs

The social fund

The social fund came fully into operation in April 1988 and replaced not just single payments but also maternity and death grants. It provides two sets of assistance.

• Under the non-discretionary part of the scheme, persons on income support, disability working allowance, income-based JSA or family credit can claim a maternity expenses payment of £100. The same groups, plus persons on housing benefit, may be able to claim help with funeral expenses. Small amounts known as cold weather payments are also payable in very restricted circumstances.

• Under the discretionary part of the scheme, persons on income support may be awarded budgeting loans, crisis loans and community care grants.

Budgeting loans can be given for occasional, exceptional items of expenditure. Crisis loans may be obtained in cases of emergency or disaster. However all loans will be recovered by direct deductions, at source, from claimants' benefits. Moreover, claimants may be refused a loan if they are deemed to be too poor and indebted to be able to repay it. Also, because the system is cash limited, a social fund officer may refuse to assist because to do so would mean exceeding the budget. For such claimants there is now no statutory safety net and an application to a charitable organisation may be the only option open to them.

Community care grants are payable to persons moving out of institutionalised care and to vulnerable groups in the community such as the elderly, the disabled and families under stress. The guidance and directions issued by the DHSS to social fund officers are very restrictive.

Claimants have no right of appeal to independent social security appeal tribunals, but they can ask for the decision to be reviewed by social fund inspectors and can appeal on a point of law to the Social Security Commissioner.

Family credit

Family credit is payable to employees and the self-employed in full-time work (16 hours or more per week) with child dependents, if their capital does not exceed £8,000 and their income falls below the prescribed level. As for income support, while those with capital of more than £8,000 are totally excluded, claimants with between £3,000 and £8,000 are deemed to have a weekly income of £1 per week for each block of £250. Capital under £3,000 is completely ignored. The assessment of entitlement is as follows:

The first step is to calculate total income, *i.e.* net wages plus benefits in payment - excluding child benefit, attendance allowance, DLA and housing benefit. £15 of any maintenance payment and up to £60 of child care costs (excluding informal care) will be disregarded. The next stage is to calculate maximum family credit (MFC), *i.e.* the most the claimant could receive. The MFC varies according to family type and the number and the ages of children. Finally, income is compared with what is known as the threshold figure – in 1997-98 this is £77.15 for all families. If income is below the threshold, benefit equals the full MFC. If income is above the threshold, benefit equals MFC less 70% of the difference between income and the threshold.

Two additional points can be made. First, family credit was presented as a more generous benefit than family income supplement, which it replaced in 1988. In practice, as family credit counts as income for housing benefit purposes, families may find that once account is taken of the reduction or loss altogether of housing benefit the net increase in resources is rather less than expected. Second, family credit does not give entitlement, as family income supplement did, to free school meals. Once again, therefore, the real gains are less than claimants may expect.

Housing benefit

Housing benefit is payable to those on low incomes (those with savings exceeding £16,000 are excluded altogether) and provides assistance with rent and rates to public and private sector tenants and owner occupiers. For income support claimants, benefit equals maximum housing benefit minus non-dependent contributions. For others the assessment of entitlement is again a complex process.

The first stage is to calculate the maximum housing benefit (MHB), *i.e.* the most that could be paid. MHB consists of rent and/or rates, less any deductions for non-dependents. In plainer English, this means that, if claimants, for example, have grown-up sons and daughters in the household, those persons are assumed to be contributing specified amounts towards housing costs regardless of whether or not they can or wish to do so.

The second stage is to calculate the claimant's "applicable amounts" *i.e.* his or her needs according, with some minor variations, to the income support rates. For example, a married couple would in 1997-98 have an applicable amount of £77.15. If income is below the applicable amount, benefit equals the MHB. If income is above the applicable amount, a percentage (65% for rent and 20% for rates) of the difference between income and the applicable amount is deducted from the MHB and the housing benefit equals whatever remains. For present purposes income means net wages (minus any "disregards" to which there is entitlement) and most benefits apart from attendance allowance and DLA.

A number of points can be made on this benefit. First, the tapers, *i.e.* the rate at which benefit is cut if income is above the applicable amounts, are much harsher than prior to 1988. Persons on very low incomes can find that they are considered too affluent to receive housing benefit. Additionally, over the past two years substantial changes have been made to curtail the assistance given to private sector tenants. The maximum housing benefit for persons aged under 26 is now normally restricted to the amount payable for a room in a shared house - regardless of the accommodation occupied. Beyond this the regulations have been amended so that private sector tenants generally are less likely to have their full rent covered and further restrictions are to be put in place.

Dissatisfied claimants can ask the housing authority to review its decision and then request a hearing by a housing benefit review board. There is no appeal beyond this and the only other option is judicial review (see Chapter 2). Few claimants make use of these appeals provisions, probably because most find housing benefit incomprehensible.

More information

The social security system is constantly changing. Readers are advised to consult the books listed in Further Reading at page 429.

The address of the Child Poverty Action Group is:

- 1-5 Bath Street
  4th floor
  London EC1V 9PY
  tel: 017 405 5942

Further Reading

Books on human rights in international law

Scott Davison, *Human Rights* (1993); Open University Press, Buckingham.

P R Ghandhi, *International Human Rights Documents* (1995); Blackstone Press, Oxford.

David Harris, Michael O'Boyle and Colin Warbrick, *Law of the European Convention on Human Rights* (1995); Butterworths, London.

Francis Jacobs and Robin White, *The European Convention on Human Rights* (2nd ed, 1996); Clarendon Press, Oxford.

A H Robertson amd J G Merrills, *Human Rights in the World* (4th ed, 1996); Manchester University Press, Manchester.

A H Robertson and J G Merrills, *Human Rights in Europe* (3rd ed, 1993); Manchester University Press, Manchester.

Rebecca Wallace, *International Human Rights: Text and Materials* (1997); Sweet & Maxwell, London.

Books on rights and liberties in the United Kingdom

S L Bailey, D J Harris and B L Jones, *Civil Liberties: Cases and Materials* (4th ed, 1995); Butterworths, London.

Brice Dickson (ed), *Human Rights and the European Convention: The Effects of the Convention on the United Kingdom and Ireland* (1997); Sweet and Maxwell, London.

Sue Farran, *The United Kingdom Before the European Court of Human Rights: Case Law and Commentary* (1996); Blackstone Press, London.

David Feldman, *Civil Liberties and Human Rights in England and Wales* (1993); Clarendon Press, Oxford.

Conor Foley, *Human Rights, Human Wrongs: The Alternative Report to the United Nations Human Rights Committee* (1995); Rivers Oram Press, London.

Richard Gordon and Richard Wilson, *Human Rights in the United Kingdom* (1996); Oxford University Press, Oxford.
Murray Hunt, *Using Human Rights Law in English Courts* (1997); Hart Publishing, Oxford.
Francesca Klug, Keir Starmer and Stuart Weir, *Three Pillars of Liberty: Political Rights and Freedoms in the United Kingdom* (1996); Routledge, London.
Christopher McCrudden and Gerald Chambers (eds), *Individual Rights and the Law in Britain* (1995); Clarendon Press, Oxford.
John Wadham, Philip Leach and Penny Sergeant, *Your Rights: The Liberty Guide* (1997); Pluto Press, London.
Michael Zander, *A Bill of Rights?* (4th ed, 1996); Sweet and Maxwell, London.

Books on rights and liberties in Northern Ireland

Kevin Boyle, Colm Campbell and Tom Hadden, *The Protection of Human Rights in the Context of Peace and Reconciliation in Ireland* (1996); Forum for Peace and Reconciliation, Dublin.
Helsinki Watch, *Human Rights in Northern Ireland* (1991); Human Rights Watch, New York.
Anthony Jennings (ed), *Justice Under Fire: The Abuse of Civil Liberties in Northern Ireland* (2nd ed, 1990); Pluto Press, London.
Lawyers Committee for Human Rights, *At the Crossroads: Human Rights and the Northern Ireland Peace Process* (1996); Lawyers Committee for Human Rights, New York.
Liberty, *Broken Covenants: Violations of International Law in Northern Ireland* (1993); Liberty, London.

Books relating to specific chapters of this book

Legal remedies

Brigid Hadfield, *Judicial Review*, chap.2 of Brice Dickson and Deborah McBride (eds), *The Digest of Northern Ireland Law* (2nd ed, 1995); SLS Legal Publications Ltd, Belfast.

Police powers

Vaughan Bevan and Ken Lidstone, *The Investigation of Crime: A Guide to Police Powers* (1991); Butterworths, London.
Andrew J. Goldsmith (ed), *Complaints Against the Police: The Trend to External Review* (1991); Clarendon Press, Oxford.
John Harrison and Stephen Cragg, *Police Misconduct: Legal Remedies* (2nd ed, 1991); Legal Action Group, London.
Clive Walker, *The Prevention of Terrorism in British Law* (2nd ed, 1992); Manchester University Press, Manchester.

Prisons

Tim Owen and Stephen Livingstone, *Prison Law: Text and Materials* (1993); Clarendon Press, Oxford.

Free speech

Patrick Birkinshaw, *Freedom of Information* (2nd ed, 1996); Butterworths, London.
Justice, *Freedom of Expression and the Law* (1990); Justice, London.

Discrimination

Christine Bell, *Discrimination Law: Religious and Political Belief,* chap.14 of Brice Dickson and Deborah McBride (eds*), The Digest of Northern Ireland Law* (2nd ed, 1995); SLS Legal Publications Ltd, Belfast.
Colin Bourn and John Whitmore, *Anti-Discrimination Law in Britain* (3rd ed, 1996); Sweet and Maxwell, London.
Brian Doyle, *Disability Discrimination: Law and Practice* (1996); Jordans, Bristol.
Denise Magill and Sarah Rose, *Fair Employment Law in Northern Ireland: Debates and Issues* (1996); Standing Advisory Commission on Human Rights, Belfast.

Family and welfare law

Child Poverty Action Group, *National Welfare Benefits Handbook* (27th ed, 1997-98); CPAG, London.

Child Poverty Action Group, *Rights Guide to Non-Means-Tested Benefits* (20th ed, 1997-98); CPAG, London.
Eileen Evason, *Social Security*, chap.10 of Brice Dickson and Deborah McBride (eds), *The Digest of Northern Ireland Law* (2nd ed, 1995); SLS Legal Publications Ltd, Belfast.
Brenda Hale, *Mental Health Law* (1996); Sweet and Maxwell, London.
Housing Rights Service, *Housing Rights Manual* (1994, looseleaf); Housing Rights Service, Belfast.
E. Knights and S. Cox, *Child Support Handbook* (1997); Child Poverty Action Group, London.
Ruth Lavery, *Child Law*, chap.13 of Brice Dickson and Deborah McBride (eds), *The Digest of Northern Ireland Law* (2nd ed, 1995); SLS Legal Publications Ltd, Belfast.
Monica McWilliams and Lynda Spence, *Taking Domestic Violence Seriously: Issues for the Civil and Criminal Justice System* (1996); The Stationery Office, Belfast.
Kerry O'Halloran, *Family Law in Northern Ireland* (1997); Gill and Macmillan, Dublin.
R. Poynter and M. Barnes, *Jobseeker's Allowance Handbook* (1997); Child Poverty Action Group, London.
Ciaran White (ed), *Law for Northern Ireland Social Workers* (1995); Gill and Macmillan, Dublin.

Education

Neville Harris, *The Law Relating to Schools* (2nd ed, 1995); Tolley Publishing, Croydon.
Simon Oliver and Lesley Austen, *Special Educational Needs and the Law* (1996); Jordans, Bristol.

Employment law

N M Selwyn, *Selwyn's Law of Employment* (9th ed, 1996); Butterworths, London.

Table of Legislation and International Law

(Page references to this volume are at the end of each entry, in italics)

Table of Cases

(Page references to this volume are at the end of each entry, in italics)

R v Entry Clearance Officer, Bombay ex parte Amin [1983] 2 AC 818
    222, 237
R v Flynn and Leonard [1972] NIJB *66*
R v Fulling [1987] QB 426 *63*
R v Gibson [1990] 2 QB 619 *286*
R v Hampshire County Council, ex parte K [1990] 2 QB 71 *301*
R v Harper [1990] 4 NIJB 75 *70, 71*
R v Howell [1982] QB 416 *28, 29, 160*
R v Ireland [1997] 4 All ER 225 *182*
R v Kane, Kelly and Timmons (unreported, 1991) *144*
R v Keys and Others (1986) 84 Cr. App. R. 204 *157*
R v MacNaughton [1975] 5 NIJB *58*
R v Martin and Others [1992] 5 NIJB 1 *74*
R v McBrien and Harman [1984] 8 NIJB *66*
R v McDonald and Others [1989] NI 37 *280*
R v Norfolk County Council, ex parte M [1989] 2 All ER 359 *295*
R v Powell [1997] 4 All ER 545 *144*
R v R [1992] 1 AC 599 *279*
R v Rowley [1991] 1 WLR 1020 *286*
R v Samuel [1988] QB 615 *71*
R v Sang [1980] AC 402 *65*
R v Saunders [1979] 2 CMLR 216 *138*
R v Self [1992] 1 WLR 657 *30*
R v Tohill [1974] NIJB *68*
Rainey v Greater Glasgow Health Board [1987] AC 224 *217*
Raymond v Honey [1983] AC 1 *98*
Rice v Connolly [1966] 2 QB 414 *26, 73*
Royal Copenhagen A/S [1995] IRLR 648 *217*

Savjani v Inland Revenue Commissioners [1981] 1 All ER 1121 *237*
Seide v Gillette Industries Ltd [1980] IRLR 427 *232*
Showboat Entertainment Centre Ltd v Owens [1984] 1 All ER 836
    229
Sibson v UK (1994) 17 EHRR 193 *142*
South Coast Shipping Co. Ltd, Ex parte [1993] 2 WLR 621 *87*
Steel v Goacher [1983] RTR 98 *35*
Stewart v UK (1985) 7 EHRR 453 *5*
Stitt, Ex parte, The Times, 3 February 1987 *138*
Sunday Times v UK (1979) 2 EHRR 245 *176*
Sutherland v UK, The Independent, 8 October 1997 *287*

Index